Java: an Object-Oriented Language

Java: an Object-Oriented Language

Michael A. Smith
School of Computing
University of Brighton

THE McGRAW-HILL COMPANIES

London · Chicago · New York · St Louis · San Francisco · Auckland
Bogotá · Caracas · Lisbon · Madrid · Mexico · Milan
Montreal · New Delhi · Panama · Paris · San Juan · São Paulo
Singapore · Sydney · Tokyo · Toronto

Published by
McGraw-Hill Publishing Company
SHOPPENHANGERS ROAD, MAIDENHEAD, BERKSHIRE, SL6 2QL, ENGLAND
Telephone +44 (0) 1628 502500
Fax: +44 (0) 1628 770224   Web site: http://www.mcgraw-hill.co.uk

---

British Library Cataloguing in Publication Data

A catalogue record for this book is available from the British Library

ISBN 007 709460 3

Library of Congress Cataloguing-in-Publication Data

The LOC data for this book has been applied for and may be obtained from the
Library of Congress, Washington, D.C.

Further information on this and other McGraw-Hill titles is to be found at
http://www.mcgraw-hill.co.uk
Author's Website address: **http://www.mcgraw-hill.co.uk/smithma**

Publishing Director: Alfred Waller
Publisher: David Hatter
Typeset by: the Author
Produced by: Steven Gardiner Ltd
Cover by: Hybert Design

345CUP3210

Printed in Great Britain

Contents

Preface

This book is aimed at students and programmers who wish to learn the object-oriented language Java. There is no prior assumption about knowledge of a computer previous language. The book uses the current version of the language, Java 2. The language is in a continual state of development and as new versions appear, the reader will find support material on the Author's website, as detailed below. Design concepts are explained using the UML notation, which is becoming the de facto industry standard.

The first chapter introduces fundamental programming ideas using simple everyday examples to illustrate the basic building blocks used in program construction. The chapter assumes no previous programming knowledge and can be used by students as a gentle introduction to program construction. Following on from the introduction to programming is a chapter that looks at basic concepts behind software construction using an object-oriented approach.

The next two chapters concentrate on the building blocks used in the construction of Java applications. These two chapters look at simple data types and their manipulation together with looping and selection control structures. The book then moves on to discuss the object-oriented features of the language, using numerous examples to illustrate the ideas of encapsulation, inheritance and polymorphism.

For those readers who wish to explore programming using a GUI (Graphic User Interface) a chapter illustrates how to create simple window based applications and applets. For those readers who have access to an integrated development environment a chapter is devoted to looking at the key components from such a framework.

The book then moves on to explore key issues in Java development. This is dealt with by chapters on the model view paradigm, serialization of objects, threads, remote method invocation and reflection. Following on from these topics is a chapter that explores the use of graphics in a Java application or applet.

Exercises and self-assessment questions are suggested for the reader at the end of each chapter to allow the reader to practise the use of the Java components illustrated and to help reinforce the reader's understanding of the material in the chapter. The answers to early exercises are given to aid the reader's understanding of the material. The book ends with a reflective chapter on the nature of the Java language and the technologies used in its implementation.

I would in particular like to thank Corinna, my wife, for putting up with my many long hours in the 'computer room' and her many useful suggestions on the presentation and style used for the material in this book.

Website

Support material for the book can be found on the Author's website, http://www.mcgraw-hill.co.uk/smithma. The material consists of further solutions, source code, artwork and general information about Java.

Further exercises may be obtained by tutors, who may contact the Author, by email.

Michael A. Smith
Brighton, February 1999
m.a.smith@brighton.ac.uk

The example programs shown in this book follow the conventions:

Item in program	Example	Convention used
Actual parameter	```value = 2;``` ```display(value);```	Is in lower case.

Class	```class Account```
	```{```
	``` // Body of class```
	```}```
		The first character of the class name is capitalised.

Class variable (A global data item that is shared between all instances of the class.)	```static float the_rate;```	Is in lower case starting with the_ and is declared in the private part of the class.
Class method	```Cars.how_many()```	The class method name is in lower case.
Constant	```public static final int MAX = 10;```	Is in upper case.

Enumeration	```class Colour {```
	``` public static final int RED = 0;```
	```}```
		Is in upper case.

Formal parameter	```void display(int amount)```	Is in lower case.
Instance variable (A data field contained in an object)	```float the_balance;```	Starts with 'the_' and is in lower case
Instance method	```picture.display()```	The method name is in lower case.
Variable name / Object	```mine```	Is in lower case.

In the visible parts of the standard Java classes the following conventions are used:

Method	```picture.displayImage()```	Starts with a lower-case letter and where appropriate uses an upper-case letter to indicate component parts of the method name.
Class name	```TextArea textArea1;```	Starts with an upper-case letter and where appropriate uses an upper-case letter to indicate component parts of the class name.

Glossary of terms used

Active object   An object that contains a separately executing thread.

Actual parameter   The physical object passed to a function. For example, in the following fragment of code the actual parameter passed to the method deposit is amount.

```
double amount = 100.00;
mas.deposit( number );
```

ADT   Abstract Data Type. The separation of a data type into two components:
● the public operations allowed on instances of the type.
● the private physical implementation of the type.
(Representation of an instance of the type plus the implementation of the operations allowed on an instance of the type.)

Bean   A re-usable visual component.

Class   The specification of a type and the operations that are performed on an instance of the type. A class is used to create objects that share a common structure and behaviour.

The class Account is as follows:

```
class Account
{
  private double the_balance     = 0.0d;  //Balance
  private double the_min_balance = 0.0d;  //Minimum bal

  public Account() {
     the_balance = the_min_balance = 0.00;
  }

  public double account_balance()
  {
     return the_balance;
  }

  // Methods for withdraw and deposit

  public void set_min_balance( double money )
  {
    the_min_balance = money;
  }
}
```

Class method   A member function in a class that only accesses class variables. For example, the method prelude in the class Account_R which sets the class variable the_no_transactions is as follows:

```
void static prelude()
{
   the_no_transactions = 0;
}
```

Note: As prelude is a class method the member function is called without reference to an instance of the class. For example:
Account_R.prelude();

Class variable   A data member that is shared between all objects in the class. In effect it is a global variable which can only be accessed by methods in the class. For example, the class variable the_no_transactions in the class Account_R is declared as follows:

```
class Account_R {
{
   private double      the_balance;
   private double      the_overdraft;
   private static int the_no_transactions;

}
```

Dynamic-   The binding between an object and the message that is sent to it is <u>not</u>
binding   known at compile-time.

Encapsulation   The provision of a public interface to a hidden (private) collection of data items and methods that provide a coherent function.

Formal   In a method body the name of the object or variable that is passed to the
parameter   function. For example, in the following method the formal parameter is money.

```
public void deposit( final double money )
{
   the_balance = the_balance + money;
}
```

Getter

A method that gets the contents of an instance variable. Usually used in connection with the building of a bean. For example, in the following fragment of a class the getter method `getThe_mes` returns the contents of the instance variable `the_mes`.

```
class TT extends Canvas implements Serializable
{
  private string the_mes;
  public synchronized void getThe_mes( String message )
  {
    the_mes = message;
  }
  // etc.
}
```

Inheritance

The derivation of a class (subclass) from an existing class (superclass). The subclass will have the methods and instance/class variables in the class plus the methods and instance/class variables defined in the superclass. The class `Account_with_statement` that extends the class `Account` is defined as follows:

```
class Account_with_statement extends Account
{

}
```

Inspector

A method that does not change the state of the object. See also Getter.

Instance method

A method in a class that accesses the instance variables contained in an object. For example, the method `account_balance` accesses the instance variable `the_balance`.

```
public double account_balance()
{
  return the_balance;
}
```

Instance variable

A member variable contained in an object. The instance variables of the class should be declared as private.

```
class Account {
{
  private double the_balance;

}
```

Member methods	The collective name for instance methods and class methods.
Member variables	The collective name for instance variables and class variables.
Message	The sending of data values to a method that operates on an object. For example, the message 'deposit £30 in account `mike`' is written in Java as:

```
mike.deposit( 30.00 );
```

Meta-class	An instance of a meta-class is a class.
Method	Implements behaviour in an object. A method may be either a class method or an instance method.
Multiple inheritance	A class derived from more than one superclass. Java does not support multiple inheritance.
Mutator	A method that changes the state of the object. See also Setter.
Object	An instance of a class. An object has a state that is interrogated / changed by methods in the class. The object mike that is an instance of `Account` is declared as follows:

```
Account mike = new Account();
```

Overloading	When an identifier can have several different meanings. For example, the method `print` in the class `PrintWriter`:

```
FileOutputStream ostream = new FileOutputStream("f.dat");
PrintWriter pw           = new PrintWriter( ostream );

pw.print( "The sum of 1 + 2 + 3 is " );
pw.print( 1 + 2 + 3 );
```

is overloaded so that objects of different types can be printed using the same method name.

Polymorphism
The ability to send a message to an object whose type is not known until run-time. For example, in the code below, the message display is sent to an object representing a picture element that is held in the heterogeneous collection picture_elements.

```
picture_elements[i].display();
```

The method called depends on the actual picture element selected to receive the message display.

Setter
A method that sets an instance variable. Usually used in connection with the building of a bean. For example, in the following fragment of a class the setter method setThe_mes sets the instance variable the_mes.

```
class TT extends Canvas implements Serializable
{
  private string the_mes;
  public synchronized void setThe_mes( String message )
  {
    the_mes = message;
  }
  // etc.
}
```

Static binding
The binding between a method in an object and the message that it is sent to the object is known at compile-time.

Subclass
A class that is inherited from another class. Also known in other languages as a derived class.

Superclass
A class from which other classes are derived. Also known in other languages as a base class.

Thread
A thread is a separate execution on the code that using the same address space as the main thread of control. In Java a thread is implemented using an instance of the class Thread. An object containing a separately executing thread is an active object.

To my wife Corinna Lord, daughter Miranda and mother Margaret Smith

and guinea pig Delphi

1. Introduction to programming

A computer programming language is used by a programmer to express the solution to a problem in terms that the computer system can understand. This chapter looks at how to solve a small problem using the computer programming language Java.

1.1 Computer programming

Solving a problem by implementing the solution using a computer programming language is a meticulous process. In essence the problem is expressed in terms of a very stylized language in which every detail must be correct. However, this is a rewarding process both in the sense of achievement when the program is completed, and usually the eventual financial reward obtained for the effort.

Like the planet on which we live where there are many different natural languages, so the computer world also has many different programming languages. The programming language Java is just one of the many computer programming languages used today.

1.2 Programming languages

In the early days of computing circa 1950's, computer programs had to be written directly in the machine instructions of the computer. Soon assembly languages were introduced that allowed the programmer to write these instructions symbolically. An assembler program would then translate the programmer's symbolic instructions into the real machine code instructions of the computer. For example, to calculate the cost of a quantity of apples using an assembly language the following style of symbolic instructions would be written by a programmer:

```
    LDA    AMOUNT_OF_OF_APPLES    ; Load into the accumulator # pounds
    MLT    PRICE_PER_POUND        ; Multiply by cost per pound of apples
    STA    COST_OF_APPLES         ; Save result
```

Note: Each assembly language instruction corresponds to a machine code instruction.

In the period 1957—1958 the first versions of the high level languages FORTRAN & COBOL were developed. In these high level programming languages programmers could express many ideas in terms of the problem rather than in terms of the machine architecture. A compiler for the appropriate language would translate the programmer's high level statements into the specific machine code instructions of the target machine. Advantages of the use of a compiler include:

- Gains in programmer productivity as the solution is expressed in terms of the problem rather than in terms of the machine.

- If written correctly, programs may be compiled into the machine instructions of many different machines. Hence, the program may be moved between machines without having to be re-written.

For example, the same calculation to calculate the cost of apples is expressed in FORTRAN as:

```
COST = PRICE * AMOUNT
```

1.3 Range of programming languages

Since the early days of computer programming languages the number and range of high level languages has multiplied greatly. However, many languages have also effectively died through lack of use. A simplistic classification of the current paradigms in programming languages is shown in the table below:

Type of language	Brief characteristics of the language	Example
Functional	The problem is decomposed into individual functions. To a function is passed read only data values which the function transforms into a new value. A function itself may also be passed as a parameter to a function. As the input data to a function is unchanged individual functions may be executed simultaneously as soon as they have their input data.	ML
Logic	The problem is decomposed into rules specifying constraints about a world view of the problem.	Prolog
Object-oriented	The problem is decomposed into interacting objects. Each object encapsulates and hides methods that manipulate the hidden state of the object. A message sent to an object evokes the encapsulated method that then performs the requested task.	Ada 95 C++ Eiffel Java Smalltalk

| Procedural | The problem is decomposed into individual procedures or subroutines. This decomposition is usually done in a top down manner. In a top down approach, once a section of the problem has been identified as being implementable by a procedure, it too is broken down into individual procedures. The data however, is not usually part of this decomposition. | C Pascal |

1.3.1 Computer programming languages

A computer programming language is a special language in which a high level description of the solution to a problem is expressed. However, unlike a natural language, there can be no ambiguity or error in the description of the solution to the problem. The computer is unable to work out what was meant from an incorrect description.

For example, in the programming language Java, to print the result of multiplying 10 by 5 the following programming language statement is written:

```
System.out.println( 10 * 5 );
```

To the non programmer this is not an immediately obvious way of expressing: print the answer to 10 multiplied by 5.

1.3.2 The role of a compiler

The high-level language used to describe the solution to the problem, must first be converted to a form suitable for execution on the computer system. This conversion process is performed by a compiler. A compiler is a program that converts the high-level language statements into a form that a computer can obey. During the conversion process the compiler will tell the programmer about any syntax or semantic mistakes that have been made when expressing the problem in the high-level language. This process is akin to the work of a human translator who converts a document from English into French so that a French speaker can understand the contents of the document.

Once the computer program has been converted to a form that can be executed, it may then be run. It usually comes as a surprise to many new programmers that the results produced from running their program is not what they expected. The computer obeys the programming language statements exactly. However, in their formulation the novice programmer has formulated a solution that does not solve the problem correctly.

1.4 A small problem

A local orchard sells some of its rare variety apples in its local farm shop. However, the farm shop has no electric power and hence uses a set of scales which just give the weight of the purchased product. A customer buying apples, fills a bag full of apples and takes the apples to the shop assistant who weighs the apples to determine their weight in kilograms and then multiples the weight by the price per kilogram.

   If the shop assistant is good at mental arithmetic they can perform the calculation in their head, or if mental arithmetic is not their strong point they can use an alternative means of determining the cost of the apples.

1.5 Solving the problem using a calculator

For example, to solve the very simple problem of calculating the cost of 5.2 kilos of apples at £1.20 a kilo using a pocket calculator the following 4 steps are performed:

Pocket calculator	Step	Steps performed
	1	Enter the cost of a kilo of apples: C 1 . 2 0
Display: 6.24 Keys: S M / * 7 8 9 - 4 5 6 + 1 2 3 C 0 . =	2	Enter the operation to be performed: *
	3	Enter the number of kilos to be bought: 5 . 2
	4	Enter calculate =

Note: The keys on the calculator are:
    C   Clear the display and turn on the calculator if off
    S   Save the contents of the display into memory
    M   Retrieve the contents of the memory
    + - * /   Arithmetic operations
         *   Multiply   /   Division
         +   plus   -   minus
    =   Calculate

When entered, these actions cause the calculation 1.20 * 5.2 to be evaluated and displayed. In solving the problem, the problem is broken down into several very simple steps. These steps are in the 'language' that the calculator understands. By obeying these simple instructions the calculator 'solves' the problem of the cost of 5.2 kilos of apples at £1.20 a kilo.

1.5.1   Making the solution more general

The calculation using the pocket calculator can be made more general by storing the price of the apples in the calculator's memory. The price of a specific amount of apples can then be calculated by retrieving the stored price of the apples and multiplying this retrieved amount by the quantity required. For example, to setup the price of apples in the calculator's memory and calculate the cost of 4.1 kilos of apples, the following process is :

Pocket calculator	Step	Steps performed
	1	Enter the cost of a kilo of apples: C 1 . 2 0
	2	Save this value to the calculator's memory: S
	3	Retrieve the value from memory: M
	4	Enter the operation to be performed: *
	5	Enter the number of kilos to be bought: 4 . 1
	6	Enter calculate =

To calculate the price for each customer's order of apples, only steps 3 — 6 needs to be repeated. In essence, a generalized solution to the problem of finding the price of any quantity of apples has been defined and implemented.

1.6 Solving the problem using the Java language

To solve the problem of calculating the cost of a quantity of apples using the programming language Java, a similar procedure to that used previously when using a pocket calculator is followed. This time, however, the individual steps are as follows:

Step	Description
1	Set the memory location `price_per_kilo` to the cost per kilogram of the apples.
2	Set the memory location `kilos_of_apples` to the kilograms of apples required.
3	Set the memory location `cost` to the result of multiplying the contents of memory location `price_per_kilo` by the contents of the memory location `kilos_of_apples`.
4	Print the contents of the memory location `cost`.

Note: Although a shorter sequence of steps can be written to calculate 1.2 multiplied by 5.2 the above solution can easily be extended to allow the price of any number of kilograms of apples to be calculated.

In Java like most programming languages when a memory location is required to store a value, it must first be declared. This is done for many reasons, some of these reasons are:

- So that the type of items that are to be stored in this memory location can be specified. By specifying the type of the item that can be stored the compiler can allocate the correct amount of memory for the item as well as checking that a programmer does not accidentally try and store an inappropriate item into the memory location.

- The programmer does not accidentally store a value into a memory location `c0st` when they meant `cost`. The programmer accidentally typed zero (0) when they meant the letter (o).

The sequence of steps written in pseudo English is transformed into the following individual Java statements which, when obeyed by a computer, will display the cost of 5.2 kilograms of apples at £1.20 a kilogram.

Step	Line	Java statements
	1	`double price_per_kilo;`
	2	`double kilos_of_apples;`
	3	`double cost;`
1	4	`price_per_kilo  = 1.20;`
2	5	`kilos_of_apples = 5.2;`
3	6	`cost = price_per_kilo * kilos_of_apples;`
4	7	`System.out.println( cost );`

Note: *Words in bold type are reserved words in the Java language and cannot be used*
for the name of a memory location.
The name of the memory location contains the character _ to make the name
more readable. Spaces in the name of a memory location are not allowed.
Each Java statement is terminated with a ;
*Multiplication is written as *.*

The individual lines of code of the Java application are responsible for the following actions:

Line	Description
1	Allocates a memory location called `price_per_kilo` that is used to store the price per kilogram of apples. This memory location is of type `double` and can hold any number that has decimal places.
2-3	Allocates memory locations: `kilos_of_apples` and `cost`.
4	Sets the contents of the memory location `price_per_kilo` to 1.20. The = can be read as 'is assigned the value'.
5	Assign 5.2 to memory location `kilos_of_apples`.
6	Sets the contents of the memory location `cost` to the contents of the memory location `price_per_kilo` multiplied by the contents of the memory location `kilos_of_apples`.
7	Displays the contents of the memory location `cost` onto the computer screen. The components of this statement are illustrated below: Memory location to be printed Method that prints memory location `System.out.println( cost );` The ( ) around the name of the memory location to be printed must be included.

This solution is very similar to the solution using the pocket calculator, except that individually named memory locations are used to hold the stored values, and the calculation is expressed in a more human readable form.

An animation of the above Java application is shown below. In the animation the contents of the memory locations are shown after each individual Java statement is executed. When a memory location is declared in Java its initial contents are set to zero. In the case of an instance of a `double` memory location this is set to 0.0.

Java statements	price_ per_kilo	kilos_ of_apples	cost

`double price_per_kilo;`
`double kilos_of_apples;`
`double cost;`
	0.0	0.0	0.0

`price_per_kilo = 1.20;`	1.20	0.0	0.0
`kilos_of_apples = 5.2;`	1.20	5.2	0.0
`cost = price_per_kilo *` `      kilos_of_apples;`	1.20	5.2	6.24
`System.out.println( cost );`	1.20	5.2	6.24

1.6.1   Running the application

The above lines of code, though not a complete Java application, form the core code for such an application. When this code is augmented with additional peripheral code, compiled and then run, the output produced will be of the form:

```
6.24
```

A person who knows what the application does, will instantly know that this represents the price of 5.2 kilograms of apples at £1.20 a kilogram. However, this will not be obvious to a casual user of the application.

1.7 The role of comments

To make a Java program easier to read, comments may be placed in the program to aid the human reader of the program. A comment starts with // and extends to the end of the line. It is important however, to realize that the comments you write in a program are completely ignored by the computer when it comes to run your program. For example, the previous fragment of code could be annotated with comments as follows:

```
double price_per_kilo;        //Price of apples
double kilos_of_apples;       //Apples required
double cost;                  //Cost of apples

price_per_kilo  = 1.20;       // Set cost of apples to £1.20
kilos_of_apples = 5.2;        // Kilos required
cost = price_per_kilo * kilos_of_apples;  // Evaluate cost
System.out.println( cost );              // print the cost
```

Note: This is an example of comments. The more experienced programmer would probably miss out many of the above comments as the effect of the code is easily understandable.

Comments that do not add to a reader's understanding of the program code should be avoided. In some circumstances the choice of meaning full names for memory locations is all that is required. As a general rule, if the effect of the code is not immediately obvious then a comment should be used to add clarity to the code fragment.

1.8   Summary

The statements in the Java programming language seen so far are illustrated in the table below:

Java statement	Description
double cost;	Declare a memory location called cost.
cost = 1.2 * 5.2;	Assign to the memory location cost the result of evaluating 1.2 multiplied by 5.2.
System.out.println("Hi");	Print the message Hi followed by a new line.
System.out.println(cost);	Print the contents of the memory location cost followed by a new line.

Statements of this form allow a programmer to write many different and useful programs.

1.9   A more descriptive application

By adding additional Java statements, the output from an application can be made clear to all who use the application. For example, the application in Section 1.6 can be modified into the application illustrated below. In this application, a major part of the application's code is concerned with ensuring that the user is made aware of what the results mean.

Line	Java statements
1	`double price_per_kilo;` `//Price of apples`
2	`double kilos_of_apples;` `//Apples required`
3	`double cost;` `//Cost of apples`
4	`price_per_kilo = 1.20;`
5	`kilos_of_apples = 5.2;`
6	`cost = price_per_kilo * kilos_of_apples;`
7	`System.out.print( "Cost of apples per kilo  £ " );`
8	`System.out.print( price_per_kilo );`
9	`System.out.println();`
10	`System.out.print( "Kilos of apples required K " );`
11	`System.out.print( kilos_of_apples );`
12	`System.out.println();`
13	`System.out.print( "Cost of apples            £ " );`
14	`System.out.println( cost );`
15	`System.out.println();`

Line	Description
1-6	Calculate the cost of 5.2 kilograms of apples at £1.20 per kilogram.
7	Displays the message `Cost of apples per kilo  £` onto the computer screen. The double quotes around the text message are used to signify that this is a text message to be printed rather than the contents of a memory location.
8	Displays the contents of the memory location `cost` onto the computer screen after the above message.
9	Starts a new line of output on the computer screen.
10—12	As for lines 7—9 but this time the message is `Kilos of apples required K` and the memory location printed is `kilos_of_apples`.
13—15	As for lines 7—9 but this time the message is `Cost of apples            £` and the memory location printed is `cost`.

1.9.1 Running the new application

With the addition of some extra lines of code, the above application can be compiled and then run on a computer system. Once executed the following results will be displayed:

```
Cost of apples per kilo   £ 1.2
Kilos of apples required K 5.2
Cost of apples           £ 6.24
```

This makes it easy to see what the application has calculated.

1.10   Types of memory location

So far the type of the memory location used has been of type `double`. A memory location of type `double` can hold any number that has a fractional part. However, when such a value is held it is only held to a specific number of decimal places. Sometimes it is appropriate to hold numbers that have an exact whole value, e.g. a memory location `people` that represents the number of people in a room. In such a case the memory location should be declared to be of type `int`.

For example, the following fragment of code uses an `int` memory location to hold the number of people in a room.

```
int room;     // Memory location
room = 7;     // Assigned the number 7
```

The choice of the type of memory location used, will of course depend on the values the memory location is required to hold. As a general rule, when an exact whole number is required, then a memory location of type `int` should be used and when the value may have a fractional part then a memory location of type `double` should be used.

Memory location	Assignment to memory location
int people	people = 2;
double weight	weight = 7.52

1.10.1   Warning

Java will not allow assignments that cause a loss of precision. This means that you cannot assign a number with decimal places or implied decimal places to a location that holds an integer value. For example, the following assignment is invalid:

Memory location	Invalid assignment	Reason
int people	people = 2.1;	You cannot assign a number with a fractional part to a memory location of type **int**.

1.11   Repetition

So far, all the Java applications used in the examples have used straight line code. In straight line code the application consists of statements that are obeyed one after another from top to bottom. There are no statements that affect the flow of control in the application. This technique has allowed us to produce a solution for the specific case of the cost of 5.2 kilograms of apples at £1.20 per kilogram.

Using this strategy, to produce an application to list the cost of apples for a series of different weights would effectively involve writing out the same code many times. An example of this style of coding is illustrated below:

```
double price_per_kilo;                    //Price of apples
double kilos_of_apples;                   //Apples required
double cost;                              //Cost of apples

price_per_kilo = 1.20;

System.out.print( "Cost of apples per kilo  : " );
System.out.print( price_per_kilo );
System.out.println();

System.out.println( "Kilo's  Cost" );
```

```
kilos_of_apples            = 0.1;
```

```
cost = price_per_kilo * kilos_of_apples;
System.out.print( kilos_of_apples );
System.out.print( "        " );
System.out.println( cost );
```

```
kilos_of_apples            = 0.2;
```

```
cost = price_per_kilo * kilos_of_apples;
System.out.print( kilos_of_apples );
System.out.print( "        " );
System.out.println( cost );
```

etc.

Whilst this is a feasible solution, if we want to calculate the cost of 100 different weights this will involve considerable effort and code. Even using copy and paste operations in an editor to lessen the typing effort, will still involve considerable effort! In addition, the resultant application will be large and consume considerable resources.

1.12 Introduction to the `while` statement

In Java a `while` statement is used to repeat program statements while a condition holds true. A `while` statement can be likened to a rail track as illustrated in Figure 1.1. While the condition is true the flow of control is along the true track. Each time around the loop the condition is re-evaluated. Then, when the condition is found to be false, the false track is taken.

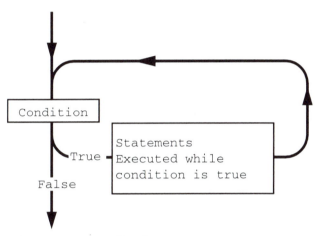

Figure 1.1 The `while` statement as a rail track.

In a `while` loop the condition is always tested first. Due to this requirement if the condition initially evaluates to false then the code associated with the `while` loop will never be executed.

1.12.1 Conditions

In the language Java, a condition is expressed in a very concise format which at first sight may seem strange if you are not used to a mathematical notation. For example, the conditional expression: 'the contents of the memory location `count` is less than or equal to 5' is written as follows:

```
count <= 5
```

Note: The memory location named `count` *will need to be declared as:*

```
int count;
```

The symbols used in a condition are as follows:

Symbol	Means	Symbol	Means
<	Less than	<=	Less than or equal to
==	Equal to	!=	Not equal to
>	Greater than	>=	Greater than or equal to

If the following memory locations contain the following values:

Memory location	Assigned the value
`int` temperature;	temperature = 15;
`double` weight;	weight = 50.0;

then the following table shows the truth or otherwise of several conditional expressions written in Java.

In English	In Java	Condition is
The temperature is less than 20	temperature < 20	true
The temperature is equal to 20	temperature == 20	false
The weight is greater than or equal to 30	weight >= 30.0	true
20 is less than the temperature	20 < temperature	false

Note: As a memory location that holds a `double` *value represents a number that is held only to a certain number of digits accuracy, it is not a good idea to compare such a value for equality* == *or not equality* != *.*

1.12.2   A `while` statement in Java

Illustrated below in a fragment of code that uses a `while` statement to write out the text message `Hello` five times:

```
int count;
count = 1;                     //Set count to 1

while ( count <= 5 )           //While count less than or equal 5
{
  System.out.print( "Hello" ); // Print Hello
  System.out.println();
  count = count + 1;           // Add 1 to count
}
```

Note: The statement: `count = count + 1;` *adds 1 to the contents of* `count` *and puts the result back into the memory location* `count`.

In this code fragment, the statements between the { and } brackets are repeatedly executed while the contents of count are less than 5. The flow of control for the above `while` statement is illustrated in Figure 1.2.

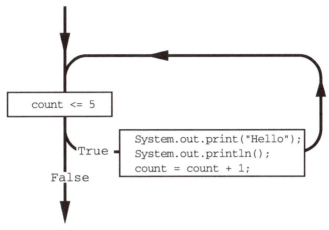

Figure 1.2 Flow of control for a `while` statement in Java.

1.12.3   Using the `while` statement

The real advantage of using a computer program accrues when the written code is repeated many times, thus saving the implementor considerable time and effort. For example, if we wished to produce a table representing the cost of different weights of apples, then a computer application is constructed that repeats the lines of Java code that evaluate the cost of a specific weight of apples. However, for each iteration of the calculation the memory location that contains the weight of the apples is changed. A fragment of Java code to implement this solution is illustrated below:

```java
double price_per_kilo;                      //Price of apples
double kilos_of_apples;                     //Apples required
double cost;                                //Cost of apples

price_per_kilo  = 1.20;

System.out.print( "Cost of apples per kilo  : " );
System.out.print( price_per_kilo );
System.out.println();

System.out.println( "Kilo's  Cost" );
kilos_of_apples           = 0.1;

while ( kilos_of_apples <= 10.0 )           //While lines to print
{
  cost = price_per_kilo * kilos_of_apples;  //Calculate cost
  System.out.print( kilos_of_apples );      //Print results
  System.out.print( "        " );
  System.out.println( cost );
  kilos_of_apples = kilos_of_apples + 0.1;  //Next value
}
```

which when compiled with suitable peripheral code produces output of the form:

```
Cost of apples per kilo  : 1.2
Kilo's  Cost
0.1     0.12
0.2     0.24
0.3     0.36
0.4     0.48
0.5     0.6
0.6     0.72
0.7     0.84
0.8     0.96
0.9     1.08
1.0     1.12
1.1     1.32
1.2     1.44
1.3     1.56
...
9.9     11.88
10.0    12.0
```

Note: There will need to be additional Java statements to control the format of the numbers output.

1.13   Selection

The `if` construct is used to conditionally execute a statement or statements depending on the truth of a condition. This statement can be likened to the rail track illustrated in Figure 1.3 in which the path taken depends on the truth of a condition. However, unlike the `while` statement there is no loop back to re-execute the condition.

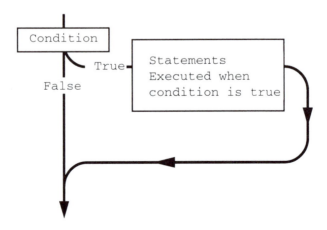

Figure 1.3 The `if` statement represented as a rail track.

For example, the following fragment of a Java application only prints out Hot! when the contents of the memory location temperature are greater than 30 degrees centigrade.

```java
int temperature;
temperature = 30;

if ( temperature > 30 )          //If temperature greater than 30
{
  System.out.print( "Hot!" );  // Say its hot
  System.out.println();
}
```

In this code fragment, the statements between the { and } brackets are only executed if the condition temperature > 30 is true. The flow of control for the above fragment of code is illustrated in Figure 1.4.

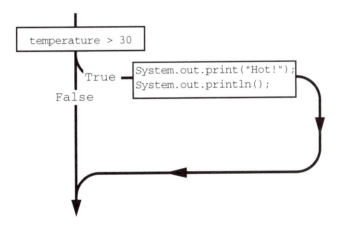

Figure 1.4 The if statement represented as a rail track.

1.13.1   Using the if statement

The fragment of application code which was used earlier to tabulate a list of the price of different weights of apples can be made more readable by separating every 5 lines by a blank line. This can be achieved by having a counter count to count the number of lines printed and after the 5th line has been printed to insert a blank line. After a blank line has been printed the counter count is reset to 0. This modified application is shown below:

```java
double price_per_kilo;              //Price of apples
double kilos_of_apples;             //Apples required
double cost;                        //Cost of apples
```

```
    price_per_kilo  = 1.20;
    kilos_of_apples = 0.1;

    System.out.print( "Cost of apples per kilo  : " );
    System.out.print( price_per_kilo );
    System.out.println();

    System.out.println( "Kilo's  Cost" );
    kilos_of_apples          = 0.0;
    int lines_output = 0;

    while ( kilos_of_apples <= 10.0 )          //While lines to print
    {
      cost = price_per_kilo * kilos_of_apples; //Calculate cost

      System.out.print( kilos_of_apples );     //Print results
      System.out.print( "         " );
      System.out.println( cost );

      kilos_of_apples = kilos_of_apples + 0.1; //Next value
      lines_output = lines_output + 1;         //Add 1

      if ( lines_output >= 5 )                 //If printed group
      {
        System.out.println();                  //  Print line
        lines_output = 0;                      //  Reset count
      }
    }
```

which when compiled with additional statements would produce output of the form shown below:

```
Cost of apples per kilo  : 1.2
Kilo's  Cost
0.0       0.0
0.1       0.12
0.2       0.24
0.3       0.36
0.4       0.48

0.5       0.6
0.6       0.72
0.7       0.84
0.8       0.96
0.9       1.08

1.0       1.2
1.1       1.32
1.2       1.44
1.3       1.56
1.4       1.68

etc.
```

1.14 Self-assessment

- What is a computer programming language?

- What do the following fragments of Java code do?

```java
int i;
i = 10;

while ( i > 0 )
{
  System.out.print( i );
  i = i - 1;
}

System.out.println();
```

```java
int temperature;
temperature = 10;

if ( temperature > 20 )
{
  System.out.print( "It's Hot!" );
}

if ( temperature <= 20 )
{
  System.out.print( "It's not so Hot!" );
}

System.out.println();
```

- What is wrong with the following fragment of Java code?

```java
double weight;
weight = 20;
```

- Write an if statement for each of the following conditions. In your answer state how any memory location you have used has been declared

  - The temperature is less than 15 degrees centigrade.
  - The distance to college is less than 15 Kilometres.
  - The distance to college is greater than or equal to the distance to the football ground.
  - The cost of the bike is less than or equal to the cost of the hi-fi system.

1.15   Paper exercises

Write down on paper Java statements to implement the following.

Note: *You do not need to run these solutions. However, if you do run your answers on a computer system you may wish to look at Chapter 11 on formatting of numbers.*

- *Name*
  Write out your name and address.

- *Weight*
  Calculate the total weight of 27 boxes of paper. Each box of paper weighs 2.4 kilograms.

- *Name*
  Write out the text message `"Happy Birthday"` 3 times using a `while` loop.

- *Times table*
  Print the 5 times table. The output should be of the form:
  ```
  5 *  1 =   5
  5 *  2 =  10
  ```
  etc.

  Hint: *Write the Java code to print the line for the 3rd row, use a variable* `row` *of type* `int` *to hold the value 3.*
  ```
      5 *  3 =  15
  ```
  Enclose these statements in a loop that varies the contents of `row` *from 1 to 12.*

- *Weight table*
  Print a table listing the weights of 1 to 20 boxes of paper, when each box weighs 2.4 kilograms.

- *Times table*
  Print a multiplication table for all values between 1 and 5. The table to look like:
  ```
        |  1   2   3   4   5
      -----------------------
      1 |  1   2   3   4   5
      2 |  2   4   6   8   10
      3 |  3   6   9   12  15
      4 |  4   8   12  16  20
      5 |  5   10  15  20  25
  ```

  Hint: *Write the Java code to print the line for the 2nd row, use a variable* `row` *of type* `int` *to hold the value 2.*
  ```
      2 | 2   4   6   8   10
  ```
  Enclose these statements in a loop that varies the contents of `row` *from 1 to 5. Add statements to print the heading:*
  ```
        | 1   2   3   4   5
      -----------------------
  ```

2. Software design

This chapter looks at software production in the large. In particular it looks at problems that occur in the development of large and not so large software systems. The notation used by UML (Unified Modelling Language) is introduced as a mechanism for documenting and describing a solution to a problem that is to be implemented on a computer system.

2.1 The software crisis

In the early days of computing, it was the hardware that was very expensive. The programs that ran on these computers were by today's standards incredibly small. In those distant times computers only had a very limited amount of storage; both random access memory and disk storage.

Then it all changed. Advances in technology enabled computers to be built cheaper, with a far greater capacity than previous machines. Software developers thought, "Great! We can build bigger and more comprehensive programs". Software projects were started with an increase in scope and great optimism.

Soon, with projects running over budget and not meeting their client's expectations, the truth dawned: large scale software construction is difficult. The early techniques that had been used in small scale software construction did not scale up successfully for large scale software production.

This can be likened to using a bicycle to travel a short distance. Whilst this is adequate for the purpose, the use of a bicycle is inappropriate if a long distance has to be travelled in a short space of time. You cannot just peddle faster and faster.

2.2 A problem, the model and the solution

In implementing any solution to a problem, we must first understand the problem that is to be solved. Then, when we understand the problem fully, a solution can be formulated.

There are many different ways of achieving an understanding of a problem and its solution. Usually, this involves modelling the problem and its solution using either a standard notation or a notation invented by the programmer. The advantage of using a standard notation is that other people may inspect and modify the description of the problem and its proposed solution. For example, in building a house, an architect will draw up a plan of the various components that are to be built. The client can view the plans and give their approval or qualified approval subject to minor modifications. The builders can then use the plan when they erect the house.

Architect's plan (model)	Finished house

Writing a computer program involves the same overall process. First, we need to understand the task that the computer program will perform. Then we need to implement a solution using the model that we have created.

An easy pitfall at this point is to believe that the model used for the solution of a small problem can be scaled up to solve a large problem. For example, to cross a small stream we can put a log over the stream or if athletic we can even jump over the stream. This approach to crossing a stream however, will not scale up to crossing a large river. Likewise to build a 100-storey tower block, an architect would not simply take the plans for a 2-storey house and instruct the builders to build some extra floors.

In software the same problems of scale exist; the techniques that we use to implement a small program cannot usually be successfully used on a large programming project. The computer literature is full of examples of software disasters that have occurred when a computer system has been started without a full understanding of the problem that is to be solved.

2.2.1   Responsibilities

Since our earliest days we have all been told that we have responsibilities. Initially, these responsibilities are very simple, but as we grow older so they increase. A responsibility is a charge, trust or duty of care to look after something. At an early age this can be as simple as keeping our room neat and tidy. In later life, the range and complexity of items that we have responsibility for, increases dramatically.

A student for example, has the responsibility to follow a course of study. The lecturer has the responsibility of delivering the course to the students in a clear and intelligible manner. The responsibilities of the student and lecturer are summarized in tabular form below:

Responsibilities of a student	Responsibilities of a lecturer
Follow the course of study.	Deliver the course.
Perform to the best of their ability in the exam / assessment for the course.	Set and mark the assessment for the course.
	Attend the exam board for the delivered course.

Software too has responsibilities. For example, a text editor has the responsibility of entering the user's typed text correctly into a document. However, if the text that is entered into the text editor is incorrect or meaningless, then the resultant document will also be incorrect. It is not the role of the text editor to make overall decisions about the validity of the entered text.

In early computing literature, a common saying was "Garbage in, garbage out". Even though the software package implements its responsibilities correctly, the results produced may be at least meaningless, at worse damaging if used.

2.3 Objects

The world we live in is composed of many different objects. For example, a person usually has access to at least some of the following objects:

- A telephone
- A computer
- A car.

Each object has its own individual responsibilities. For example, some of the responsibilities associated with the above objects are:

Object	Responsibilities
Telephone	• Establish contact with another phone point. • Convert sound to / from electrical signals.
Computer	• Execute programs. • Provide a tcp/ip connection to the internet.
Car	• Move • Go faster / slower • Turn left / right • Stop

A responsibility here, is a process that the object performs. For example, a car can move forwards or backwards. However, the car has to be instructed by the driver to perform this task. The object is passive, and only performs an action when instructed to do so.

2.3.1 The car as an object

A car is made up of many components or objects. From a user's perspective some of the major objects that make up a car are:

- The shell or body of the car.
- The engine.
- The gearbox.
- The clutch.
- The battery that provides electric power.

We can think of the body or shell of the car as a container for all the other objects, that when combined, form a working car. These other objects are hidden from the driver of the car. The driver can, however, interact with these objects by using the external interfaces that form part of the car shell. This arrangement of objects is expressed diagrammatically using the UML notation in Figure 2.1.

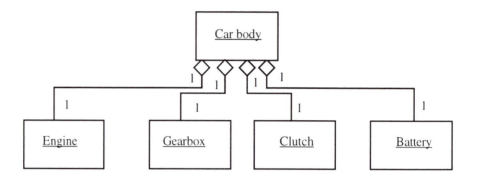

Figure 2.1 Objects that make up a car.

In Figure 2.1 the following style of notation is used:

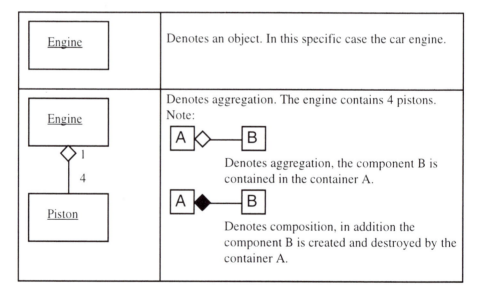

By using this notation, we can express the 'part of' relationship between objects. The engine, gearbox, clutch and battery are 'part of' a car.

2.4 The class

In object-oriented terminology a class is used to describe all objects that share the same responsibilities and internal structure. A class is essentially the collective name for a group of like objects. For example, the following objects all belong to the class car:

Corinna's red car	Mike's silver car	Paul's blue car

Although the objects differ in detail, they all have the same internal structure and responsibilities. Each object is an instance of the class Car. The notation for a class is slightly different from that of an object. The UML notation for a class and an object are illustrated below:

A class	An object (an instance of a class)
Car	Corinna's car

Note: The name of the object is underlined.

It is important to distinguish between a class and an object. A very simple rule is that objects usually have a physical representation, whereas classes are an abstract concept.

2.5 Methods and messages

A method implements a responsibility for a class. For example, some of the responsibilities for the class Car are as follows.

Responsibilities of the class Car
- Start / stop engine
- Go faster / slower
- Turn left / right
- Stop

An instance of the class Car is an object. By sending a message to the object a hidden method inside the object (a responsibility of the class Car) is invoked to process the message. For example, the driver of the car by pressing down on the accelerator, sends the message 'go faster'. The implementation of this is for the engine control system to feed more petrol to the engine. Normally however, the details of this operation are not of concern to the driver of the car.

2.6 Class objects

We have looked at a car's shell as a container for objects and can look at a laptop computer as a container for several computing devices or objects. A laptop computer is composed of:

- The shell of the laptop, that has external interfaces of a keyboard, touch pad and display screen.

- The local disk drive.
- The network file system.
- The CPU.
- The sound and graphics chipset.

In this analysis, the networked file system is shared between many different laptops, each individual laptop having access to the networked file system. In object-oriented terminology the networked file system is a class object which is shared between all the notebooks.

The concept of a shared object is important as it allows all instances of a class to have access to the same information. Thus, if one instance of a laptop computer creates a file on the network file system, the other notebooks will be able to access the contents of this file.

This arrangement of objects for a laptop computer can be expressed diagrammatically as illustrated using the UML notation in Figure 2.2. Unfortunately in UML there is no way to show diagrammatically that a class item is shared between many classes.

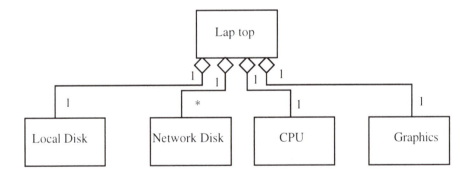

Figure 2.2 Objects that make up a laptop computer from a user's perspective.

Another interesting property of a class object, is that to access it you do not need an instance of the container object. For example, the network file system can be used by devices other than the laptop computers.

2.7 Inheritance

A typical office will usually contain at least the following objects:

- A telephone.
- A fax machine with a telephone hand set.
- A computer.

Each of these objects has their own individual responsibilities. For example, some of the responsibilities of these office objects are:

Object	Responsibilities
Telephone	• Establish contact with another phone point. • Convert sound to / from electrical signals.
Fax machine with a telephone hand set	• Establish contact with another phone point. • Convert sound to / from electrical signals. • Convert images to / from electrical signals.
Computer	• Execute programs. • Provide a tcp/ip connection to the internet.

Looking at these responsibilities shows that the telephone and fax machine share several responsibilities. The fax machine has two of the responsibilities that the telephone has. We could say that a fax machine is a telephone that can also send and receive images. Another way of thinking about this is that the fax machine can be used as if it were only a telephone. This relationship between classes that represent all telephones and fax machines is shown diagrammatically in Figure 2.3 using the UML notation. In this relationship a fax machine is inherited (or formed from the components) of a telephone.

Inheritance diagram	Responsibilities:
Telephone △ Fax machine	Establish contact with another phone point. Convert sound to / from electrical signals. All the responsibilities of a telephone plus: Convert images to / from electrical signals.

Figure 2.3 Relationship between a telephone and a fax machine.

Note: The superclass (telephone) is the class from which a subclass (fax machine) is inherited.
Inheritance requires you to take all the responsibilities from the superclass; you cannot selectively choose to take only some. However, even though you inherit the responsibilities you do not need to use them.

The inheritance relationship is an important concept in object-oriented programming as it enables new objects to be created by specializing an existing object. In creating the new object, only the addition, responsibilities have to be constructed. The development time for a new software object is reduced as the task of creating the inherited responsibilities has already been done. This process leads to a dramatic reduction in the time and effort required to create new software objects.

2.8 Polymorphism

In a collection of different objects if all the objects are capable of receiving a specific message then this message may be sent to any object in the collection. The method executed when this message is received by an object will depend on the type of the object that receives the message.

For example, in a group of individuals if you ask a person how to take part in their favourite sport, you will probably get many different answers. In effect the message "How to take part in your favourite sport" is polymorphic in that the answer you get depends on the individual person you select to ask. A tennis player for example, would give a different answer than a golfer.

2.9 Self-assessment

- Explain why the solution to a small problem may not always scale up to solve a much larger and complex problem.

- What is a "Responsibility"?

- What are the responsibilities of:
  - A video camera.
  - An alarm clock.
  - A traffic light.
  - An actress playing the role of Olgar in the Three sisters by Chekov.

- What is the relationship between an object, message and a method?

- What classes do the following objects belong to?

apartment	cat	crayon	crystal	dog
guinea pig	igloo	house	ink pen	library
mansion	office block	pencil	rabbit	sheep

  Identify which classes are subclassed from other classes?

- Identify several objects and classes around you at the moment. Can you find responsibilities that any of the objects or classes have in common ?

3. Java the language basics — part 1

This chapter looks at some simple Java applications, which introduce the basic control structures of the language. The applications shown in this chapter write directly into a console window and are termed console applications.

3.1 A first Java application

Like many books on programming, this Chapter also uses an example program that writes the traditional greeting of Hello world to the user's terminal. The Java term for a program that runs directly on a computer is an application. Hence from now on all programs in this book will be called applications.

```java
class Hello
{
  public static void main( String args[] )
  {
    System.out.println("Hello world");
  }
}
```

The above application, when compiled and run, displays the following message on the user's terminal:

```
Hello world
```

In this example the Java application consists of a single class Hello which contains a single method main which is invoked when the application is run. The method main contains the line:

```
System.out.println("Hello world");
```

that is responsible for outputting the greeting "Hello world".

3.1.1 Components of: `System.out.println("Hello world");`

This Java statement is responsible for outputting the message `"Hello world"` to the console window and is composed of the components illustrated in Figure 3.1 below.

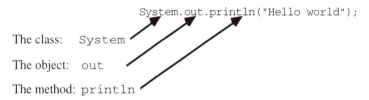

```
System.out.println("Hello world");
```

The class: `System`

The object: `out`

The method: `println`

Figure 3.1 Components of the statement: `System.out.println("Hello world")`.

The object `out` is an instance of the class `PrintStream`. The class `System` contains a visible instance of this class called `out`. A programmer can refer to this object directly by using the notation `System.out`.

Hence, the above statement should be read as, send the message `println` with a parameter of `"Hello world"` to the object `out` that is a static member of the class `System`.

Note: A static object in a class is shared between all instances of the class and can be accessed directly by prefixing the object with the name of the class in which it occurs.

See Chapter 6 on anatomy of a method.

3.2 Structure of a Java application

A Java application is made up of at least the following components:

● A class:
In the example application shown in Figure 3.2 the class is `Hello`.

● A special method called `main`:
The method `main` is special as its name signifies to the Java compiler that this method is to be executed when the application is run.

The structure of the class `Hello` is illustrated in Figure 3.2 below:

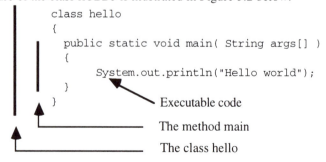

```
class hello
{
    public static void main( String args[] )
    {
        System.out.println("Hello world");
    }
}
```

Executable code

The method main

The class hello

Figure 3.2 Structure of a Java class `Hello`.

Note: The symbols { and } are used to delimit the body of the class and the method.

3.2.1   Layout of a Java application

A Java application can be written without regard to format provided that the individual components that make up the application can be recognized. For example, the following is a valid Java application:

```
class Hello{public static void main(String args[]){
System.out.println("Hello world");}}
```

Note: At least one white space character is required between words in the application so that each word can be distinguished. In the above example space is used to separate the words `class` *and* `Hello`.

However, to make the application easy to read, follow and modify, a Java application should be written using indentation and suitable comments.

3.3   The methods `println` and `print`

The methods `print` and `println` are used to write information into the console window of a Java application. These methods have the following responsibilities:

Message	Responsibility
print(arg)	Writes the argument to the console window.
println(arg) println()	As for print except that a new line character is added at the end of the output.

Note: If the argument is a variable, then the contents of the variable are written in character form.

3.3.1   Example of use

The previous application can be re-written as follows:

```
class Hello
{
  public static void main( String args[] )
  {
    System.out.print( "hello " );
    System.out.print( "world" );
    System.out.println();
  }
}
```

Note: Even when a method has no parameters' the ( )'s are still required.

3.3.2   Printing the contents of a variable

The contents of a variable may also be output using `print` or `println`. For example, the following demonstration application outputs the sum of 1+2+3:

```
class Calculate
{
  public static void main( String args[] )
  {
    int sum;
    System.out.print( "The sum of 1 + 2 + 3 is " );
    sum = 1 + 2 + 3;
    System.out.print( sum );
    System.out.println();
  }
}
```

which, when compiled and run, will produce the following output to the user's screen:

```
The Sum of 1+2+3 is 6
```

3.4 Comments

Java has three ways of introducing comments into an application. The first two styles are for normal comments that are to be read by a developer or maintainer of the code and the third style is captured and used in program documentation. The style of these comments is illustrated below:

Style 1

```
/* This is a comment */
```

where the comment is bracketed between /* and */ although it is more usual to write this in the form:

```
/*
 *   This is also a comment
 */
```

Note: The / */ comment delimiters may not be nested.*

Style 2

```
//The rest of the line is a comment
```

Here the comment is introduced by // and is terminated by the new line.

Style 3

```
/**
 * Comment to appear in automatically generated documentation.
 *   @tag description
 */
```

The third comment form is used for a document comment. A documentation comment is processed by a documentation application such as `javadoc` that produces cross referenced documentation about the items used in the application. Appendix G contains a list of the different tags that can be used in a documentation comment.

It is good programming practice to write comments for any code section that is not immediately obvious to a reader of the code. A // comment can be inside a /* */ comment and a /* */ comment can be inside a // comment. However, a /* */ comment cannot contain another /* */ comment.

3.5   The concatenation operator +

In Java the + operator is also used to concatenate strings together. For example, the hello world application could have been written as:

```
class Hello
{
  public static void main( String args[] )
  {
    System.out.println( "hello " + "world" );
  }
}
```

If at least one of the operands to the + operator is a string, then the other operand will be converted to a string so that the concatenation may take place. This is usually only meaningful if the other operand is one of the standard types.

This automatic conversion is very useful is simplifying the code required to output results from an application. For example, the following application outputs the sum of 1 + 2 + 3.

```
class Example
{
  public static void main( String args[] )
  {
    int sum = 1 + 2 + 3;
    System.out.println( "The sum of 1 + 2 + 3 is " + sum );
  }
}
```

The above application can be further simplified to:

```
class Example
{
  public static void main( String args[] )
  {
    System.out.println( "The sum of 1 + 2 + 3 is "  + (1+2+3) );
  }
}
```

Note: The use of brackets around the expression 1+2+3.

3.5.1   Warning

The + operator needs to be used with care. As the following statement:

```
System.out.println( "The sum of 1 + 2 + 3 is " + 1 + 2 + 3 );
```

when it is compiled and run will print:

```
The sum of 1 + 2 + 3 is 123
```

The reason for this, is that the expression is evaluated left to right as follows:

Original expression	"The sum of 1 + 2 + 3 is " + 1 + 2 + 3
After evaluating 1st +	"The sum of 1 + 2 + 3 is 1" + 2 + 3
After evaluating 2nd +	"The sum of 1 + 2 + 3 is 12" + 3
After evaluating 3rd +	"The sum of 1 + 2 + 3 is 123"

3.6 A larger Java application

A complete Java application to produce a simulated countdown for the launch of a space craft is shown below. In this application several constructs that affect the flow of control are introduced.

```
class Countdown
{
  public static void main( String args[] )
    throws java.lang.InterruptedException
  {
    int countdown=10;                    //Start from 10
    while ( countdown > 0 )              //While greater than 0
    {
      System.out.println(countdown);     // Write contents of countdown
      if ( countdown == 3 )              // If equal to 3
      {
        System.out.println("Ignition");  //  Write Ignition
      }
      countdown--;                       // Decrement countdown by 1
      Thread.sleep( 1000 );              // 1000 milliseconds delay
    }
    System.out.println( "Blast Off");    //Write Blast off
  }
}
```

Note: The expression countdown-- *is an idiom in Java that decrements the contents of* countdown *by* 1.

When compiled and run, this application produces the following results:

```
10
9
8
7
6
5
4
3
Ignition
2
1
Blast Off
```

Note: There is a 1 second delay between writing the individual numbers in the countdown.

3.6.1   The static method **Thread.sleep**

In the application the statement:

```
Thread.sleep( 1000 );
```

causes a delay of 1000 microseconds (1 second). The declaration of the method `main` needs modification because this delay may be interrupted. The declaration of `main` is now:

```
public static void main( String args[] )
    throws java.lang.InterruptedException
```

This simply states that the interruption to the enforced delay will not be handled in the method `main`. If such an exception does occur, because there is no handler for the exception, the exception will be propagated out of `main` and cause the application to fail with an appropriate run-time error message. Chapter 13 discusses the role of exceptions in a Java application in more detail.

3.7   Repetition: the `while` statement

The `while` statement is used to repeatedly execute line(s) of code while a condition holds. For example, in the countdown application the `while` construct is used to repeatedly execute the lines of code that write the current time in seconds to the launch.

```
while ( countdown > 0 )
{
  // Body of loop
}
```

The above `while` statement repeatedly executes the code between { and } until the condition `countdown > 0` is no longer true.

Note: The ( )s around the condition are mandatory. The { and } brackets are only required if there is more than one statement to execute repeatedly. Many people, however, would always put in the {} brackets to show the bounds of the loop.

3.8   Selection: the `if` statement

The `if` statement allows a run-time choice to be made about which lines of code are to be or not to be executed. For example, in the countdown application the message `Ignition` is only written when the countdown is at 3 seconds to launch.

```
if ( countdown == 3 )
{
  // Body of if statement
}
```

In the fragment of code above, the lines between { and } are only executed if the condition `countdown == 3` is true. That is, the contents of the variable `countdown` contain 3.

Note: Equality is written ==. It is an error to write equality as =.

Not equality is written as !=. For example, to test if the current month number is not February the following style of code is written:

```java
if ( month != 2 )
    System.out.println("The month is not February");
```

Note: As only one statement was selected to be executed when the condition was true, the enclosing brackets { and } were not required. However, this will lead to an error if at a later stage another statement is added without enclosing both statements in enclosing { } brackets.

3.8.1 if else

An else part may be added to an if statement to select a statement or statements that will be executed when the condition is false.

```java
if ( month == 2 )
    System.out.println("The month is February");
else
    System.out.println("The month is not February");
```

Note: The ; before the else must be present as it terminates the previous statement.

3.9 Other repetition constructs

In addition to the general while statement, Java contains two other looping constructs these are: the for statement and the do while statement.

3.9.1 The for statement

The for statement in Java is written as:

```java
for ( int countdown = 10; countdown >= 1; countdown-- )
{
  // Body of for statement
}
```

Note: The variable controlling the for loop countdown may be declared inside the ( ) brackets. When the control variable is declared in this way within the for statement its scope is the body of the loop.

which in this example steps countdown through the values 10 to 1. This is equivalent to the following `while` statement:

```
{
  int countdown = 10;
  while ( countdown  >= 1 )
  {
    // Body of loop
    countdown--;
  }
}
```

Note: `countdown--;` *is the Java idiom for:* `countdown = countdown - 1;`
In the `for` *statement any of the components between the* `;`*'s may be omitted.*

3.9.2   The `do while` statement

In some cases it is a requirement that the loop should be executed at least once, in which case the `do  while` statement may be used. For example, the above `for` statement could have been written as:

```
int countdown = 10;
do
{
  // Body of loop
  countdown--;
} while ( countdown >= 1 );
```

Note: However, if the variable `countdown` *had an initial value of 0 the loop would be executed once.*

3.10   Other selection constructs

In addition to the `if` statement there are two other statements that allow code to be selectively executed. The first of these, the `switch` statement, allows an elegant way of choosing which of several different code sequences should be executed. Whilst the second allows an expression to contain a choice about which value is to be selected.

3.10.1   The `switch` statement

The following rather inelegant series of `if` statements when executed will print the name of the current month contained in the integer variable `month`:

```
if ( month == 1 )
    System.out.print( "January" );
else if ( month == 2 )
    System.out.print( "February" );
else if ( month == 3 )
    System.out.print( "March" );
else System.out.print( "Not January, February or March" );
System.out.println();
```

Note: 1 represents January, 2 represents February etc.

can be re-written in an elegant way using a `switch` statement as follows:

```
switch ( month )
{
    case 1 :
        System.out.print("January");
        break;
    case 2 :
        System.out.print("February");
        break;
    case 3 :
        System.out.print("March");
        break;
    default:
        System.out.print( "Not January, February or March" );
}
System.out.println();
```

In the `switch` statement however, an explicit break-out must be specified, otherwise control will drop to the next switch label. This break-out of the `switch` statement is performed by the `break` statement.

Note: The value switched must be an instance of a byte, short, char or int. The case label must be a compile time constant value of type byte, short, char or int.
If break is omitted execution will continue through the case label to the next statement.

3.10.2   Conditional expression statement

The expression:

```
month == 2 ? "February" : "not February"
```

delivers the string "February" or "not February" depending on the value of `month`. This can be used as illustrated below to print whether the current month is February or not. By using a conditional expression, source code may often be simplified and in many cases made more elegant and easy to follow. For example, the following code fragment:

```java
if ( month == 2 )
  System.out.println( "The month is February" );
else
  System.out.println( "The month is not February" );
```

can be re-written as follows:

```java
System.out.println( "The month is " +
                    (month == 2 ? "" : "not ") +
                    "February" );
```

3.11   The **break** statement

As shown above, the break statement may be used to cause control to be passed to the end of a `switch` statement. The `break` statement may also be used to terminate early the execution of the looping constructs `while`, `do while` and `for`. For example, the following while loop steps `counter` from 10 to 1, but the break statement causes a break-out of the loop when `counter` reaches 3.

```java
int counter = 10;
count: while ( counter >= 1 )              //Named while loop count
{
  System.out.print( counter + " " );       //print counter
  if ( counter == 3 ) break count;         //break-out of "count"
  counter--;
}
System.out.println();
```

Note: The `while` loop is named `count` so that the break statement can break-out of an explicit loop. By naming the loop, the programmer is sure which loop is to be broken out of.

When combined into a complete application and run, the following results will be produced:

```
10 9 8 7 6 5 4 3
```

A `break` statement may also be un-labelled as in the case below:

```
int counter = 10;
while ( counter >= 1 )
{
  System.out.print( counter + " " );      //print counter
  if ( counter == 3 ) break;              //break out
  counter--;
}
System.out.println();
```

The danger in using this form is, that if the while loop were removed, the break statement would cause an exit from any surrounding loop. This may not be the effect the programmer intended when they removed the original loop. By naming the loop, a compile-time error would be generated if the named loop were removed.

3.12   The `continue` statement

The `continue` statement is rather unusual in that its effect is to abandon the current execution path through the loop, and proceed to the next iteration. For example, the following `for` loop steps `counter` from 1 to 10.

```
count: for ( int counter=1; counter<=10; counter++ )
{
  if ( counter == 3 ) continue count;    //continue "count"
  System.out.print( counter + " " );     //print counter
}
System.out.println();
```

Note: *That in the above example the* `for` *statement is named* `loop` *so that there is no ambiguity about which* `for` *statement is being continued.*

The result of the above code is simply that the number 3 is not printed.

```
1 2 4 5 6 7 8 9 10
```

Although not recommended the `continue` statement may also be written without naming the loop that is to be continued as follows:

```
for ( int counter=1; counter<=10; counter++ )
{
  if ( counter == 3 ) continue;          //continue
  System.out.print( counter + " " );     //print counter
}
System.out.println();
```

3.13   Exiting from an inner loop

By naming a looping construct, a safe break-out of an inner loop to the end of an outer loop may be made. For example, the following application prints successively longer and longer lines of stars. However, this process is terminated when the fifth star in a line is printed.

```java
class Main
{
  public static void main( String args[] )
  {
    loop_outer: for( int i=1; i<99; i++ )     //FOR loop outer
    {
      System.out.print("Stars " + i + " "); //Outer loop
      loop_inner: for( int s=1; s<=i; s++ ) // FOR loop inner
      {
        System.out.print( "*" );              //  print *
        if (s >= 5) break loop_outer;         //  Exit loop outer
      }                                       // End loop inner
      System.out.println();
    }                                         //End loop outer
    System.out.println();
  }
}
```

Note: The statement break loop_outer; *will cause an exit from the* for
statement named loop_outer.

When compiled and run, the following results are produced:

```
Stars 1 *
Stars 2 **
Stars 3 ***
Stars 4 ****
Stars 5 *****
```

3.14   The **try catch** block

When executing an application there is always the possibility of failure. One of the areas that can cause failure is the reading of information that has been input by a user. The user may type in the wrong data values. For example, when asked to input a number, the user might enter alphabetic characters instead.

Rather than have to test each action individually for failure, Java uses an exception mechanism to indicate exceptional events. An exception is generated in an application in cases when processing cannot be sensibly continued. The exception mechanism is controlled by the construct:

```
try
{
    // Some code that may fail
}
catch ( )
{
    // Action taken if failure in try block
}
```

Note: Chapter 13 explains the exception mechanism in more detail.

The code in the catch block is only executed if a failure occurs. The catch construct nominates which exceptions are to be caught. If there is more than one type of exception to be caught then several catch constructs are used.

For example, the following code converts a number represented as characters held in a string into a numerical value held in the variable value. If the process fails then the code in the catch block is executed. However, if the process succeeds, then the code in the catch block is not executed.

```
int value = 0;                                //
try
{
    value = Integer.parseInt( "123" );       //Convert
}
catch ( NumberFormatException ex )           //Problem
{
    System.out.println("Problem with conversion");
}
```

Note: The methods Integer.parseInt *converts the characters in its string argument into an integer number. If this process fails then the exception* NumberFormatException *is thrown. Chapter 7 describes in more detail the major methods of the class* Integer. *The exception mechanism is discussed in more detail in Chapter 13.*

3.15   Input / Output using the class System

The class System contains objects that allow input and output for console based applications. The class System contains the following visible objects:

Field / Object	Instance of class	Object used for:
in	InputStream	Reading from the standard output stream.
out	PrintStream	Writing to the standard output stream.
err	PrintStream	Writing to the standard error stream.

These stream objects normally take input from the keyboard and write output to the console window. However, many operating systems allow these input and output streams to be redirected to allow the input for an application to be taken from a file and the output from the application to be written to a file.

On a DOS / Unix based system input or output is taken from / directed to a file by using the following command line syntax to run the application:

`java count < data.txt`	Input taken from file `data.txt`.
`java count > results.txt`	Output written to the file `results.txt`.
`java count < data.txt > results.txt`	Input taken from the file `data.txt` and output written to the file `results.txt`.

Note: The above application is called `count` and is run using the Java interpreter directly. Some operating systems will recognize a Java bytecode file and automatically create the Java virtual machine in which the application is run. In which case the application could be run using the following command line invocation: `count < data.txt` which runs the application `count` taking its input from the file `data.txt`.

Appendix G details the parameters to the JDK command line compiler `javac` and interpreter `java`.

3.15.1   Input from the standard input stream

The method `read` is a member of the class `InputStream`. It reads a character from the standard input and returns its integer representation. If the end of file is reached the value -1 is returned. The following fragment of code:

```
int c; c = System.in.read();
```

reads the next character from the standard input stream into the variable c.

The following demonstration application calculates statistics relating to the characters read from the standard input. In this application the following class methods from the class `java.lang.Character` are used to determine the type of a letter:

Method	Responsibility
`Character.isDigit(c)`	Returns true if the character passed as a parameter is a digit.
`Character.isLetter(c)`	Returns true if the character passed as a parameter is a letter.

Note: Section 6.3 describes the concept of class methods. Appendix F has a fuller list of the methods in `Character`.

```
import java.io.IOException;       // Required to import these classes
import java.lang.Character;       // See Chapter 17 on Packages

class Count
{
  public static void main( String args[] )
  {
    int letters   = 0;
    int digits    = 0;
    int total     = 0;
    try
    {
      int c;
      while ( ( c = System.in.read() ) != -1 )
      {
        char ch = (char) c;
        total++;
        if ( Character.isDigit( ch ) )   digits++;
        if ( Character.isLetter( ch ) )  letters++;
      }
    }
    catch ( IOException name )
    {
      System.err.println("IO error");
    }
    System.out.println("Number of characters   : " + total );
    System.out.println("              letters   => : " + letters );
    System.out.println("              digits    => : " + digits );
  }
}
```

Note: The use of a try catch *block to capture input errors. If there is an input error,
control will be passed out of the* while *loop to the code in the* catch *block.
This code writes an appropriate message to the error stream.*

When compiled and run, typical results from the application would be as follows:

```
Number of characters   : 318
          letters   => : 253
          digits    => : 0
```

3.15.2   Output to the standard error stream

As seen earlier the methods print and println are used to output textual
information to the standard output stream. Output to the standard error stream is effected
in the same way using the object err that is a visible field of the class System. For
example, the following code will write the error message it failed to the error
stream.

```
System.err.println("It failed");
```

3.16   Self-assessment

- What are the major differences so far between Java and any other computer programming languages known to you?

- What are the = and == operators used for?

- Why does Java allow the naming of a looping statement such as `while`?

- Why does Java have two looping constructs `while` and `do while`?

- When should comments be introduced into an application?

- Can any sequence of `if else` statements be replaced by a single `case` statement?

3.17   Exercises

Construct the following Java applications using the object `out` in the class `System` for all output.

- *Numbers*
  An application to write out the numbers 1 to 25 in descending order.

- *Times table*
  An application to print the multiplication table for 7 from 1 to 12.

- *Miles to kilometres*
  An application to print out a conversion table of miles to kilometres from 1 mile to 25 miles. There are approximately 1.609244 kilometres to a mile.

- *Fibonacci series*
  An application to print out numbers in the fibonacci series 1 1 2 3 5 8 13 21 ... until the last number is larger than 50000. The next number in the series is formed from the sum of the previous last two terms.

- *Times table*
  An application to print a multiplication table for all values between 1 and 5. The table to look like:

```
   | 1   2   3   4   5
   ----------------------
1  | 1   2   3   4   5
2  | 2   4   6   8   10
3  | 3   6   9   12  15
4  | 4   8   12  16  20
5  | 5   10  15  20  25
```

4. Java the language basics — part 2

This chapter looks at the inbuilt data types in Java together with the operations that may be performed on instances of these types.

4.1 Fundamental types in Java

The Java language supports the following fundamental data types:

Integer data types	`byte, short, int, long`
Real data types	`float, double`
Character data type	`char`
Boolean data type	`boolean`

Unlike many languages, instances of these types have a precise representation and a defined initial value. For example, an instance of an `int` is represented by a 32 bit 2's complement number that has an initial value of 0. It may, however, be explicitly initialized by the user to another value.

The complete collection of inbuilt data types together with their initial default values is shown in the table below:

Type	Comment	Representation	Initial value
`boolean`	A boolean value	1 bit	`false`
`byte`	A whole number	8 bit 2's complement no.	0
`short`	A whole number	16 bit 2's complement no.	0
`char`	A character	16 bit Unicode character	`'\u0000'`
`int`	A whole number	32 bit 2's complement no.	0
`float`	A number with decimal paces	32 bit IEEE 754	`0.0`
`long`	A whole number	64 bit 2's complement no.	0
`double`	A number with decimal places	64 bit IEEE 754	`0.0`

Note: The precision, range of values and initial value of instances of these data types. The declaration of a variable may occur anywhere an executable statement may occur.

4.1.1   The types `byte`, `short`, `int` and `long`

An instance of any of the integer data types holds a number to a precise amount, the only difference between instances of the types is the range of numbers that can be represented in an instance of the types. For example, the following table below shows the range of values that can be held in instances of the integer data types.

Type	Range of values that can be held	Size (bits)
byte	−128 ... +127	8
short	−32768 ... +32767	16
int	−2147483648 ... +2147483647	32
long	−9223372036854775808 ... +9223372036854775807	64

4.1.2   The types `float` and `double`

An instance of the type `int` holds numbers to an exact whole value. However, in solving some problems it is required to hold values to several decimal places. For example, the distance by road between central Brighton and central London is 104.6 kilometres. In an application dealing with road distances the distance from Brighton to London is expressed as follows:

```
double brighton_to_london = 104.6;
```

A `float` or `double` is implemented as a floating point number. A floating point number holds a value to a specific number of digits. This will, in many cases be an approximation to the exact value which the programmer wishes to store. For example, a 1/3 will be held as 0.333 ... 33. The following table shows how various numbers are effectively stored in floating point form to 6 decimal places:

Number	Scientific notation	Floating point form
12.34	$0.1234 * 10^2$	+123400 +02
0.001234	$0.1234 * 10^{-2}$	+123400 −02
0.333333	$0.333333 * 10^0$	+333333 +00

Note: However, inside the computer a floating point number is held in binary.

The major consequence of using a floating point number is that the numbers are held to an approximation of their true value. Any calculations that use floating point numbers will usually only give an approximation to the true answer. In many cases this approximation will not cause any problems. However, one area where this approximation to the real value will cause problems is when the value represents a large monetary amount that has to be held to the exact amount in pounds and pence.

The range of values that can be held in an instance of a `float` or `double` is shown below:

Type	Range of values that can be held (approximately)	
float	+/− $1.4 * 10^{-45}$	... $3.4 * 10^{38}$
double	+/− $4.9 * 10^{-324}$	... $1.8 * 10^{308}$

4.1.3   The type `char`

An instance of the type `char` holds a Unicode character. This is a 16 bit variable that can contain the characters of most known languages. The table below shows the character values used for some of the alphabets that an instance of the type `char` can represent.

Character value	Language
0x0000 – 0x007F	Control and Basic Latin characters. Characters 0x00 - 0x7F are ASCII
0x0080 – 0x00FF	Latin-1 Supplement (£ sign is here 0xA3)
0x0370 – 0x03FF	Greek
0x0600 – 0x6FF	Arabic
0x0F00 – 0xFBF	Tibetan

The characters represented by the first few positions in the Unicode character set are illustrated in the table below. In this table the explanation mark (!) has a decimal value of 33 and the lower-case letter z has decimal value of 122.

```
     |  0  1  2  3  4  5  6  7  8  9
---------------------------------------
 30  |           !  "  #  $  %  &  '
 40  |  (  )  *  +  ,  -  .  /  0  1
 50  |  2  3  4  5  6  7  8  9  :  ;
 60  |  <  =  >  ?  @  A  B  C  D  E
 70  |  F  G  H  I  J  K  L  M  N  O
 80  |  P  Q  R  S  T  U  V  W  X  Y
 90  |  Z  [  \  ]  ^  _  `  a  b  c
100  |  d  e  f  g  h  i  j  k  l  m
110  |  n  o  p  q  r  s  t  u  v  w
120  |  x  y  z  {  |  }  ~
```

Note: Characters with decimal values 30, 31, 127, 128 and 129 are not represented.
Space has a decimal value of 32.

4.1.4   The type `boolean`

An instance of this type holds a boolean value that is either true or false. By using `boolean` values in an application the logic of the code can often be expressed in a more elegant form.

4.2   Const declarations

To make an application more readable, constants can be given symbolic names. The declaration of a constant is very similar to that of a normal variable. The only difference is, of course, that no value can subsequently be assigned to it. For example, the value of π which represents the ratio of a circle's circumference to its diameter (Circumference = π * diameter) is defined as:

```
final double PI  = 3.14159265358979323846;
```

Note: It is good programming practice to use a constant declaration for any value other than 0 or 1. To differentiate easily between constant items and variable items, constant items are shown in UPPER case.

4.3   Widening of variables

Variables of one type may be assigned to variables of another type provided that there is no information loss. This type conversion is called widening. Permitted widening of the standard variables are as follows:

Items of type	May be widened to any of the following types
byte	short int long float double
short	int long float double
char	int long float double
int	long float double
long	float double
float	double

Note: A widening to a floating point type may result in loss of precision. This will be due to the inability of the floating point number to hold all the digits of the original number. However, the magnitude of the number is not affected.

4.4   Narrowing conversions

A narrowing conversion will lose information. The following narrowing conversions may be performed provided a cast is used to specify the narrowing performed:

Items of type	May be narrowed to any of the following types
short	byte char
char	byte short
int	byte short char
long	byte short char int
float	byte short char int long
double	byte short char int long float

For example, to assign an instance of a `long` to an instance of an `int`, the following assignment statement is used:

```
int   as_int   = (int) as_long;
```

The cast (`int`) converts the `long` value into an `int` value. However, there will be information loss if the value contained in the `long` variable `as_long` contains a number outside the range $-2147483648 \ldots +2147483647$. The narrowing is performed by simply truncating the `long` value to 32 bits.

4.4.1 Assignments that result in a potential loss of precision

Java will flag a compile-time error if an assignment will result in a potential loss of information, as in the assignment of `as_int` to `as_short` shown below:

```
int   as_int   = 999999;
short as_short = as_int;   // Compile-time error
```

that will result in a compile-time error as a `short` cannot contain all the information that an `int` can hold. Remember, an `int` is represented in 32 bits whilst a short is represented in 16 bits.

A cast to a new type is written (`Type`) where `Type` is one of the standard types. For example, the previous code is correctly written as:

```
int   as_int   = 999999;
short as_short = (short) as_int; // OK

System.out.println("as_int    : " + as_int );
System.out.println("as_short   : " + as_short );
```

which when combined into a complete application and run produces the following results:

```
as_int     : 999999
as_short   : 16959
```

which may not be what was wanted. What happens is that the contents of `an_int` are truncated to the bottom 16 bits and then assigned to `as_short`.

Remember, it is up to the programmer to make sure that assignment produces a consistent result. Casts are usually used when the programmer knows that the value can be converted successfully without any loss of information.

4.5 Binary numeric promotions

When an operation is performed between instances of the standard types. the following promotion model is used when the operands differ in type or involve instances of `byte`, `short` or `char`. In an expression involving `Operand1 operator Operand2`.

If either `Operand1` or `Operand2` is a:

`double`	then the other operand is converted to a	`double`
`float`	then the other operand is converted to a	`float`
`long`	then the other operand is converted to a	`long`

otherwise both operands are converted to an `int`. For example, with the following declarations of instances of the standard types:

```
byte    a_byte;
int     an_int;
float   a_float;
```

The effect of the following expressions is as follows:

Expression	Results in
`a_byte + an_int`	The contents of a_byte promoted to an int.
`a_byte + a_byte`	The contents of both operands promoted to an int.
`a_float + a_byte`	The contents of a a_byte promoted to a float.

This means that any operation delivering a numeric result involving instances of `byte`, `short` or `char` will result in the delivery of an `int` value as the result of the computation.

4.6 Arithmetic operators in Java

In Java the following arithmetic operators are used to form arithmetic expressions:

Operator	Represents
+	plus
–	minus
*	multiplication
/	division than
%	remainder

4.7 Relational operators in Java

In Java the following relational operators are used in constructing boolean expressions:

Operator	Represents
==	equal
!=	not equal
<	less than
>	greater than
<=	less than or equal
>=	greater than or equal

Note: That equality is written as == and not as =.

The following fragment of code ascertains if the current month is in the last quarter of the year:

```java
// month is 1 for January 2 for February etc.
if ( month >= 10 )
    System.out.println("In the last Qtr of the year");
```

4.8 Logical operators

The following logical operators are used to form complex conditional expressions:

Operator	Represents
&&	logical and between boolean values
||	logical or between boolean values

For example the && operator is used in the following logical expression to test that both the day number is 25 and the month number is 12.

```java
if ( day == 25 && month == 12 )
    System.out.println("Happy Christmas");
```

In the next conditional expression a test is made to ascertain if the year is a leap year.

```java
if ( year%4 == 0 &&
    ( year%100 != 0 || year%400 == 0 ) )
{
    System.out.print( year + " is a leap year ");
}
```

Note: Remember, a century year is only a leap year if it is also divisible by 400.

4.8.1   Logical operators summary

The following truth tables illustrate the result of using the logical operators on truth values:

Logical and `&&`	Logical or `||`
`false && false => false`	`false || false => false`
`false && true  => false`	`false || true  => true`
`true  && false => false`	`true  || false => true`
`true  && true  => true`	`true  || true  => true`

4.8.2   Lazy evaluation

In evaluating a logical expression lazy evaluation is performed. In lazy evaluation once the truth of the expression is established no further evaluation of the expression is performed. For example, in the expression:

```
if ( day == 25 && month == 12 )
   System.out.println("Happy Christmas");
```

if the `day` is not `25` then the expression `month == 12` will not be evaluated. A consequence of this is that if the expression had been:

```
if ( day == 25 && object.method() )
```

then `object.method()` would not be called.

The effect of lazy evaluation is summarized in the table below where the LHS of the expression is either true or false and the RHS is a boolean expression which is only evaluated if required.

Logical expression	(`boolean expression`) evaluated
`truth && (boolean expression)`	✓
`false && (boolean expression)`	✗
`truth || (boolean expression)`	✗
`false || (boolean expression)`	✓

4.9 Bitwise operators

Individual bits in an instance of the integer data types can be manipulated with the following operators:

Operator	Implements
a << b	a is left shifted by b bits
a >> b	a is right shifted by b bits the sign bit is propagated
a >>> b	a is right shifted by b bits the sign bit is **not** propagated
a & b	the bitwise and of a and b is formed
a | b	the bitwise or of a and b is formed
a ^ b	the bitwise xor of a and b is formed

Figure 4.1 illustrates the result of the bitwise operations on a single bit. For example, the result of 1 ^ 1 is 0.

& (Bitwise and)		| (Bitwise or)		^ (Bitwise xor)	
	0 1		0 1		0 1
0	0 0	0	0 1	0	0 1
1	0 1	1	1 1	1	1 0

Figure 4.1 The bitwise operators &, | and ^ in Java.

The following fragment of code prints out a 32 bit IP (Internet Protocol) address contained in the `int` variable `ip_address` as 4 decimal octets:

```java
for ( int i=3; i>=0; i-- )
{
  int octet = ( ip_address >>> (i*8) ) & 0xFF;
  System.out.print( octet );
  if ( i !=0 )
    System.out.print(".");
}
System.out.println();
```

Note: It would be wrong to declare octet *as a byte, as a byte is signed and we wish to print out the octet as an unsigned value.*

When the above code is combined into a larger application and run, a possible output is shown below:

```
192.173.134.35
```

4.10   Shortcuts

In Java there are several shortcuts for adding or subtracting an amount from a variable. The most widely used are the increment and decrement operators ++ and --. For example, to add 1 to the contents of day, the following code is written:

```
day++;
```

Whilst initially looking strange, this does promote a leanness and simplicity in many code sequences. Likewise the -- operator is used to take 1 away from a variable.

4.10.1   Using the -- and ++ operator in expressions

Care needs to be taken when using -- or ++ in an expression as the placement of the operator will cause different values to be delivered. The following table illustrates the exact effect of these operators:

Operator	Before a value e.g. ++cost	After a value e.g. cost++
++	Increments the value by 1 unit then delivers the result	Delivers the value then increments the value by 1 unit
--	Decrements the value by 1 unit then delivers the result	Delivers the value then decrements the value by 1 unit

For example, if cost has an initial value of 100 in each case, then:

Java expression	Delivered as the result of the expression	Value of cost after the evaluation of the expression
++cost	101	101
cost++	100	101
--cost	99	99
cost--	100	99

Note: These operators can be applied to any of the inbuilt types.

4.10.2   Other shortcuts

Another common construct that can be shortened in Java, is the statement:

```
item = item operator expression;
```

where operator is one of the Java operators such as + - * / etc. This can be rewritten in a shorter form, as:

```
item operator= expression;
```

For example:

Long form	Shortened form
`items = items + 100;`	`items += 100;`
`items = items * 2;`	`items *= 2;`

4.11   Expressions

In Java a statement is actually an expression that delivers the result of the assignment. Hence, a programmer can write an expression that contains several assignment statements. For example, the following code sets the variables a, b and c to 10.

```
int a,b,c;
a = b = c = 10;
```

Source code reduction can be achieved by using an assignment in the middle of an expression. However, this technique can lead to code that is difficult to follow.

4.12   Summary of binary operators

In Java the operations allowed on the standard data types are indicated below.

Operator	Description	Allowed on instances of				
		`boolean`	`char`	`byte / short`	`int / long`	`float / double`
+	Addition		✓ [1]	✓ [1]	✓	✓
–	Subtraction		✓ [1]	✓ [1]	✓	✓
/	Division		✓ [1]	✓ [1]	✓	✓
*	Multiplication		✓ [1]	✓ [1]	✓	✓
%	Remainder		✓ [1]	✓ [1]	✓	✓ [2]
<<	Left shift		✓ [1]	✓ [1]	✓	
>>	Right shift [3]		✓ [1]	✓ [1]	✓	
>>>	Right shift [4]		✓ [1]	✓ [1]	✓	
&	bitwise and		✓ [1]	✓ [1]	✓	
|	bitwise or		✓ [1]	✓ [1]	✓	
^	bitwise xor		✓ [1]	✓ [1]	✓	
&&	logical and	✓				
||	logical or	✓				

Key: ✓   Allowed.
   [1]   Both sides promoted to an `int` before the operation is performed. Thus an `int` result is returned from the expression.
   [2]   The floating point remainder.
   [3]   The right shift operator >> propagates the sign bit.
   [4]   The right shift operator >>> does **not** propagate the sign bit.

4.13   Summary of monadic arithmetic operators

In Java the monadic operators allowed on the standard data types are indicated below:

		Allowed on instances of				
Operator	Description	`boolean`	`char`	`byte` / `short`	`int` / `long`	`float` / `double`
+	Monadic plus		✓ [1]	✓ [1]	✓	✓
–	Negation		✓ [1]	✓ [1]	✓	✓

Key: ✓   Allowed.
         [1]   The result will be converted to an `int`.

4.14   Use of strings

An instance of the class `String` is an object that holds a read only string that is used like a normal variable. For example, the following code fragment sets the string object `town` to the string `"Brighton"` and the string object `university` to the string `"University of"` concatenated with the contents of the string object `town`.

```
String town      = "Brighton";
String university = "University of " + town;
```

The contents of the two `String` objects are printed using the normal output methods of `print` or `println` as follows:

```
System.out.println( town );
System.out.println( university );
```

which, when combined with suitable code and run will produce the following results:

```
Brighton
University of Brighton
```

An instance of a standard type concatenated with an instance of a string will result in the contents of the standard type in character form being concatenated. For example, the following fragment of code:

```
String month    = "December ";
String christmas = month + 25;
System.out.println( christmas );
```

when combined with suitable code and run, will produce the following result:

```
December 25
```

4.14.1 Comparing strings

The correct way of comparing strings for equality requires the use of the method equals as demonstrated in the following fragment of code:

```
String town = "Brighton";

if ( town.equals("Brighton") )
{
    // Executed when the string in town equals "Brighton"
}
```

4.14.2 Warning

Even though it will compile, it is wrong to write:

```
String town = "Brighton";

if ( town == "Brighton" )
{
    // Will not always give the expected result
}
```

as it will not always give the expected result. The reason for this is explained in more detail in Section 14.1.2. However, for the time being, when comparing strings, always use the method equals.

4.15   Self-assessment

● How are variables declared in Java, and where may a declaration appear?

● What is the range of values that an instance of an int and short can hold respectively?

● In assigning instances of the standard data types, what restrictions apply? For example, are the following assignments legal?

```
int i = 0;   double d = 0.0;
i = d;                      // Is this legal ?
d = i;                      // Is this legal ?
```

● What is the result of executing the following Java statements?

```
int i = 10; System.out.println( i++ );
int i = 10; System.out.println( ++i );
```

● With the following declarations:

```
char c;     int i;      double d;     short s;
```

what is the type of the result of the following expressions?

```
c + i;          d + s;                  i + d;
c + c;          i + i;                  s + s;
(char) i + c;   (double) i + i;         c + s;
```

● When does the division operator deliver an integer, and when does it deliver a floating point number?

● What is wrong with the following fragment of code?

```
String product = "Apples";

if ( product == "Apples" )
{
  System.out.println( "Processing apples" );
  // etc.
}
```

4.16   Exercises

Construct the following applications:

● *Character codes*
An application to write out the characters that are internally represented by the integers 65 to 91.

The output should look like this:

```
The Unicode character A has internal value 65
The Unicode character B has internal value 66
```

● *Character count*
An application to count the number of characters taken from the standard input. This application can then be used as a software tool to count the number of characters in a text file.

- *Upper case*
  An application to make sure that the first character of each sentence is capitalised. The output from this application is a file that has capitalised the first letter of each sentence. Assume that a full stop is only used at the end of a sentence.

- *Primes*
  An application to print all prime numbers between 3 and 1000.
  A prime number is divisible only by itself and 1.

- *Perfect numbers*
  An application to print all perfect numbers between 3 and 1000. A perfect number is a number with factors which, when added together, add up to the number. For example 6, is a perfect number (factors 1,2,3) and 28 is also a perfect number (factors 1,2,4,7,14). The output should be of the form:

  ```
  6 is a perfect number
  Factors are:  1 2 3
  28 is a perfect number
  Factors are:  1 2 4 7 14
  etc.
  ```

- *Number of 1 bits in a character*
  An application which will input characters and print out their representation in binary. For example, if the characters ABC were input, the output would be in the form:

  ```
  Character    In binary

  A            0000 0000 0100 0001
  B            0000 0000 0100 0010
  C            0000 0000 0100 0011
  ```

- *Encrypt*
  A simple encryption algorithm for encrypting a message is to exclusively or (Java operator ^) each character of the message with a bit pattern before writing it out in its now secret form. Then the same process can be repeated on the encrypted text to reveal the original message. Write an application to carry out this encryption / decryption. Only use a 7 bit character, so avoiding binary data.

  For example:

  ```
  'A'          01000001      Encrypted    01110001
  key          01110000      key          01110000
    xor        -------        xor         --------
  Encrypted    00110001      decrypted    01000001
  ```

  Devise and implement a better encryption / decryption algorithm.

5. The class

At the centre of Java programming is the class. The class is a description of all objects that share the same member variables and member methods. A class is used as a mould to create the objects used in a Java application or applet. In effect a class allows a user to create new data types.

5.1 Introduction to the class construct

In Java a class is used as a description or mould for the creation of objects. For example, a class `Account` would be used in a Java application to create specific instances of individual people's bank accounts. Each bank account would contain potentially a different balance but the actions performed on individual person's bank accounts would be the same.

This is illustrated in Figure 5.1 where Mike's account contains £100.00 and the minimum balance allowed is £0.00 and Corinna's account contains £200.00 with a minimum allowed balance of -£10.00. Each account is able to process the transactions of: deposit money into the account, return the balance of the account, withdraw money from the account and set the minimum balance that the account must hold.

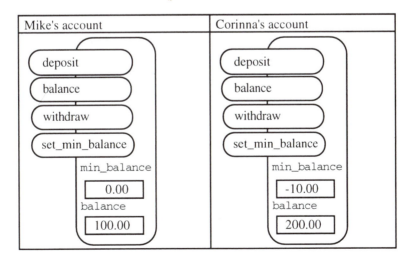

Figure 5.1 Instances of the class `Account`.

In the implementation of objects, the code for methods will not be duplicated for each object. Rather there will be a single copy of the code for each method that is used by all objects that belong to the same class. This optimization means that an object only contains its state information represented by instance variables. For example, the state information for an instance of an `Account` is contained in the instance variables `min_balance` and `balance`.

5.1.1   A class diagram showing a class

A class diagram for the class `Account` using the UML notation is illustrated in Figure 5.2.

Class Diagram	Components

Account
the_balance
the_min_balance
deposit
withdraw
account_balance
set_min_balance
	The class `Account` is composed of the instance variables:
	    `the_balance` and `the_min_balance`
	and the methods:
	    `deposit`, `withdraw`, `account_balance`
	    and `set_min_balance`.

Figure 5.2 Class diagram for the class `Account`.

5.2 Class, objects, messages and methods

The objects `mike` and `corinna` are instances of the class `Account`. Messages that may be sent to these objects are:

- Withdraw money from this account.
- Deposit money into this account.
- Return the account balance of this account.
- Set the minimum balance for this account.

To deposit £100.00 into Mike's account the message `deposit` is sent with a parameter of 100.00 to the object `mike`. This invokes an internal hidden method to processes the transaction. In processing the transaction, the instance variable representing the current balance of the account is modified.

In the above description of processing a deposit transaction on a bank account many object-oriented terms have been used, these are:

class	A collective name for all objects that have the same instance methods and variables. However, the contents of the instance variables may be different.

instance variables	The variables contained within the object that represent its internal state.
message	A request sent to an object to obey one of its hidden methods.
method	An action that manipulates or accesses the internal state of the object. The implementation of this action is however hidden from a client who sends messages to this object.
object	An item that has a hidden internal structure. The hidden structure is manipulated or accessed by messages sent to the object.

5.2.1 Declaring an object in Java

An object is declared in exactly the same way as variables are declared in Java. However, the declaration allocates no storage for the object. The storage for the object must be created either explicitly at a later stage, or as part of the declaration. Assuming that a class Account has already been created then the declaration and allocation of storage for an object to hold Mike's bank account is as follows:

```
Account mike    = new Account();
```

This consists of two parts:

1	The declaration of the object	Account mike
2	The allocation of storage for the object.	= new Account()

This process is explained in more detail in Section 5.3. The nature of an object in Java.

5.2.2 Sending a message to an object

The following notation is used to send the message deposit with a parameter of 100.00 to the object mike:

```
mike.deposit(100.00);
```

This is read as send the message deposit with a parameter of 100.00 to the object mike.

The components of this Java statement are illustrated in Figure 5.3 opposite.

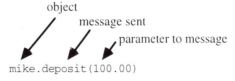

Figure 5.3 Sending a message to an object.

5.2.3   Using the class `Account`

The class `Account` is used in the following application to create the objects `mike` and `corinna`. After these objects have been created a series of simple banking transactions are performed on the accounts.

```
class Main
{
  public static void main(String args[])
  {
    Account mike    = new Account();
    Account corinna = new Account();

    double obtained;

    System.out.println( "Mike's Balance    = " +
                        mike.account_balance() );

    mike.deposit(100.00);
    System.out.println( "Mike's Balance    = " +
                        mike.account_balance() );

    obtained = mike.withdraw(20.00);
    System.out.println( "Mike has withdrawn  : " + obtained );
    System.out.println( "Mike's Balance    = " +
                        mike.account_balance() );

    corinna.deposit(50.00);
    System.out.println( "Corinna's Balance   = " +
                        corinna.account_balance() );
  }
}
```

Which when compiled and run produces the following results.

```
Mike's Balance      = 0.0
Mike's Balance      = 100.0
Mike has withdrawn  : 20.0
Mike's Balance      = 80.0
Corinna's Balance   = 50.0
```

5.2.4   Specification of the class `Account`

The class `Account` described above contains the following methods and variables:

● Methods in the class

Name	Remarks
account_balance	Returns the current balance of the account.
withdraw	Withdraws money from the account. Naturally money can only be withdrawn if the account balance stays above or equal to the minimum balance allowed.
deposit	Deposits money into the account.
set_min_balance	Sets the minimum balance that the account must hold. A negative amount indicates an overdraft is allowed.

● Instance variables in the class

Name	Remarks
the_balance	Holds the current balance of the account.
the_min_balance	The minimum balance that the account is allowed to go to. If the account holder was allowed an overdraft of £200.00 then the_min_balance would contain -200.00.

Note: To distinguish easily member variables from other data items the member variable name is prefixed with the_.

5.2.5   The Java class Account

The implementation of the class for Account is shown below:

```
class Account
{
```

Contained within the class declaration is the declaration of the instance variables that hold the state information for each individual object. These declarations are prefixed with the reserved word private to indicate that they are not accessible outside of the class.

```
private double the_balance     = 0.0d;   //Balance of account
private double the_min_balance = 0.0d;   //Minimum bal (Overdraft)
```

Following this the methods contained in the class are defined. The first method is special and is called automatically whenever an instance of the class is created. This special method is called a constructor and has the same name as the class. For the class Account the constructor sets the instance variables in the object to a zero value.

```
public Account() {
   the_balance = the_min_balance = 0.00;
}
```

*Note: As the instance variables are given initial values of zero there is no need to have
a constructor. The constructor is shown here to illustrate the use of a constructor
in a class.*
The reserved word `public` *indicates that the constructor is visible to a user of
the class. A constructor must be visible if an instance of the class is to be created.*

5.2.5.1   The method `account_balance`

The next method returns the balance of the account contained in the instance variable
`the_balance`.

```
public double account_balance()
{
   return the_balance;
}
```

Note: This method is necessary as the state of the object is hidden from the user.

Figure 5.4 below illustrates the components of this method.

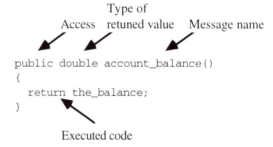

Figure 5.4 Components of the method `account_balance`.

5.2.5.2   The method `withdraw`

The method `withdraw` has a single parameter `money`. In the implementation of the
method a check is made to ensure that there are sufficient funds in this instance of
`Account` to allow the transaction to be made. The result of executing the method is the
amount of money that has been successfully withdrawn from the account. If no money
can be withdrawn from the account then 0.00 is returned.

```
public double withdraw( final double money )
{
  if ( the_balance - money >= the_min_balance )
  {
    the_balance = the_balance - money;
    return money;
  } else {
    return 0.00;
  }
}
```

Note: The use of the reserved word final *to indicate that the formal parameter*
money of type double *cannot be written to.*
Parameters are more fully discussed in Chapter 6 on Anatomy of a method.

Figure 5.5 below illustrates the components of this method.

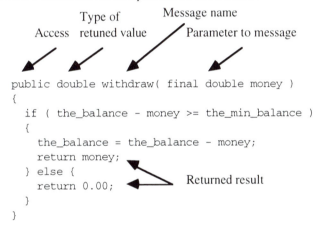

Figure 5.5 Components of the method withdraw.

5.2.5.3   The method deposit

The method deposit adds the contents of the parameter money to the instance
variable the_balance. The reserved word void is used to indicate that this method
returns no result.

```
public void deposit( final double money )
{
  the_balance = the_balance + money;
}
```

Figure 5.6 below illustrates the components of this method.

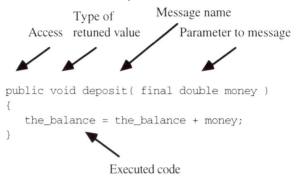

```
public void deposit( final double money )
{
    the_balance = the_balance + money;
}
```

Figure 5.6 Components of the method deposit.

The method set_min_balance overwrites the instance variable the_min_balance with the new value supplied as a parameter.

```
public void set_min_balance( final double money )
{
   the_min_balance = money;
}
```

The class definition is terminated by a closing }.

```
}
```

5.3 The nature of objects in Java

In Java an object is represented by a handle. The handle points to the physical storage of the object. For example, the storage for the object mike is shown in Figure 5.7.

Figure 5.7 Storage for a Java object.

Provided that a Java programmer never copies an object, this implementation detail can be ignored. However, if a programmer copies an object as in the following code, the semantics of the copy are that of a shallow copy. The concept of a shallow copy is more fully explored in Section 14.1.1.

```
Account mike                 = new Account();
Account shallow_copy_mike    = mike;
mike.deposit(100.00);
System.out.println("Balance account mike                = " +
                    mike.account_balance() );
System.out.println("Balance account shallow copy mike = " +
                    shallow_copy_mike.account_balance() );
```

Which when combined into a Java application and run produces the following results:

```
Balance account mike             = 100.0
Balance account shallow copy mike = 100.0
```

The reason for this is that only the handle for the object `mike` is copied to `shallow_copy_mike`. Hence though the handle has been copied the underlying storage has not. This is illustrated in Figure 5.8.

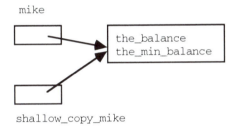

Figure 5.8 Storage after a shallow copy of an object.

Chapter 14 describes how to duplicate the storage for an object. This process is termed a deep copy of an object.

5.3.1   The value `null`

An objects handle may be assigned the value `null` to indicate that currently the handle does not point to any storage. When an object's handle is initially created it has an initial value of `null`. This `null` value can be tested for, so that a programmer can ascertain whether or not storage has been allocated for the object.

```
Account mike = null;    // The default value

if ( mike == null )
{
   // No storage allocated for object
}
```

5.4 Garbage collection

In Java an object consists of two components: the handle or reference to the object and the actual storage for the object. The storage for the handle for an object is returned back to the system when the method in which the handle was declared is exited. However, the storage for the object will not be returned to the system. This means that the Java run-time system has storage allocated for objects that can never be accessed. To prevent the eventual consumption of all available storage the Java run-time system periodically runs a garbage collector that searches for orphaned objects that cannot be accessed. When found by the garbage collector the storage for these orphaned objects is returned back to the systems pool of available storage.

However, this process takes a finite time to run. The consequence of this is that there may be times when a Java application appears less responsive than might be expected, due to the resources consumed by the running garbage collector.

5.4.1 An example

The following method declares an instance of the class `Account`, the storage for which is orphaned once the method is exited.

```
public void process()
{
   Account mike    = new Account();

   // Processing on the object

}
```

Note: The storage for the object `mike` *is allocated in two distinct phases.*

Allocation of the handle   `Account mike`
Allocation of the objects storage   `= new Account();`

The storage for the object will be returned back to the pool of available storage when the garbage collector is called.

5.4.2 Explicitly calling the garbage collector

The garbage collector can be explicitly called by evoking the following static method:

```
System.gc();
```

5.5 A personal account manager

A personal account manager, implemented on a small electronic notebook with an LCD display, presents the user with a menu on the first few lines of the display, in the form:

```
[a]   Deposit

[b]   Withdraw

[c]   Balance

Input selection:
```

The bottom lines of the display would enable the user to provide any input values required and also provide room to display any results.

In the example screens below, the user input is shown in **bold** type. For example, if option a were selected, then after the user had input £100, the bottom of the display would look like:

```
Input selection: a
Amount to deposit = 100
```

Then if option c where selected the bottom of the screen would display

```
Input selection : c
Balance = #100.0
```

5.5.1   The class TUI

To simplify the implementation of this application an instance of a TUI (Text User Interface) class is used to implement the interactions between the end user and the application.

The responsibilities of the class TUI are:

Method	Responsibility
menu	Sets up the menu that will be displayed to the user. Each menu item is described by a string.
chose_option	Returns the menu item selected by a user of the TUI.
message(s)	Display the message s to a user.
dialogue(s)	Displays the message prompt s to a user returning the string they type as a response.
dialogue_int(s)	Displays the message prompt s to a user returning the number they type as an int.
dialogue_double(s)	Displays the message prompt s to a user returning the number they type as a double value.

In implementing this class in Java a class that just contains static fields is created to represent an enumeration for the menu items selected.

```
class Menu_item
{
  public static final int M_1 = 1;
  public static final int M_2 = 2;
  public static final int M_3 = 3;
  public static final int M_4 = 4;
  public static final int M_5 = 5;
  public static final int NONE = 0;
}
```

Note: An instance of the class Menu_item *does not need to be declared to use the static fields representing the enumeration's.*
The use of static fields are more fully discussed in Chapter 6 on the Anatomy of a method.

The class TUI contains 5 string variables to hold the names of the 5 possible menu choices that may be displayed.

```
class TUI
{
  private String men_1 = "";       //Name of 1st menu item
  private String men_2 = "";       //Name of 2nd menu item
  private String men_3 = "";       //Name of 3rd menu item
  private String men_4 = "";       //Name of 4th menu item
  private String men_5 = "";       //Name of 5th menu item
  private static final int EOF = -1;
```

The method menu stores the 5 possible menu items that a user may select from. To allow some flexibility if a menu item is the empty string then it will not be displayed.

```
  public void menu( final String m1, final String m2, final String m3,
                    final String m4, final String m5 )
  {
    men_1 = m1; men_2 = m2; men_3 = m3;
    men_4 = m4; men_5 = m5;                  //Store names
  }
```

A menu choice is presented to the user by the method chose_option. This method displays the individual menu items onto the user's screen. The private method display_menu_item will only write an individual menu item if it is not an empty string.

```
public int chose_option()
{
  int choice = Menu_item.NONE;
```

The code decoding a users response is repeated until a valid response is given.

```
while ( choice == Menu_item.NONE )              //While no valid reply
{
  char selection = ' ';  System.out.println("");
  display_menu_item( "[a]  ", men_1 );          //First menu item
  display_menu_item( "[b]  ", men_2 );          //Second ..
  display_menu_item( "[c]  ", men_3 );          //Third
  display_menu_item( "[d]  ", men_4 );          //Fourth
  display_menu_item( "[e]  ", men_5 );          //Fifth
```

The user's response to the list of menu items is obtained by using the method `dialogue` that returns the user's response as a string. If it exists then the first non-white space character from the string is taken as the response typed by the user.

```
String res = dialogue("Input selection");  //Response
res        = res.toLowerCase().trim();     //Lower case
if ( res.length() >= 1 )
  selection = res.charAt(0);               //First char
```

Note: Individual characters in a string are accessed by using the method charAt. The first character in a string is at position 0, the second character at position 1 etc. The method length() returns the number of characters in a string.

A check is made to determine if the response given is a valid menu item and also if it can be selected. For example, a menu item that is the empty or null string cannot be selected.

```
switch ( selection )
{
  case 'a' :
    if ( ! men_1.equals( "" ) ) choice = Menu_item.M_1; break;
  case 'b' :
    if ( ! men_2.equals( "" ) ) choice = Menu_item.M_2; break;
  case 'c' :
    if ( ! men_3.equals( "" ) ) choice = Menu_item.M_3; break;
  case 'd' :
    if ( ! men_4.equals( "" ) ) choice = Menu_item.M_4; break;
  case 'e' :
    if ( ! men_5.equals( "" ) ) choice = Menu_item.M_5; break;
  }
  if ( choice == Menu_item.NONE ) message( "Invalid response" );
}
return choice;                                 //User selection
}
```

Note: The use of the method equals("") to test for any empty string.

The method `display_menu_item` will only display menu items that are not the null or empty string.

```
private void display_menu_item( String prompt, String name )
{
  if ( ! name.equals( "" ) )  //Not null String so print
  {
    System.out.println( prompt  + name );
    System.out.println( "" );
  }
}
```

A response is sent to the users screen by using the method `message`. This simply writes the supplied string onto the users terminal.

```
public void message( final String mes )
{
  System.out.println( mes );
}
```

Information is obtained from a user by requesting a string response to a dialogue message. The input line is read character by character and converted into a string. To simplify processing, the end of file character causes an immediate termination of the application.

```
public String dialogue( final String mes )
{
  String line = "";                            //Line read
  int    ch;
  System.out.print( mes + " : " );             //Prompt
  try
  {
    ch = System.in.read();                      //Read ch
    while ( ch != '\n' && ch != EOF )           //While !EOL
    {
      line += (char) ch;                        // append ch
      ch = System.in.read();                    // next ch
      if ( ch == '\r' ) ch = System.in.read();  // Skip ''
    }
    if ( line.equals("") && ch == EOF )
      System.exit(-1);                          //Exit **
    return line;                                //return line
  }
  catch( IOException exp )                       //Problem
  {
    System.exit(-1);                            //Exit **
  }
  return "";                                    //Blank line
}
```

To read a floating point number from the user the method `dialogue_double` is used. This method calls the method `dialogue` to return the user's response as a string. Then the wrapper class `Double` is used to convert this string into an instance of a `double`.

```
public double dialogue_double( final String mes )
{
  String res = dialogue( mes );            //Read line
  double value = 0.0;                      //
  try
  {
    value = Double.parseDouble( res );     //Convert
  }
  catch ( NumberFormatException ex )       //Problem
  {                                        // ignore
  }
  return value;                            //return
}
```

Note: The use of wrapper classes is more fully explained in Chapter 7 on Wrapper classes.

In a similar way the method `dialogue_int` returns an instance of an `int` as the number input by a user.

```
public int dialogue_int( final String mes )
{
  String res = dialogue( mes );            //Read line
  int value = 0;                           //
  try
  {
    value = Integer.parseInt( res );       //Convert
  }
  catch ( NumberFormatException ex )       //Problem
  {                                        // ignore
  }
  return value;                            //return
}
}
```

5.5.2   The main application

Having created a class `TUI` and re-using the existing class `Account` the implementation of the personal account manager is achieved in only a few lines of code. In essence the application is an endless loop that requests a menu choice from the end user.

```
class Main
{
  public static void main( String args[] )
  {
    Account mine    = new Account();    //My Account
    TUI     screen = new TUI();         //Interaction screen
    double  amount;                     //money

    screen.menu("Deposit", "Withdraw", "Balance", "", "" );

    while ( true )
    {
      switch ( screen.chose_option() )
      {
```

When deposit is selected the user is interrogated for the amount that they wish to deposit. If this is a valid amount then the money is deposited into the user's account.

```
        case Menu_item.M_1 :
          amount = screen.dialogue_double("Amount to deposit");
          if ( amount >= 0.0 )
          {
            mine.deposit( amount );
          } else {
            screen.message("Amount must be positive");
          }
          break;
```

Likewise for withdraw after a validation on the amount to be withdraw the transaction is performed. If the transaction fails due to insufficient funds the user's is informed of the situation.

```
        case Menu_item.M_2 :
          amount = screen.dialogue_double("Amount to withdraw");
          if ( amount > 0.0 )
          {
            double get = mine.withdraw( amount );
            if ( get <= 0.0 )
              screen.message("Sorry not enough funds");
          } else {
            screen.message("Amount not valid");
          }
          break;
```

The code for balance converts the result from applying the transaction account_balance into a string so that it can be displayed using the method message.

```
        case Menu_item.M_3 :
          {
            String mes = "Balance = #"  +
                        String.valueOf(mine.account_balance());
            screen.message( mes );          //"Bal ... "
          }
          break;
      }
    }
  }
}
```

5.5.3   Putting it all together

When compiled and run a typical series of interactions with the running application are shown below:

Deposit an initial 100.00 into the account.

```
[a]   Deposit

[b]   Withdraw

[c]   Balance

Input selection : a
Amount to deposit : 100.00
```

Try and take 200.00 from the account.

```
[a]   Deposit

[b]   Withdraw

[c]   Balance

Input selection : b
Amount to withdraw : 200.00
Sorry not enough funds
```

Show the balance

```
[a]   Deposit

[b]   Withdraw

[c]   Balance

Input selection : c
Balance = #100.0
```

5.6 Interfaces

An interface defines a set of methods that a class must implement. When a class implements an interface a user of the class knows that all the methods in the interface have a concrete implementation. If all the methods in the interface were not implemented then a compile time error message would be generated when an instance of the class was compiled.

For example, a designer of a banking system might create the following interface:

```
interface Account_protocol
{
  public double account_balance();
  public void    deposit( final double money);
  public double withdraw( final double money );
}
```

Note: An interface is like a class except that there is only a signature for the methods in the interface.

Implementors of classes representing bank accounts would be required to implement this interface. By insisting that each implementor of a class implements the interface `Account_protocol` guarantees that each instance of an account must be able to: deposit money into, withdraw money from and return the balance of the account. For example, a simple bank account that implements the `Account_protocol` is defined as follows:

```
class Simple_Account implements Account_protocol
{
  private double the_balance     = 0.0d;   //Balance of account

  public double account_balance()
  {
    return the_balance;
  }

  public double withdraw( final double money )
  {
    if ( the_balance - money >= 0.00 )
    {
      the_balance = the_balance - money;
      return money;
    } else {
      return 0.00;
    }
  }

  public void deposit( final double money )
  {
    the_balance = the_balance + money;
  }
```

The method `transfer` may be passed as its first parameter any type of bank account that implements the `Account_protocol`. This is a great advantage as it means that in the future if a new type of bank account is created that implements the interface `Account_protocol` then an instance of this new account may be passed to the method `transfer`.

```java
public double transfer( Account_protocol other, final double money )
{
  if ( money > 0.00 )
  {
    double obtain = other.withdraw( money );
    if ( obtain != 0.00 )
    {
      deposit( money );
      return money;
    }
  }
  return 0.00;
}
```

Note: *A class may implement many protocols.*
The method `transfer` *may be passed any object that implements the*
`Account_protocol`.

5.6.1   Putting it all together

The following class will test the class `Simple_Account`.

```java
class Main
{
  public static void main( String args[] )
  {
    Simple_Account mike    = new Simple_Account();
    Simple_Account corinna = new Simple_Account();

    double obtained;

    mike.deposit(100.00);
    System.out.println( "Mike's Balance      = " +
                        mike.account_balance() );

    corinna.deposit(150.00);
    System.out.println( "Corinna's Balance   = " +
                        corinna.account_balance() );

    corinna.transfer( mike, 80.00 );

    System.out.println( "Mike's Balance      = " +
                        mike.account_balance() );
    System.out.println( "Corinna's Balance   = " +
                        corinna.account_balance() );
  }
}
```

Which when compiled and run will produce the following output:

```
Mike's Balance      = 100.0
Corinna's Balance   = 150.0
Mike's Balance      = 20.0
Corinna's Balance   = 230.0
```

5.7 Nested classes

A class declared inside another class is termed a nested class. The nested class can access all of the members of its enclosing class. There are two types of nested class:

A static nested class	This may only access the enclosing classes class variables or methods.
A non static nested class also called an inner class.	This may access all the enclosing classes member variables or methods.

For example, the following class Car contains an inner class Engine.

```
class Car
{
  class Engine                            //Inner class
  {
    private double the_capacity;          //Engine Capacity

    public Engine( double engine_capacity )  //Constructor
    {
      the_capacity = engine_capacity;
    }

    public double engine_size()           //Return Engine size
    {
      return the_capacity;
    }

  }

  Engine the_engine = new Engine( 1.3 );  //Instance of engine

  public double capacity()                //Return capacity
  {
    return the_engine.engine_size();
  }

}
```

5.8 Self-assessment

- How can a user of an object request the execution of a method in that object?

- What are the advantages of holding data and the code that manipulates the data in a single unit?

- Should a method in a class be private? Explain your answer.

- Should an instance variable in a class be public? Explain your answer.

- How should an implementor of a class allow access to instance variables contained in an object?

5.9 Exercises

Construct the following classes:

- *Cinema performance attendance*
  A class Performance, an instance of which represents the seats at a particular showing of a film, has the following methods:

Method	Responsibility
book_seats	Books n seats at the performance.
cancel	Un-books n seats.
seats_free	Returns the number of seats that are still unsold.
seats_booked	Returns the number of seats sold for this performance.

  Thus on an instance of Performance the following actions can be performed:

  - Book a number of seats.
  - Return the number of remaining seats at the performance.
  - Return the number of seats sold.

  Remember to make sure that the transactions that you process are valid. For example, booking -5 seats will result in the number of booked seats going down.

- *Library book*
  A class to represent a book in a library, such that the following operations can be processed:

  - Loan the book.

  - Mark the book as being reserved. Only one outstanding reservation is allowed on a book.

  - Cancel a reservation on a book.

  - Ask if a book can be loaned. A book can only be loaned if it is not already on loan or is not reserved.

  - Return the book.

Construct the following application:

- *Cinema*
  An application to deal with the single day's administration of bookings for a cinema. Each day there is a single performance at 8pm.
  The application should display a menu of the possible options that may be selected. There should be checking for invalid data items such as booking -5 seats.

  Hint: *Use the class TUI to provide a simple menu system.*
  Use a single instance of the class Performance to represent the 8pm performance.

6. Anatomy of a method

This chapter looks in detail at the construction and use of methods. In particular the following topics are considered: parameter passing, class methods and variables, recursive methods.

6.1 Parameter passing

The process of passing additional information to a method is implemented by the parameter mechanism. For example, in Chapter 5 on classes the amount of money to be deposited into an account is passed to the method `deposit`. The process of passing data values to a method is illustrated in the fragment of code below:

```
Account mike    = new Account();
double payment = 50.00;

mike.deposit(payment);
```

The implementation of the method `deposit` is:

```
public void deposit( final double money )
{
   the_balance = the_balance + money;
}
```

Note: The prefix final indicates that the formal parameter can not be changed.

6.1.1   Terminology

The following terminology is used when describing the parameter passing mechanism associated with a method:

Terminology	Explanation	Example
Actual parameter	The variable or literal value passed with the message to the method	payment
Formal parameter	The name of the parameter when accessed inside the method	money

For the above code fragment, when the method deposit is invoked it is passed a single actual parameter payment. In the implementation of the method deposit the formal parameter money is used when access to the passed parameter is required. As it is declared as final the formal parameters state can not be changed.

In Java, all parameters are passed by value. When a parameter is passed by value a copy of the actual parameter is assigned to the formal parameter.

When an object is passed as an actual parameter to a method, its handle (pointer to its storage) is assigned to the formal parameter. There is no copying of the state of the object. Hence any changes to the object's state by using the formal parameter handle will change the state of the actual parameter.

The following table summarizes these effects when passing a variable m and an object a.

Method signature	Code in method	Parameter changed Actual	Formal	Code Compiles
void deposit(**final double** m)	m = 2.0;			✗ [3]
void deposit(**double** m)	m = 2.0;	✗	✓	✓
void gift(**final** Account a)	a.deposit(5.00);	✓ [1]	✓ [1]	✓
void gift(Account a)	a.deposit(5.00);	✓ [1]	✓ [1]	✓
void gift(**final** Account a)	a=**new** Account();			✗ [3]
void gift(Account a)	a=**new** Account();	✗	✓ [2]	✓

Key   [1]   The state of the object represented by the handle is changed
         [2]   The formal parameter's handle is changed
         [3]   The compiler detects that this is an invalid operation.

Note: The actual parameter refers to the actual variable or object passed as a parameter to the method.

Hence, when an object is passed as an actual parameter to a method, a shallow copy is used to copy the actual parameter to the formal parameter. Even if the formal parameter is declared as final, the storage for the object can still be changed.

6.2   Class methods

A class method is special as it may be called without reference to any object. Because of this, a class method may not access instance variables in the class.

6.2.1   Class methods as functions

Java does not allow functions. A function is a stand alone code sequence that is called in a program to perform some action. The effect of a function can be created by defining a static method in a class. For example, the class Functions shown below contains the class method is_vowel. This method returns true if the character passed as a parameter is a vowel. A class method is indicated by prefixing its return type with the reserved word static. The class Functions that contains the class method is_vowel is defined as follows:

```
class Functions
{
  public static boolean is_vowel( final char c )
  {
    switch ( c )
    {
      case 'A' : case 'E' : case 'I' : case 'O' : case 'U' :
      case 'a' : case 'e' : case 'i' : case 'o' : case 'u' :
        return true;
      default  :
        return false;
    }
  }
}
```

Note: *This is a naive implementation of* is_vowel *as it only works for the English*
language.

Many of the standard Java classes use class methods to provide useful functions. For
example, the class Character implements many useful character handling functions.
Appendix F lists the members of this class.

6.2.2 Putting it all together

The following code illustrates the use of the static method is_vowel:

```
class Main
{
  public static void main( String args[] )
  {
    char c = 'A';
    System.out.println( "Character " + c + " is a " +
                    (Functions.is_vowel(c) ? "vowel" : "consonant") );
  }
}
```

which, when compiled and run produces the following output:

```
Character A is a vowel
```

6.3 Parameter passing and static methods

The following demonstration class contains a static method bonus that adds a bonus of
£50 to a person's, bank account, and a static method details that prints information
about an account.

```
class Account_handling
{
  public static void bonus( final Account acc )
  {
    acc.deposit( 50.00 );
  }

  public static String details( final String name, final Account cur )
  {
    return "Account balance for " + name + " " +
            new Double( cur.account_balance() ).toString();
  }
}
```

The class `Account_handling` is used in the following application to show that even though a formal parameter for an object is declared as final the actual parameter may be changed from within a method.

```
class Main
{
  public static void main( String args[] )
  {
    Account mike    = new Account();
    Account corinna = new Account();
    corinna.deposit( 100.00 );

    Account_handling.bonus( mike );
    Account_handling.bonus( corinna );

    System.out.println(Account_handling.details("Mike", mike ) );
    System.out.println(Account_handling.details("Corinna",corinna) );
  }
}
```

Note: The qualifier `final` is applied to the handle or pointer to the formal parameters in the class methods `bonus` and `details`.

When compiled and executed, the results produced are as follows:

```
Account balance for Mike 50.0
Account balance for Corinna 150.0
```

6.4 Class variables

A class variable is shared between all members of the class. In Java, a class variable is signified by prefixing its declaration with the reserved word `static`. A class variable is used when a variable is to be shared between all instances of the class. For example, a class representing a bank account could have a static variable that contained the total of the amount invested by all customers. This class variable is changed when the messages deposit or withdraw are sent to an instance of an account. This new class Account has the following responsibilities:

Method	Responsibility
account_balance	Returns the current balance of the account.
withdraw	Withdraws money from the account. Naturally money can only be withdrawn if the account balance stays above or equal to the minimum balance allowed.
deposit	Deposits money into the account.
set_min_balance	Sets the minimum balance that the account must hold. A negative amount indicates an overdraft is allowed.
grand_balance	Returns the grand total of the money invested by account holders in the bank.

The new class Account is implemented as follows:

```java
class Account
{
  private double the_balance     = 0.0d;  //Balance of account
  private double the_min_balance = 0.0d;  //Minimum bal
  static  double the_g_balance   = 0.0d;  //Grand balance

  public double account_balance()
  {
     return the_balance;
  }

  public double withdraw( final double money )
  {
     if ( the_balance - money >= the_min_balance )
     {
       the_balance = the_balance - money;
       the_g_balance = the_g_balance - money;
       return money;
     } else {
       return 0.00;
     }
  }

  public void deposit( final double money )
  {
     the_balance  = the_balance + money;
     the_g_balance = the_g_balance + money;
  }

  public void set_min_balance( double money )
  {
     the_min_balance = money;
  }

  public static double grand_balance()
  {
     return the_g_balance;
  }
}
```

6.4.1   Putting it all together

The following code illustrates the use of the new class `Account`:

```java
class Main
{
  public static void main( String args[] )
  {
    Account mike    = new Account();
    Account corinna = new Account();

    double obtained;

    mike.deposit(100.00);
    System.out.println( "Mike's Balance       = " +
                         mike.account_balance() );

    obtained = mike.withdraw(20.00);
    System.out.println( "Mike has withdrawn    : " + obtained );
    System.out.println( "Mike's Balance       = " +
                         mike.account_balance() );

    corinna.deposit(50.00);
    System.out.println( "Corinna's Balance    = " +
                         corinna.account_balance() );

    System.out.println( "Bank holds           = " +
                         Account.grand_balance() );
  }
}
```

which, when compiled and run, produces the following output:

```
Mike's Balance       = 100.0
Mike has withdrawn    : 20.0
Mike's Balance       = 80.0
Corinna's Balance    = 50.0
Bank holds           = 130.0
```

6.5   A recursive method

Recursion is the ability of a method to call itself from within its own code body. Whilst this initially may seem a strange idea, it can lead to very elegant code sequences that otherwise would require many more lines of code. In certain exceptional cases, recursion is the only way to implement a solution to a problem.

An example of a recursive static method to return a string containing the characters that represent an integer number is shown below:

- Create a string `res` to hold the result of the calculation
- Split the number into two components:
  - (a)   The first digit (remainder when number divided by 10)
  - (b)   The other digits (number divided by 10).

For example:
123 would be split into:
3   (first digit)
12   (other digits).

- If the other digits are greater than or equal to 10 then append to the string `res` a string representing the other digits. This string is generated by recursively calling this process.

- Append to the string `res` a character representation of the number held in the first digit.

- Return the string `res` as the result of the method.

The sequence of calls made is:

Call	Implemented as
`toString( 123 )`	`toString( 12 ) + '3'`
`toString( 12 )`	`toString( 1 ) + '2'`
`toString( 1 )`	`'1'`

This process is expressed diagrammatically in Figure 5.9.

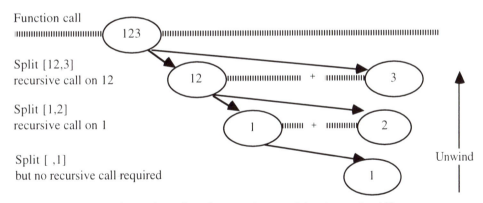

Figure 5.9 Illustration of recursive calls to form a string containing the number 123.

The process works by solving a small part of the problem; in this case how to turn a single digit into a string, then re-executing the code to solve the remainder of the problem, i.e. to convert the other digits into a string. In this particular example, the recursive call is made before the remainder of the problem is solved. This still works as the problem to be solved 'the conversion of an instance of a `long` into a string' is reduced in size (the number is smaller) in each recursive call.

It is important to remember that for recursion to work, the code must reduce the problem to be solved before recalling itself recursively. If this does not take place then endless recursive calls will ensue, which will cause eventual application failure when the system cannot allocate any more memory to support the recursion. Stack space is used on each recursive call to store any parameters or local variables plus the function support information.

```
class Useful
{
  public static String toString( final long number )
  {
    String res = "";
    long number_to_print = number;          //For number = 123
    if ( number < 0 )                        //Is -ve
    {
      number_to_print= -number; res += "-";  // Leading -
    }
    long first_digit  = number_to_print%10;  //Split  ..3 - first
    long other_digits = number_to_print/10;  //        12. - rest
    if ( number_to_print >= 10 )             //More than 1 digit
    {
      res += toString( other_digits );       //Other digits [12]
    }
    res += (char) (first_digit + '0');       //First digit  [3]
    return res;
  }
}
```

6.5.1   Putting it all together

The following code illustrates the use of the class method `to_string`:

```
class Main
{
  public static void main( String args[] )
  {
    System.out.println( Useful.toString( 12345 ) );
    System.out.println( Useful.toString( -12345 ) );
    System.out.println( Useful.toString( -123456789 ) );
  }
}
```

which, when run produces the following output:

```
12345
-12345
-123456789
```

Note: A recursive method can of course also be a normal method as well as a class method.

6.6 Self-assessment

- What is the relationship between an actual and a formal parameter.

- Why when changing a formal parameter is the actual parameter:
  changed when the formal parameter is an object,
  not changed when the item passed is a variable?

- What is the effect of declaring a formal parameter final?

- What is the difference between an instance variable and a class variable?

- What is the difference between a class method and an instance method.

- How is a class method called?

6.7 Exercises

Construct the following class methods in the class `Useful` that have the following signature:

- `boolean prime( final long n )`
  A class method to return true if the number n is prime.

- `String string_mult( final String s, final int n )`
  A class method to return a string that is the string s repeated n times. For example, `Useful.string_mult( "*", 4 )` would deliver `"****"`.

Construct the following application:

- *Cinema*
  An application to deal with a single day's administration of bookings for a cinema. Each day there are four separate performances: an early afternoon performance at 2pm, an early evening performance at 5.30pm, the main performance at 8.00pm and the late performance at 11.00pm.
     The application should be able to handle the booking of cinema seats for any of these four performances. In addition a management summary of the total number of seats sold for each performance should be included.

Hints: Use the class TUI (Section 5.5.1) to provide a simple menu system.
Use four instances of the class Performance.
(See the exercise in the previous chapter for its specification.)
Create a class Transaction that has a static method process this is responsible for processing transactions on an instance of the class Performance passed as a parameter.

7. Wrapper classes

This chapter discusses the role of wrapper classes. Instances of wrapper classes are used to hold instances of the standard types. In addition useful functions are implemented as static methods in many of the wrapper classes.

7.1 Introduction

In the language Java, some processes can only be performed using an object or objects. For example, the container classes can only store and manipulate objects. This prevents a user from using the standard container classes to store instances of the standard types. Remember an instance of `int`, `double` etc. is not an object.

To solve this and other similar problems, the standard class library defines wrapper classes for many of the standard types. A wrapper class allows the conversion of a standard type into an object and vice-versa. However, to access the instance of the standard type contained in an instance of the wrapper class requires the use of an access method.

7.2 The wrapper class `java.lang.Double`

The wrapper class `Double` (`java.lang.Double`) is used to hold a `double` value as an object. This class has the following constructors:

Constructor	Responsibility
Double(d)	Constructs an instance of a Double from the double parameter d.
Double(s)	Constructs an instance of a Double from the value contained in the String parameter s.

The major methods of the class `Double` are:

Method	Type	Responsibility
doubleValue()	I	Returns a double representation of the object.
parseDouble(s) Since JDK 1.2	I	Returns a double representation of the value represented as digits in the String s.
toString()	I	Returns a String representation of the object.

valueOf(s)	S	Returns a new object of type `Double` that represents the value contained in the string parameter s. The exception `NumberFormatException` is thrown if the number contained in the string cannot be parsed.

Note: Type I Instance method S Static method

7.2.1   Converting a string to a `double`

The method `parseDouble` returns the double representation of the number stored in character form in a string. Hence a very simple way of converting a floating point number held in a string to an instance of a `double` is as follows:

```
String number = "123.45"
double i      = Double.parseDouble( number );
```

A less elegant approach is to use the static method `valueOf` to create an instance of the class `Double` as follows:

```
String number = "123.45"
double d      = (Double.valueOf(number)).doubleValue();
```

7.2.2   Converting a `double` to a string

Likewise a `double` is converted to a string using the following process:

```
String s   = (new Double(123)).toString();
```

Though in this case it is more elegant and shorter to write:

```
String s   = "" + 123;
```

Note: This works as + between a string and a standard type is defined to convert the standard type to a string.

7.3 The wrapper class `java.lang.Integer`

The wrapper class `Integer` is used to hold an `int` value as an object. This class has the following constructors:

Constructor	Responsibility
`Integer( i )`	Constructs an instance of an `Integer` from the `integer` parameter i.
`Integer( s )`	Constructs an instance of an `Integer` from the value contained in the `String` parameter s.

The major methods of the class are:

Method	Type	Responsibility
`intValue()`	I	Returns an `int` representation of the object.
`toString()`	I	Returns a `String` representation of the object.
`valueOf( s )`	S	Returns a new object of type `Integer` that represents the value contained in the string parameter s. The exception `NumberFormatException` is thrown if the number contained in the string cannot be parsed.
`parseInt( s )`	S	Returns an `int` representation of the value represented as digits in the `String` s.

Note: Type I Instance method S Static method

7.3.1 Converting a string to an `int`

The method `parseInt` returns the `int` representation of the number stored in character form in a string. Hence a very simple way of converting an integer number held in a string to an instance of an `int` is as follows:

```
String number = "123"
int i   = Integer.parseInt( number );
```

7.3.2 Converting an `int` to a string representation

The same strategy as used with a `double` can be used to convert an instance of an `int` to a string namely:

```
String s   = "" + 123;
```

7.4   The wrapper classes in general

Wrapper classes are implemented in the standard library for the following standard types:

Standard type	Wrapper class	Standard type	Wrapper class
boolean	Boolean	byte	Byte
char	Character	short	Short
int	Integer	long	Long
float	Float	double	Double

The wrapper classes are inherited from `Object` as shown in Figure 7.1. The class `Number` is an abstract class from which the numeric wrapper classes are derived:

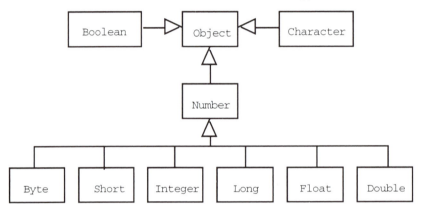

Figure 7.1 The wrapper classes.

A summary of the major extraction and interrogation methods that are implemented in each wrapper class is illustrated in the table below:

Method	Byte	Short	Integer	Long	Float	Double	Boolean	Character
byteVal() [1]	✓	✓	✓	✓	✓	✓		
shortVal() [1]	✓	✓	✓	✓	✓	✓		
intVal() [1]	✓	✓	✓	✓	✓	✓		
longVal() [1]	✓	✓	✓	✓	✓	✓		
floatVal() [1]	✓	✓	✓	✓	✓	✓		
doubleVal() [1]	✓	✓	✓	✓	✓	✓		
booleanVal() [1]							✓	
charVal() [1]								✓
valueOf() [2]	✓	✓	✓	✓	✓	✓	✓	

Note	Explanation
1	The methods byteVal(), shortVal() .. charVal() deliver the contents of the wrapper class as the specified type.
2	Delivers the contents of the wrapper class as a string.

7.5 The wrapper class **`java.lang.Character`**

The wrapper class Character (java.lang.Character) contains many useful static methods that interrogate and transform characters. An abridged list of these static methods is shown in the table below:

Static Method	Responsibility
isLetter(c)	Returns true if c is a letter (upper or lower case).
isDigit(c)	Returns true if c is a digit.
isLetterOrDigit(c)	Returns true if c is a letter or digit.
isLowerCase(c)	Returns true if c is a lower-case letter.
isSpaceChar(c)	Returns true if c is a Unicode space character.
isUpperCase(c)	Returns true if c is an upper-case letter.
isWhiteSpace(c)	Returns true if c is a white space character.
toLowerCase(c)	Returns the lower-case representation of c.
toUpperCase(c)	Returns the upper-case representation of c.

Note: Appendix F lists all the major methods of the wrapper class Character. *The 1st parameter* c *is of type* char.

7.6 Self-assessment

● Why are there wrapper classes in Java?

● How can you convert a number held in string into a data value held in a variable?

● Describe two different ways of converting an integer value into a string?

8. Windowed programming

This chapter looks at building an application or applet that uses standard visual components to display information using a GUI (Graphical User Interface).

8.1 Introduction

There are two types of windowed Java programs that can be created:

- **An Application**
  That runs as a stand alone program, and may access resources on the local machine.

- **An Applet**
  That runs inside a web browser, and may **not** access resources on the local machine. However, a running applet can deny resources to the user of a computer by making excessive use of CPU time and memory. This is termed a denial of resources attack.

A software solution developed both as an application and an applet would share a large amount of common code.

8.1.1 Inheritance

Inheritance is the ability for a new class to inherit all the methods and instance variables from an existing class. Inheritance is a useful way of re-using existing code. For example, a class B inheriting from a class A is shown below:

Class A	Class B inheriting from class A
```class A { public void method_in_a() { } }```	```class B extends A { public void method_in_b() { } }```

Class B contains the following methods: method_in_b and the inherited method method_in_a from class A. Inheritance is fully discussed in Chapter 12, for now treat inheritance as simply a way of automatically including all the methods from an existing class (the superclass) into a new class (the subclass).

Many of the classes used for implementing windowed programming are inherited from other classes. This approach to the design of the GUI library has prevented considerable code duplication as well as saving time and effort in its production.

8.1.2   The awt package

A windowed based Java application or applet uses classes in the awt package to create visual components on the user's screen. The simplest of these classes are:

Class	Implements	Example
Frame	A window container for visual components in an application or applet.	
Button	The representation of a labelled button on the screen. The button may be pressed to affect an action inside the application or applet.	Button
List	An area on the screen representing a list box into which is displayed lines of text.	Line 1 Line 2
TextArea	An area on the screen into which results from the application or applet are written.	Line 1 Line 2
TextField	An area on the screen representing a text field into which the user can enter text.	Entered

Using instances of these classes a straightforward application that uses a GUI can be created. Many development environments provide a GUI builder that allows the creation of the front end of the GUI using a graphical editor. The GUI builder in essence generating the skeleton code for the application and leaves the user with the task of creating the code that processes interactions generated by a user of the GUI.

8.1.3 Selected methods in major `awt` components

The class `java.awt.Component` is the superclass for many visual components. The major responsibilities of this class are:

Method	Responsibility

setFont(f)	Sets the font used in the visual representation of the component. For example:
	`Font f = new Font("Monospaced",Font.PLAIN,9);`
	`visual_component.setFont( f )`

setBounds(x,y,w,h)	Sets or resizes a visual instance of the class `Component` in pixels. The new location of the component's top left-hand corner is at position x,y with a width of w pixels and a height of h pixels.
setName(str)	Sets the component's name.
setSize(w, h)	Resizes to be w pixels wide by h pixels high.

Note: All visual components inherited from this class will also contain these methods. Chapter 12 describes inheritance in detail.

The class `java.awt.Container` that is inherited from the class `Component` implements the following major responsibilities:

Method	Responsibility
remove(vc)	Removes a visual component from the window.
setLayout(lm)	Sets the layout manager. Layout managers are discussed in Chapter 27.
add(vc)	Adds a new visual component to the window.
setSize(w, h)	Sets the size of the window in pixels.

The class `java.awt.Frame` that is inherited from the class `Container` implements the following major responsibilities:

Method	Responsibility
Frame() Frame(str)	The constructor for a frame. May be constructed with a specific title `str`.
setTitle(str)	Sets the title for the frame.

The class `java.awt.Button` that is inherited from the class `Component` implements the following major responsibilities:

Method	Responsibility
Button() Button(str)	The constructor for a button. May be constructed with a specific label `str`.
addActionListener(l)	Sets a listener to which notification will be sent when a user 'presses' the visual representation of the button.
getLabel()	Returns the label associated with this button.
setLabel(str)	Sets the name of the button's label.

The class `java.awt.List` that is inherited from the class `Component` implements the following major responsibilities:

Method	Responsibility
List() List(rows)	The constructor for a list. May be constructed to display # rows. (May be more if size permits.)
add(s)	Adds a string to the list box.
removeAll()	Removes all the text messages from the visual representation of the list.

The class `java.awt.TextComponent` that is inherited from the class `Component` implements the following major responsibilities:

Method	Responsibility
getText()	Returns as a string the text that is presented by this component.
setText(str)	Sets the text presented by the visual component to be `str`.

The class `TextField` that is inherited from the class `TextComponent` that itself is inherited from `Component` implements the following major responsibilities:

Method	Responsibility
TextField() TextField(cols) TextField(str) Textfield(str,cols)	The constructor for an instance of a text field. May be constructed to be `cols` wide with an initial string of `str`.
addActionListener(l)	Sets a listener to which notification will be sent when a user completes an input into the visual text field.
setColumns(n)	Sets the number of columns in the text field.

The class `java.awt.TextArea` that is inherited from the class `TextComponent` that itself is inherited from `Component` implements the following major responsibilities:

Method	Responsibility
TextArea() TextArea(rows,cols) TextArea(str) Textfield(str,rows,cols)	The constructor for an instance of a text field. May be constructed to be `rows` deep by `cols` wide with an initial string of `str`. (May be more if current size permits.)
append(str)	Appends the `str` to the textarea. A new line character is required to start a new line.

8.1.4   Relationship between illustrated **awt** classes

The inheritance relationship between the awt components described above is illustrated in Figure 8.1 below. The class `TextArea` contains in addition to the methods in its own class the methods inherited from class `TextComponent` and class `Component`. Whilst the class `Button` in addition to the methods in its own class also contains the inherited methods from the class `Component`.

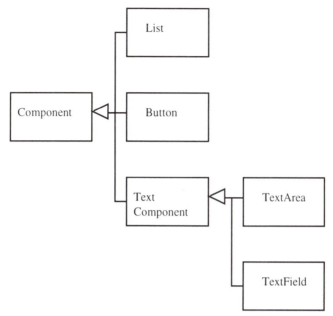

Figure 8.1 Inheritance diagram of selected awt components.

Note: Inheritance is discussed in detail in Chapter 12.

8.2 A GUI application

A simple GUI based application consists of a single instance of the class `TextField` and `TextArea` that are used for input and output respectively. The visual representation of this application is illustrated in Figure 8.2.

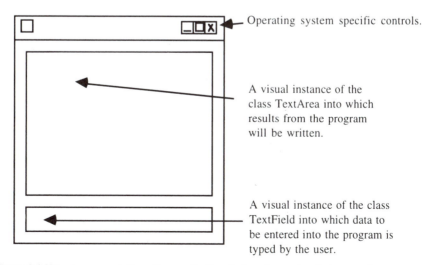

Figure 8.2 Visual representation of an application that performs simple input and output.

The components to create the application shown in Figure 8.2 are detailed below. In the application the following class libraries are used:

```
import java.awt.*;
import java.awt.event.*;
```

*Note: The use of * to indicate that all units in the hierarchy are to be made available to the application.*

The class `Application` is inherited from the class `Frame`. Inheritance is a way of adding all the existing methods and instance variables of an existing class to a new class. This in effect specializes an existing class without having to modify the code of the specialized class. Inheritance is discussed in more detail in Chapter 12 on Inheritance.

```
class Application extends Frame
{
  private static final int H = 400;      // Height of window
  private static final int W = 300;      // Width  of window

  private TextField    the_input;        //Visual Text Field (Input)
  private TextArea      the_output;       //Visual Text Area  (Output)
```

The constructor for the class is responsible for creating the instances of `TextField` and `TextArea`. Once created, the size and font used for the visual object is set and the visual object is then added to the visual window.

```
  public Application()
  {
    setLayout(null);                      //Set layout manager (none)
    setSize( W, H );                      //Size of Window

    Font font = new Font("Monospaced",Font.PLAIN,12);

    the_input = new TextField();          //Input area
    the_input.setBounds(10,H-50,W-20,40);  //              Size
    the_input.setFont( font );            //              Font
    add( the_input );                     //Add to canvas

    the_output = new TextArea( 10, 40 );  //Output area
    the_output.setBounds(10,30,W-20,H-100); //              Size
    the_output.setFont( font );           //              Font
    add( the_output );                    //Add to canvas
  }
}
```

Note: The class application has in addition to the constructor all the methods in the class Frame. Inheritance is fully explained in Chapter 12.

Chapter 9 describes a hypothetical development environment that is based on existing environments that allow the creation of the user interface in a visual way. This is achieved by using in effect a graphical editor to position the visual components on the screen. By using such an environment the programmer is freed from having to calculate many details such as the coordinates of the individual visual components.

This GUI based application is run by creating an instance of the class `Application` and sending the instance the message `show`. This process is illustrated below:

```
class Main
{
  public static void main( String args[] )
  {
    (new Application()).show();
  }
}
```

Note: The expression (new Application()).show() delivers an instance of the class Application to which the message show is sent.

8.3 Listener objects

In a GUI solution, user interactions, are processed by methods in a listener object. The methods in the listener object act like call-back functions. A call-back function is a body of code that is called in response to a user interaction. The object containing the call-back functions is nominated as the listener to a visual object that a user will interact with. When a user interacts with the visual object, the visual object calls the software developers nominated call-back function to process the interaction.

The following is a partial list of the different interactions generated by a user that can have call-back code associated with them.

- Selecting an option in the application or applet
- Opening or closing a window
- Entering text to be processed
- Change the focus
- Pressing a button.

Each visual object may have one or more call-back functions associated with it. For example, the class `TextField`'s call-back function is called after the user has entered data into the visual text field and pressed return.

8.3.1   Nominating a listener

An interface is a specification of a protocol that a class has to implement. For example, the interface ActionListener is defined as follows:

```
interface ActionListener
{
    public void actionPerformed( ActionEvent e );
}
```

A listener object for events from a visual text field implements the interface ActionListener. For example, the class Transaction that implements the interface ActionListener is defined as follows:

```
class Transaction implements ActionListener
{
  public void actionPerformed( ActionEvent e )
  {
      // Code to process users entered data
  }
}
```

Note: The class Transaction *overrides the method* actionPerformed *from the interface* ActionListener *with a concrete implementation.*

An instance of the class Transaction is used as a listener object for the visual component of a text field.

The following code registers the object the_cb an instance of Transaction with the object the_input an instance of the class TextField using the method addActionListener.

```
private TextField    the_input   = new TextField();
private Transaction  the_cb      = new Transaction();

input.addActionListener( the_cb );
```

8.4 A personal bank account application

An application to maintain the balance of a person's private bank account on a dedicated electronic personal assistant is developed below. In this complete application the interface described in Section 8.2 is used. The class diagram for the application is shown in Figure 8.3 below.

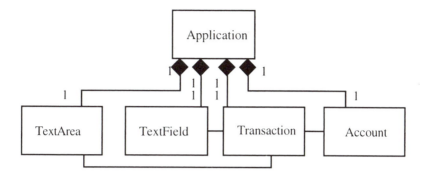

Figure 8.3 Class diagram for the visual personal bank account application.

8.4.1   The complete code

As the application uses a GUI the awt classes are imported together with the classes responsible for handling events from these classes:

```
import java.awt.*;
import java.awt.event.*;
import Account;
```

The class Application's constructor creates instances of the visual components used in the GUI. The inner class Transaction is responsible for processing the user's entered data. An instance of this class the_cb is registered as a listener to the visual object the_input an instance of the class TextField with the statement:

```
the_input.addActionListener( the_cb );    // Listener
```

The code for the class Application is:

```
class Application extends Frame
{
  private static final int H = 400;       //Height of window
  private static final int W = 300;       //Width  of window

  private TextField    the_input;         //Visual Text Field (Input)
  private TextArea     the_output;        //Visual Text Area  (Output)
  private Transaction  the_cb      = new Transaction();
  private Account      the_account = new Account();


  public Application()
  {
    setLayout(null);                      //Set layout manager (none)
    setSize( W, H );                      //Size of Window
```

```
Font font = new Font("Monospaced",Font.PLAIN,12);

the_input = new TextField();              //Input area
the_input.setBounds(10,H-50,W-20,40);     //             Size
the_input.setFont( font );                //             Font
add( the_input );                         //Add to canvas
the_input.addActionListener( the_cb );    //Add listener
the_output = new TextArea( 10, 40 );      //Output area
the_output.setBounds(10,30,W-20,H-100);   //             Size
the_output.setFont( font );               //             Font
add( the_output );                        //Add to canvas
}
```

The class `Transaction` is an inner class to `Application`. An inner class can access the instance variables of the containing class. However, an inner class cannot be accessed from outside the containing class. Inner classes are described in more detail in Section 5.7.

The method `actionPerformed` in the class `Transaction` extracts the characters that have been input into the visual object `input` into a transaction character stored in `action` and the rest of the input stored as a string into `rest`. For example, if the users input was `"D 23.50"` then `action` would contain the character `'D'` and `rest` would contain `"23.50"`. After the characters have been extracted from the text field the contents of the text field are cleared.

```
class Transaction implements ActionListener
{
  public void actionPerformed( ActionEvent e )
  {
    String user_input = the_input.getText() + "  ";//Make safe
    the_input.setText( "" );                        //Clear input
    char action      = user_input.charAt(0);        //Transaction
    String rest      = user_input.substring( 1 );  //Data
```

Note: This is an inner class as it is contained within another class. Section 10.9 describes the class `String` in detail.

The static method `parseDouble` in the wrapper class `Double` is used to convert the string `rest` into an instance of a `double`. This code returns an amount of 0.00 if the number is invalid or less than zero.

```
double value      = 0.00;
try
{
  value = Double.parseDouble( rest );              //Data val
}
catch ( NumberFormatException ex ) { }
```

Note: The wrapper classes are discussed in Chapter 7 and the exception mechanism is discussed in Chapter 13.

In the following case statement the appropriate action for the transaction submitted by the user is selected. For deposit, a health check on the value supplied is performed, then if valid this amount is deposited into the account. Appropriate messages are written onto the screen using the_output an instance of the class TextArea.

```
double res = 0.0;
switch ( action )
{
  case 'D' : case 'd' :                        //Deposit
    if ( value >= 0.00 )
    {
      the_account.deposit( value );
      the_output.append( "Deposited  : " + value + "\n");
    } else {
      the_output.append( "Amount must be positive\n" );
    }
    break;
```

The transactions of withdraw and balance are handled in a similar way.

```
  case 'W' : case 'w' :                        //Withdraw
    if ( value >= 0.00 )
    {
      res = the_account.withdraw( value );
      if ( res == value )
        the_output.append( "Withdrawn  : " + value + "\n");
      else
        the_output.append( "Sorry not possible\n" );
    } else {
      the_output.append( "Amount must be positive\n" );
    }
    break;
  case 'B' : case 'b' :                        //Balance
    res = the_account.account_balance();
    the_output.append( "Balance    : " + res + "\n" );
    break;
```

The transaction clear removes all the display items from the visual instance of the class TextArea.

```
  case 'C' : case 'c' :                        //Clear area
    the_output.setText( "" );
    break;
  default  :
    the_output.append( action + " - Error\n" );
  }
 }
 }
}
```

8.4.2   Putting it all together

To run the application the message `show` is sent to an instance of the class `Application`.

```
class Main
{
  public static void main( String args[] )
  {
    (new Application()).show();
  }
}
```

Figure 8.4 illustrates a typical interaction using this application.

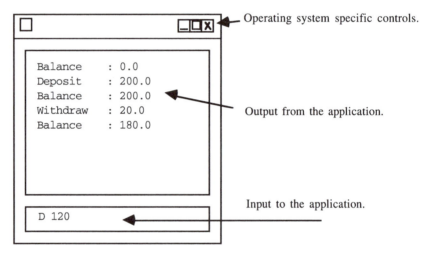

Operating system specific controls.

Output from the application.

Input to the application.

Figure 8.4 Example interaction using the application.

8.5 Processing events from the main window

The main window for the application can also generate events. The interface `WindowListener` contains the following methods:

Method	Called when
WindowActivated	The window is activated.
windowClosed	The window has been closed.
windowClosing	The window is being closed.
windowDeactivated	The window is deactivated.
windowDeiconfied	The window is restored from an iconified state.
windowIconified	The window has been iconified. On a Microsoft system the window is shrunk to the taskbar.
windowOpened	The window is opened.

However, if only one or two of these events is to be processed it is tedious to have to define null implementations for all the other methods for a listener class. The class WindowAdapter implements all of the above methods with a null body. An implementor can then inherit from this class to provide new definitions for only the actions that they wish to process. Section 12.4 describes in more detail the process of overriding a method in the superclass.

8.5.1   A listener object for handling window closing

The following inner class Window_Action is used as a listener for the main window. When the user closes the main window the method windowClosing will be called which will immediately exit the application.

```
class Window_Action extends WindowAdapter
{
  public void windowClosing( WindowEvent e )
  {
    System.exit(0);                          //Just exit
  }
}
```

Note: *The class* Window_Action *inherits all the methods from the class*
WindowAdapter *and overrides the method* windowClosing *with a new*
definition.

An event is registered with the main window by calling the method addWindowListener. For example, in the previous application a listener for a window closing would be registered by adding the following code in the constructor:

```
Window_Action  wa  = new Window_Action();
addWindowListener( wa );
```

and of course the code for the inner class Window_Action.

8.5.2   Other events from the main window

Other user generated events may be actioned by providing an implementation of the method detailed in the interface WindowListener.

8.6 Using menus

The same application as seen above in Section 8.4 can be built using pull-down menus. In implementing this solution two new classes are used MenuBar and Menu. Figure 8.5 illustrated below shows a menu-bar containing two pull-down menus: Transaction and System. As the mouse is moved over the menu-bar the pull-down menus are exposed.

The menu System contains a single item named Clear.

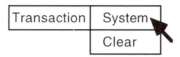

Figure 8.5 A menu-bar and pull-down menu.

8.6.1   Selected methods of `MenuBar` and `Menu`

The class `Menu` or its subclasses implements the following major responsibilities:

Method	Responsibility
Menu() Menu(str)	Constructs a new menu and a menu labelled `str`.
add(str)	Adds a menu item named `str`.
addActionListener(c)	Adds a function object `c` that implements the call-back function.
addSeparator	Adds a line separator in the menu.

The class `MenuBar` implements the following major responsibilities:

Method	Responsibility
MenuBar()	Creates a new menu-bar.
add	Adds a new pull-down menu to the menu-bar.

For example, to set-up a menu-bar that contains two pull-down menus that contain the following menu items.

- *Transaction:*
  Contains pull-down menu items for (Deposit, Withdraw and Balance)
- *System:*
  Contains the single pull-down menu items (`Clear`)

The following code is used:

```
the_menubar = new MenuBar();              //MenuBar across the top
the_menu1  = new Menu("Transaction");     // Transaction
the_menu1.add( "Deposit" );               //   Contains Deposit
the_menu1.add( "Withdraw" );              //   Contains Withdraw
the_menu1.addSeparator();                 //   Contains --------
the_menu1.add( "Balance" );               //   Contains Balance
the_menubar.add( the_menu1 );             //
the_menu2  = new Menu("System");          // System
the_menu2.add( "Clear" );                 //   Contains Clear
the_menubar.add( the_menu2 );             //
```

8.6.2   A new version of the personal bank account application

A new version of the application uses pull-down menus to select the appropriate transactions. When either of the transactions deposit or withdraw is selected an instance of the class `TextField` appears at the bottom of the screen for the user to enter the amount of money. The input area is removed after the user has signified that they wish their inputted value to be used by pressing return. This application is illustrated in Figure 8.6 below:

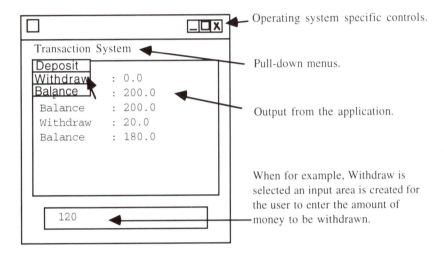

Figure 8.6 The personal bank account application using pull-down menus.

In the implementation of the application a class `M_Name` holds the names of the strings used in each pull-down menu. This is for two reasons:

- At a later stage the code to determine which item in the pull-down menu was selected will return the name of the menu item selected. By using a constant for the name any mismatches in spelling can be avoided.

- It allows the application to be easily customised for other languages.

```
class M_Name
{
  public static final String TRANS    = "Transaction";
  public static final String DEPOSIT  = "Deposit";
  public static final String WITHDRAW = "Withdraw";
  public static final String BALANCE  = "Balance";
  public static final String SYSTEM   = "System";
  public static final String CLEAR    = "Clear";
}
```

The code for the application is as follows:

```
class Application extends Frame
{
  private static final int H = 400;        // Height of window
  private static final int W = 300;        // Width  of window

  private TextField    the_input;          //Visual Text Field (Input)
  private TextArea     the_output;         //Visual Text Area   (Output)
  private MenuBar      the_menubar;
  private Menu         the_menu1, the_menu2;
  private Transaction  the_cb      = new Transaction();
  private Account      the_account = new Account();
```

The constructor for the application creates the output area and the pull-down menus as follows:

```
public Application()
{
  setLayout(null);                         //Set layout manager (none)
  setSize( W, H );                         //Size of Window

  Font font = new Font("Monospaced",Font.PLAIN,12);

  the_output = new TextArea( 10,40 );      //Output area
  the_output.setBounds(10,50,W-20,H-100);  //            Size
  the_output.setFont( font );              //            Font
  add( the_output );                       //Add to canvas

  the_menubar = new MenuBar();             //Menu Bar across the top
  the_menu1   = new Menu( M_Name.TRANS );  // Transaction
  the_menu1.add( M_Name.DEPOSIT );         //   Contains Deposit
  the_menu1.add( M_Name.WITHDRAW );        //   Contains Withdraw
  the_menu1.addSeparator();                //   Contains --------
  the_menu1.add( M_Name.BALANCE );         //   Contains Balance
  the_menubar.add( the_menu1 );            //
  the_menu2   = new Menu( M_Name.SYSTEM ); // System
  the_menu2.add( M_Name.CLEAR );           //   Contains Clear
  the_menubar.add( the_menu2 );            //

  the_menu1.addActionListener( the_cb );   //To process menu events
  the_menu2.addActionListener( the_cb );   //To process menu events

  setMenuBar( the_menubar );
}
```

Note: That a single function object the_cb *is used as the listener for both pull-down menus.*

The listener for the pull-down menus, interrogates the object e an instance of

`ActionEvent` to discover which of the menu items was selected. The class `ActionEvent` implements the following major responsibilities:

Method	Responsibility
getActionCommand()	Returns the command string associated with this event.
getModifiers()	Returns the sum of the modifier keys held down during this event.

Note: In the case of a listener for a pull-down menu the method
     getActionCommand will return the name of the menu item selected.

```
class Transaction implements ActionListener
{
  Transaction_deposit  cb_deposit  = new Transaction_deposit();
  Transaction_withdraw cb_withdraw = new Transaction_withdraw();

  public void actionPerformed( ActionEvent e )
  {
    String action_is = e.getActionCommand();
    char action      = ' ';
    if ( action_is.equals( M_Name.DEPOSIT  ) ) action = 'D';
    if ( action_is.equals( M_Name.WITHDRAW ) ) action = 'W';
    if ( action_is.equals( M_Name.BALANCE  ) ) action = 'B';
    if ( action_is.equals( M_Name.CLEAR    ) ) action = 'C';
```

For the transaction Deposit an instance of the class `TextField` is created to allow the user to enter the amount to be deposited. This object `the_input` itself has a listener `cb_deposit` which will be called when the user has entered the amount to be deposited into the text area and pressed return.

```
double res    = 0.0;
switch ( action )
{
  case 'D' : case 'd' :                      //Deposit
    the_input = new TextField( "", 1 );      //For input
    the_input.setBounds(30,H-45,W-60,40);    // Size
    the_input.addActionListener( cb_deposit ); // CB to process
    add( the_input );                        // Add to window
    break;
```

The transaction withdraw is implemented in a similar way to deposit.

```
case 'W' : case 'w' :                      //Withdraw
  the_input = new TextField( "", 1 );      //For input
  the_input.setBounds(30,H-45,W-60,40);    // Size
  the_input.addActionListener( cb_withdraw );// CB to process
  add( the_input );                        // Add to window
  break;
```

The transactions of balance and clear are implemented directly as follows:

```
      case 'B' : case 'b' :                          //Balance
        res = the_account.account_balance();
        the_output.append( "Balance    : " + res + "\n");
        break;
      case 'C' : case 'c' :                          //Clear area
        the_output.setText( "" );
        break;
      default  :
        the_output.append( action + " - Error\n" );//Will not occur
    }
  }
}
```

The listener for deposit extracts the amount entered by the user, performs the transaction and writes suitable messages onto the screen using the object the_output an instance of the class TextArea. The visual object the_input an instance of the class TextField is then removed from the screen.

The local method has_value converts a number held in a string into an instance of a double.

```
class Transaction_deposit implements ActionListener
{
  public void actionPerformed( ActionEvent e )
  {
    double value = has_value( the_input.getText() ); //to double
    if ( value >= 0.00 )
    {
      the_account.deposit( value );
      the_output.append( "Deposited  : " + value + "\n");
    } else {
      the_output.append( "Amount must be positive\n");
    }
    remove( the_input );                          //Remove from display
    the_input = null;                             //Remove references
  }
}
```

Likewise, the listener for withdraw process the transaction using the amount entered by the user.

```
class Transaction_withdraw implements ActionListener
{
  public void actionPerformed( ActionEvent e )
  {
    double value = has_value( the_input.getText() ); //to double
```

```
    if ( value >= 0.00 )
    {
      double res = the_account.withdraw( value );
      if ( res == value )
        the_output.append( "Withdrawn  : " + value + "\n");
      else
        the_output.append( "Sorry not possible\n" );
    } else {
      the_output.append( "Amount must be positive\n");
    }
    remove( the_input );                    //Remove from display
    the_input = null;                       //Remove references
  }
}
```

The method `has_value` converts the potential number held in the string s into an instance of a `double`. If the converted number is invalid then 0.00 is returned.

```
private double has_value( String s )
{
  double value   = 0.00;
  try
  {
    value = Double.parseDouble( s );        //Data val
  }
  catch ( NumberFormatException ex ) { }
  return value;
}
```

Note: The wrapper classes are discussed in Chapter 7 and the exception mechanism is discussed in Chapter 13.

8.6.3   Putting it all together

To run the application the message `show` is sent to an instance of the class `Application`.

```
class Main
{
  public static void main( String args[] )
  {
    (new Application()).show();
  }
}
```

8.6.4   Pull-down menus not allowed with applets

Unfortunately the awt classes do not allow pull-down menu to be used with an applet.

8.7 Building an applet

An applet is like an application except that it runs within an applet viewer or a web browser. To make running an arbitrary applet downloaded from the web safe, an applet is not allowed to access resources on the user's machine. Though draconian this restriction prevents unfortunate incidents happening when running an arbitrary applet on your machine.

Strictly speaking, there is one way that an applet can cause problems on your machine. As the applet is a running program it can deny resources to other running programs by consuming resources on your machine.

An applet is created by inheriting from the class `Applet`.

8.7.1   The class `Applet`

The class `Applet` that is inherited from the class `Panel` that itself is inherited from `Component` implements the following major responsibilities:

Method	Responsibility
`init()`	Called when the applet has been loaded into the system.
`start()`	Called when the applet should start executing.
`stop()`	Called when the applet should stop executing.
`destroy()`	Called when the applet is just about to be destroyed.
`getCodeBase()`	Returns an instance of the class URL that is the URL of the applet. The major methods of the class URL are detailed in Section 19.4.4.
`getParameter( str )`	Returns the string associated with the parameter `str` used when the applet is called.

On a leading web browser the following effects were observed when running an applet. Of course the web browser that you are using may do things differently.

Applet in a web page	Effect
The web page is first loaded.	The constructor for the applet is called. The methods `init` and `start` are called.
The web page is replaced by a new page (For example, The user follows a hypertext link.)	The method `stop` is called.
The web page is re-displayed Use of back/forward button on browser.	The method `start` is called.
The web page is re-loaded.	The methods `stop` and `destroy` are called. The constructor for the applet is called. The methods `init` and `start` are called.
The web page is re-visited by following a hypertext link to it.	The constructor for the applet is called. The methods `init` and `start` are called.

8.7.2   Comparison of an application and an applet

In essence there are very few difference between the code required for an application and an applet. However, it is important to remember what an application and applet can and cannot do. This relationship is summarized in the table below:

Criteria	Application	Applet
Can access and change resources on the local machine.	✓	✗
Is run as a stand alone entity.	✓	✗
Is run in a web browser or applet viewer.	✗	✓

8.8 A personal bank account applet

The application developed in Section 8.4 is now developed as a web-based applet. Unfortunately the version of the personal account manager using pull-down menus cannot be developed as a pull-down menu is not allowed in an applet using the `awt` classes. In re-implementing this as an applet, the basic structure of the code stays the same. The major differences are:

- The class `Web_menu` representing the applet inherits from the class `Applet`.

- The class `Web_menu` overrides the method `init`. The method `init` performs the Initialization of setting up the visual components.

- An HTML file counting the `<APPLET>` tag is used to load the applet into a web browser or applet viewer. Appendix H illustrates some basic HTML tags.

8.8.1   The complete code for the applet

The complete applet for the dedicated personal assistant is shown below. Firstly the classes that the application will use:

```
import java.awt.*;
import java.awt.event.*;
import java.applet.*;
import Account;
```

Note: That in additional to the `awt` *components we also need to use the package* `java.applet`.

The class Web_menu is inherited from the class `Applet`. Inheritance is a way of adding all the existing methods and instance variables of an existing class to a new class. This in effect specializes an existing class without having to modify the code of the specialized class. Inheritance is discussed in detail in Chapter 12.

```java
public class Web_menu extends Applet
{
  private static final int H = 400;        // Height of window
  private static final int W = 300;        // Width  of window

  private TextField    the_input;          //Visual Text Field (Input)
  private TextArea     the_output;         //Visual Text Area  (Output)
  private Transaction  the_cb      = new Transaction();
  private Account      the_account = new Account();

  public void init()
  {
    setLayout(null);                       //Set layout manager (none)
    setSize( W, H );                       //Size of Window
    Font font = new Font("Monospaced",Font.PLAIN,12);

    the_input = new TextField();           //Input area
    the_input.setBounds(10,H-50,W-20,40);  //            Size
    the_input.setFont( font );             //            Font
    add( the_input );                      //Add to canvas
    the_input.addActionListener( the_cb );

    the_output = new TextArea( 10,40 );    //Output area
    the_output.setBounds(10,30,W-20,H-100);//            Size
    the_output.setFont( font );            //            Font
    add( the_output );                     //Add to canvas
    the_output.append("Bank Account\n");
  }
```

Note: The method `init` is called when the applet is loaded. In this case it sets up the
awt components and adds a listener to process user transactions.
Public classes are discussed in Chapter 17 packages.

The class `Transaction` that implements the call-back functionality is identical to that seen earlier for the bank account implemented as a GUI based application.

```java
class Transaction implements ActionListener
{
  public void actionPerformed( ActionEvent e )
  {
    String user_input = the_input.getText() + "  ";//Make safe
    char action       = user_input.charAt(0);      //Transaction
    String rest       = user_input.substring( 1 ); //Data
    double value      = 0.00;

    try
    {
      value = Double.parseDouble( rest );          //Data val
    }
    catch ( NumberFormatException ex ) { }
```

Once the type of transaction and the amount have been extracted the following code is responsible for processing these transactions.

```
    double res = 0.0;
    switch ( action )
    {
      case 'D' : case 'd' :                      //Deposit
        if ( value >= 0.00 )
        {
          the_account.deposit( value );
          the_output.append( "Deposited  : " + value + "\n");
        } else {
          the_output.append( "Amount must be positive\n" );
        }
        break;
      case 'W' : case 'w' :                      //Withdraw
        if ( value >= 0.00 )
        {
          res = the_account.withdraw( value );
          if ( res == value )
            the_output.append( "Withdrawn  : " + value + "\n");
          else
            the_output.append( "Sorry not possible\n" );
        } else {
          the_output.append( "Amount must be positive\n" );
        }
        break;
      case 'B' : case 'b' :                      //Balance
        res = the_account.account_balance();
        the_output.append( "Balance    : " + res + "\n" );
        break;
      case 'C' : case 'c' :                      //Clear area
        the_output.setText( "" );
        break;
      default   :
        the_output.append( action + " - Error\n" );
    }
   }
  }
}
```

To run the applet using a web browser or applet viewer the following HTML page is used to load the applet into the web browser or applet viewer.

```
<HTML>
  <HEAD> <TITLE>Account Applet</TITLE> </HEAD>

  <BODY>
    <H2>Account Applet</H2>
    <APPLET CODE="web_menu.class" WIDTH=300 HEIGHT=400></APPLET>
  </BODY>
</HTML>
```

Note: Appendix H illustrates some basic HTML tags.

The HTML tag:

```
<APPLET CODE="web_menu.class" WIDTH=300 HEIGHT=400></APPLET>
```

loads the applet web_menu.class into a window 300 pixels wide by 400 pixels high in the web browser. Figure 8.7 illustrates a typical interaction using this applet.

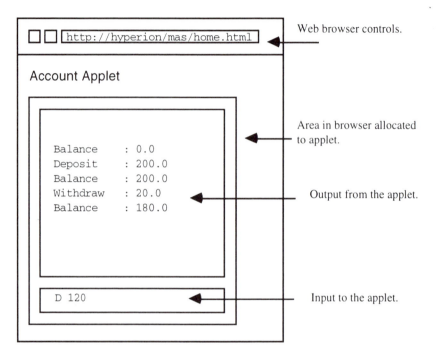

Figure 8.7 Example interaction using the application.

8.9   Passing parameters to an applet

The HTML tag <PARAM> is used to pass a string to the applet. For example, to pass the initial amount on deposit in the personal bank account applet the following HTML tags would be used.

```
<APPLET CODE="web_menu.class" WIDTH=300 HEIGHT=400>
   <PARAM NAME="IA" VALUE="20.00">
</APPLET>
```

The <PARAM> tag has the element NAME that names a parameter and VALUE that gives its value. In the above example, the name of the parameter is "IA" and it has a value of "20.00".

The class `Applet` has the following method:

Method	Responsibility
getParameter(str)	Returns as a string the value associated with the parameter named in the string str.

8.9.1 Putting it all together

The following method `set_initial_value` deposits a value taken from the applet parameter named `IA` into a bank account.

```
public void set_initial_value( Account the_account )
{
  double value = 0.00;
  String start_with = getParameter( "IA" );          //Value
  try
  {
    value = Double.parseDouble( start_with );          //Data val
  }
  catch ( NumberFormatException ex ) { }
  the_account.deposit( value );                      //Deposit
}
```

By adding the above method `set_initial_value` to the class `Web_menu` and the following code to the end of its method `init`:

```
set_initial_value( the_account );          //Initial amount
```

an initial amount of money managed by the personal account manager can be set.

8.10 Using buttons to initiate an interaction

The interface for the personal account manager can be recast to use buttons to initiate the interactions. An area is provided at the bottom of the screen for the user to enter the amount of money involved in the transaction. This new interface is illustrated in Figure 8.8 below.

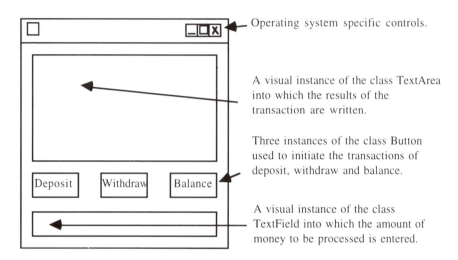

Operating system specific controls.

A visual instance of the class TextArea into which the results of the transaction are written.

Three instances of the class Button used to initiate the transactions of deposit, withdraw and balance.

A visual instance of the class TextField into which the amount of money to be processed is entered.

Figure 8.8 The new personal account manager interface.

8.10.1   Building the new interface

The interface for the application is built using the same style of code as illustrated in Section 8.2. Firstly constants are defined to hold the names of the buttons:

```
class M_Name
{
  public static final String  DEPOSIT  = "Deposit";
  public static final String  WITHDRAW = "Withdraw";
  public static final String  BALANCE  = "Balance";
}
```

The code for the application is developed in the class `Application` as follows:

```
class Application extends Frame
{
  private static final int H = 400;      //Height of window
  private static final int W = 300;      //Width  of window

  private TextField    the_input;        //Visual Text Field (Input)
  private TextArea     the_output;       //Visual Text Area  (Output)
  private Button       the_dep_bt;       //Deposit  button
  private Button       the_wit_bt;       //Withdraw button
  private Button       the_bal_bt;       //Balance  button
  private Account      the_account = new Account();
```

The constructor is responsible for creating the visual interface and is implemented as follows:

```
public Application()
{
  setLayout(null);                        //Set layout manager (none)
  setSize( W, H );                        //Size of Window

  Font font = new Font("Monospaced",Font.PLAIN,12);

  the_input = new TextField();            //Input area
  the_input.setBounds(10,H-70,W-20,40);   //              Size
  the_input.setFont( font );              //              Font
  add( the_input );                       //Add to canvas

  the_output = new TextArea( 10,40 );     //Output area
  the_output.setBounds(10,30,W-20,H-160); //              Size
  the_output.setFont( font );             //              Font
  add( the_output );                      //Add to canvas

  the_dep_bt = new Button( M_Name.DEPOSIT );
  the_dep_bt.setBounds( 10, H-120, W/3-20, 40);
  the_dep_bt.addActionListener( new Transaction_deposit() );

  the_wit_bt = new Button( M_Name.WITHDRAW );
  the_wit_bt.setBounds( W/3+10,  H-120, W/3-20, 40);
  the_wit_bt.addActionListener( new Transaction_withdraw() );

  the_bal_bt = new Button( M_Name.BALANCE );
  the_bal_bt.setBounds( W/3*2+10,H-120, W/3-20, 40);
  the_bal_bt.addActionListener( new Transaction_balance() );

  add( the_dep_bt );
  add( the_wit_bt );
  add( the_bal_bt );

  Window_Action  wa  = new Window_Action();
  addWindowListener( wa );
}
```

Note: Each button has a unique call-back function allocated to process events from the button.

The inner class `Transaction_deposit` contains the single method `actionPerformed` that implements the call-back function for the button labelled 'Deposit'.

```
class Transaction_deposit implements ActionListener
{
  public void actionPerformed( ActionEvent e )
  {
    double value = has_value( the_input.getText() + " " );
    the_input.setText( "" );                    //Clear input
    double res = 0.0;
    if ( value >= 0.00 )
    {
      the_account.deposit( value );
      the_output.append( "Deposited  : " + value + "\n");
    } else {
      the_output.append( "Amount must be positive\n" );
    }
  }
}
```

Likewise the inner class `Transaction_withdraw` contains the single method `actionPerformed` that implements the call-back function for the button labelled 'Withdraw'.

```
class Transaction_withdraw implements ActionListener
{
  public void actionPerformed( ActionEvent e )
  {
    double value = has_value( the_input.getText() + " " );
    the_input.setText( "" );                    //Clear input
    if ( value >= 0.00 )
    {
      double res = the_account.withdraw( value );
      if ( res == value )
        the_output.append( "Withdrawn  : " + value + "\n");
      else
        the_output.append( "Sorry not possible\n" );
    } else {
      the_output.append( "Amount must be positive\n" );
    }
  }
}
```

Likewise the inner class `Transaction_balance` contains the single method `actionPerformed` that implements the call-back function for the button labelled 'Balance'.

```
class Transaction_balance implements ActionListener
{
  public void actionPerformed( ActionEvent e )
  {
    double value = has_value( the_input.getText() + " " );
    the_input.setText( "" );                    //Clear input
    double res = the_account.account_balance();
    the_output.append( "Balance    : " + res + "\n" );
  }
}
```

8.10.2 Putting it all together

The application is completed by adding code for the class `Window_Action` illustrated in Section 8.5.1 and the method `has_value` illustrated in Section 8.6.2.

8.10.3 Using a single event handler for all buttons

Rather than have a separate call-back function for each button, a single call-back function may be nominated for all buttons. Using this approach the event generated is interrogated to discover its source. When the call-back function is called it is passed an instance of the class `ActionEvent` that may be interrogated to discover the source of the event. Using the method `getActionCommand` to interrogate the instance of `ActionEvent` will result in the return of the string used as the label for the button.

The application shown in Section 10.2.1 could be implemented using a single event handler for all three buttons. In this style of implementation the skeleton code for the event handler would be as follows:

```
class Transaction implements ActionListener
{
  public void actionPerformed( ActionEvent e )
  {
    // Get input from the text field
    String action_is = e.getActionCommand();

    if ( action_is.equals( M_Name.DEPOSIT  ) )
    {
      // Process the transaction Deposit
    }

    if ( action_is.equals( M_Name.WITHDRAW  ) )
    {
      // Process the transaction Withdraw
    }

    if ( action_is.equals( M_Name.BALANCE  ) )
    {
      // Process the transaction Balance
    }
  }
}
```

8.11   Swing

The swing classes allow an application to have the look and feel of native applications on the host machine. Though based around the awt classes the swing classes provided additional and enhanced features that allow a programmer a greater degree of control over the resultant visual interface.

8.11.1   The personal bank account application using swing classes

In essence for this simple application the differences using swing rather than awt are as follows:

●   The visual interface classes are now JTextArea, JTextField, JButton and JFrame, rather than TextArea, TextField, Button and Frame respectively.

●   To add a component to an instance of a JFrame the method getContentPane().add(the_component) is used.

●   To set a null layout manager for the application or applet the method getContentPane().setLayout(null) is used.

Note: The window produced by default for an instance of JTextArea is non-scrolling.

8.11.2   Implementation

In the implementation of the application shown below only the new swing classes are shown in detail, the core code that drives the application in the call-back functions is omitted. Also omitted is the class M_Name that contains constants for the names used in the three buttons.

```
class Application extends JFrame
{
  private static final int H = 400;        //Height of window
  private static final int W = 350;        //Width  of window

  private JTextField   the_input;          //Visual JText Field (Input)
  private JTextArea    the_output;         //Visual JText Area  (Output)
  private JButton      the_dep_bt;         //Deposit  button
  private JButton      the_wit_bt;         //Withdraw button
  private JButton      the_bal_bt;         //Balance  button
  private Account      the_account = new Account();
```

The constructor that creates the visual interface using the swing components is as follows:

```
public Application()
{
   getContentPane().setLayout(null);       //Set layout manager (none)
   setSize( W, H );                        //Size of Window

   Font font = new Font("Monospaced",Font.PLAIN,12);

   the_input = new JTextField();           //Input area
   the_input.setBounds(10,H-70,W-20,40);   //          Size
   the_input.setFont( font );              //          Font
   getContentPane().add( the_input );      //Add to canvas

   the_output = new JTextArea( 10,40 );    //Output area
   the_output.setBounds(10,30,W-20,H-160); //          Size
   the_output.setFont( font );             //          Font
   getContentPane().add( the_output );     //Add to canvas

   the_dep_bt = new JButton( M_Name.DEPOSIT );
   the_dep_bt.setBounds( 10, H-120, W/3-20, 40);
   the_dep_bt.addActionListener( new Transaction_deposit() );

   the_wit_bt = new JButton( M_Name.WITHDRAW );
   the_wit_bt.setBounds( W/3+10, H-120, W/3-20, 40);
   the_wit_bt.addActionListener( new Transaction_withdraw() );

   the_bal_bt = new JButton( M_Name.BALANCE );
   the_bal_bt.setBounds( W/3*2+10, H-120, W/3-20, 40);
   the_bal_bt.addActionListener( new Transaction_balance() );

   getContentPane().add( the_dep_bt );
   getContentPane().add( the_wit_bt );
   getContentPane().add( the_bal_bt );

   Window_Action  wa  = new Window_Action();
   addWindowListener( wa );
}

}
```

The code for call-back functions is the same as seen previously in the implementation using the awt classes.

8.12   Self-assessment

● What classes are used to create a GUI based application and applet?

● What visual components are available to display information?

● What visual components are available to receive input?

● What is a listener object, and how is it used?

● What are the major differences between an applet and an application.\?

● What other visual controls may be used for input to a Java application or applet?

8.13   Exercises

● *Personal bank account applet*
Re-write the application for a personal bank account manager shown in section 8.10 as an applet.

● *Windowed based cinema attendance (Application)*
Using as a base the cinema attendance application constructed as an exercise in Chapter 5, re-implement the application using a GUI for all interactions.

● *Windowed based cinema attendance (Applet)*
Using as a base the cinema attendance application constructed as an exercise in Chapter 5, re-implement this as an applet.

9. Development environments

This chapter looks at a hypothetical visual development environment for Java. Though not representing an actual environment it does contain the essence of many visual Java development environments.

9.1 Introduction

As the `awt` contains standard components, developers have sought ways other than programming for creating the visual interface used by the end user. The design of the visual interface is a visual activity and as such, is much easier to perform using a wysiwyg (what you see is what you get) environment than having to explicitly create the code that will produce the desired interface.

A common solution is a visual development environment, that allows a programmer to create the visual interface for a Java application or applet using a software tool akin to a graphic editor. Using such a software tool, visual and non visual interface components are placed onto the form representing the visual interface of the user's application or applet. The form is the design view of the interface that the end user of the application or applet will see.

Using the development environment a programmer adds additional code to implement the functionality of the application or applet. The complete code for the application or applet is then generated and compiled by the visual development environment. The time taken to implement an application or applet using such an approach can be significantly reduced.

9.2 A hypothetical visual development environment

A minimal hypothetical visual development environment consists of the following components:

- *An application menu-bar banner:*
  This allows the user to create, save, edit and generally manage the project that contains the application or applet that is being developed. The project contains all the files required for the application or applet in addition to intermediate files that detail the relationship between the visual components and the generated code.

- *A component tool-bar:*
  This contains the visual components and non-visual components that can be added to the form, this usually consists of the awt visual components, although additional manufacturer specific components are also increasingly supplied.

- *Project:*
  A menu box that details the components in the current project.

- *A properties list:*
  This allows the programmer to amend properties of visual and non-visual components that have been added to the form. For example, the colour of a button may be specified.

- *A Java form:*
  This represents the interface that an end user will see when they run the application or applet.

Illustrated in Figure 9.1 is a screen shot of the hypothetical visual development environment. In this environment the major components are highlighted. The screen shot in Figure 9.1 shows an applet being created, but as yet, no components have been added to the form.

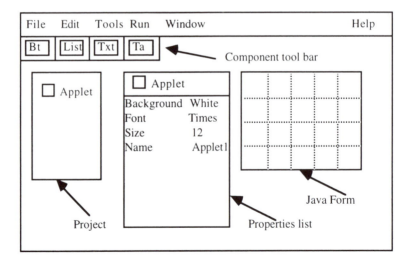

Figure 9.1 Hypothetical visual development environment for Java.

9.2.1   The application menu-bar

This allows a programmer to perform the following major actions using the pull-down menus in the applications menu-bar.

- *Menu File:*
  Create, and save the project that contains the files representing the application or applet.
- *Menu Edit:*
  Edit various fields on the form. This can include setting of options that effect the generated application or applet.
- *Menu Tools:*
  Various tools, used to help in the building of the application or applet. For example, select if an applet or application is to be built.
- *Menu Run:*
  Run the generated application or applet within the development environment.
- *Menu Window:*
  Select a window in the development environment.
- *Menu Help:*
  Provide on-line help on how to use the environment as well as details about the class libraries and language features.

9.2.2   The component tool bar

Allows a programmer to add instances of the visual components to the Java form. In this hypothetical development environment the awt components that can be added are:

Component	Is used to create the following component on the form
Bt	An instance of an awt Button.
List	An instance of an awt List.
Txt	An instance of an awt TextField.
Ta	An instance of an awt TextArea

Note: It is usual to have many more components. In particular, other components from the awt as well as manufacturer supplied components.

9.2.3   The project

The project window shows the components that make up the project. This will usually detail the relationship between the visual and non-visual components that have been added to the form. In addition the interactions that have been specified will also be listed.

9.2.4   The properties list

Allows a programmer to set various properties for an instance of a visual or non-visual component that has been added to the form. Figure 9.2 illustrates the properties of the Java form itself.

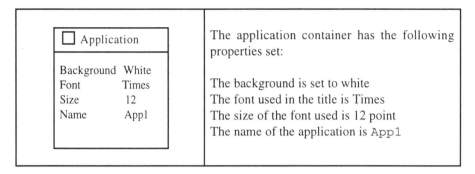

☐ Application Background White Font Times Size 12 Name App1	The application container has the following properties set: The background is set to white The font used in the title is Times The size of the font used is 12 point The name of the application is App1

Figure 9.2 The properties sheet for the applets window.

By using the properties list, a designer can change aspects of the visual components such as: size and position, font used, colour displayed in.

9.2.5   The Java form

The Java form represents a design view of the interface that is to be created for the application or applet. Onto the Java form are placed the visual or non-visual components from the component tool-bar that are required for the specific application or applet. The form has a grid to help objects align so that the designer can generate a pleasing interface. Figure 9.3 illustrates the form on which the Java components are placed.

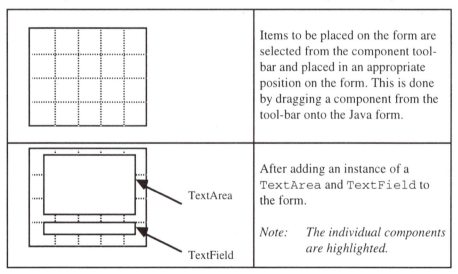

	Items to be placed on the form are selected from the component tool-bar and placed in an appropriate position on the form. This is done by dragging a component from the tool-bar onto the Java form.
TextArea TextField	After adding an instance of a `TextArea` and `TextField` to the form. *Note: The individual components are highlighted.*

Figure 9.3 The Java form.

9.3 Building an application

Using the hypothetical development environment outlined in this chapter the following stages are required to build the bank account application developed in Section 8.8:

● Create a new project for an application.

- Add the awt visual components of a TextField and TextArea to the Java form.

- Modify properties for the TextField and TextArea. For example, the font used to display the response.

- Add the call-back code that is to be executed when an end user of the application enters data into the instance of the TextField displayed on the form.

- Save and compile the application.

9.3.1   Create a new project for the application

The File menu is used to create a new project. Then the Tools menu is used to specify that an application is to be built. If an applet had been selected to be created then the code generated would contain minor differences.

9.3.2   Add **awt** components to the Java form

The awt components are dragged from the component tool-bar onto the Java form. In placing the awt components on the form the user may re-size the components to create a visually pleasing interface for the end user. For example, Figure 9.4 illustrates one possibility of the layout of the components:

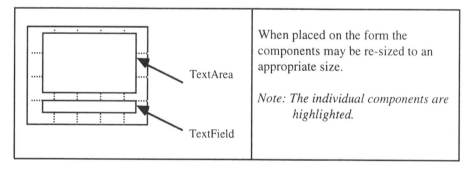

Figure 9.4 The Java form with added visual components.

The actual instances of these objects are named:

Visual object class name	Instance of visual object named
TextArea	textArea1 for the first instance then textArea2 etc.
TextField	textField1 for the first instance then textField2 etc.

Note: The same would be true for instances of the awt components Button and List.

9.3.3   Modifying properties of visual objects

By selecting the properties for the object `textField1` individual attributes of the component may be changed. For example, by selecting the object `textField1` on the form, the following properties may be changed:

- The background colour of the text field.
- The font used for the entered text.
- The size of the font for the entered text.

It is usual however, to allow additional properties to be changed.

Note: The other visual objects properties can be modified in the same way.

9.3.4   Adding the call-back code

As well as being able to change properties of an object on the Java form, call-back code may also be associated with the object. This call-back code is implemented as methods in an inner class. The methods in the inner class will be called when a specific user interaction is performed on the visual component.

For example, it is usual to allow a method to be associated with at least the following user interactions:

Interaction	Explanation
Key typed	A user typed a character.
Enter	The user pressed return.
MousePress	The user presses the mouse button.
ComponentResize	The end user tries to resize the component.
GotFocus	The focus of interaction is switched to this component.
LostFocus	The focus of interaction is moved from this component.

Note: Not all objects will be able to support these specific actions. Likewise objects may support additional interactions.

When an interaction is associated with a visual component the visual development environment will add skeleton code for its call-back method in the code for the application. For example, if the event `Enter` is associated with the object `textField1` then the following skeleton style of code is generated:

```
void cb_texField1_Enter( java.awt.event.ActionEvent event )
{
  // Add code here that will be called when an end user
  // presses enter when this component is selected
}
```

In implementing the bank account application the code that the programmer would add would be:

```java
void cb_texField1_Enter( java.awt.event.ActionEvent event )
{
  String user_input = the_input.getText() + "   ";//Make safe
  char action        = user_input.charAt(0);       //Transaction
  String rest        = user_input.substring( 1 ); //Data
  double value       = 0.00;

  try
  {
    value = Double.parseDouble( rest );           //Data val
  }
  catch ( NumberFormatException ex ) { }

  double res = 0.0;
  switch ( action )
  {
    case 'D' : case 'd' :                          //Deposit
      if ( value >= 0.00 )
      {
        the_account.deposit( value );
        the_output.append( "Deposited  : " + value + "\n");
      } else {
        the_output.append( "Amount must be positive\n" );
      }
      break;
    case 'W' : case 'w' :                          //Withdraw
      if ( value >= 0.00 )
      {
        res = the_account.withdraw( value );
        if ( res == value )
          the_output.append( "Withdrawn  : " + value + "\n");
        else
          the_output.append( "Sorry not possible\n" );
      } else {
        the_output.append( "Amount must be positive\n" );
      }
      break;
    case 'B' : case 'b' :                          //Balance
      res = the_account.account_balance();
      the_output.append( "Balance    : " + res + "\n" );
      break;
    case 'C' : case 'c' :                          //Clear area
      the_output.setText( "" );
      break;
    default  :
      the_output.append( action + " - Error\n" );
  }
}
```

Note: So far we have not declared the object the_account. *This needs to be an object whose life-time is the lifetime of the application and hence cannot be declared as a local variable inside the method.*

9.3.5   Creating the object `the_account`

The only minor step left is to create the instance of the class `Account` that is used to hold the state of a person's bank account. However, this object must have the same lifetime as the application and hence must be declared outside of the method `cb_texField1_Enter`.

By selecting the Java form, the generated code for the application can be edited. In the code for the class `Application` will be the declaration of the visual objects `textField1` and `textArea1`. For example, one possible form for the generated could would be as follows:

```
class Application extends Frame
{
  private TextField    the_input;        //Visual Text Field (Input)
  private TextArea     the_output;       //Visual Text Area  (Output)
  private Transaction  the_cb = new Transaction();

  public Application()
  {
    setLayout(null);                     //Set layout manager (none)
    setSize( W, H );                     //Size of Window

    Font font = new Font("Monospaced",Font.PLAIN,12);

    textfield1 = new TextField();        //Input area
    textfield1.setBounds(10,350,280,40); //          Size
    textfield1.setFont( font );          //          Font
    add( textfield1 );                   //Add to canvas

    textfield1.addActionListener( the_cb );   //Add listener

    textArea1 = new TextArea( 10,40 );   //Output area
    textArea1.setBounds(10,30,280,300);  //          Size
    textArea1.setFont( font );           //          Font
    add( textArea1 );                    //Add to canvas
  }

// etc.
```

At an appropriate point in the declarations of the visual objects, add the following line to declare an instance of the class `Account`:

```
private Account  the_account    = new Account();
```

9.3.6   Putting it all together

The run menu allows the implementor to compile and run the completed applet. A successful compile and run is illustrated in Figure 9.5. Of course, if the implementor has made any mistakes, these will be reported in a log window. Once the errors have been corrected, another attempt at compiling and running the application may be made.

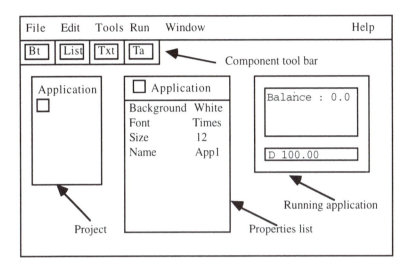

Figure 9.5 Running the application.

9.4   Self-assessment

- How does the visual development environment that you use differ from the hypothetical visual development environment described above?

- What additional facilities does the visual environment that you use, have over the hypothetical environment described in this chapter?

- What are the advantages or disadvantages of using a visual development environment against creating all the code directly.

9.5   Exercises

- *Windowed personal account manager*
  Create the account manager application and applet using your visual development environment.

10. Arrays

This chapter looks at how collections of variables and objects are held and manipulated using Java's inbuilt container: the array. Chapters 21 and 22 will look at other containers that provide more flexibility in accessing and storing data values.

10.1   Introduction

An array allows the construction of containers for objects or variables of the same type. However, the array container is restrictive in how it can be used and manipulated. In particular:

- Once allocated the size of the array may not be changed.
- Values in the array are selected using an index. However, the index value must be an integer in the range 0 .. length-1. Where length is the number of elements in the array.

10.1.1   Array declaration

The following fragment of code illustrates the declaration of an array of 4 integer elements. In this fragment of code individual elements are initialized to the values 50, 100, 120, 40 respectively.

```
int size_of_rooms[] = new int[4];

size_of_rooms[0] =  50;
size_of_rooms[1] = 100;
size_of_rooms[2] = 120;
size_of_rooms[3] =  40;
```

The array declaration shown above consists of two distinct components:

1	Declaration of a handle for the array	int size_of_rooms[]
2	Allocation of storage for the array	= new int[4]

The storage for the array after assigning the values 50, 100, 120, 40 to individual elements is illustrated in Figure 10.1.

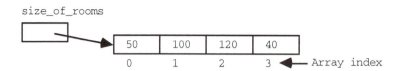

Figure 10.1 Storage for the array `size_of_rooms`.

This declaration of an array is similar to the declaration of an instance of a class, first storage for the handle is allocated then the storage for the actual array elements is allocated. If an attempt is made to access an array element without allocating storage for the array a run-time error will occur.

10.1.2   Access to individual elements of the array

Individual elements of the array are accessed using an array subscript as follows:

```
System.out.println("The size of room 2 is " +
                   size_of_rooms[2] + " square metres" );
```

which when combined with suitable code and run would produce the following results:

```
The size of room 2 is 120 square metres
```

A variable may be used as the array index. For example, the following code fragment prints the size of all the rooms.

```
    for ( int i=0; i<4; i++ )
    {
      System.out.println("The size of room " + i + " is " +
                       size_of_rooms[i] + " square metres" );
    }
```

Which when combined with suitable code and run would produce the following results: .

```
The size of room 0 is 50 square metres
The size of room 1 is 100 square metres
The size of room 2 is 120 square metres
The size of room 3 is 40 square metres
```

10.1.3   Accessing undefined array elements

Any attempt to access an array element that is not contained in the array will result in a run-time error. For example, if the following code were executed:

```
System.out.println("The size of room 5 is " +
                    size_of_rooms[5] + " square metres" );
```

then the run-time exception `ArrayIndexOutOfBoundsException` would be generated. The Exception mechanism is discussed fully in Chapter 13.

10.1.4   Initializing an array on creation

The array `size_of_rooms` could have been declared and initialized as follows:

```
int size_of_rooms[] = { 50, 100, 120, 40 };
```

In this case the array consists of 4 elements, with the `size_of_rooms[0]` set to 50, `size_of_rooms[1]` set to 100 etc.

10.1.5   The length attribute of an array

The attribute `length` of an array object delivers the number of elements in the array. For example, the following fragment of code populates the array `size_of_rooms` with the values 50, 100, 120 and 40 then prints the size of the individual rooms:

```
int size_of_rooms[] = { 50, 100, 120, 40 };

for ( int i=0; i<size_of_rooms.length; i++ )
{
   System.out.println("The size of room " + i + " is " +
                       size_of_rooms[i] + " square metres" );
}
```

Note: `size_of_rooms.length` *returns the number of elements in the array.*

Which when combined into a complete Java application and run produces the following results:

```
The size of room 0 is 50 square metres
The size of room 1 is 100 square metres
The size of room 2 is 120 square metres
The size of room 3 is 40 square metres
```

10.2   Multi-dimensional arrays

The following table illustrates the declaration and allocation of storage for a 1, 2 and 3 dimensional `int` array in Java

Declaration of array handle	Conceptual model of storage	Allocation of physical storage for array	Access to shaded element
`int vector[];`		`vector = new int[4];`	`vector[2]`
`int table[][];`		`table = new int[3][4];`	`table[1][2]`
`int cube[][][];`		`cube = new int[2][3][4];`	`cube[0][1][2]`

Note: In Java there is no limit to the number of dimensions that an array may have.

10.3   Initialization of multi-dimensional arrays

In the same way that a single dimension array may be initialized with pre-defined values so multi-dimensional arrays may also be initialized. For example, the following table illustrates the Initialization of a 2D array `table` and a 3D array `cube`.

`int table[][];`	`table = { {1,2,3,4}, {5,6,7,8}, {9,10,11,12}  };`
`int cube[][][];`	`cube = { { {1,2,3,4}, {5,6,7,8}, {9,10,11,12}  },` `          { {1,2,3,4}, {5,6,7,8}, {9,10,11,12}  } };`

10.3.1   Elements in a multi-dimensional array

The following declaration allocates storage for a cube:

```
int cube[][][] = new int[2][3][4];
```

the following table illustrates how to obtain the number of elements in each dimension of the cube illustrated above:

Length of:	1st dimension	2nd dimension	3rd dimension
Obtained with:	`cube.length`	`cube[0].length`	`cube[0][0].length`

Note: The array index when used must be valid.

10.3.2 Arrays of arrays

An array may be composed of individual elements that are themselves arrays. For example, the following code creates the following triangular structure:

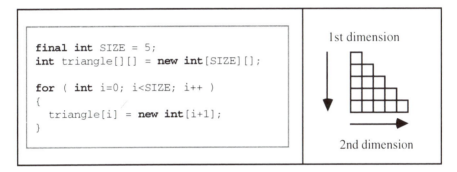

The array declaration shown above consists of three distinct components:

1	Declaration of a handle for the array of arrays	`int triangle[][]`
2	Allocation of storage for the 1st dimension	`= new int[SIZE][];`
3	Allocation of storage for each row in the 2nd dimension.	`triangle[i] = new int[i+1];`

The following fragment of code would print out the numbers held in the triangular array.

```
for ( int i=0; i<triangle.length; i++ )
{
  for ( int j=0; j<triangle[i].length; j++ )
    System.out.print( triangle[i][j]  + " " );
  System.out.println();
}
```

However, it would be unusual to use such a complex data structure in most applications or applets.

10.4   Command line parameters to a Java application

When a Java application is run from the command line, any command line arguments are passed to the application as an array of strings. Remember the declaration for the method main is:

```
public static void main( String args[] )
```

Note: This signifies that the actual parameter to the method is an array of strings.

An application to echo the command line arguments to the console is implemented as follows:

```
class Echo
{
  public static void main( String args[] )
  {
    for ( int i=0; i<args.length; i++ )   //Arg 0 is the 1st arg
    {
      System.out.print( args[i] );        //Write argument
      if ( i != args.length )
        System.out.print( " " );          //Separator
    }
    System.out.println( "" );             //New line
  }
}
```

Note: On a DOS / Unix system this would implement part of the functionality of the program echo.

10.4.1   Putting it all together

When compiled the above application Echo will print out its command line arguments. This is very similar to the DOS / Unix command echo. For example, when run as a command line application as follows:

```
java Echo Hello world
```

the output produced is as follows:

```
Hello world
```

10.5 Returning an array as the result of a method

Java arrays are first class objects and can be returned as the result of a method. For example, the following demonstration method returns an array containing terms from the fibonacci series.

```
class Useful
{
  public static long[] fibonacci( final int terms )
  {
    int no_of_terms = (terms >= 90 || terms <= 2) ? 2 : terms;

    long values[] = new long[no_of_terms];
    values[0] = 1;
    values[1] = 1;
    for ( int i=2; i<no_of_terms; i++ )
    {
      values[i] = values[i-1] + values[i-2];
    }
    return values;
  }
}
```

The following test class, illustrates using the method `fibonacci` in the class `Useful`.

```
class Main
{
  public static void main( String args[] )
  {
    long numbers[] = Useful.fibonacci(8);
    for ( int i=0; i<numbers.length; i++ )
    {
        System.out.print( numbers[i] + " " );
    }
    System.out.println();
  }
}
```

When compiled and run, this application produces the following results:

```
1 1 2 3 5 8 13 21
```

10.6   The game of noughts and crosses

The game of noughts and crosses or tick tack toe is played on a square board of 3 by 3 cells. Players take it in turn to place their counter on the board. The first player to have three of their counters in a row either vertically, horizontally or diagonally wins. If no more moves can be made and no player has a row of three of their counters then the game is a draw. An example game between two players who play with black and white counters is shown below in Figure 10.2:

	For ◯	For ●
First move	◯	◯ ●
Second move	◯ ◯ ●	◯ ◯ ● ●
Third move	◯ ◯ ◯ ● ●	◯ ◯ ◯ ● ● ●
Final move	◯ ◯ ◯ ◯ ● ● ●	

Figure 10.2 A game of noughts and crosses.

In looking at a game between two players in an object-oriented way several objects can be identified. These objects are the two players, the black and white counters and the board. These objects are shown below in Figure 10.3

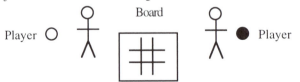

Figure 10.3 Object-oriented view of the game of noughts and crosses.

In this implementation of the noughts and crosses application, the class `Player` is not created, interactions with the human players are performed directly by the main processing code. The only class that will be used is a class to represent the board on which the game is played and a class responsible for playing the game.

The responsibilities of the class `Board` are as follows:

Method	Responsibility
add	Adds the player's counter to the board. The player's move is specified by a number in the range 1 to 9 and their counter by a character. X for ● and O for ○.
check_move	Returns true if the presented move is valid. The method checks that the move is in the range 1 to 9 and that the specified cell is not occupied.
position	Returns the character occupying a specific cell on the noughts and crosses board.
situation	Returns the current state of the noughts and crosses board. Is the game won, drawn or is still playable?

10.6.1 The main class `Play`

The main class `Play` contains the static method `main` that creates an instance of the class `Play` that is then sent the message `play_game`. By using this approach an actual instance of the class `Play` is created.

The method `play_game` organises the interaction between the outside environment and an instance of the class `Board`. In essence this consists of a loop that asks alternatively for moves for `'X'` the black counter and `'O'` the white counter. To simplify the interaction between the game player and the application the class `TUI` (see Section 5.5.1) is used for all input-output interactions.

```
class Play
{
  private char   the_player;                      //Either 'X' or 'O'
  private TUI    the_screen  = new TUI();         //I/O
  private Board  the_oxo     = new Board();       //Instance of Board
  private int    the_game_is = Board_state.PLAYABLE; //State of Board

  public static void main( String args[] )
  {
    (new Play()).play_game();
  }

  public void play_game()
  {
    the_player = 'X';                             //First the_player
    while ( the_game_is == Board_state.PLAYABLE ) //While playable
    {
      String who = "Player " + the_player;
      int move = the_screen.dialogue_int(who + " enter move: ");
      if ( the_oxo.check( move ) )                // Valid
      {
        the_oxo.add( move, the_player );          //Add to board
        display();                                //Display board
        the_game_is = the_oxo.situation();        //Game is
```

Once the state of the game has been established an appropriate action is then taken.

```
switch ( the_game_is )
  {
    case Board_state.WIN  :                    // Won
      the_screen.message(who + " wins");
      break;
    case Board_state.DRAW :                    // Drawn
      the_screen.message("It's a draw" );
      break;
    case Board_state.PLAYABLE :
      switch ( the_player )                    // Playable
      {
        case 'X' : the_player='O'; break;     //  'X' -> 'O'
        case 'O' : the_player='X'; break;     //  'O' -> 'X'
      }
      break;
  }
} else {
  the_screen.message("Move is invalid" );
  }
}
}
```

The following methods `display` and `display_line` are responsible for displaying the current state of the board in a pictorial format. The method `position` delivers the character (player's counter) that is stored in the board. Figure 10.4 below indicates the position of each of the cells in the noughts and crosses board as envisaged by a player of the game.

1	2	3
4	5	6
7	8	9

Figure 10.4 Position of player's counters on the noughts and crosses board.

The method `display_line` displays an individual line (row) of the board. The parameter passed is the number of the first cell in the row to be displayed.

```
private void display_line( final int pos )
{
  the_screen.message( the_oxo.position( pos   )  + " | " +
                      the_oxo.position( pos+1 )  + " | " +
                      the_oxo.position( pos+2 )  );
}
```

The method `display` calls the method `display_line` three times once for each of the three rows of the noughts and crosses board.

```
public void display()
{
  the_screen.message( "" );
  display_line( 1 );
  the_screen.message( "---------" );
  display_line( 4 );
  the_screen.message( "---------" );
  display_line( 7 );
  the_screen.message( "" );
}
}
```

10.6.2   The class `Board_state`

The class `Board_state` acts as a container for the following enumeration's which are used to define the current state of play for the game.

```
class Board_state {
  public static final int WIN     = 0;
  public static final int DRAW    = 1;
  public static final int PLAYABLE = 2;
}
```

Note: By defining the values as `static final` *they are implemented as constants.*

10.6.3   The class `Board`

The class `Board` implements the validation of moves and the determination of the current state of a game of noughts and crosses. Internally the noughts and crosses board is represented as a one-dimensional array of characters. An occupied square has either the value `'X'` or `'O'`, whilst an empty square is represented by the character `' '`. These values are a convention and it is assumed that the user of the class `Board` will only supply `'X'` and `'O'` as representations of moves.

```
class Board
{
  private char    the_sqrs[];              //Playing grid
  private int     the_moves;               //Moves made
  private boolean the_end_of_game = false; //Game finished

  private static final int SIZE_TTT = 9;   //Squares on board
```

The constructor for the class `Board` resets all the squares on the board to the initial state of empty.

```java
public Board()
{
  the_sqrs = new char[SIZE_TTT];        // Allocates storage
  for ( int i=0; i<SIZE_TTT; i++ )      // Populate with ' '
  {
    the_sqrs[i] = ' ';
  }
  the_moves = 0;
}
```

The method `check` checks if the supplied move is reasonable, is a valid move for the current state of the game and that the game has not ended. If any of these checks fail a result of `false` is returned.

```java
public boolean check( final int pos )
{
  return (pos >= 1 && pos <= SIZE_TTT) &&
         the_sqrs[pos-1] == ' '         &&
         ! the_end_of_game;
}
```

Note: As Java uses lazy evaluation, if the move is outside the range 1 .. 9 then the corresponding square is not checked for a previous counter.
That the square number on the noughts and crosses board is converted into an array index by subtracting 1.

The method `add` adds a new counter onto the board. It is a prerequisite of using this method that the method `valid` has been called to check that such a move is possible.

```java
public void add( final int pos, final char piece )
{
  the_sqrs[ pos-1 ] = piece;
  the_moves++;
}
```

The method `position` returns the character stored in the board. By using this method the code that is responsible for displaying a representation of the board can be written independently of this class. In particular, if the representation of the board changed then a user of the class `Board` would not need to change their code that accesses the board.

```java
public char position( int i )
{
  return the_sqrs[i-1];
}
```

The method `situation` evaluates the current state of the game. The strategy used to evaluate the current state of the game is as follows:

- Look at the 8 possible win lines for a line of three squares whose contents though the same are not the space character. If such a line exists then the last player played a winning move.

- If 9 moves have been played then the game is a draw.

- If the above two conditions are false then the game is deemed still playable. This last condition is naive as there are situations in the game where even though there are unoccupied squares no player can win.

In the body of the method the two-dimensional array `win_lines` first dimension represents the 8 win lines (0..7) and the second dimension represents the square numbers for that win line (0..2). This arrangement is illustrated in Figure 10.5. By selecting the board's cell positions from `win_lines` the actual cells in the array `the_sqrs` can be checked.

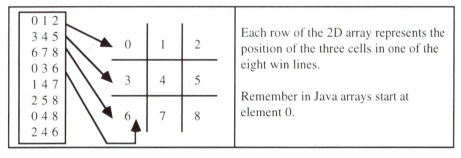

Figure 10.5 Representing the eight win lines.

The code for the method `situation` is as follows:

```java
public int situation()
{
  int WL = 8;      //Number of win lines
  int LL = 3;      //Length of a line
  int win_lines[][]    = { {0,1,2}, {3,4,5}, {6,7,8},
                           {0,3,6}, {1,4,7}, {2,5,8},
                           {0,4,8}, {2,4,6} };
  for ( int i=0; i<WL; i++ )
  {
    char first_cell = the_sqrs[ win_lines[i][0] ];
    if ( first_cell != ' ' &&
         first_cell == the_sqrs[ win_lines[i][1] ] &&
         first_cell == the_sqrs[ win_lines[i][2] ] )
    {
      the_end_of_game = true;
      return Board_state.WIN;
    }
  }
}
```

```
  if ( the_moves >= SIZE_TTT )
   {
     the_end_of_game = true;
     return Board_state.DRAW;
   }

   return Board_state.PLAYABLE;
  }

}
```

10.6.4 Putting it altogether

When compiled and run, a possible interaction between two players is as follows:

X's first move	O's first move	X's second move	O's second move

`X | | `
`---------`
` | | `
`---------`
` | | `
	`X | | `
	`---------`
	` | | `
	`---------`
	` | O | `
		`X | | X`
		`---------`
		` | | `
		`---------`
		` | O | `
			`X | O | X`
			`---------`
			` | | `
			`---------`
			` | O | `

X's third move	O's third move	X's fourth move	

`X | O | X`
`---------`
` | X | `
`---------`
` | O | `
	`X | O | X`
	`---------`
	` | X | `
	`---------`
	`O | O | `
		`X | O | X`
		`---------`
		` | X | `
		`---------`
		`O | O | X`
			As can be seen to go first is a clear advantage

10.7 A GUI version of the noughts and crosses application

The noughts and crosses application can be recast to work in a GUI environment. This demonstration application uses the same style of GUI interface as seen earlier in Chapter 8. The application consist of two windows in a frame:

- An instance of `TextField` for input.
- An instance of `TextArea` for output.

Input to the application is entered into the visual instance of the `TextField`, the listener for this object implements the processing of the individual moves. The class `Application` that implement the GUI interface is shown below:

```
import java.awt.*;
import java.awt.event.*;
class Application extends Frame
{
  private static final int H = 400;          // Height of window
  private static final int W = 300;          // Width  of window

  private TextField    the_input;            //Visual Text Field (Input)
  private TextArea     the_output;           //Visual Text Area  (Output)
  private Transaction  the_cb = new Transaction();

  public Application()
  {
    setLayout(null);                         //Set layout manager (none)
    setSize( W, H );                         //Size of Window

    Font font = new Font("Monospaced",Font.PLAIN,12);

    the_input  = new TextField();            //Input area
    the_input.setBounds(10,H-50,W-20,40);    //          Size
    the_input.setFont( font );               //          Font
    add( the_input );                        //Add to canvas

    the_input.addActionListener( the_cb );   //Add listener

    the_output = new TextArea( 10, 40 );     //Output area
    the_output.setBounds(10,30,W-20,H-100);  //          Size
    the_output.setFont( font );              //          Font
    add( the_output );                       //Add to canvas
    View.display( the_output );              //Display board
    View.display_who_plays( the_output );    //Display player to move
  }
  class Transaction implements ActionListener
  {
    public void actionPerformed( ActionEvent e )
    {
      String user_input = the_input.getText(); //User input
      View.action( the_output, user_input );   //Process
    }
  }
}
```

The class `View` contains the methods responsible for the presentation of the current view of the game. As the class contains only static methods (class methods) and no instance of the object is ever created static fields (class variables) are used to hold state information between calls to its static methods.

```
class View
{
  private static char   the_player = 'X';
  private static Board  the_oxo    = new Board();
  private static int    the_game_is= Board_state.PLAYABLE;
```

The class method `action` is responsible for the processing of the entered moves. The user's move is first converted to an `int` value for later processing by the remaining code.

```
static void action( TextArea the_output, String user_input )
{
  int move = 0;
  try
  {
    move = (new Integer( user_input )).intValue();
  }
  catch ( NumberFormatException err )
  {
    the_output.append( err + "\n");              //Java error message
  }
```

Note: If an error occurs in conversion of the string to an integer, then move *will still have the value 0. However, a value of 0 will be detected as an invalid move later on in the code:*

The processing of the move follows the same strategy as seen earlier. Except that this time the results of the interaction are written into an instance of the class `TextArea`.

```
  String who = "Player " + the_player;
  if ( the_oxo.check( move ) )              // Valid
  {
    the_oxo.add( move, the_player );         //Add to board
    display( the_output );                   //Display board
    the_game_is = the_oxo.situation();       //Game is
    switch ( the_game_is )
    {
      case Board_state.WIN  :                // Won
        the_output.append(who + " wins"+ "\n");
        return;
      case Board_state.DRAW :                // Drawn
        the_output.append("It's a draw"+ "\n");
        return;
      case Board_state.PLAYABLE :
        switch ( the_player )                // Playable
        {
          case 'X' : the_player='O'; break;//  'X' -> 'O'
          case 'O' : the_player='X'; break;//  'O' -> 'X'
        }
        break;
    }
  } else {
    display( the_output );                    //Display board
    the_output.append( "\n" );
    the_output.append( "Invalid move for " + who + "\n");
  }
  display_who_plays( the_output );
}
```

The class method `display_who_plays` simply writes a prompt for the next player to enter a move.

```
static void display_who_plays( TextArea the_output )
{
  the_output.append( "\n" );
  the_output.append( "Next move for player " + the_player + "\n");
}
```

The displayable representation of the board is generated by the following two class methods:

```
static void display_line( TextArea the_output, final int pos )
{
  the_output.append( the_oxo.position(pos)   + " | " +
                     the_oxo.position(pos+1) + " | " +
                     the_oxo.position(pos+2) + "\n" );
}

static void display( TextArea the_output )
{
  the_output.append( "\n" );
  display_line( the_output, 1 );
  the_output.append( "---------" + "\n" );
  display_line( the_output, 4 );
  the_output.append( "---------" + "\n" );
  display_line( the_output, 7 );
  the_output.append( "\n" );
}
}
```

10.7.1 Putting it altogether

The application is run by creating a instance of the class `Application` and sending it the message `show`.

```
class Play
{
  public static void main( String args[] )
  {
    (new Application()).show();
  }
}
```

When compiled and run a typical screen shot of the application is shown below:

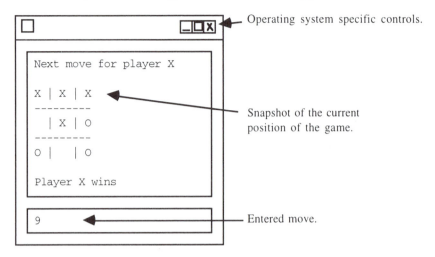

Operating system specific controls.

Snapshot of the current position of the game.

Entered move.

Note: As the application declares a static instance of the class Board *the application is not serially re-usable. The consequence of this is that to play a second game the application must be re-loaded.*

10.8   A piggy bank

Arrays in Java can hold objects as well as instances of the inbuilt types. For example, to build an application to implement the computer system for a very simple bank would require an array of bank accounts. To implement this a class Bank is defined which has the following responsibilities:

Method	Responsibility
deposit	Deposits money into a numbered account.
withdraw	Withdraws money from a numbered account.
account_balance	Returns the balance from a numbered account.
new_account_no	Delivers an account number for a new account. If cannot allocate an account throws the exception Bank_Exception.

A simple application that allocates a new account for Mike and then performs some transactions on the newly allocated account is shown below:

```
class Main
{
  public static void main( String args[] )
  {
    try
    {
      Bank piggy = new Bank();
      int  mike  = piggy.new_account_no();

      piggy.deposit( mike, 100.00 );
```

```
      double obtained;

      System.out.println( "Mike's Balance    = " +
                          piggy.account_balance(mike) );

      piggy.deposit(mike, 100.00);
      System.out.println( "Mike's Balance    = " +
                          piggy.account_balance(mike) );

      obtained = piggy.withdraw(mike, 20.00);
      System.out.println( "Mike has withdrawn: " + obtained );
      System.out.println( "Mike's Balance    = " +
                          piggy.account_balance(mike) );

      piggy.deposit(mike, 50.00);
      System.out.println( "Mike's Balance    = " +
                          piggy.account_balance(mike) );
   }
   catch ( Bank_Exception err )
   {
      System.out.println("Error : " + err.getMessage() );
   }
  }
}
```

Note: The exception `Bank_Exception` is thrown if a new account cannot be
       allocated. Exceptions are fully discussed in Chapter 13.

Which when compiled with the classes Bank and Account and run will deliver the
following results:

```
Mike's Balance    = 100.0
Mike's Balance    = 200.0
Mike has withdrawn: 20.0
Mike's Balance    = 180.0
Mike's Balance    = 230.0
```

10.8.1   The class **Bank**

The class Bank is in effect a container for a collection of accounts. The collection is
implemented using an array. Later in Chapters 21 and 22 other and more flexible
container objects will be examined.

When an array of objects is created, there are three stages to its creation. For
example, to create the_accounts an array of 10 instances of class Account
requires the following code:

Stage	Action	Java code
1	Declaration of the array object `the_accounts`	`Account the_accounts[];`
2	Allocation of storage for the array	`the_accounts = new Account[10];`
3	Allocation of storage for the objects contained in the array	`the_accounts[ 0] = new Account();` `the_accounts[ 1] = new Account();` `etc .`

The storage for the object `the_accounts` is illustrated in Figure 10.6.

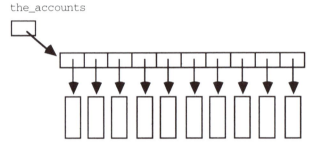

Figure 10.6 Storage for the populated array `the_accounts`.

Note: In creating an array of objects it is all to easy to forget to allocate storage for the stored objects.

The exception `Bank_Exception` is defined as follows:

```
class Bank_Exception extends Throwable
{
  public Bank_Exception( String s )
  {
    super( s );
  }
}
```

Note: How to create an exception class is fully explained in Chapter 13.

The class `Bank` is implemented as follows:

```
import Account;

class Bank
{
  private static int MAX_ACCOUNTS = 10; //Maximum # of Accounts

  private Account the_accounts[];       //Collection of Accounts
  private int the_next_account_no;      //Next account number
```

The constructor allocates storage for the array but does not allocate storage for the individual accounts that will be held in the array.

```
public Bank()
{
  the_accounts = new Account[MAX_ACCOUNTS];   //Storage for array
  the_next_account_no = 0;                    //Next account no
}
```

The method new_account_no allocates an account number for a new account and then allocates storage for the account in the array. If an account cannot be allocated, then the exception Bank_Exception is thrown.

```
public int new_account_no() throws Bank_Exception
{
  if ( the_next_account_no < MAX_ACCOUNTS-1 )
  {
    the_accounts[ the_next_account_no] = new Account();
    return the_next_account_no++;
  }
  else
    throw new Bank_Exception( "No new accounts" );
}
```

Note: The exception Bank_Exception is thrown if a new account cannot be allocated. Chapters 21 and 22 illustrates better ways of storing collections of objects, when the maximum number of objects that will be placed in the collection is not known in advance.

The other methods in the class Bank call the similarly named method in the class Account. For example, the method deposit calls the method deposit in the class Account as illustrated in Figure 10.7.

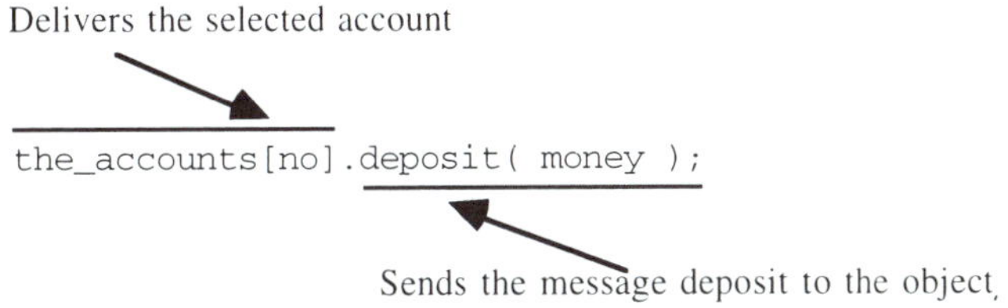

Delivers the selected account

```
the_accounts[no].deposit( money );
```

Sends the message deposit to the object

Figure 10.7 Calling the method deposit in the class Account.

The code for the methods account_balance, withdraw, deposit and set_min_balance is shown below:

```
public double account_balance( final int no )
{
  return the_accounts[no].account_balance();
}
```

```
public double withdraw( final int no, final double money )
{
   return the_accounts[no].withdraw( money );
}

public void deposit( int no, double money )
{
   the_accounts[no].deposit( money );
}

public void set_min_balance( final int no, final double money )
{
   the_accounts[no].set_min_balance( money );
}
}
```

10.9   Introducing the class `String`

Though not specifically an array a string can be regarded as a collection of characters, from which individual characters can be extracted. The class `String` allows the easy manipulation and processing of strings. As an instance of the class `String` is a read only object the user does not need to worry that only a shallow copy is performed when an instance of the `String` class is copied.

However, the user does need to remember that a comparison operation using == and != is a deep comparison. Hence, when comparing strings, the methods `equals` and `compareTo` must usually be used.

The `String` class has the following major methods:

Methods	Responsibility

`String()`
`String( String s )`
`String( StringBuffer stb )`
`String( char chs[] )`
	A constructor to create a new instance of a `String`.

`charAt( pos )`	Returns the character at position `pos` in the object. The first character is at position 0.
`compareTo( s )`	Compares s lexicographically using the Unicode character set. For `a.compareTo(b)` the value returned is an `int` that is: 0 if a == b. <0 if a < b. >0 if a > b.
`equals( s )`	Returns `true` if s equals the string held in the object.
`lastIndexOf( ch )`	Returns the index of the last character `ch` in the object.
`lastIndexOf( s )`	Returns the index of the first character in the last occurrence of string s in the object.

Methods	Responsibility
`length()`	Returns the number of characters in the string.
`replace( ch_old, char_new)`	Replaces all occurrences of character `ch_old` with the character `ch_new` in the object.
`substring( from )`	Returns a substring that extends from the character at position `from` to the end of the string. The string starts at position 0.
`substring( from, to )`	Returns a substring that extends from character at position `from` to the character at position `to-1`.
`toCharArray()`	Returns a `char` array of the characters in the string.
`toLowerCase()`	Converts the string to lower case.
`toUpperCase()`	Converts string to upper case.
`trim()`	Removes leading and trailing white space.
`valueOf( arg )`	Returns the string representation of `arg` where arg is an instance of a `boolean`, `char`, `char[]`, `double`, `float`, `int`, `long`, `object`.

Note: On some Java compilers `"Str" == "Str"` *will deliver* `true` *as the compiler only stores 1 copy of like strings.*

10.9.1   Using the class `String`

The following table illustrates the effect of using some of the methods illustrated above on an instance of the class `String` that is declared and initialized as follows:

```
String name = "University-of-Brighton";
```

Call of	Will deliver
`name.charAt(14)`	`B`
`name.lastIndexOf('t')`	`19`
`name.lastIndexOf("Brighton")`	`14`
`name.length()`	`22`
`name.replace( '-', ' ' )`	`University of Brighton`
`name.substring(0,10)`	`University`
`name.substring(14)`	`Brighton`
`name.toLowerCase()`	`university-of-brighton`
`name.toUpperCase()`	`UNIVERSITY-OF-BRIGHTON`

10.10   The class `StringBuffer`

An instance of the class `StringBuffer` is an object that holds a writeable string. A newly created instance of the class `StringBuffer` has by default an additional capacity of 16 extra locations. This means that the initial value in an instance of the class `StringBuffer` may be extended by 16 characters before a new area of storage has to be claimed.

The `StringBuffer` class has the following major methods:

Methods	Responsibility

`StringBuffer()`
`StringBuffer( s )`
`StringBuffer( capacity )`
	A constructor to create a new instance of a `StringBuffer`.

`charAt( pos )`	Returns the character at position `pos` in the stringbuffer.
`append( s )` `append( standard_type )`	Appends the string `s` to the buffer. Will also work to append character representations of instances of the standard types. For example, `append( 2 )` and `append( 1.2 )`.
`insert( pos, s )` `insert( pos, standard_type )`	Inserts string `s` at position `pos` in the stringbuffer. Will also work to insert character representations of instances of the standard types.

10.10.1   Using the class `StringBuffer`

The following fragment of code when combined with suitable declarations and run:

```
StringBuffer town       = new StringBuffer( "Brighton" );
StringBuffer university = new StringBuffer();
university.append( new String( town ) );
university.insert( 0, "University of " );

System.out.println( town );
System.out.println( university );
```

will produce the following output:

```
Brighton
University of Brighton
```

Likewise, when the following fragment of code is combined with suitable declarations and run:

```
StringBuffer month = new StringBuffer( "December " );
StringBuffer today = month.append(25);
System.out.println( today );
```

this will produce the output:

```
December 25
```

10.11 Self-assessment

● How are arrays in Java declared?

● What is wrong with the following fragment of code?

```
int numbers[];

numbers[0] = 2;
```

● In the game of noughts and crosses how could you prevent a programmer ever creating an instance of the class `View`?

10.12 Exercises

Construct the following class methods in the class `Useful`. that have the following signature:

● *String strip(String s)*
A class method to return a string that is the string s with all spaces removed.

● *String format(final String f, final int n)*
A class method to return a string representing the number n formatted according to the pattern specified by the string f. The format string f can take the following form:

Format string f	Explanation
"DDDDDD"	In a field width of 6 characters. Leading 0's are printed as spaces.

- `String format( final String f, final double n )`
  A class method to return a string representing the number n formatted according to the pattern specified by the string f. The format string f can take the following form:

Format string f	Explanation
"DDDD.DD"	In a field width of 7 characters with 2 decimal places. Leading 0's are printed as spaces.

Construct the following applications:

- *Noughts and crosses (many plays)*
  Create a new version of the noughts and crosses game so that several games can be played in succession. Include a feature that allows an undo facility.

- *Battleships*
  The game of battleships is played on a two-dimensional board. The objective of the game is to destroy all the opponent's battleships in the minimum number of moves. If the player correctly identifies a square which contains a battleship, then the battleship is destroyed and removed from the board. If the player guesses a square that is next to a battleship then the board identifies a near miss.

  Hint: To populate the board with battleships you may wish to use the static method random() *in the class* java.lang.Math *that delivers a pseudo random number in the range 0.0 to 1.0.*

11. Formatting

This chapter looks at the ways of formatting numbers and currency values in Java. Java provides a series of locales that provide country specific formatting for currency, date and number values. By using a specific locale application or applet code can be kept independent of country when dealing with monetary amounts, dates, and formatted numbers. Only the locale need be changed to customize the application or applet for a specific country.

11.1   Introduction

One of the problems in writing software is that if it is to be made available in several countries then provision must be made for the different way numbers, dates and monetary values are represented. For example, the date, the 25 December 2001 is expressed in the following formats:

Country	Representation of 25 December 2001
UK	25 December 2001
US	Tuesday, December 25, 2001
France	mardi 25 décembre 2001
Germany	Dienstag, 25. Dezember 2001

11.2   The class `java.text.DecimalFormat`

To simplify the formatting of decimal numbers, Java provides the class `DecimalFormat` that has the following major methods:

Method	Responsibility
`DecimalFormat()`	Creates a decimal format using the default locale.
`DecimalFormat( str )`	Creates a decimal format using the default locale and the format string defined by `str`.
`format( d )`	Returns a string representing the `double` d formatted using the held format.
`format( l )`	Returns a string representing the `long` l formatted using the held format.

`DecimalFormat`'s superclass `NumberFormat` contains the following major methods:

Method	Responsibility
`getInstance(c)` `getInstance()`	Returns a number format for `c`. Where `c` is the `locale` for a particular country. If no parameter then the default format.
`getCurrencyInstance(c)` `getCurrencyInstance()`	As for `getInstance` but a currency format.

11.2.1   Using `DecimalFormat`

Like dates, different countries have different ways of formatting numbers. For example, the following code

```
NumberFormat df =  DecimalFormat.getInstance(country);

System.out.println( df.format( 12345.67 ) );
```

Note: `DecimalFormat.getInstance` returns an object of type `NumberFormat`.

will print numbers in the following format when `country` is replaced by the appropriate `locale`.

Number	using `Locale.UK`	using `Locale.US`
12345.67	12,345.67	12,345.67

Style	using `Locale.FRANCE`	using `Locale.GERMANY`
12345.67	12 345,67	12.345,67

Note: `DecimalFormat.getInstance()` returns a general purpose number format for the default country.

11.2.2   Using a specific format

The format string is composed of the following symbols that define how the number is to be formatted in the returned string.

Symbol	Meaning
0	A single digit
#	A single digit or empty if no digit to print
.	A decimal point
,	A comma separator in a number
–	Show as negative
%	Multiply by 100 and show as a percentage.
?	Multiply by 1000 and show as mille.
¤	Replace by the current currency symbol, if ¤¤ then the international currency symbol ¤. Note: When present in a pattern the currency format is used.
	Used in a prefix or suffix to quote special characters

Symbol	Meaning
X	Any other character

For example, when the following fragment of code is run:

```
double number     = 1234.567;
String fs         = "format string";
DecimalFormat df = new DecimalFormat( fs );
String answer     = df.format( number );
```

the following table illustrates the contents of the variable `answer` for various formatting strings set in the variable `fs`.

Contents of `fs`	`answer`	Commentary
00000.00	01234.57	The number is formatted to two decimal places rounded.
00	1234	Even though only two digits for the whole part of the number specified, the number is returned in full.
####0.00	1234.57	# is for a digit or empty. It does not reserve spaces in the output format.
#,###,##0.00	1,234.57	Only the first , is printed

11.2.3 Components of the format pattern

The pattern used to format a number is defined by the following BNF grammar.

Notes	BNF Rule
1	pattern := subpatern(;subpatern)
2	subpatern := (prefix)integer(.fraction)(suffix)
3	prefix := '\\u0000' .. '\\uFFFD' - Special characters
3	suffix := '\\u0000' .. '\\uFFFD' - Special characters
4	Integer := '#' * '0' * '0'
5	fraction := '#' * '0' *

Notes	Explanation
1	The meta symbols ( ) are used to represent an optional part. The optional part is used to specify the -ve form of the number.
2	The number represented by the subpattern may have an optional prefix, fraction and suffix.
3	The prefix and suffix may be any Unicode character except for some special characters.
4	The meta character * means 0 or more occurrences. Thus the pattern for an integer is composed of 0 or more '#' characters followed by 0 or more '0' characters followed by one '0' character.
5	The pattern for a fraction is composed of 0 or more '#' characters followed by 0 or more '0' characters.

11.2.4   Putting it all together

The following fragment of code:

```
DecimalFormat df = new DecimalFormat( "####0.00" );
double val  = 123.456;
System.out.println( "The length to 2 decimal places is " +
                    df.format( val ) );
```

when combined into a complete application and run will print:

```
The length to 2 decimal places is 123.46
```

11.3   Currency formatting

Formatting of a monetary amount requires a different format for each currency. For example, to format a monetary amount in the UK the following code is used:

```
double owed = 123.45;
NumberFormat  cf = NumberFormat.getCurrencyInstance(Locale.UK);
System.out.println( "The amount owed is " + cf.format( owed ) );
```

Which when combined with suitable code and compiled and run will produce the following output:

```
The amount owed is £123.45
```

11.3.1   Other countries

Canned formats are provided for the following countries.

Country	Locale for formatting.	Country	Locale for formatting.
Canada	Locale.CANADA	Canada	Locale.CANADA_FRENCH
China	Locale.CHINA	France	Locale.FRANCE
Germany	Locale.GERMANY	Italy	Locale.ITALY
Japan	Locale.JAPAN	Korea	Locale.KOREA
PRC	Locale.PRC	Taiwan	Locale.TAIWAN
UK	Locale.UK	US	Locale.US

Note: Locale.UK is equivalent to new Locale("en", "GB", "").
Locale.PRC and Locale.CHINA are identical.

Thus to print an amount in US dollars, the following code is used:

```
double owed = 123.45;
NumberFormat   cf = NumberFormat.getCurrencyInstance(Locale.US);
System.out.println( "The amount owed is " + cf.format( owed ) );
```

Which when combined with suitable code and compiled and run will produce the following output:

```
The amount owed is $123.45
```

Note: *This mechanism does not understand about exchange rates, it only understands how to write an amount in a particular currency for a particular language.*

11.4 Date formatting

The class `java.util.Date` has the following major methods:

Method	Responsibility
`Date()` `Date( m )`	Constructs a new date object initialized to the current time. May also be initialized to the date of m milliseconds past the 1st January 1970.
`after( when )`	Returns true if the date is after the instance of `Date when`.
`before( when )`	Returns true if the date is before the instance of `Date when`.
`equals( when. )`	Returns true if the dates are equal

The class `java.util.GregorianCalendar` has the following major methods:

Method	Responsibility
`GregorianCalendar()` `GregorianCalendar(m)`	Constructs a new date object initialized to the current time. May also be initialized to the date of m milliseconds past the 1st January 1970.
`getTimeInMillis()`	Returns the time set in the object as milliseconds past the 1st January 1970.
`set(year,month,day,` `    hour,minit,secs)`	Sets the date. For example: `miranda_born.set(1998,9,21,15,35,0)` is the 21st October 1998 at 3.35pm 1998. Note that for the month field January =0, February =1 etc.

The following fragment of code prints the current date and time using the format locale for the UK.

```
Date now = new Date();                // The time now
DateFormat df_uk;
DateFormat tf_uk;
DateFormat dtf_uk;
df_uk  = DateFormat.getDateInstance( DateFormat.FULL, Locale.UK );
tf_uk  = DateFormat.getTimeInstance( DateFormat.FULL, Locale.UK );
dtf_uk = DateFormat.getDateTimeInstance( DateFormat.FULL,
                                         DateFormat.FULL,
                                         Locale.UK );

String line1 =  df_uk.format( now );
String line2 =  tf_uk.format( now );
String line3 = dtf_uk.format( now );

System.out.println( line1 );
System.out.println( line2 );
System.out.println( line3 );
```

Which when combined into a complete application and run on the 25th December 2001 at 9:30 will print:

```
25 December 2001
09:30:00 o'clock GMT+00:00
25 December 2001 09:30:00 o'clock GMT+00:00
```

The first parameter to `getDateInstance`, `getTimeInstance` and `getDateTimeInstance` selects the format of the output.

11.4.1 Using `getDateInstance`

The following table illustrates the different formats for a date that can be extracted using the following fragment of code:

```
DateFormat df = DateFormat.getDateInstance( style, country );
System.out.println( dtf.format( now ) );
```

where `style` and `country` are:

Style	using Locale.UK	using Locale.US
`DateFormat.DEFAULT`	25-Dec-01	Dec 25, 2001
`DateFormat.FULL`	25 December 2001	Tuesday, December 25,
`DateFormat.SHORT`	25/12/01	12/25/01
`DateFormat.MEDIUM`	25-Dec-01	Dec 25, 2001
`DateFormat.LONG`	25 December 2001	December 25, 2001

Style	using Locale.FRANCE	using Locale.GERMANY
DateFormat.DEFAULT	25 déc. 01	25.12.2001
DateFormat.FULL	mardi 25 décembre 2001	Dienstag, 25. Dezember 2001
DateFormat.SHORT	25/12/01	25.12.01
DateFormat.MEDIUM	25 déc. 01	25.12.2001
DateFormat.LONG	25 décembre 2001	25. Dezember 2001

11.5   Self-assessment

● What do the following characters in a formatting pattern represent?
  `'#', '0', ','`

● Is it possible to format a number in a fixed size field width regardless of how many leading spaces there will be to the number.

11.6   Exercises

● *Multilingual calculator*
  Write an application that acts as a simple currency calculator, but displays the output suitable for `Germany`, France, US and the UK.

12. Inheritance

This chapter looks at how an existing class may be extended to provide additional features. However, when a class is extended the new class (subclass) only has access to the public members of the original class (superclass).

12.1   Introduction

The class `Account` shown in Chapter 5 has the following methods and instance variables.

Methods of `Account`	Instance variables of `Account`
`account_balance`	`the_balance`
`withdraw`	`the_min_balance`
`deposit`	
`set_min_balance`	

At a later date it is decided that it would be useful if a bank account was able to display a mini-statement for an individual's bank account. This afterthought about the inclusion of additional responsibilities for the class `Account` is typical of the requests made of software developers.

One approach would be to create a new class `Account_with_statement` by copying the code for the class `Account` and adding the following method and member variables:

● Additional method

Name	Remarks

`statement`	Return a string representing a mini-statement for the account. For example:
	
	`Mini-statement #1  for Mike`
	`The balance of your account is : £0.0`

● Additional member variables

Name	Remarks
`the_account_name`	Holds the account holder's name
`the_statement_no`	A unique serial number identifying this mini-statement.

However, this has several serious drawbacks

- The code copied from the class `Account` must be re-tested, in case any errors were introduced during copying or there are undesirable interactions between the old and the new code.

- If the original code for the class `Account` is modified the new class must also be modified.

Inheritance removes these problems by allowing a user to create a new class by specializing an existing class. The class to be specialized is known as the superclass and the specialized class that is created is known as the subclass. However, the subclass has only the access rights to the superclass that a client of the class would have. In particular, the private components of the superclass cannot be accessed. Only the public components can be accessed from the subclass. This process is illustrated in Figure 12.1 below:

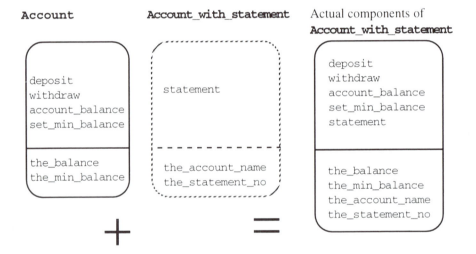

Figure 12.1 Illustration of inheritance.

12.1.1　Terminology

The following terminology is used when discussing inheritance.

Terminology	Explanation
superclass / base class	A class from which other classes are derived from.
subclass / derived class	A new class that specializes an existing class

12.1.2　A class diagram showing the inheritance relationship

The above relationship of inheritance is shown in the UML class diagram illustrated in Figure 12.2.

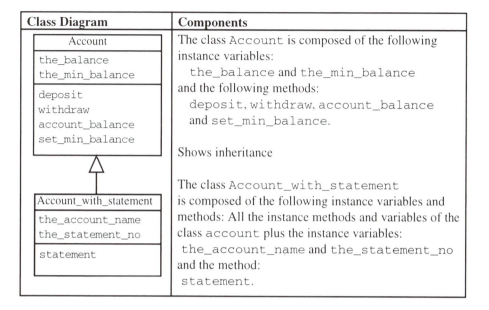

Class Diagram	Components

Account
the_balance
the_min_balance
deposit
withdraw
account_balance
set_min_balance
 	
Account_with_statement
the_account_name
the_statement_no
statement
	The class `Account` is composed of the following instance variables:
	　`the_balance` and `the_min_balance`
	and the following methods:
	　`deposit`, `withdraw`, `account_balance`
	　and `set_min_balance`.
	
	Shows inheritance
	
	The class `Account_with_statement` is composed of the following instance variables and methods: All the instance methods and variables of the class `account` plus the instance variables:
	　`the_account_name` and `the_statement_no`
	and the method:
	　`statement`.

Figure 12.2 Class diagram showing inheritance.

12.2　The class `Account_with_statement`

The class `Account_with_statement` that extends the account class is developed below. Firstly the class `Account` is made available in the application by using the `import` statement. Importing the code for the class `Account`, ensures that there need only be one copy of the classes code on the system.

```
import Account;
```

Note:　The code for the class `Account` is held in a directory that is known to the Java compiling system. The environment variable CLASSPATH contains a list of directories containing previously written classes. Section 17.4.1 describes the environment variable CLASSPATH in more detail .

Next the new class is developed. The format of this class is identical to a normal class except that the class name is followed by `extends Account` to indicate to the compiler that this new class will inherit from the previously defined class `Account`.

```
import Account;

class Account_with_statement extends Account
{
```

The additional instance variables are declared in the normal way.

```
private String the_account_name = "Anonymous";
private long   the_statement_no = 1;
```

The constructor initializes the new instance variables. Before these variables are initialized there is an implicit call to the constructor in the superclass `Account`. However, if there was a parameter to the constructor then it would have to be explicitly called.

```
public Account_with_statement()
{
   the_account_name = "Anonymous";       //Account name Anonymous
   the_statement_no = 1;                 //First statement
}
```

Note: This constructor is not really required as the state variables are initialized with their declaration.

An additional constructor is provided so that an account may be named, again there is an implicit call to the constructor in the superclass `Account`.

```
public Account_with_statement( final String name )
{
   the_account_name = name;              //Account name
   the_statement_no = 1;                 //First statement
}
```

The method `statement` returns a string containing details about the account. A string is returned so that the client of the class can choose how this information is to be printed or displayed.

```
public String statement()
{
   return "Mini-statement £" + the_statement_no++ + "  for " +
          the_account_name + "\n" +
          "The balance of your account is : £" + account_balance() +
          "\n";
}
}
```

Figure 12.3 illustrates the syntax for deriving a new class from an existing class.

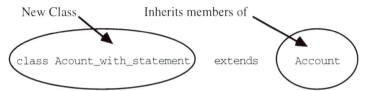

Figure 12.3 `Account_with_statement` inheriting from the class `Account`.

12.2.1 Putting it all together

A complete application to test the class `Account_with_statement` is shown below:

```java
import Account_with_statement;

class Main
{
  public static void main(String args[])
  {
    Account_with_statement mike    =
      new Account_with_statement( "Mike" );
    Account_with_statement corinna =
      new Account_with_statement( "Corinna" );

    double obtained;

    System.out.println( mike.statement() );

    mike.deposit(100.00);
    System.out.println( mike.statement() );

    obtained = mike.withdraw(20.00);
    System.out.println( "Mike has withdrawn   : " + obtained );
    System.out.println( mike.statement() );

    corinna.deposit(50.00);
    System.out.println( corinna.statement() );
  }
}
```

When compiled and run will produce the following results:

```
Mini-statement #1  for Mike
The balance of your account is : £0.0

Mini-statement #2  for Mike
The balance of your account is : £100.0

Mike has withdrawn   : 20.0
Mini-statement #3  for Mike
The balance of your account is : £80.0

Mini-statement #1  for Corinna
The balance of your account is : £50.0
```

12.3   The class `Object`

In Java the class `Object` is the superclass of all other classes. When a class is created that does not extend an existing class it implicitly extends the class `Object`. Hence the class `Object` contains methods that are available to all other classes. Appendix F lists the methods of the class `Object`.

12.4   Overriding a superclass method

As well as extending a class by adding new methods, existing methods in the superclass may be overridden to provide a different functionality. For example, a class `Restricted_Account` that restricts an account holder to only 3 withdrawals in a particular accounting period has the following additional two responsibilities to those of the class `Account`:

Method	Responsibility
reset	Resets the withdrawal counter so 3 more withdrawals can be made.
withdraw	Allows the withdrawal if there has been no more than 3 withdrawals in the current accounting period and the withdrawal will not take the user below their approved minimum balance.

An implementation of this restricted account is:

```java
class Restricted_Account extends Account
{
  private static final int MAX_WITHDRAWALS = 3;
  private int the_no_withdrawals_to_go = MAX_WITHDRAWALS;

  public void reset()
  {
    the_no_withdrawals_to_go = MAX_WITHDRAWALS;
  }
}
```

Note: No constructor is required, as there is no Initialization required for instances of the class `Restricted_Account`. However, a default constructor will be created which will call the constructor in the superclass `Account`.

In the implementation of the overridden method `withdraw` the method withdraw in the superclass is used to implement part of the functionality of the method. The method `withdraw` in the superclass is called by the statement:

```java
super.withdraw( amount )
```

Had just the statement withdraw(amount) been used then the method withdraw in the subclass would have been called. This would result in endless recursion that would eventual cause failure of the application when all the memory allocated for stack space was consumed. The overriding method withdraw is implemented as follows:

```java
public double withdraw( final double amount )
{
  if ( the_no_withdrawals_to_go > 0 )
  {
    the_no_withdrawals_to_go--;
    return super.withdraw( amount );
  } else {
    return 0.00;
  }
}
```

12.4.1   Putting it all together

A complete application to test the class Restricted_Account is shown below.

```java
class Main
{
  public static void main( String args[] )
  {
    Restricted_Account mike     = new Restricted_Account();

    double obtained;

    System.out.println( "Mike's Balance       = " +
                        mike.account_balance() );

    mike.deposit(100.00);
    System.out.println( "Mike's Balance       = " +
                        mike.account_balance() );

    for ( int i=1; i<=4; i++ )
    {
      obtained = mike.withdraw(20.00);
      System.out.println( "Mike has withdrawn   : " + obtained );
      System.out.println( "Mike's Balance       = " +
                          mike.account_balance() );
    }
  }
}
```

The output from the test application is:

```
Mike's Balance      = 0.0
Mike's Balance      = 100.0
Mike has withdrawn  : 20.0
Mike's Balance      = 80.0
Mike has withdrawn  : 20.0
Mike's Balance      = 60.0
Mike has withdrawn  : 20.0
Mike's Balance      = 40.0
Mike has withdrawn  : 0.0
Mike's Balance      = 40.0
```

Note: The methods in the class Account *of course do not need to be tested.*
That the fourth call of the method withdraw *fails.*

12.4.2   Restrictions in overriding methods in a superclass

When a method is overridden it cannot be overridden to give a lesser access. For example, the table below illustrates what types of method may override a method in the superclass.

Method in superclass is:	May be overridden by a method that is:
private	Not visible, hence meaningless
protected	protected or public
public	public

Note: The scope protected *is discussed in detail in Section 12.8.*

12.5   An interest bearing account

An interest bearing account in addition to the responsibilities of a normal account has the following additional responsibilities:

Method	Responsibility
Interest_Account	Creates an interest bearing account. A single parameter indicates the initial opening balance of the account.
end_of_day	Performs end of day processing on the account. In particular calculates the interest gained this day.
interest_accumulate	Accumulates the daily interest on the account in a running total.
interest_credit	Credits any accumulated interest to the account. This is actioned at the end of the accounting period.
set_min_balance	Performs no action. As the account is interest bearing, overdrafts are forbidden.
set_rate	Sets the interest rate for all interest bearing accounts.

Note: *The method* `end_of_day` *calls the method* `interest_accumulate` *to accumulate the interest gained each day. The method* `interest_credit` *deposits this accumulated interest into the account at the end of the accounting period.*

A class `IA_Const` is used to hold the default interest rate (10% annual interest calculated on a daily basis) that is applied to interest bearing accounts:

```
class IA_Const
{
  public static final double RATE = 0.00026116;    //10% interest
}
```

The class `Interest_Account` is defined as follows:

```
class Interest_Account extends Account
{
  private static double the_interest_rate = IA_Const.RATE;
  private double        the_accumulated_interest;
```

Note: *The class variable* `the_interest_rate` *that is shared between all instances of an account.*

The first constructor sets the `the_accumulated_interest` to 0.00.

```
  public Interest_Account()
  {
    the_accumulated_interest = 0.0d;
  }
```

Note: *There is an implicit call to the constructor in the superclass* `Account` *before the first line of executable code in the constructor for* `Interest_Account`.

The second constructor, allows an initial amount to be set in the account. This is implemented by calling the method `deposit` in the class `Account`. Rather than repeat the code body for the 1st constructor in this constructor a call to the 1st constructor is explicitly made. This is written as `this()`. The reserved word `this` represents the current object.

```
  public Interest_Account(final double initial)
  {
    this();                            //Constructor in this class
    deposit( initial );                //Set initial amount
  }
```

Note: The call to the method deposit *could have been written as:*

```
        this.deposit( initial );          //Set initial amount
```

The class method set_rate sets the class variable the_interest_rate that represents the rate of interest to be applied to all interest bearing accounts.

```
public static void set_rate(final double ir)
{
   the_interest_rate = ir;
}
```

At the end of the day the method end_of_day is called to calculate the daily interest and add this to a running total. The adding of today's interest to an accumulating total is implemented by the method interest_accumulate. This is so that any subclass of Interest_account will be able to call this method to form the total. Remember, the instance variable the_accumulated_interest is private to this class.

```
public void end_of_day()
{
   interest_accumulate(
     account_balance() * the_interest_rate );
}
```

At the end of the accounting period the accumulated interest is deposited in the account.

```
public void interest_credit()
{
  deposit( the_accumulated_interest );
  the_accumulated_interest = 0.0d;
}
```

As interest bearing accounts are not allowed to be overdrawn the method that allows an overdraft is overridden with a method that performs no action.

```
public void set_min_balance( double money )   //Deny access
{
   return;
}
```

The method `interest_accumulate` is responsible for accumulating the daily interest. This method is `protected`, this means that the method is not visible to a user of an instance of the class, but is visible to an inheriting class. The scope of items in a class is discussed in detail in Section 12.8.

```
  protected void interest_accumulate( final double ai )
  {
    the_accumulated_interest += ai;
  }
}
```

12.5.1 Putting it all together

A complete application to test the class `Interest_Account` is shown below:

```
import Interest_Account;

class Main
{
  public static void main(String args[])
  {
    Interest_Acount mike = new Interest_Account();
    DecimalFormat     nf = new DecimalFormat( "#######0.00" );

    double obtained;

    System.out.println("Mike's Balance = " +
                       nf.format( mike.account_balance() ) );

    mike.deposit(100.00);

    mike.end_of_day();
    mike.interest_credit();

    System.out.println("Mike's Balance = " +
                       nf.format( mike.account_balance() ) );
  }
}
```

The above application, when compiled and run, displays the following message on the user's terminal:

```
Mike's Balance = 0.00
Mike's Balance = 100.02
```

12.6 A special interest bearing account

A subclass can itself be inherited from. For example, to create a special interest bearing account that has 2 rates of interest. A low rate for deposits of under £1,000 and a higher rate for accounts that contain more than £1,000.

A special interest bearing account in addition to the responsibilities of an interest account has the additional responsibilities:

Method	Responsibility
Special_Interst_Account	Creates a special interest bearing account. A single parameter indicates the initial opening balance of the account.
set_rate	Sets the interest rate for all special interest bearing accounts.
end_of_day	Performs end of day processing on the account. In particular calculates the interest gained this day.

The class SIA_Const is used to hold the default values for the two interest rates.

```
class SIA_Const
{
  public static final double R1 = 0.00026116;    //10%
  public static final double R2 = 0.00028596;    //11%
}
```

The class Special_Interest_Account is defined as follows:

```
class Special_Interest_Account extends Interest_Account
{

  static double the_interest_band_1 = SIA_Const.R1;
  static double the_interest_band_2 = SIA_Const.R2;
```

The first constructor for the class is defined as follows:

```
public Special_Interest_Account()
  {
  }
```

Note: This constructor is required explicitly as a default constructor is only generated if there are no explicitly defined constructors.
The constructor will make an implicit call to the constructor in the superclass Interest_Account.

The second constructor calls the constructor in Interst_Account to set an initial amount in the account.

```
public Special_Interest_Account( final double initial )
{
  super( initial );      //Constructor in Interest_Account
}
```

Note: The explicit call to the constructor in the superclass `Interest_Account`*.*
The reserved word super is the direct superclass of this class.

The method `set_rate` sets the interest rates for all special interest bearing
accounts.

```
public static void set_rate(final double ir1, final double ir2)
{
  the_interest_band_1 = ir1;
  the_interest_band_2 = ir2;
}
```

The method `end_of_day` overrides the method `end_of_day` in the class
`Interest_Account` to implement this account's formula for calculating the rate of
interest due on the outstanding balance.

```
public void end_of_day()
{
  double money =  account_balance();
  if ( money < 1000 )
    interest_accumulate( account_balance()*the_interest_band_1 );
  else
    interest_accumulate( account_balance()*the_interest_band_2 );
}
}
```

12.6.1   Putting it all together

A complete application to test the class `Special_Interest_Account` is shown
below:

```
import Special_Interest_Account;

class Main
{
  public static void main(String args[])
  {
    double DAILY_RATE_R1 = 0.00026116;  //10% Annual rate
    double DAILY_RATE_R2 = 0.00028596;  //11% Annual rate
    Special_Interest_Account.set_rate(SIA_Const.R1, SIA_Const.R2);

    Special_Interest_Account mike = new Special_Interest_Account();
    DecimalFormat nf          = new DecimalFormat( "#######0.00" );
```

```
      double obtained;

      System.out.println("Mike's Balance = " +
                        nf.format(mike.account_balance() ) );

      mike.deposit(20000.00);
      System.out.println("Mike's Balance = " +
                        nf.format( mike.account_balance() ) );

      obtained = mike.withdraw(2000.00);
      System.out.println("Withdraw 2000.00" );
      System.out.println("Mike's Balance = " +
                        nf.format( mike.account_balance() ) );

      System.out.println("Deposit 50.00" );
      mike.deposit(50.00);
      System.out.println("Mike's Balance = " +
                        nf.format( mike.account_balance() ) );

      mike.end_of_day();
      mike.interest_credit();
      System.out.println("End of day processing" );
      System.out.println("Mike's Balance = " +
                        nf.format( mike.account_balance() ) );
   }
}
```

The above application, when compiled and run, displays the following results on the console:

```
Mike's Balance = 0.00
Mike's Balance = 20000.00
Withdraw 2000.00
Mike's Balance = 18000.00
Deposit 50.00
Mike's Balance = 18050.00
End of day processing
Mike's Balance = 18055.16
```

12.7   Using constructors and destructors

If a class has a constructor, then when an instance of the class is created, the code for the constructor is executed. Likewise, if an object has a destructor then its code will be called just before the storage for the object is released. In Java a destructor in a class is specified by defining a method with the following signature:

```
protected void finalize() throws Throwable
```

However, if an exception occurs in the method `finalize` then it will not be propagated out of the method. If an exception occurs then the method `finalize` terminates and the application continues.

12.7.1 Inheritance

Constructors and destructors are not inherited. Thus if the superclass has a constructor with a parameter, and it is required to construct the subclass using this parameter, then the subclass must itself have a constructor that is passed this parameter and the body of the constructor must explicitly call the superclass's constructor.

12.7.2 A class to describe a room

A demonstration class to describe a room in a building has the following responsibilities:

Method	Responsibility
Room	Constructs an instance of a Room.
finalize	Destructs an instance of a Room.
size	Returns the size in square metres.

The following Java class implements these responsibilities of the class Room. In the implementation code for the class messages are written to indicate the construction and destruction of the room.

```
class Room
{
  private int the_size_sq_metres;    //Size of room in Square Metres

  public Room( final int sq_metres )
  {
    the_size_sq_metres = sq_metres;
    System.out.println( "Constructor Room    :"   +
                        " size square metres = " +
                        the_size_sq_metres          );
  }
```

The method `finalize` contains a call to the method `super.finalize()` that is the destructor for the classes superclass. This is called after any code in the classes destructor.

```
  protected void finalize() throws Throwable
  {
    System.out.println( "Destructor Room    : " +
                        the_size_sq_metres + " sq Metres " );
    super.finalize();
  }
```

Note: The explicit call of the superclass method `finalize` *is required.*

The method `size` prints the size of the room in square metres.

```
public void size()
{
   System.out.println( "Method size()       :"    +
                       " size square metres = " +
                       the_size_sq_metres          );
  }
}
```

12.7.3   Putting it all together

The class `Room` is used in the following application that explicitly calls the garbage collector `System.gc()` and the method `System.runFinalization()` to call any finalization code for inactive objects.

```
class Main
{
  public static void main( String args[] )
  {
    Main.method_using_room();    //Method creates instance of Room
    System.gc();                 //Force Garbage collector
    System.runFinalization();    //Force run of Finalization code
  }

  public static void method_using_room()
  {
    Room w413 = new Room( 60 );
    w413.size();
  }
}
```

The output from the application when it is compiled and run is:

```
Constructor Room    : size square metres = 60
Method size()       : size square metres = 60
Destructor Room     : 60 sq Metres
```

Note: *That if the methods* `System.gc()` *and* `System.runFinalization()`
        *where not explicitly called then there may be no output from the finalize method
        as the input output system may have been closed down before the finalize method
        in the class Room was called. Remember if there is an exception in the*
        `finalize` *method it will not be propagated out of the method.*

12.7.4 A class to describe an office

This demonstration class is derived from the class `Room` and describes an office in a building. The class `Office` is initialized with the size of the office and the number of staff members who can be accommodated.

The Java implementation of this class is:

```java
class Office extends Room
{
  private int the_no_staff;              //Number of staff in Office
```

The constructor for `Office` needs to explicitly call the constructor of its superclass `Room` with the size of the room. This is achieved by the call `super( size )`. If this had not been done a compile time error message would be generated as the compiler does not know what actual parameter to call the superclass constructor with.

```java
  public Office( final int size, final int no_staff )
  {
    super( size );
    the_no_staff = no_staff;
    System.out.println( "Constructor Office :" +
                        " number of staff   = " + the_no_staff );
  }
```

The destructor in the superclass `Room` must be explicitly called with `super.finalize();` if this is not done then the destructor code for the class Room would not be executed.

```java
  protected void finalize() throws Throwable
  {
    System.out.println( "Destructor Office  : " +
                        the_no_staff + " staff ");
    super.finalize();
  }
```

The method `staff`, writes out details about the number of staff in the office.

```java
  void staff()
  {
    System.out.println( "Method staff()     :" +
                        " number of staff   = " + the_no_staff ) ;
  }
}
```

12.7.5   Putting it all together

The class Room and Office are used in the following application that explicitly calls the garbage collector System.gc() and System.runFinalization() to call any finalization code for inactive objects.

```
class Main
{
  public static void main( String args[] )
  {
    Main.method_using_office();   //Method creates instance of Room
    System.gc();                  //Force Garbage collector
    System.runFinalization();     //Force run of Finalization code
  }

  public static void method_using_office()
  {
    Office w425 = new Office( 140, 4 );
    w425.size(); w425.staff();
  }
}
```

The output from the application is as follows:

```
Constructor Room    : size square metres = 140
Constructor Office  : number of staff    = 4
Method size()       : size square metres = 140
Method staff()      : number of staff    = 4
Destructor Office   : 2 staff
Destructor Room     : 140 sq Metres
```

Note: The order in which the constructors and destructors are called for an instance of a class which is derived from a superclass.

12.8   Visibility of fields in a class

The visibility of a fields in a class to the outside world, classes in the same package and to other classes which may inherit from the class, depends on the access specifier given to the field. In essence there is a hierarchy of visibility.

```
class Example
{
public
  // Visible to all
protected
  // Visible to an inheriting class
  // Visible to other classes in the same package
private
  // Not visible
no access specifier given
  // Visible to other classes in the same package
}
```

The following table summarizes the visibility of class fields. For each case, possible items that may be described in this way are suggested.

Access specifier	Visible to items in:			Examples of items which might be declared in this way
	the program	a subclass	same package	
public	✓	✓	✓	Functions visible to a client of the class.
protected		✓ [2]	✓	Functions which are used to build the functions that are visible to a client of the class and would be useful to a subclass.
private				Variables, and any functions which should not be seen even by a subclass.
[1]			✓	Shared data.

Key   ✓   Has visibility to

           [1]   No access specifier.

           [2]   But cannot access a protected field in a class that is in another package unless it inherits from that class.

Note: Irrespective of the access specifier of a field it is visible to all other fields in the same class.

12.9   Preventing overriding of methods and subclassing

When a class is written it is possible to prevent:

●   A method in the class been overridden by a subclass.

●   The class itself been subclassed.

To prevent a subclass from overriding a method in a class, the method is declared as `final`. For example, in the class `Room` below a subclass of `Room` is prevented from overriding the method `about`.

```
class Room
{
  final public String about()
  {
    // code of the method about
  }
}
```

To prevent the class itself from being subclassed, the class is declared as `final`. For example, the class `Room` shown below cannot be subclassed:

```
final class Room
{
  public String about()
  {
    // code of the method about
  }
}
```

12.9.1   Reasons why this should be done

By using the above techniques a builder of a class can guarantee that no-one can subvert their intention. For example, if in the class `Account` (see Chapter 5) the method `set_min_balance` had been made `final` then no subclass of class `Account` could be created that prevented a minimum balance being set.

However, excessive use of this feature may prevent people from making effective use of your classes.

12.10   Constructors

A constructor will implicitly call its superclass constructor with no parameter, before the code of the constructor is executed. If a different constructor in the superclass is to be called then this must be done explicitly before any code in the constructor is executed.

12.10.1 Calling a constructor in the current class and superclass

The following table summarizes the ways of calling constructors in the current class and the superclass.

Called constructor is in:	Construct is called using
the same class	`this`()
the superclass	`super`()

Note: The same mechanism is used if the constructor had parameters, except of course the actual parameters are used in the call.

12.10.2 Default constructor

If there are no constructors in a class a default constructor with no formal parameters is implicitly created that will implicitly call its superclass constructor **super**(). However, if a constructor with parameters is provided then a default constructor with no parameters will not be implicitly created. The consequence of this is that its subclass must now explicitly call one of the user created constructors in the super class. For example, the following demonstration code will fail to compile:

```
class Base                          class Derived extends Base
{                                   {
  private int the_number = 2;         public Derived()
                                      {
  public Base(int number)               // code
  {                                   }
    the_number = number;            }
  }
}
```

as the constructor in the class `Derived` does not explicitly call the constructor in the class `Base` that has a parameter.

12.11 Abstract classes

An implementor may create a class in which some or all of the methods are left unimplemented. To use such a class a subclass has to be created which overrides the unimplemented methods with a concrete implementation. For example, an implementor can create a class `Abstract_Account` in which the methods for: obtaining the account balance, depositing money and withdrawing money are defined, but the method that delivers a string representing the state of the account is left undefined. This class is illustrated below:

```
abstract class Abstract_Account
{
  private double the_balance    = 0.0d;  //Balance of account

  public double account_balance()
  {
    return the_balance;
  }

  public double withdraw( final double money )
  {
    // Code for withdraw
  }

  public void deposit( final double money )
  {
    the_balance = the_balance + money;
  }

  abstract public String statement();
}
```

Note: The class is declared as `abstract`, *the method that has no implementation is also declared as abstract.*

An implementor can then use this abstract account class in the production of a normal account. The implementor only has to provide an overridden method for `statement` plus any other methods or constructors they require to specialise the class for their use. For example, the following class `Normal_Account` overrides `statement` to return a string with the account holder's name plus their current balance.

```
class Normal_Account extends Abstract_Account
{
  private String the_name = "";

  Normal_Account( String name )
  {
    the_name = name;
  }

  public String statement()
  {
    return the_name + " balance is " + account_balance();
  }
}
```

When compiled and run with the following test application:

```
class Main
{
  public static void main( String args[] )
  {
    Normal_Account mike    = new Normal_Account("Mike's     ");
    Normal_Account corinna = new Normal_Account("Corinna's   ");

    double obtained;

    mike.deposit( 100.00 );
    System.out.println( mike.statement() );

    corinna.deposit( 150.00 );
    System.out.println( corinna.statement() );

    corinna.deposit( mike.withdraw( 80.00 ) );

    System.out.println( mike.statement() );
    System.out.println( corinna.statement() );
  }
}
```

would produce the following output:

```
Mike's      balance is 100.0
Corinna's   balance is 150.0
Mike's      balance is 20.0
Corinna's   balance is 230.0
```

12.11.1 Pure abstract class

If all the methods in a class are abstract then the class is pure abstract. For example, the following class:

```
abstract class Pure_Abstract_Account
{
  abstract public double account_balance();
  abstract public void   deposit( final double money);
  abstract public double withdraw( final double money );
}
```

is pure abstract. This is similar to an interface in that a user of the pure abstract class has to provide an implementation for all the methods.

12.12 Self-assessment

- How can inheritance increase programming productivity?

- If a method is `private` in the superclass can it be overridden to be `public` in the subclass?

- If a method is `public` in the superclass can it be overridden to be `private` in the subclass?

- From a subclass how is a constructor in the superclass called?

- How is a constructor called from another constructor in the same class?

- Are there any dangers with using inheritance?

- Why might you want to prevent another programmer overriding a method that you have written in a new class?

- What is an abstract class?

- Why might you want to define an abstract class?

12.13 Exercises

Construct the following class using inheritance

- *Account_with_close*
  A class which has all the methods of `Account` plus the additional method of `can_close` and `close`. The responsibilities of these methods are:

Method	Responsibility
can_close	Determines if the account can be closed. An account can only be closed if there is no overdraft.
close	Withdraws the outstanding balance of the account.

This however, is only allowed to happen if the account is not overdrawn.

Construct the following application

● *Test*
An application to test the class Account_with_close.

Construct the following classes:

● *Employee_pay*
A class Employee_pay which represents a person's salary has the following methods:

Method	Responsibility
set_hourly_rate	Sets the hourly rate.
add_hours_worked	Accumulates the number of hours worked so far.
pay	Delivers the pay for this week.
reset	Resets the hours worked back to zero.
hours_worked	Delivers the number of hours worked so far this week.
pay_rate	Delivers the hourly pay rate.

Tax is to be deducted at 20% of total pay.

● *Better_employee_pay*
A class Better_employee_pay which represents a person's salary. This extends the class Employee_pay to add the additional methods of:

Method	Responsibility
set_overtime_pay	Sets the overtime pay rate.
normal_pay_hours	Sets the number of hours in a week that have to be worked before the overtime pay rate is applied.
pay	Delivers the pay for this week. This will consist of the hours worked at the normal pay rate plus the hours worked at the overtime rate.

Construct the following application

● *test*
An application to test the classes Better_employee_pay and Employee_pay.

Construct the following class:

● *Employee_pay_with_repayment.*
A class Employee_pay_with_repayment which represents a person's salary after the deduction of the weekly repayment of part of a loan for travel expenses. This extends the class Better_employee_pay to add the additional methods of:

Method	Responsibility
set_deduction	Sets the weekly deduction
pay	Delivers the pay for this week. This will include the deduction of the money for the employee loan if possible.

Remember to include the possibility of an employee not being able to repay the weekly repayment of their loan as they have not worked enough hours.

● *Test*
An application to test the class Employee_pay_with_repayment.

● *Company*
A class Company that has the following methods:

Method	Responsibility
add_hours_worked	Accumulates the number of hours worked so far for a particular employee.
normal_pay_hours	Sets the number of hours in a week that have to be worked before the overtime pay rate is applied for a particular employee.
pay	Delivers the pay for this week for a particular employee. This will consist of the hours worked at the normal pay rate plus the hours worked at the overtime rate.
reset	Resets the hours worked back to zero for a particular employee.
set_hourly_rate	Sets the hourly rate for a particular employee.
set_overtime_pay	Sets the overtime pay rate for a particular employee.

Note: *The class is a container class for an array of 100 instances of the class* Better_employee_pay. *The messages sent to an instance of this class are delegated to the object for the specific employee.*

● *Payroll*

An application that implements the payroll for a small company of up to 100 employees. An individual transaction with the application consists of a single line of the form:

<Action> <Employee Number> [<Parameters>]

Where:

<Action> is

S	Sets the hourly rate for this employee.
O	Sets the overtime hourly rate for this employee.
N	Sets the number of hours normally worked in a week for this employee. If an employee work's over this number of hours then they will be paid at an overtime rate.
A	Enters hours worked by this employee so far this week.
P	Prints the pay earned by the employee for this week. This includes the deduction of 20% tax on total pay.
R	Reset the number of hours worked back to zero so that data for the next week can be entered.

<Employee Number> is
A number in the range 1 to 100;

<Parameters> are
Any additional values associated with the transaction.

Typical transactions

S 1 5.00	Set the hourly rate for employee 1 as £5.00 per hour
O 2 7.50	Set the overtime rate for employee 2 to be £7.50 per hour.
P 2	Print the total pay earned by employee 2 for this week. [Remember tax is deducted as 20% of total pay]
A 3 5	Employee 3 has worked 5 hours today

● *Payroll GUI*

Re-implement the payroll application described above, using a graphical user interface.

13. Exceptions

This chapter examines the exception mechanism. The exception mechanism is used to process unexpected errors in a safe and consistent way. However, this mechanism is not intended as a substitute for careful error checking in the written code. An example of acceptable use is when a method is supplied with incorrect data and no sensible processing decision can be made.

13.1   Introduction

An exception is an event generated in an application or applet in exceptional circumstances. For example, an exception could be raised when an attempt is made to process too many data items. The raised exception can be caught and an appropriate recovery action taken. An exception is in effect a clean way for application or applet code to abandon processing and return control to the wrapper code that initiated the processing.

The wrapper or calling code has the responsibility of handling the exception in a clean and consistent way. If the code does not capture the exception the exception is propagated up until either it is handled by an exception handler provided in the application or applet or is caught by the system exception handler. If caught by the system exception handler, the application or applet is abandoned with an appropriate but caustic error message.

13.1.1 Raising and capturing an exception

An exception is raised by the `throw` construct. For example, while processing user supplied data, the application or applet code could abandon the process as insufficient storage is available to store an audit trail. The writer of this processing code raises an exception with the following statement:

```
throw new Throwable("Too many items");
```

Note: The item throw is an instance of the class `Throwable`, which is constructed with an optional string parameter representing the nature of the error.

The caller of this code has the responsibility of capturing the exception. This is achieved with a `try` block as follows:

```
  try {

    if ( position > MAX_VALUE )
      throw new Throwable("position = " + position );

  }
  catch ( Throwable exc )
  {
    System.out.println( "Fail : " + exc.getMessage() );
  }
```

Note: An instance of the class Throwable *is thrown.*
The method getMessage() *delivers the string that the instance of the class*
Throwable *was created with.*

The code in the try block, is executed in the normal way. However, if during executing this code an exception is generated then control is passed to the catch block to process the exception. After the exception has been processed or the code completes without an exception, control passes to the next statement after the try catch block. Remember, if no exception occurs the code in the catch block will not be executed.

13.1.2 Major methods in the class `java.lang.Throwable`

The class Throwable contains the following major methods

Method	Responsibility
getMessage()	Returns the string that is passed as a parameter to the construction of an instance of the class.
printStackTrace(stream)	Prints a stack trace. Where stream is an instance of PrintWriter or PrintStream.
printStackTrace()	Prints a stack trace on the standard error stream.

13.1.3   The exception classes

The class Throwable is the superclass to a family of subclasses that represent specific types of exceptions that may be thrown. In addition by inheriting from the class Throwable user defined exceptions can be created. For example, the exception Range_Error_Exception is created as follows:

```
class Range_Error_Exception extends Throwable
{
  public Range_Error_Exception( String s )
  {
    super( s );
  }
}
```

This exception, is used in the following fragment of code:

```
try {

  if ( position > MAX_VALUE )
    throw new Range_Error_Exception("position = " + position );

}
catch ( Range_Error_Exception exc )
{
  System.out.println();
  System.out.println( "Range error : " + exc.getMessage() );
}
```

13.1.4   Propagating an exception out of a method

The class `Prime` contains the class method `is_prime` that delivers the truth of whether an integer number is a prime or not. If the number tested is less than or equal to zero the exception `Range_Error_Exception` is raised. The class `Prime` is defined as follows:

```
class Prime
{
  public static boolean is_prime( long n ) throws Range_Error_Exception
  {
    if (n < 0) throw new Range_Error_Exception("Negative");

    if ( n%2 == 0) return false;                      //Even
    long root_n = (long) ( Math.sqrt( (double) n ) ) + 1; //upto
    for ( long i = 3; i<=root_n; i+=2 )               //Odd numbers
    {
      if ( n % i == 0 ) return false;                 //Divisible
    }
    return true;                                      //Prime
  }
}
```

The method `is_prime` first checks if the supplied parameter is less than or equal to zero. If the parameter is less than or equal to zero then the exception `Range_Error_Exception` is raised with the statement:

```
throw new Range_Error_Exception("Negative");
```

As the exception `Range_Error_Exception` is not caught inside the method, the methods signature must indicate that this exception will be propagated out of the method. This is indicated as follows on the signature of the method:

```
public static boolean is_prime( long n ) throws Range_Error_Exception
```

Note: If this information is not made part of the signature of the method and there is no
catch block for the exception in the method then a compile-time error will be
generated, unless the exception is a subclass of Error or
RuntimeException.

By including this information with the signature of the method a client user knows
exactly what exceptions may be generated when they call this method. They can choose
to catch the exception or let it be passed on to whoever called their code. Of course, they
too must indicate that the method they have written will propagate this exception.

13.1.5   Putting it all together

The following application illustrates the use of the class method is_prime:

```
class Main
{
  public static void main( String args[] )
  {
    try {
      System.out.print("Primes between 20 ... -1 are   : ");
      for ( int i=20; i>=-1; i-- )
      {
        if ( Prime.is_prime( i ) ) System.out.print( i + " " );
      }
      System.out.println();
    }
    catch ( Range_Error_Exception exc )
    {
      System.out.println();
      System.out.println( "Range_Error_Exception : " +
                             exc.getMessage() );
    }
  }
}
```

Which when compiled and run will produce the following output:

```
Primes between 20 ... -1 are   : 19 17 13 11 7 5 3 1
Range_Error_Exception : Negative
```

13.2   The **finally** clause

The finally clause allows a code sequence to be specified that will be executed
regardless of how the try catch block is exited. For example, in the following method
list_primes:

```java
class Useful
{
  public static void list_primes( final int start,
                                   final int stop
                                 )
                                 throws Range_Error_Exception
  {
    try {
      System.out.println("Primes between " + start + " ... " + stop);
      for ( int pos_prime=start; pos_prime<=stop; pos_prime++ )
      {
        if ( Prime.is_prime( pos_prime ) )
          System.out.println( pos_prime );
      }
    }
    finally
    {
      System.out.println("List of primes finished");
    }
  }
}
```

the message `"List of primes finished"` will always be printed, even when an
exception occurs that is not caught by the `try catch` block. By using this form of the
try block the need to repeat code can be avoided.

13.2.1   Putting it all together

The following applications illustrates the use of the `finally` clause.

```java
class Main
{
  public static void main( String args[] )
  {
    try {
      Useful.list_primes( 1, 12 );
      Useful.list_primes( -5, 12 );
    }
    catch ( Range_Error_Exception exc )
    {
      System.out.println( "Range_Error_Exception : " +
                          exc.getMessage() );
    }
  }
}
```

Which when compiled with suitable declarations and run will produce the following output:

```
Primes between 1 ... 12
1
3
5
7
11
List of primes finished
Primes between -5 ... 12
List of primes finished
Range_Error_Exception : Negative
```

Note: That the message `List of primes finished` *is printed for both calls of* `Useful.list_of_primes` *even though in the second call an exception is generated.*

13.3   Capturing any exception

A catch block for the class `Throwable` will catch an instance of any subclass of `Throwable`. This is a consequence of an instance of a subclass being able to be assigned to any instance of its superclass. The following code will capture the exception `Prime_Exception` plus any exception whose superclass is `Throwable`.

```java
class Main
{
  public static void main( String args[] )
  {
    try {
      System.out.print("Primes between 20 ... -1 are   : ");
      for ( int i=20; i>=-1; i-- )
      {
        if ( Prime.is_prime( i ) ) System.out.print( i + " " );
      }
      System.out.println();
    }
    catch ( Prime_Exception exc )
    {
      System.out.println();
      System.out.println( "Prime Exception : " + exc.getMessage() );
    }
    catch ( Throwable err )
    {
      System.out.println( "Unexpected : " + err.getMessage() );
    }
  }
}
```

Note: Be careful in using `Throwable` *to capture any exception as you may wish to handle different exceptions in separate ways.*

13.4   The classes **RuntimeException** and **Exception**

The hierarchy for the exception classes is illustrated in Figure 13.1 below.

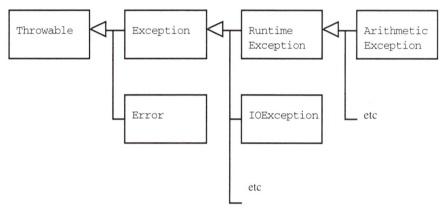

Figure 13.1 Outline of exception class hierarchy.

Note: Subclasses of Error *indicate a serious error and are not normally caught.*
Subclasses of RuntimeException *are exceptions that would usually be*
caught so that a recovery action could be taken.

A method is not required to declare in its throw class any exception that is inherited
from the class RuntimeException or Exception. The implication of this is that
the normal run-time errors generated by the virtual machine for arithmetic errors etc. do
not explicitly have to be included in a throw clause for each method that may cause the
exception to be generated. For example, the following code is valid:

```
class Useful
{
  public static int calculate( final long number )
  {
    if ( number > BIG_NUMBER )
    {
      throw new ArithmeticException("number too big");
    }

    // Code for calculation

  }
}
```

13.5   Self-assessment

- When should an exception be used, when should an exception not be used?

- How may a programmer capture the thrown exception Prime_Exception?

- How can a programmer create there own exceptions?

- How can a programmer guarantee that they will catch every exception that is thrown?

- How can an application or applet guarantee that code will be executed regardless of how the try block is left?

- If an exception is propagated out of a method is it necessary to have a throws clause?

13.6 Exercises

Construct the following class:

- *DataStore*
  A store for objects has the following methods:

Method	Responsibility
put(str,o)	Adds the object o to the data store using the key str. The key is an instance of the class String.
get(str)	Retrieves the object stored under the key str.
contains(str)	Returns true if the key string str is present.

The following code fragment illustrates the storing and retrieving of items in this simple container.

```
DataStore store = new DataStore();

try
{
  store.add( "Mike",    new Account() );
  store.add( "Corinna", new Account() );

  Account mike = ((Account) store.get( "Mike" );

  System.out.println("Mike's balance is " +
                     mike.account_balance() );
}
catch ( DS_Full exc )
{
    System.out.println( "Fail : " + err.getMessage() );
}
```

Build the class DataStore that throws the following exceptions:

- DS_Full
  When the Data store is full

- DS_Not_There
  When the item requested is not held in the data store.

14. Assigning and comparing objects

This chapter illustrates how objects may be assigned and compared. Unfortunately these operations are implemented in two distinct ways that will produce different results. For the unwary programmer this may lead to some unexpected results in their application or applet.

14.1   Introduction

As objects are represented by a handle, that references the storage of the object, the operations of assignment and comparison for equality may be performed in two distinct ways. The table below summarizes the two distinct ways that the operations of assignment and compassion for equality are made in Java.

Operation	Implemented as	Implemented as	Know as a
Assignment	Assigning the handle of the object	`a = b;`	Shallow copy
	Assigning the storage of the underlying object that the handle references.	`a = b.clone();`	Deep copy
Comparison for equality	Comparing the handle	`if ( a = b )`	Deep equality comparison
	Comparing the storage of the underlying objects that the handles reference.	`if ( a.equal(b) )`	Shallow equality comparison

Note: The comparison operators <, <=, >=, and > are not defined between instances of objects.
The method `clone` returns the cloned object as type `Object`. It is thus usual to cast this returned object back to its original type.

14.1.1   Assignment: deep and shallow copy

Figure 14.1 below illustrates graphically the effect of performing a shallow and deep copy of instances of the class `Account`.

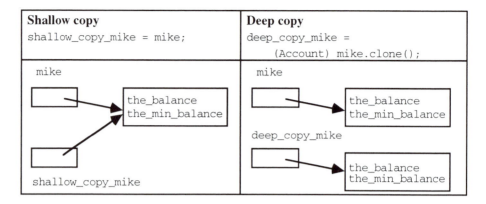

Figure 14.1 Illustration of a deep and shallow copy of an object.

14.1.2   Comparison for equality

Figure 14.2 below graphically illustrates deep and shallow equality when comparing instances of the class `Account`.

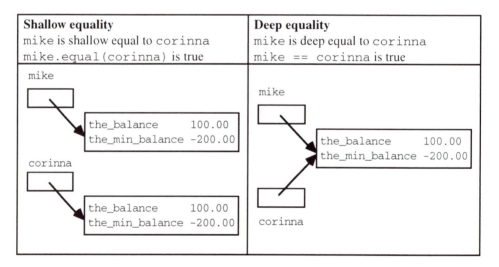

Figure 14.2 Illustration of deep and shallow equality.

14.2   Assignment of objects

In Java the normal assignment operator = implements a shallow copy of an object. For example, in the following code, a shallow copy of the object `mike` is made to the object `shallow_copy_mike`.

```
public static void main(String args[])
{
  Account mike                 = new Account(50.0);
  Account shallow_copy_mike    = mike;
  mike.deposit(100.00);
  System.out.println("Balance account mike             = " +
                     mike.account_balance() );
  Account copy_mike = mike;
  System.out.println("Balance account shallow copy mike = " +
                     shallow_copy_mike.account_balance() );
}
```

Note: Remember in Java all objects are represented by a handle or pointer to the objects storage.

which when compiled and run would produce the following results:

```
Balance account mike               = 150.0
Balance account shallow copy mike = 150.0
```

The important point is that in a shallow copy the storage for the object is not duplicated whereas in a deep copy the storage is. In particular if a shallow copy of an object is made any changes to the object will be reflected in all the shallow copies.

14.2.1   Making an object cloneable: Deep copy

To make an instance of a class cloneable a class must:

- Implement the interface Cloneable.

- Override the method clone in the class Object.

the interface Cloneable contains no methods and is defined as follows:

```
public interface Cloneable {}
```

The method clone in the class Object has the following signature:

```
protected Object clone() throws CloneNotSupportedException
```

Hence an implementor of a class that implements the Cloneable interface is required to provide a method clone with the following signature:

```
public Object clone()
```

This is necessary as a user of the class would not be able to see the method clone in the superclass Object if it were not overridden with a public version of the method.

14.2.2　An example

For a simple class that contains only variables the overridden method `clone` can call the method `clone` in the superclass `Object` to implement the copy. For example, a cloneable class `Account` is implemented as follows:

```
class Account implements Cloneable
{
  private double the_balance    = 0.0d;  //Balance of account
  private double the_min_balance = 0.0d;  //Minimum bal (Overdraft)

  public Account( final double opening_balance )
  {
    the_balance = opening_balance;
  }

  public Account( final double opening_balance,
                  final double min_balance )
  {
    this( opening_balance );
    the_min_balance = min_balance;
  }

  public Object clone()
  {
    try {
      return super.clone();                //Type is Object
    }
    catch ( CloneNotSupportedException e )  //Just in case
    {
      System.exit(-1);                     //Exit **
    }
    return new Object();                   // Keep compiler happy
  }

// Code for the methods
//    account_balance, withdraw, deposit, set_min_balance

}
```

Note:　*The code for the methods (`deposit`, `withdraw`, `account_balance` and `set_min_balance`) previously seen in Section 5.2.5 for the class `Account` are not shown.*

The method `clone` returns a clone copy of the object that is of type `Object`. This must be cast to an instance of an `Account` before it can be assigned.

14.2.3　Putting it all together

The following code illustrates the use of the method `clone` to perform a deep copy of an instance of the class `Account`.

```
class Main
{
  public static void main(String args[])
  {
    Account mike              = new Account(50.00);
    Account deep_copy_mike = (Account) mike.clone();
    mike.deposit(100.00);
    System.out.println("Balance account mike               = " +
                        mike.account_balance() );
    Account copy_mike = mike;
    System.out.println("Balance account deep copy mike     = " +
                        deep_copy_mike.account_balance() );
  }
}
```

Which when compiled and run produces the following output:

```
Balance account mike             = 150.0
Balance account deep copy mike   = 50.0
```

14.2.4   Duplicating the instance variables of a class directly

The body of the method `clone` can be used to copy the individual instance variables of the class directly. If any of the instance variables are themselves objects then they are deep copied using their clone method.

```
class Account implements Cloneable
{
  private double the_balance     = 0.0d;  //Balance of account
  private double the_min_balance = 0.0d;  //Minimum bal (Overdraft)

  public Object clone()
  {
   Account copy = new Account();          //New Account
   copy.the_balance     = the_balance;    //Copy fields
   copy.the_min_balance = the_min_balance;
   return copy;                           //Return new copy
  }

 // Code for the methods
 //    The constructor(s)
 //    account_balance, withdraw, deposit, set_min_balance

}
```

Note: If any of the fields of the class contain objects them this form of the code must be used to copy the objects using their `clone` method.

14.3   Deep and shallow equality

As for deep and shallow assignment the same principles hold for equality. This time if the objects share the same storage they are deeply equal. However, if the objects do not share the same storage but they do contain the same state information then they are shallow equal. Instances of the class `Account` that are shallow and deep equally are shown below in Figure 14.3:

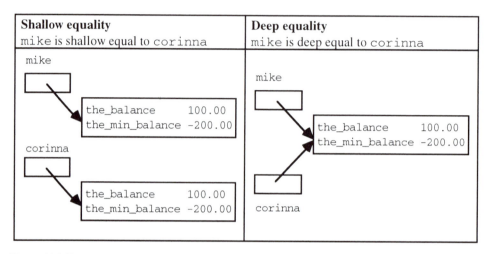

Figure 14.3 Illustration of deep and shallow equality.

14.3.1   Use of == for equality of objects: Deep equality

The normal operator `==` implements deep equality of objects. Hence, the results obtained from its use are not always what are wanted. For example, using the class `Account` seen in Section 14.2.4 the following test class:

```
class Main
{

  public static void test( final String mes, final boolean res )
  {
    System.out.println("Assertion: " + mes + " is " +
                    ( res ? "true" : "false " ) );
  }

  public static void main(String args[])
  {
    Account mike        = new Account(50.00);
    Account corinna     = new Account(50.00);
    Account miranda     = new Account(100.00);

    test( "mike == mike   " , mike == mike );
    test( "mike == corinna" , mike == corinna );
    test( "mike == miranda" , mike == miranda );
  }
}
```

When compiled and run will produce the following results:

```
Assertion: mike == mike    is true
Assertion: mike == corinna is false
Assertion: mike == miranda is false
```

14.3.2   Use of `equal` for equality of objects: Shallow equality

By overriding the method `equal` (in the class `Object`) the user can implement appropriate code to test the equality of the two objects. For example, if the class `Account` in Section 14.2.2 had the additional method:

```java
public boolean equals( Account other )
{
    return ( ( the_balance == other.the_balance ) &&
             ( the_min_balance == other.the_min_balance ) );
}
```

Then the result of running the following test class `Main` that used this new version of `Account`:

```java
class Main
{
    public static void test( final String mes, final boolean res )
    {
        System.out.println("Assertion: " + mes + " is " +
                           ( res ? "true" : "false " ) );
    }

    public static void main(String args[])
    {
        Account mike       = new Account(50.00);
        Account corinna    = new Account(50.00);
        Account miranda    = new Account(100.00);

        test( "mike == mike   " , mike.equals( mike ) );
        test( "mike == corinna" , mike.equals( corinna ) );
        test( "mike == miranda" , mike.equals( miranda ) );
    }
}
```

would be as follows:

```
Assertion: mike == mike    is true
Assertion: mike == corinna is true
Assertion: mike == miranda is false
```

14.4   Self-assessment

● What is the difference between a deep and a shallow copy?

● What is the difference between a deep and a shallow comparison?

● Why is the cloneable interface required?

● As the superclass `Object` contains the method `clone` why do objects have to implement the `cloneable` interface?

● Why is their not an interface for equals?

● Why did the designers of Java not have the assignment operator = implement a deep copy and the equality operator == implement shallow equality?

14.5   Exercises

Construct the following class:

● *Person*
A class `Person` which represents details about a person has the following methods:

Method	Responsibility
Person	Constructs a new instance of a person with their name and height.
clone	Returns a deep copy of the object.
equals	Returns true if two objects are shallow equal.
get_height	Returns the person's height in metres.
get_name	Returns the person's name as a string.
set_height	Sets the person's height.
set_name	Sets the person's name.

Construct the following test application

● *test*
An application to test the class `Person`.

15. The game of draughts

This chapter illustrates the construction of an application to play the game of draughts between two human players. A cut down version of the UML object-oriented design method is used to analyse and help design the solution.

15.1 Draughts

The draughts board is composed of 64 cells in an 8-by-8 grid. Figure 15.1 illustrates the draughts board at the start of a game. The aim of the game is to capture all of your opponent's counters. Contestants take it in turn to move one of their counters (men) on the board (chequerboard) into a vacant cell. A valid move is either a diagonal move forward of one cell into an empty cell or a diagonal move forward jumping over your opponent's counter to a vacant cell. The latter move captures the opponent's counter jumped over. The jumped over counter is removed from the board. A player must capture an opponent's counter if a capture is possible.

After capturing an opponent's counter, the same capturing procedure may be repeated using the same counter to capture further counters.

If a player can move one of their counters to their opponent's end of the board, then this counter is promoted to a king. A king has special powers and in addition to being able to move diagonally forward, can also move diagonally backwards.

The game is won when a player has captured all of their opponent's counters. A tied game occurs when either a player cannot move due to the position of their opponent's counters, or neither player can remove all their opponent's counters.

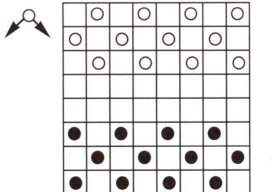

Figure 15.1 Starting position for the game of draughts.

The arrows by the side of the board indicate the direction of play for the player counters.

15.2 The game of draughts

The table below illustrates three examples of a move for black on a fragment of the draughts board.

	Before black's move	After black's move
1	Black to play	The board after black has captured white's counter.
2	Black to move, black must make a double capture.	The board after capturing white's counters
3	Black cannot capture any of his opponents counters.	The board after black plays a 'safety' move.

15.2.1   An application to play draughts between two human players

A controller of the game (game's master) asks each player in turn for a move. When a move is received from a player, the board is asked to validate the move. If this is a valid move the counter of the current player is moved on the board. If an opponent's counter is captured then this is removed from the board. The board is displayed and the new state of the game is evaluated. This process is repeated until either a player wins by removing all of his opponent's counters or a stalemate position is reached. The player making the last move is asked to announce the result of the game.

The interactions by the controller with the system are shown in Figure 15.2.

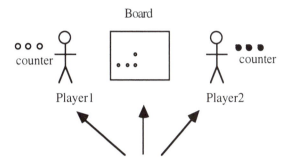

Figure 15.2 Interactions by the controller with the objects in the system.

In the English description of the problem, nouns indicate potential objects and verbs indicate potential messages sent to these objects.

With the major **nouns** indicated in bold and the major ***verbs*** indicated in bold italics, the specification for the game can now be read as:

The draughts **board** is composed of 64 **cells** in an 8-by-8 grid. The aim of the game is to capture all of your opponent's **counters**. Contestants take it in turn to ***move*** one of their **counters** (men) on the **board** (chequerboard) into a vacant **cell**. A valid ***move*** is either a diagonal ***move*** forward of one **cell** into an empty **cell** or a diagonal ***move*** forward jumping over your opponent's counter to a vacant **cell**. The latter ***move*** captures the opponent's **counter** jumped over. The jumped over **counter** is ***removed*** from the **board**. A player must capture an opponent's **counter** if a capture is possible.

After capturing an opponent's **counter**, the same capturing procedure may be repeated using the same counter to capture further counters.

If a player can ***move*** one of their **counters** to their opponent's end of the board, then this **counter** is promoted to a king. A king has special powers and in addition to being able to ***move*** diagonally forward, can also ***move*** diagonally backwards.

The **ga**me is won when a player has captured all of their opponent's counters. A tied **game** occurs when either a **player** cannot ***move*** due to the position of their opponent's counters, or neither **player** can ***remove*** all their opponent's **counters**.

A controller of the **game** (game's master) asks each **player** in turn for a **move** . When a **move** is received from a **player**, the **board** is asked to ***validate*** the **move**. If this is a valid **move** the counter of the current player is moved on the board. If an opponent's **counter** is captured then this is removed from the **board**. The **board** is displayed and the new state of the **game** is ***evaluated***. This process is repeated until either a **player** wins by removing all of his opponent's **counters** or a stalemate position is reached. The **player** making the last ***move*** is asked to ***announce*** the result of the **game**.

The major objects and verbs identified are:

Objects (nouns)	Messages (verbs)
board	announce
cell	ask
counter	display
game	evaluated
move	move
player	removed
	validate

Using the above list a first draft of objects and messages sent to the objects can be created. This first draft of possible objects and messages is shown below:

```
board
        Display a representation of the board.
        Move a counter on the board.
        Remove a counter from the board.
        Evaluate the current state of the board.
        Validate a proposed move.
player
        Announce the result of the game.
        Ask for the next move.
cell
        Display a representation of the game.

counter
        Display a representation of the counter.
move

game
        Play the game.
```

15.2.2   Working with classes

It is more appropriate to deal with classes than to deal with objects. For example, Board is the class to which the object board belongs. In producing this list several refinements have been made to the methods in the classes. In particular the class Move now has methods that allow the saving and retrieving of a move and its individual constituent elements. The refined methods for the classes are:

Class	Message	Responsibility
Board	colour	Returns the colour of the counter in cell #,#.
	display Δ	Displays a representation of the board.
	evaluate	Evaluates the current state of the game: win, draw or still playable.
	move	Moves a counter on the board from cell #,# to cell #,#.
	remove	Removes the counter from the board at cell #,#.
	valid_move	Implements the move and return true if it is a valid move.
Player	announce Δ	Announces that the player has either won or draws the game.
	counter_is	Returns the counter used by the player.
	get_move Δ	Returns the move made by the player.
Cell	clear	Clears a cell.
	colour	Returns the colour of the counter contained in the cell.
	coloured_rank	Returns a representation of the counter in the cell.
	contents	Returns the counter in the cell.
	drop	Drops a counter into a cell
Counter	colour	Returns the colour of the stored counter.
	empty	Returns the colour that is used to represent no counter.
	promote	Promotes the counter to a King
	valid_move	Implement the move and return true if the whole move is valid.
	coloured_rank	Returns a representation of the counter.
Move	add	Adds the (row, column) that makes up part of a move.
	colour	Returns the colour of the player who made this move.
	column	Returns the column position of the current component of the move. See from and to.
	from	Access methods row and column extract from the from part of the move component.

Class	Message	Responsibility
	next	Selects the next move component.
	part_of_move	Returns the index of the current move component. 0 -> first, 1-> second etc.
	row	Returns the row position of the current component of the move. See from and to.
	special_move	Returns true if the move is a resignation or an agreed draw.
	start	Sets extract the first move element.
	to	Access methods row and column extract from the to part of the move component.
	to_be_made	Returns true if still move elements to be processed.

Game	play	Plays the game.

Note: Methods marked with a Δ involve I/O.
Some of the original messages (verbs) have been renamed to a more specific name when producing this list.
This refinement process involves careful consideration of the interaction between classes.

15.2.3 The class Move

The class Move is in essence a container for a series of (column, row) pairs of numbers. Each component of a move consists of two (column, row) pairs, the first pair represents the from part of the move, the second pair the to part of the move. For example, Figure 15.3 illustrates a multiple move from position (8, 1) to first (6, 3) and then onto (4, 5).

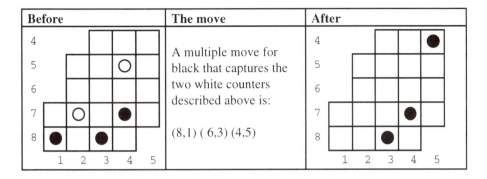

Figure 15.3 A multiple move in the game of draughts.

For example, to enter the multiple move (8, 1) (6, 3) (4, 5) into an instance of the class Move the following code fragment is used:

```
Move move = new Move( black );   // Move for black player

move.add( 8,  1 );
move.add( 6,  3 );
move.add( 4,  5 );
```

Note: This move consists of two components, the first component of the move is from (8,1) to (6,3) and the second component of the move is from (6, 3) to (4, 5).

Access to the stored moves is made using a iterator that allows access to each component of the move. The iterator is part of the class Move. As a component of a move consists of two parts a from part and a to part the methods from and to are used respectively to set which part of the move component is accessed. The methods row and column return the respective row and column from the selected part of the move component. The method next steps the iterator onto the next component of the move.

For example, the following code fragment prints the parts of the individual components of the move held in the object move:

```
int part_no = 1;
move.start();                                //Set start
while ( move.to_be_made() )                  //While parts
{
  System.out.println("Move part " + part_no++ ); // Part #
  move.from();                               // From
  System.out.println(" From " + move.row() +  //  extract
                   ", " + move.column() );
  move.to();                                 // To
  System.out.println(" To   " + move.row() +  //  extract
                   ", " + move.column() );
  move.next();                               // next
}                                            //End while
```

Note: In the class Move there is no checking for the validity of the entered move.

When run with the addition of appropriate surrounding code the above fragment of code will print:

```
Move part 1
 From 8, 1
 To   6, 3
Move part 2
 From 6, 3
 To   4, 5
```

15.2.4   The classes `Player` and `Board`

In looking at the methods that belong to the above list of classes, methods that belong to the classes `Player` and `Board` are split into two distinct categories:

- Methods that perform I/O, or will have an interaction with objects that perform I/O.

- Methods that deal with changing the state or examining the state of the object but involve no direct or indirect I/O.

Inheritance is used to split each of the classes `Player`, and `Board` into two classes:

- A superclass whose methods involve no I/O.

- A subclass that inherits from the superclass and adds methods that perform I/O or have an I/O interaction.

15.2.5   Classes in the application

The classes used in building an implementation of the game draughts will now be:

Class	An instance of which is:
Board	The board for the draughts game, that communicates with the outside world using the TUI class for I/O.
Basic_board	The board for the draughts game.
Player	A player of the game draughts, that communicates with the outside world using the TUI class for I/O.
Basic_player	A player of the game draughts.
Cell	One of the 64 cells held in the draughts board.
Counter	A counter used in playing the draughts game, that returns a representation that the TUI class can print.
Basic_counter	A counter used in playing the draughts game.
Move	Used to hold the moves suggested by the player.
TUI	Used to communicate with the outside world. The class is shown in Section 5.5.1.
Game	Used to play the game draughts.

This decomposition allows many of the classes to be re-used when building a graphical version of draughts.

15.2.6   Object diagram

An object diagram for the game draughts using the above classes is illustrated in Figure 15.4. In this object diagram no methods are shown to conserve space. When developing the class `Basic_board` several protected methods must be added to facilitate the implementation of the subclass `Board`. In particular to implement the method `display` in the class `Board` a mechanism must be provided to inspect the contents of individual cells so that a representation of the board can be displayed.

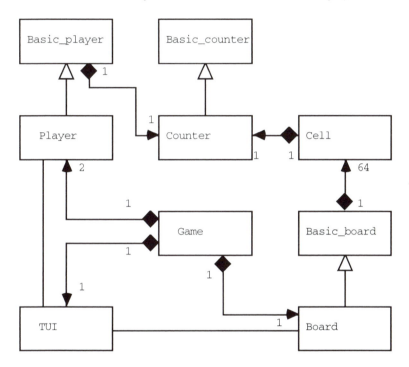

Figure 15.4 Object diagram for the game of draughts.

15.2.7   Sequence diagram for the game of draughts

The messages sent to instances of the major classes in the class `Game` are show below in Figure 15.5.

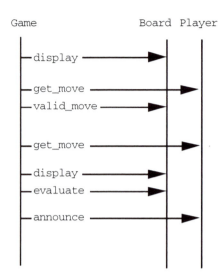

```
                                              Game              Board Player
Display initial state of board            ─display ─────────────►│      │
While game playable                            │                 │      │
  Copy board                               ─get_move ───────────────────►
  Get move                                     │                 │      │
  While not a valid move                   ─valid_move ──────────►│      │
    Restore board from copy                    │                 │      │
    Get move                                ─get_move ───────────────────►
  End while                                    │                 │      │
  Display new state of board               ─display ─────────────►│      │
  Evaluate state of board                  ─evaluate ────────────►│      │
  If game not playable                         │                 │      │
    Let player announce result             ─announce ───────────────────►
  End if                                       │                 │      │
End while                                      │                 │      │
```

Figure 15.5 Sequence diagram for the game of draughts.

15.2.8   The implementation of the class Game

In the implementation of the game the class C_Colour is used to hold enumeration's of the representation of the colour of a counter. The value NONE signifies that there was no counter.

```
class C_Colour
{
  public static final char NONE  = ' ';   //When no counter present
  public static final char WHITE = 'o';   //White
  public static final char BLACK = 'x';   //Black
}
```

The class Game contains a single method play that is responsible for the implementation of the playing of the game of draughts between two human players.

```
class Game
{
  private TUI    the_scrn = new TUI();              //Vdu/keyboard
  private Board  the_db  = new Board();             //The playing board
  private Player the_ply[] = {                      //The the_ply
      new Player( new Counter(C_Colour.BLACK) )
      new Player( new Counter(C_Colour.WHITE) )
    };
```

```
void play()
{
  int state = Board_state.PLAYABLE;
  int no = 0;                                     //First player

  the_db.display(the_scrn);                       //Display the board
  while ( state == Board_state.PLAYABLE )         //While playable
  {
    Board copy = (Board) the_db.clone();          //Before move
    Move move_is = the_ply[no].get_move(the_scrn);
    while ( !the_db.valid_move(move_is) )
    {
      the_db = copy;                              //Restore
      the_scrn.message("Invalid move");
      move_is = the_ply[no].get_move(the_scrn);   //New move
    }

    the_db.display(the_scrn);                      //Display new board
    state = the_db.evaluate();
    if ( state == Board_state.PLAYABLE )
      no = ( no == 0 ? 1 : 0 );                    //Next Contestant
    else
      the_ply[no].announce(the_scrn,state);        //The result
  }
}
```

15.2.9   The implementation of the class `Counter`

Before each move is made on the board a copy of the board is taken so that if the move is invalid then the original position of the board can be restored from the copy. However, this means that the class `Board` and any of its instance variables must be cloneable. Hence, the class `Counter` must implement the interface `Cloneable`. The responsibilities of the class `Counter` are as follows:

Method	Responsibility
clone	Delivers a new copy of a counter.
colour	Delivers a character representation of the colour of the counter. x - Black , o - White.
coloured_rank	Delivers a character representation of the coloured rank of the counter. x - Black pawn, X - black King, o - White pawn, O - White king.
empty	Delivers a character representation ` ` of no counter (static method)
promote	Promotes a pawn to a king.
valid_move	Returns true if the move is valid.

Note: The methods `colour`, `coloured_rank` *and* `empty` *return a character representation of the rank and colour of the counter.*

The implementation of the class Counter is as follows:

```
class Counter implements Cloneable
{
  private char the_colour;                     //The counters colour
  private char the_rank = C_Rank.PAWN;         //Rank of counter
```

The constructor is used to create a pawn in a particular colour.

```
  public Counter( final char colour )          //New counter
  {
    the_colour = colour;
  }
```

The overridden method clone creates a new copy of a counter. As the instance variables of the class are simple variables then a bit by bit copy of the object can be performed using the method clone in the superclass Object.

```
  public Object clone()                        //Clone object
  {
    try {
      return super.clone();
    }
    catch ( CloneNotSupportedException e )
    {
      System.err.println("Internal error: Clone Counter");
      System.exit(-1);
      return new Object();                      //Keep compiler happy
    }
  }
}
```

Note: If a copy cannot be made then the application is abandoned.

The methods colour and coloured_rank return the colour of the counter as a character representation. The following table illustrates the different values that can be returned from these two methods:

Methods	Values returned
colour	x or o
coloured_rank	x, o, X, or O

The implementation of the methods is as follows:

```
  public char colour()                         //It's colour
  {
    return the_colour;
  }
```

```
public char coloured_rank()                //It's coloured rank
{
  return the_rank == C_Rank.PAWN
    ? the_colour : Character.toUpperCase( the_colour );
}
```

The static method `empty` is used to give a representation of an empty cell.

```
public static char empty()                 //No counter
{
    return C_Colour.NONE;
}
```

The method `promote` promotes a pawn to be a king.

```
public void promote()                       //Promote
{
    the_rank = C_Rank.KING;
}
```

The only complex public method in the class is `valid_move` that determines if the move is valid. A move made by a player may involve the capture of several of their opponent's counters.

In essence the code is a loop that checks that each component of the move is valid. The task of validating the individual components of the move is performed by the private method `part_move`. The method `part_move` will deliver `true` if the current component of the move in the player's direction is valid. Special processing is required when the counter is a king as there are now two valid directions for the move forward and reverse.

```
public boolean valid_move( Basic_board b, Move move )
{
  if ( move.special_move() ) return true;
  int dir = ( the_colour == C_Colour.WHITE ? +1 : -1 );
  move.start();                             //1st move
  boolean valid     = true;                 //Move valid
  boolean move_made = false;                //
  while ( move.to_be_made() )               //Moves
  {
    move_made = true;
    if ( the_rank == C_Rank.PAWN )
    {
      valid = valid && part_move(b, move, dir);      //Forward
    } else {
      valid = valid && (part_move(b, move, dir) ||   //Forward
                        part_move(b, move, dir*-1) );//Reverse
    }
    move.next();                            //next move
  }
  return move_made && valid;
}
```

The private method `part_move` extracts the coordinates of the current move component (from, to) and checks if this is valid for the current counter. In essence there are two cases a capturing move and a positioning move.

```
private boolean part_move( Basic_board b, Move m, final int dir )
{
  int opp = ( the_colour == C_Colour.WHITE ?
              C_Colour.BLACK : C_Colour.WHITE );
  m.from();                                    //From part
  int cp_r = m.row();                          //Cur row
  int cp_c = m.column();                       //    col
  m.to();                                      //To part
  int np_r = m.row();                          //New row
  int np_c = m.column();                       //    col

  if ( cp_r + dir == np_r )                    //[] To unoccupied
  {                                            //    square
    if ( cp_c == np_c+1 || cp_c == np_c-1 )    // Col OK
    {
      if (b.colour(np_r, np_c) == C_Colour.NONE) // Cell free
      {
        b.move( cp_r, cp_c , np_r, np_c );     // Implement
        return m.part_of_move() == 0;          // Only if 1st
      }
    }
    return false;                              // Invalid
  }
  if ( cp_r + dir + dir == np_r )              //[] A capture
  {                                            //   of opponent
    int jp_r =  (cp_r + np_r)/2;               //Jumped row
    if ( (cp_c + 2 != np_c) &&
         (cp_c - 2 != np_c) ) return false;
    int jp_c =  (cp_c + np_c)/2;               //          col
    if ( b.colour( jp_r, jp_c ) == opp )       //Capture OK
    {
      if (b.colour(np_r, np_c) == C_Colour.NONE) //Into OK
      {
        b.move( cp_r, cp_c , np_r, np_c );
        b.remove( jp_r, jp_c );
        return true;                           //OK
      }
    }
    return false;                              //Invalid
  }
  return false;                                //Invalid
}
```

15.2.10 The implementation of the class `Move`

An instance of the class `Move` provides an interrogative container for the individual components of a complete move. By using an object to hold the components of a complete move the rest of the application is considerably simplified. The responsibilities of the class `Move` are as follows:

Method	Responsibility
Move	Constructor to create a new move for a particular player.
add	Adds the (row, column) that makes up part of a move.
colour	Returns the colour of the player who made this move.
column	Returns the column position of the current component of the move. See from and to.
from	Access methods row and column extract from the from part of the move component.
next	Selects the next move component.
part_of_move	Returns the index of the current move component. 0 -> first, 1-> second etc.
row	Returns the row position of the current component of the move. See from and to.
special_move	Returns true if the move is a resignation or an agreed draw.
start	Sets extract the first move element.
to	Access methods row and column extract from the to part of the move component.
to_be_made	Returns true if still move elements to be processed.

In the implementation of the class Counter shown below the inner class Position is used to record the row, column pairs that represent part of a move.

```
class Move
{
  class Position                      //Position on board
  {
    public int the_row;
    public int the_col;

    public Position( final int row, final int col )
    {
      the_row = row; the_col = col;
    }
  }
}
```

The physical storage used for the move components is a one-dimensional array of instances of the class Position. By using an array a maximum number of components for the move is set. This restriction can easily be removed by using one of the standard container classes described later in Chapters 21 and 22.

```
private final static int MAX_MOVES = 17;
private final static int MOVE_PART_FROM = 0;
private final static int MOVE_PART_TO   = 1;
private Position the_moves[] = new Position[MAX_MOVES];
private int       the_next_move = 0;      //Next move no
private int       the_move_no   = 0;      //Move no
private int       the_move_part = 0;      //Move part 0 from 1 too
private Counter   the_counter;            //Of player moving
```

The constructor records the colour of the player making the move.

```
public Move( Counter c )
{
   the_counter = c;
}
```

The method add adds a new move component. If there is insufficient space then the move component is discarded.

```
public void add( final int row, final int col )
{
   if ( the_next_move < MAX_MOVES )
     the_moves[the_next_move++] = new Position( row, col );
}
```

The method special_move return true if the move is a special non-counter moving move. A special move is a non-playing move such as the player passing on their turn as they are unable to move or resigning as they consider their position hopeless.

```
public boolean special_move()
{
   return the_next_move >= 1 &&
          (the_moves[0].the_row <0 || the_moves[0].the_col < 0);
}
```

Note: A special move is indicated by the first coordinate pair indicating the type of special move.

The method colour returns the colour of the counter used by the player making this move.

```
public char colour()
{
   return the_counter.colour();
}
```

The method `row`, `column`, `to_be_made`, `start`, `next`, `part_of_move`, `from` and `to` are the iterator methods that allow access to the individual components of the move. These are implemented as follows:

```
public int row()
{
   return the_moves[the_move_no+the_move_part].the_row-1;
}

public int column()
{
   return the_moves[the_move_no+the_move_part].the_col-1;
}

public boolean to_be_made()
{
   return the_move_no < the_next_move-1;
}

public void start()                    //Start at first move
{
   the_move_no   = 0;                  //1st Move
   the_move_part = MOVE_PART_FROM;     //Part from
}

public void next()                     //Next move
{
   the_move_no++;
}

public int part_of_move()              //Current part of move is
{
   return the_move_no;
}

public void from()                     //From part of move
{
   the_move_part = MOVE_PART_FROM;
}

public void to()                       //To part of move
{
   the_move_part = MOVE_PART_TO;
}
}
```

15.2.11 The implementation of the class `Cell`

As an instance of the class `Board` is copied and it contains cells then the class `Cell` must implement the interface `Cloneable`. The responsibilities of the class `Cell` are as follows:

Method	Responsibility
Cell() Cell(Counter c)	Constructs a new cell.
clone	Returns a copy of the cell.
clear	Removes the counter from the cell.
drop	Drops a counter into the cell.
colour	Returns the colour of the counter in the cell.
coloured_rank	Returns the coloured rank of the counter in the cell.
contents	Returns the counter in this cell.

In the implementation of the class Cell shown below, the constructors create an empty cell and a populated cell respectively.

```
class Cell implements Cloneable
{
  private Counter the_counter;                //The counter

  public Cell()                              //Empty cell
  {
    the_counter = null;
  }

  public Cell( final Counter c )             //With a counter
  {
    the_counter = c;
  }
```

The method clone returns a new instance of a cell containing a copy of the original cells contents.

```
public Object clone()                        //Clone Cell
{
  return new Cell( (Counter) the_counter.clone() );
}
```

The method clear removes any counter in the cell by setting its handle to null. The storage for the lost counter will eventually be reclaimed when the garbage collector runs.

```
public void clear()                          //Clear cell
{
  the_counter = null;
}
```

The method `drop` drops a new counter into a cell. Likewise, the storage for the lost counter will eventually be reclaimed when the garbage collector runs.

```
public void drop( final Counter c )              //Drop into cell
{
   the_counter = c;
}
```

The methods `colour, coloured_rank` return the colour of the counter in the cell and the method `contents` returns the actual counter in the cell respectively.

```
public char colour()                             //Colour of counter
{
   return the_counter != null
      ? the_counter.colour()
      :  Counter.empty();
}

public char coloured_rank()                       //Rank of counter
{
   return the_counter != null
      ? the_counter.coloured_rank()
      :  Counter.empty();
}

public Counter contents()                         //Actual counter
{
   return the_counter;
}
}
```

15.2.12 The implementation of the class `Basic_player`

The class `Basic_player` is responsible for recording which counter a player plays with. The methods of this class are:

Method	Responsibility
Basic_player(Counter c)	Constructs a new Basic_player who players with counter c.
counter_is	Returns the counter that a player plays with.

The implementation of this class is shown below:

```
class Basic_player
{
   private Counter the_players_counter;          //Plays with counter ...
```

```
public Basic_player( Counter plays_with ) //Player playing ?
{
  the_players_counter = plays_with;
}

public Counter counter_is()                    //Player plays with
{
  return the_players_counter;
}
}
```

15.2.13 The implementation of the class `Player`

The class Player is responsible for the input and output activity associated with a player. By factoring the input and output from the class Basic_player other implementations of the game can use a different form of input and output, for example a graphical version of the game could use the awt classes. The responsibilities of the class player are as follows:

Method	Responsibility
Player(Counter c)	Constructor a new player who plays with counter c.
get_move	Returns the move made by the player.
announce	Announces to all that result of the game.

The class C_Move_type is used as a container for the enumeration's of the special moves that may be made.

```
class C_Move_type
{
  public static final int DRAW   = -2;   //Draw game
  public static final int RESIGN = -1;   //Resign from game
}
```

The implementation of the class Player is shown below:

```
class Player extends Basic_player
{

  Player( Counter plays_with )
  {
    super( plays_with );
  }
```

The method `get_move` uses an instance of the class `TUI` (see Section 5.5.1) passed as a parameter to help read in a complete move that is to be made by a player. The private method `valid` performs some basic error checking on the inputted move coordinates.

```
public Move get_move( TUI vdu )
{
  Move move = new Move( counter_is() );              //Move for

  vdu.message( "Move for player " +
               counter_is().colour() + " is " );     //Ask
  int row, col;
  do
  {
    row = vdu.dialogue_int("From row    = " );        // start row
    col = vdu.dialogue_int("From column = " );        // start col
  } while ( ! (valid( row ) && valid( col )) );
  move.add( row, col );                               //Add from

  do
  {
    row = vdu.dialogue_int("Too  row    = " );        // to row
    if ( row != 0 )
    {
      col = vdu.dialogue_int("Too  column = " );      // to col
      if ( valid( row ) && valid( col ) )
        move.add( row, col );                         //Add to
      else
        vdu.dialogue("Invalid move");
    }
  } while ( row != 0 );                               //End move
  return move;
}
```

The private method `valid` performs rudimentary error checking on the inputted coordinates. Though not complete, it does determine if the move is on the board or is a special move.

```
private static boolean valid( final int cord )
{
  switch ( cord )
  {
    case 1: case 2: case 3: case 4:
    case 5: case 6: case 7: case 8:
    case C_Move_type.DRAW :
    case C_Move_type.RESIGN :
      return true;                                    //Valid move
    default :
      return false;                                   //Invalid
  }
}
```

The method `announce` announces to all the result of the game. The exception `InternalError` should never happen. However, during testing the exception did occur due to a programming error.

```java
public void announce( TUI vdu, final int what )
{
  String message = "";
  switch ( what )
  {
    case Board_state.WIN :
      message = "Player " + counter_is().colour() + " wins";
      vdu.message( message );
      break;
    case Board_state.DRAW :
      vdu.message( "The game is a draw" );
      break;
    case Board_state.RESIGN :
      message = "Player " + counter_is().colour() + " resigns";
      vdu.message( message );
      break;
    case Board_state.PLAYABLE :
      vdu.message( "The game is still playable" );
      break;
    default :
      throw new InternalError("Player.announce()");
  }
}
```

15.2.14 The implementation of the class `Basic_board`

The class `Basic_board` is responsible for maintaining the state of the playing board. As an instance of the class `Basic_board` is copied the class is required to implement the interface `Cloneable`. The responsibilities of the class are:

Method	Responsibility
Basic_board()	Constructs to create a new board.
clone	Returns a duplicate copy of the board.
colour	Returns the colour of a counter in a cell on the board.
contents	Returns the contents of a cell on the board.
evaluate	Returns the current state of the game.
move	Moves a counter from one cell to another cell on the board.
valid_move	Returns true if the suggested move is valid.

The class `Board_state` is used as a container for the enumeration's that represent the state of the game.

```
class Board_state
{
  public static final int DRAW = 0;
  public static final int WIN  = 1;
  public static final int PLAYABLE = 2;
  public static final int RESIGN = 3;
}
```

The implementation of the class `Basic_board` is as follows:

```
class Basic_board implements Cloneable
{
  public  static final int SIZE   = 8;         //Size of Board
  private Cell the_grid[][];                    //Basic_board played on

  private int the_white_counters = 12;
  private int the_black_counters = 12;
  private int the_game_is        = Board_state.PLAYABLE;

  private static final int EVEN[] = { 0,2,4,6 };
  private static final int ODD[]  = { 1,3,5,7 };
```

The constructor for the class first populates the board with empty cells. Then the population of the cells with counters is performed by the method `populate`.

```
public Basic_board()
{
  the_grid = new Cell[SIZE][SIZE];            //Create grid
  for ( int r=0; r<SIZE; r++ )                //Populate
  {
    for ( int c=0; c<SIZE; c++ )
    {
      the_grid[r][c] = new Cell();            // with cells
    }
  }
  populate();
}
```

The method `populate` populates the draughts board with the appropriate counters for the players.

```
private void populate()
{
  pop_row( 0, EVEN, C_Colour.WHITE );         //White back row
  pop_row( 1, ODD,  C_Colour.WHITE );         //     middle row
  pop_row( 2, EVEN, C_Colour.WHITE );         //     1st row
  pop_row( 5, ODD,  C_Colour.BLACK );         //Black 1st row
  pop_row( 6, EVEN, C_Colour.BLACK );         //     middle row
  pop_row( 7, ODD,  C_Colour.BLACK );         //     back row
}
```

```
    the_white_counters = 12;              //White has 12 counters
    the_black_counters = 12;              //Black has 12 counters

    the_game_is        = Board_state.PLAYABLE;//State of game
}
```

The private method `pop_row` is responsible for populates a row with a particular coloured counter. To this method is passed: the row number, an array of positions for counters that are to be dropped in the row and the colour of the counter that is to be dropped.

```
private void pop_row( final int row, final int piece_on[],
                      final char colour )
{                                          //Populate board

  for ( int i=0; i<piece_on.length; i++ )
  {
    the_grid[row][ piece_on[i] ].drop( new Counter( colour ) );
  }

}
```

The method clone is responsible for creating a duplicate copy of the board. The expression:

```
(Basic_board) getClass().newInstance();
```

is used to returns a new instance of the class `Basic_board`. The methods used are:

Method	Responsibility
getClass	Returns an instance of the class `Class` that represents the class Basic_board. This method is a member of the class `Object`, that is the superclass of `Basic_board`.
newInstance	Delivers a new instance of the class represented by an instance of the class `Class`. This method is a member of the class `Class`.

Note: A fuller description of the reflection mechanism is given in Chapter 26.
This rather perverse mechanism is required as the method is inherited in the class Board. When used as an inherited method of the class Board it will return an instance of a Board.

In the code to populate the new basic board the method `drop` is used to drop a clone copy of each counter into the respective cell positions of the copy of the basic board.

```java
public Object clone()
{
  Basic_board copy = null;                    //Keep compiler happy

  try
  {
    copy = (Basic_board) getClass().newInstance();
  }

  catch ( Throwable ex )
  {
    System.err.println("Internal error: Clone Basic_board");
    System.exit(-1);
  }

  for ( int r=0; r<copy.the_grid.length; r++ )
  {
    for ( int c=0; c<copy.the_grid[r].length; c++ )
    {
      if ( the_grid[r][c].colour() != Counter.empty() )
      {
        Counter co = (Counter) the_grid[r][c].contents().clone();
        copy.the_grid[r][c].drop( co );
      } else {
        copy.the_grid[r][c].clear();
      }
    }
  }

  return copy;
}
```

Note: *The object* `copy` *an instance of* `Basic_board` *is a fully initialized board with the full set of counters in their starting positions. This object* `copy` *is then modified to be the same as the original object.*

The method `colour` returns the colour of the counter in a particular cell on the board.

```java
public char colour( final int r, final int c )
{
  return the_grid[r][c].colour();
}
```

The method `valid_move` checks if the move is valid. The main body of the work is done by asking the counter that is to be moved if this is a valid move for it.

```
public boolean valid_move( Move move )
{
  move.start();
  if ( move.special_move() )                      //Resign / Draw
  {
    switch ( move.row() )
    {
      case C_Move_type.DRAW :
        the_game_is = Board_state.DRAW;           //Draw
        break;

      case C_Move_type.RESIGN :
        the_game_is = Board_state.RESIGN;         //Resign
        break;

      default :
        return false;                             //Invalid
    }
    return true;                                  //OK special move
  }

  Cell cell = the_grid[move.row()][move.column()];

  if ( cell.colour() != move.colour() )           //Not yours
    return false;

  return cell.contents().valid_move( this, move ); //Can it be done
}
```

The method `move` moves a counter from one cell to another cell. If in moving the cell it reaches the edge of the board then it is promoted to a king.

```
public void move( int f_r, int f_c, int to_r, int to_c )
{
  Counter to_move = the_grid[f_r][f_c].contents();

  the_grid[to_r][to_c].drop( to_move );
  the_grid[f_r][f_c].clear();

  if ( (to_move.colour() == C_Colour.BLACK && to_r == 0) ||
       (to_move.colour() == C_Colour.WHITE && to_r == 7) )
  {
    to_move.promote();
  }
}
```

The method `remove` removes a counter from the board and updates the running total of counters on the board.

```
public void remove( int r, int c )
{
  switch ( the_grid[r][c].colour() )
  {
    case C_Colour.WHITE : the_white_counters--;
    case C_Colour.BLACK : the_black_counters--;
  }
  the_grid[r][c].clear();
}
```

The method `evaluate` returns the currents state of the game. The instance variable `the_game_is` contains the current state of the game. This instance variable is set by the method `valid_move` to indicate a resignation or a recognition that the game is drawn.

```
public int evaluate()
{
  if ( the_white_counters == 0 || the_black_counters == 0 )
    return Board_state.WIN;
  return the_game_is;
}
}
```

The method `position` returns a string representing the counter in each cell on the board. In this string the following characters are used to represent the counter contained in an individual cell:

Character	Represents	Character	Represents
X	A black king	x	A black pawn
O	A white king	o	A white pawn
space	Empty cell		

```
public String position()
{
  String text  = "";
  for (int r=0; r<SIZE; r++ )                   //For each row
  {
    for (int c=0; c<SIZE; c++ )                 // For each column
    {
      text += the_grid[r][c].coloured_rank();   //Representation
    }
  }
  return text;
}
```

15.2.15 The implementation of the class `Board`

The class `Board` is responsible for the output activity associated with the board. By factoring the output from the class `Basic_board` other implementations of the game can use a different form of output, for example a graphical version could use instances of the `awt` classes. The responsibility of the class `Board` is as follows:

Method	Responsibility
display	Displays a representation of the board using an instance of the class `TUI`.

The implementation of the class `Board` retrieves the state of the board using the method `position`. From this is constructed a new string representing a character description of the board. The character representation of the board uses the characters `'|'` and `'-'` to help represent the individual cells on the board.

```java
class Board extends Basic_board
{
  public void display( TUI vdu )
  {
    String rep = position();
    int     pos = 0;
    String text  = "\n" + "     ";
    for (int c=1; c<=SIZE; c++)          //Board column number
      text += c + "    ";
    text += "\n" + "     ";
    for (int c=1; c<=SIZE; c++)          //Top of board
      text += "----";
    text += "-" + "\n";                  //

    for (int r=0; r<SIZE; r++ )          //For each row in Board
    {
      text +=  (r+1) + " | ";
      for (int c=0; c<SIZE; c++ )        // For each column
      {
        text += rep.charAt(pos++);       //  Extract cell contents
        text += " | ";
      }
      text += "\n" + "     ";            //End of row
      for (int c=1; c<=SIZE; c++)
      {
        text += "----";
      }
      text += "-\n";
    }
    text += "\n" + "\n";                 //

    vdu.message( text );                 //Write to TUI
  }
}
```

15.3 Putting it all together

Which when compiled and run would allow the following partial game to be played:

```
    1   2   3   4   5   6   7   8            1   2   3   4   5   6   7   8
   ---------------------------------        ---------------------------------
1  | o |   | o |   | o |   | o |   |     1  | o |   | o |   | o |   | o |   |
   ---------------------------------        ---------------------------------
2  |   | o |   | o |   | o |   | o |     2  |   | o |   | o |   | o |   | o |
   ---------------------------------        ---------------------------------
3  | o |   | o |   | o |   | o |   |     3  | o |   | o |   | o |   | o |   |
   ---------------------------------        ---------------------------------
4  |   |   |   |   |   |   |   |   |     4  |   |   |   |   |   |   |   |   |
   ---------------------------------        ---------------------------------
5  |   |   |   |   |   |   |   |   |     5  | x |   |   |   |   |   |   |   |
   ---------------------------------        ---------------------------------
6  |   | x |   | x |   | x |   | x |     6  |   |   |   | x |   | x |   | x |
   ---------------------------------        ---------------------------------
7  | x |   | x |   | x |   | x |   |     7  | x |   | x |   | x |   | x |   |
   ---------------------------------        ---------------------------------
8  |   | x |   | x |   | x |   | x |     8  |   | x |   | x |   | x |   | x |
   ---------------------------------        ---------------------------------
Move for player x is                    Move for player o is
From row      =  : 6                    From row      =  : 6
From column =    : 2                    From column =    : 2
Too   row     =  : 5                    Too   row     =  : 5
Too   column =   : 1                    Too   column =   : 1
Too   row     =  : 0                    Too   row     =  : 0
```

Note: Representation of the initial state of the board and after 'x' has moved their counter.

15.4 Self-assessment

- Why must the class `Basic_board` implement the interface `Cloneable`?

- What would have to be changed to play the game on other board sizes, for example a board 9 by 9?

- What changes would need to be done to the code of the method `clone` in the class `Basic_board` to make the operation more effective? In particular to remove making the object `copy` initially an instance of a fully populated class `Basic_Board`.

15.5   Exercises

Implement the following games:

- *Draughts_better*
  Modify the above game of draughts so that a check is made that a player always plays a capturing move when possible.

- *Reversi*
  Implement the game of reversi. In the game of reversi two players take it in turn to add counters to a board of 8-by-8 cells. Each player has a stack of counters, black one side and white the other. One player's counters are placed white side up, whilst the other player's are black side up. The object of the game is to capture all your opponent's counters. You do this by adding one of your counters to the board so that your opponent's counter(s) are flanked by two of your counters. When you do this, the counters you have captured are flipped over to become your counters. If you can't capture any of your opponent's counters during your turn, you must pass and let your opponent go.
  The game is won when you have captured all your opponent's counters. If neither player can add a counter to the board, then the player with the most counters wins. If the number of counters for each player is equal, then the game is a draw.
  The initial starting position is set so that the 4 centre squares in the 8-by-8 board of cells is as follows:

The first two moves in a game of reversi are shown below:

Blacks first move captures a white counter.	White responds by recapturing the counter.

● *Four counters*

Implement the game of four counters. This game is played on a vertical board of cells, six rows by seven columns. Each player takes it in turn to drop a coloured counter into one of the columns of cells on the board. The dropped counters pile up on top of each other to form a vertical column of counters in the cells. A player announces a win when they have four of their counters next to each other in the board either vertically, horizontally, or diagonally.

For example, in a game between two people using black and white counters the board might be as follows, after:

7 moves with white to play next

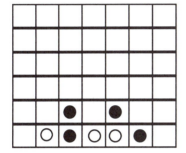

9 moves with white to play next

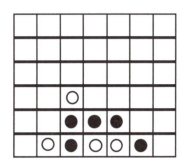

11 moves and a win for black

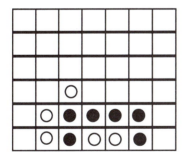

Commentary:

After move 7, white has made a tactical error by not dropping a counter into column 4.

After move 9, black is in an unassailable position and wins easily on move 11.

16. The model-view paradigm

This chapter looks at a technique for splitting the code that represents and manipulates the state of an object from the code that is responsible for displaying a representation of that object.

16.1　Introduction

A danger in writing any application or applet is that input and output of data values become entangled in the body of the code of the application or applet. When this happens the application or applet becomes less easy to maintain and will require major changes if the format of the input or output changes. By separating the input and output from the functionality of the application or applet allows a cleaner solution to be formulated.

The model-view paradigm in essence consists of:

- An observer: An object that has responsibility for displaying a representation of another object.

- The observed: An object that has one or more observers who will display the state of the object.

In the game of noughts and crosses, for example, the observed object would be the object representing the board. The observer would be an object that has responsibility for displaying a representation of the board onto the computer screen. There could be several implementations of the observer, depending on how the information is to be displayed. For example, the observer may be implemented to display the board as a:

- Textual representation: When a console application is written.

- As a graphical image: When an application with a graphical interface is developed.

This separation of responsibility is illustrated in Figure 16.1. In which the observed object `oxo` is interrogated by the object `oxo_observer` so that it can display a graphical representation of the noughts and crosses board on the computer screen.

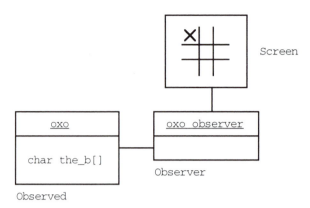

Figure 16.1 Oxo observer and observed oxo board.

The observed object oxo is unaware of how its representation will be displayed, whilst the observer object oxo_observer is unaware of how the observed object oxo represents and manipulates the board.

16.2   The interface `java.util.Observer`

An observer class for an observed object implements the Observer interface. This interface has a single method update and is defined as follows:

```
interface Observer extends object
{
  public abstract void update( Observable o, object arg );
}
```

An implementor of the Observer interface overrides the method update with a method that displays an appropriate representation of the observed object passed as the formal parameter o to the method. The method update is called when the state of the object being observed changes and user written code requests an update of the representation of the objects state.

16.3   The class `java.util.Observable`

A class that wishes instances of its objects to be observed needs to extend the class Observable. The class Observable contains the following methods:

Method	Responsibility
addObserver(ob)	Adds an observer ob.
clearChanged()	Sets no changes. The current view of the object is considered correct.
countObservers()	Returns the number of observers of this object.
deleteObserver(ob)	Removes an observer.
hasChanged()	Returns true if the object has changed.

notifyObservers()	If the object has changed, tells all observers to update their view of the object. Uses method hasChanged() to determine if the object has changed, calls observers and then calls clearChanged() to reset.
notifyObservers(arg)	As for notifyObservers() but argument passed.
setChanged()	Sets a flag to indicate that the object has changed. The method hasChanged() will now return true.

Note: *ob*   *Is of type* Observer
        arg   *Is of type* Object

16.4   A simple example of observer/observed

In the following demonstration application, an instance of the class Notice has the responsibility of holding a message that will be displayed by an instance of the class Notice_observer.

The responsibilities of the class Notice are:

Method	Responsibility
setThe_notice	Sets a notice.
getThe_notice	Returns the current notice.

The class is implemented as follows:

```java
import java.util.*;

class Notice extends Observable
{
  private String the_notice = "";

  public void setThe_notice( final String notice )
  {
    the_notice = notice;                    //Set new Notice
    setChanged();                           //State changed
  }

  public String getThe_notice()
  {
    return the_notice;
  }
}
```

Note: *The mutating method* setThe_notice *calls as a final act the method*
        setChanged *to indicate to the superclass that it has changed its state.*

The responsibilities of the class Notice_observer are:

Method	Responsibility
update	Writes a representation of the notice onto the console.

The class is implemented as follows:

```
class Notice_observer implements Observer
{

  public void update( Observable o, Object arg )
  {
    System.out.println( ((Notice) o).getThe_notice() );
  }

}
```

Note: The class `Notice_observer` *overrides the method* `update` *that is inherited from the class* `Observer`. *The method* `update` *is passed the object that is being observed. As this is described by the formal parameter as being of type* `Object` *it must be cast to a* `Notice` *before being sent the message* `getThe_notice`.

16.4.1 Putting it all together

The following code illustrates the use of the classes `Notice` and `Notice_observer`.

```
class Main
{
  public static void main( String args[] )
  {
    Notice          message     = new Notice();
    Notice_observer an_observer = new Notice_observer();


    message.addObserver( an_observer );             //Add observer
    message.setThe_notice( "Its a holiday" );       //Set Notice
    message.notifyObservers();                      //Ask for update
  }
}
```

In the above code the only reference to the observer is:

- When it is created:
  `Notice_observer an_observer = new Notice_observer();`

- When the object representing the observer is added to the observed object:
  `message.addObserver( an_observer );`

By using this technique, the code responsible for displaying a representation of an object can be totally isolated from the actual object that it is observing.

16.5 Noughts and crosses using the model-view paradigm

The noughts and crosses application seen in Section 10.7 can be recast to work using the model-view paradigm. In this recasting of the solution:

- An instance of the class Board is the observed object.

- An instance of the class Board_observer is responsible for displaying a representation of the board.

In the class Board the mutating methods now call setChanged to indicate that the state of the board has changed. The implementation of the class board is now:

```java
// import of java.awt.* java.awt.event.* java.util.*
class Board_state {
  public static final int WIN     = 0;
  public static final int DRAW    = 1;
  public static final int PLAYABLE = 2;
}

class Board extends Observable
{
  private char      the_sqrs[];          //Playing grid
  private int       the_moves;           //Moves made
  private boolean   the_end_of_game = false; //Game finished
  private static final int SIZE_TTT = 9;  //Squares on board

  public Board()
  {
    the_sqrs = new char[SIZE_TTT];
    for ( int i=0; i<SIZE_TTT; i++ )
    {
      the_sqrs[i] = ' ';
    }
    the_moves = 0;
  }

  public boolean check( final int pos )
  {
    return (pos >= 1 && pos <= SIZE_TTT) &&
           the_sqrs[pos-1] == ' '         &&
           ! the_end_of_game;
  }

  public void add( final int pos, final char piece )
  {
    the_sqrs[ pos-1 ] = piece;
    the_moves++;
    setChanged();
  }

  public char position( int i )
  {
    return the_sqrs[i-1];
  }
```

```
public int situation()
{
  int WL = 8;      //Number of win lines
  int LL = 3;      //Length of a line
  int win_lines[][]     = { {0,1,2}, {3,4,5}, {6,7,8},
                            {0,3,6}, {1,4,7}, {2,5,8},
                            {0,4,8}, {2,4,6} };
  for ( int i=0; i<WL; i++ )
  {
    char first_cell = the_sqrs[ win_lines[i][0] ];
    if ( first_cell != ' ' &&
         first_cell == the_sqrs[ win_lines[i][1] ] &&
         first_cell == the_sqrs[ win_lines[i][2] ] )
    {
      the_end_of_game = true;
      return Board_state.WIN;
    }
  }

  if ( the_moves >= SIZE_TTT )
  {
    the_end_of_game = true;
    return Board_state.DRAW;
  }

  return Board_state.PLAYABLE;
}
}
```

The class `Board_observer` is now responsible for writing the current state of the game board into an instance of the class `TextArea` that is displayed in the application's window. The responsibilities of this class are:

Method	Responsibility
Board_observer	Constructs a board observer that holds the instance of the class TextArea used for output.
update	Displays a representation of the board onto the remembered instance of TextArea.

The implementation of the class `Board_observer` is as follows:

```
class Board_observer implements Observer
{
  private TextArea    the_output;            //Output object

  public Board_observer( TextArea output )
  {
    the_output = output;
  }
```

```
public void update( Observable o, Object arg )
{
  Board oxo = (Board) o;
  the_output.setText( "" );                    //Clear output area
  the_output.append( "\n" );
  display_line( the_output, oxo, 1 );
  the_output.append( "---------\n" );
  display_line( the_output, oxo, 4 );
  the_output.append( "---------\n" );
  display_line( the_output, oxo, 7 );
  the_output.append( "\n" );
}

private void display_line( TextArea the_output, final Board brd,
                         final int pos )
{
  the_output.append( brd.position( pos   )  + " | " +
                     brd.position( pos+1 )  + " | " +
                     brd.position( pos+2 )  + "\n" );
}
}
```

Note: The private method `display_line` *used to display a single line of the noughts and crosses board.*

The class `application` that sets up the GUI (Graphical User Interface) now has the additional responsibility of creating an instance of the class `Board_observer` and notifying the object `the_oxo`, an instance of the class `Board`, that this is its observer. The code for the application is now:

```
class Application extends Frame
{
  private static final int H = 400;       // Height of window
  private static final int W = 300;       // Width  of window

  private TextField       the_input;      //Visual Text Field (Input)
  private TextArea        the_output;     //Visual Text Area  (Output)
  private Transaction     the_cb   = new Transaction();
  private Board           the_oxo  = new Board();
  private Game            the_game = new Game( the_oxo );
  private Board_observer the_observer;

  public Application()
  {
    setLayout(null);                      //Set layout manager (none)
    setSize( W, H );                      //Size of Window

    Font font = new Font("Monospaced",Font.PLAIN,12);

    the_input  = new TextField();         //Input area
    the_input.setBounds(10,H-50,W-20,40); //             Size
    the_input.setFont( font );            //             Font
    add( the_input );                     //Add to canvas
```

```
    Transaction cb  = new Transaction();
    the_input.addActionListener( cb );        //Add listener

    the_output = new TextArea( 10,40 );       //Output area
    the_output.setBounds(10,30,W-20,H-100);   //              Size
    the_output.setFont( font );               //              Font
    add( the_output );                        //Add to canvas
    the_observer = new Board_observer( the_output );
    the_oxo.addObserver( the_observer );
    the_oxo.notifyObservers();                //Initial display
  }

  class Transaction implements ActionListener
  {
    public void actionPerformed( ActionEvent e )
    {
      String user_input = the_input.getText();
      the_game.action( the_output, user_input );
    }
  }
}
```

The logic of the game is contained in the class `Game`. When a mutating method is performed on the object `the_oxo`, an instance of the class `Board`, and no more changes will be made to the board for some time the message `notifyObservers` is sent to the board so that its state will be re-displayed by the observer.

```
class Game
{
  private char   the_player = 'X';
  private int    the_game_is= Board_state.PLAYABLE;
  private Board the_oxo;

  public Game( Board oxo )
  {
    the_oxo = oxo;                            //Board played on
  }

  public void action( TextArea output, String user_input )
  {
    int move = 0;

    try
    {
      move = (new Integer( user_input )).intValue();
    }
    catch ( NumberFormatException err )
    {
      output.append( err  + "\n" );           //Java error message
    }
```

```
   String who = "Player " + the_player;
   if ( the_oxo.check( move ) )              // Valid
   {
     the_oxo.add( move, the_player );        //Add to board
     the_oxo.notifyObservers();              //Board changed

     the_game_is = the_oxo.situation();      //the_game is
     switch ( the_game_is )
     {
       case Board_state.WIN  :               // Won
         output.append(who + " wins\n");
         return;
       case Board_state.DRAW :               // Drawn
         output.append("It's a draw\n");
         return;
       case Board_state.PLAYABLE :
         switch ( the_player )               // Playable
         {
           case 'X' : the_player='O'; break;//  'X' -> 'O'
           case 'O' : the_player='X'; break;//  'O' -> 'X'
         }
         break;
     }
   } else {
     output.append( "\n" );
     output.append( "Invalid move for " + who + "\n");
   }
   display_who_plays( output );
 }

 public void display_who_plays( TextArea the_output )
 {
   the_output.append( "\n" );
   the_output.append( "Next move for player " + the_player + "\n");
 }
}
```

16.5.1 Putting it altogether

The application is run by creating an instance of the class Application and sending it the message show.

```
class Play
{
  public static void main( String args[] )
  {
    (new Application()).show();
  }
}
```

When compiled and run the application would display a screen similar to the one shown below:

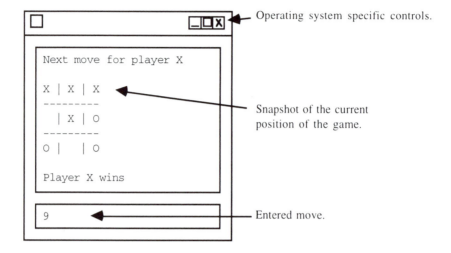

Operating system specific controls.

Snapshot of the current position of the game.

Entered move.

16.6   Self-assessment

● What are the advantages of using the model-view paradigm?

● Are there any disadvantages of using the model-view paradigm?

● Would it have been better to use the model-view paradigm in implementing the game of draughts shown in the previous chapter?

16.7   Exercises

Implement the following games using the model-view paradigm:

● *Battleships*
The game of battleships is played on a two-dimensional board. The objective of the game is to destroy all the opponent's battleships in the minimum number of moves. If the player correctly identifies a square which contains a battleship, then the battleship is destroyed and removed from the board. If the player guesses a square that is next to a battleship then the board identifies a near miss.

Hint: *To populate the board with battleships you may wish to use the static method* random() *in the class* java.lang.Math *that delivers a pseudo random number in the range 0.0 to 1.0.*

● *Better draughts*
Re-implement the game of draughts using the model-view paradigm this time to remove the input and output operations from the classes Player and Board.

17. Packages

This chapter looks at the package statement. In essence a package allows an implementor of classes to place the code for the compiled classes into a hierarchical name space. This allows other developers the ability to access the compiled code for the classes without fear of any name clashes, hence helping prevent the pollution of the global name space.

17.1   Introduction

So far the compiled code for the classes developed has been placed in the same location, the current directory. In essence all classes have been developed in an anonymous package. This will soon causes problems if you wish to share your compiled classes with other developers. A single central directory for the compiled code for all developed classes would soon create problems due to the inevitable name clashes.

In Java the `import` statement can refer to an individual class in a hierarchy as shown below:

```
import java.lang.Float;
```

The above `import` statement refers to the class `Float` that is in the package `lang` which itself in the package `java`. By placing the compiled code of a class in a particular name space, the problem of clashing names is easily avoided. However, this does pre-suppose a central allocation of the top level packages used in the name space. Once the top level packages are established, responsibility for managing names contained within the top level packages is devolved to the package owner. This process is repeated for each package level.

To include all the classes in the package `java.lang` the following import statement is used:

```
import java.lang.*;
```

*Note: The * indicates all classes and interfaces in the package `lang`.*

The Java system partitions its compiled classes into a hierarchy, part of which is illustrated in Figure 17.1.

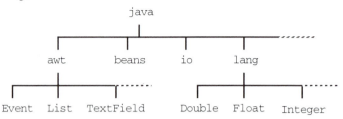

Figure 17.1 Illustration of part of the hierarchy for the system classes in Java.

In the `lang` part of the hierarchy is the class `Double`, hence to import this class the statement **import** `java.lang.Double` is used. The last part of the `import` statement names the class that is to be imported.

In essence this mechanism is akin to the internet way of resolving the problem about clashes of names. My mail address is `mas@brighton.ac.uk` that is read as in the domain `uk` (United Kingdom) then in the domain `ac` (Academic) there in the domain `brighton` (University of Brighton) there is a user named `mas`.

17.1.1 Access to items in the same package

If an item in a class is declared without an access modifier, then it is visible to all other classes in the same package. For example, in the following demonstration class shown below:

```
class Example
{
   final static int SIZE = 100;    // Maximum size of storage area
}
```

the integer field `SIZE` is visible to all other classes in the same package.

17.2 The package

To incorporate the class `Account` seen previously in Section 5.2.5 into the package `bank` a `package` statement is added at the top of the file. For example, the class `Account` is now defined as follows:

```
package bank;

public class Account
{
   // Implementation as before
   // See Section 5.2.5
}
```

A class that is to be made visible in a package must be marked as public, and a public class must be in a file which has the same name as the class with an extension of .java. For example, the above class Account must be in a file named Account.java. A direct consequence of this is that there can be only one public class in each individual file.

17.2.1 The class `Interest_Account`

The class Interest_Account as seen in Section 12.5 can also be placed in the package hierarchy. Other classes can be contained in the file containing the class to be placed in a package, but as these classes cannot be public they will not be visible outside of the package. For example, the class Interest_Account that is in the package bank.interest is defined as follows:

```
package bank.interest;

import bank.Account;

class IA_Const
{
  public static final double RATE = 0.00026116;      //Default
}

public class Interest_Account extends Account
{
  // Implementation as before
  // See Section 12.5
}
```

In this example the class IA_Const is used purely to define the initial value for the interest rate. However, the class IA_Const will not be visible to a programmer who imports the class Interest_Account.

Note: The Java statement **import** bank.interest.IA_Const; *cannot be used as the class* IO_Const *is not a public class.*

17.2.2 The class `Special_Interest_Account`

Likewise, the class Special_Interest_Account seen in Section 12.6 can be developed as part of the package hierarchy as follows:

```
package bank.interest;

import bank.interest.Interest_Account;

class SIA_Const
{
  public static final double R1 = 0.00026116;     //10%
  public static final double R2 = 0.00028596;     //11%
}
```

```
public class Special_Interest_Account extends Interest_Account
{
  // Implementation as before
  // See Section 12.6
}
```

Note: The use of the import statement to import the superclass Interest_Account.

17.2.3 Classes in the hierarchy

The hierarchy created is illustrated below in Figure 17.2 below:

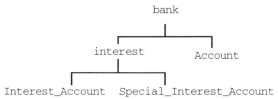

Figure 17.2 Classes in the bank hierarchy.

17.3 Using the classes

The following example application illustrates the use of classes: Interest_Account and Special_Interest_Account in the bank hierarchy:

```
import bank.interest.Interest_Account;
import bank.interest.Special_Interest_Account;

class Main
{
  public static void main( String args[] )
  {
    Special_Interest_Account mike    = new Special_Interest_Account();
    Interest_Account         corinna = new Interest_Account();
    DecimalFormat            nf      = new DecimalFormat( "####0.00" );

    mike.   deposit( 2000.00 );
    corinna.deposit( 2000.00 );

    mike.end_of_day();        corinna.end_of_day();
    mike.interest_credit();   corinna.interest_credit();

    System.out.println("Mike's    Balance = " +
                    nf.format( mike.account_balance() ) );
    System.out.println("Corinna's Balance = " +
                    nf.format( corinna.account_balance() ) );
  }
}
```

17.3.1 Putting it all together

Which when compiled and run, produces the following results:

```
Mike's    Balance = 2000.57
Corinna's Balance = 2000.52
```

17.4 Implementation of the name space

The name space is implemented as a hierarchy of directories, each directory contains all the .class files for that named part of the package hierarchy. For example, the package hierarchy bank contains the following files:

Directory	Files in each directory
bank	Account.class
bank/special	Interest_Acount.class, Special_Interest_Acount.class

Note: bank/special is the directory special in the directory bank.

17.4.1 CLASSPATH

The CLASSPATH environment variable defines the base directory in which to look for the top level directory used in the import statement. As there may be several locations where the different hierarchies are held the CLASSPATH environment variable may specify several different root directories. For example, on a DOS system where the bank directory is in the directory c:\mas and other useful classes are in the directory d:\other then the following DOS command will set c:\mas and d:\other in the CLASSPATH environment variable.

```
set CLASSPATH=c:\mas;d:\other
```

Note: The search order for packages and classes is the order in which directories appear in the CLASSPATH environment variable.

17.5   Self-assessment

- What are the advantages/disadvantages of using the package statement?

- What restrictions are imposed when using the package statement?

17.6   Exercises

- Re-write the noughts and crosses application using the package statement to place each class in a different file. In particular make it possible for the individual classes to be accessed using:

```
import oxo.*;
```

18. Polymorphism

This chapter looks at polymorphism. Using polymorphism when a message is sent to an object the binding of the message to the method is evaluated at run-time rather than compile-time. The implication of this is that when a message is sent to an object whose type is not know until run-time then the method appropriate for the object will be called. For example, the message draw sent to a box object in a collection of objects that represent different shapes will cause a box to be drawn. Whilst the same message sent to a circle object would cause a circle to be draw.

18.1   Introduction

When a message is sent to an object, the type of the object that the message is sent to has so far been known at compile-time. In Java it is possible to send a message to an object whose type is not know until run-time. For example, this can happen, when dealing with a collection of different objects. Figure 18.1 illustrates a collection of objects representing cars and houses.

Figure 18.1 A collection of car and house objects.

The collection of objects contains two different types of object, these are instances of the classes House and Car. When a message is sent to an arbitrary object in the collect the actual method that will be called cannot be resolved until run-time as the type of the object selected and hence the method that it contains will not be know at compile-time.

When the binding of the message to the method is resolved at run-time this is referred to as polymorphism or run-time dispatch. The only restriction is that the message sent must be able to be bound to a method at run-time.

This is easily achieved by insisting that the collection is declared as containing:

- Instances of a specific class.
  The collection can contain objects that belong to the specific class or are instances of subclasses of the specific class. Naturally the subclasses of the specific class may override existing methods with a new implementation.

- Instances of objects that implement a specific interface.

Hence, there must be a method that can be called, when a message that corresponds to a method in either the specific class or the specific interface of which the collection is declared as being composed of is sent to an arbitrary object in the collection.

18.2 Example of polymorphism

The demonstration class `Built` contains a single method `identity` that delivers a generic description of the object.

```
class Built
{
  public String identity()
  {
    return "Built object";
  }
}
```

From this class `Built` are subclassed two other classes `House` and `Car` that override the method `identity` with a new method that delivers a description about the specific object. The two classes `House` and `Car` are defined as follows:

The class **Car**	The class **House**
``class Car extends Built
{
  private static int the_next= 1;
  private int the_instance   = 0;

  public Car()
  {
    the_instance = the_next++;
  }

  public String identity()
  {
    return "car #" + the_instance;
  }
}``` | ```class House extends Built
{
  private static int the_next= 1;
  private int the_instance   = 0;

  public House()
  {
    the_instance = the_next++;
  }

  public String identity()
  {
    return "house #"+the_instance;
  }
}``` |

18.2.1 A collection of items that can be built

The following code fragment assigns instances of the classes `Car` and `House` to an array `item`. The array `item` is declared as an array of instances of the class `Built`. Though Java has strict type checking, an instance of a subclass may be assigned to an instance of its superclass. This slight breach to the strict type checking of Java allows polymorphism to take place. For example, the following code when combined with other appropriate code and executed:

```
    Built item[] = { new Car(), new House(), new Car() };

    for ( int i=0; i<item.length; i++ )
    {
      System.out.println(" Item[" + i + "] is " + item[i].identity() );
    }
```

will produce the following results:

```
Item[0] is Car #1
Item[1] is House #1
Item[2] is Car #2
```

What happens is that when the message `identity` is sent to an arbitrary object in the collection `item` the message is bound at run-time to the appropriate method. For example, when the first item in the collection is selected (`i` contains 0):

```
  item[i].identity()
```

then the message `identity` is bound at run-time to the method `identity` in the class `Car`. Whilst when the second item in the collection is selected (`i` contains 1):

```
  item[i].identity()
```

then the message `identity` is bound at run-time to the method `identity` in the class `House`.

18.2.2   Using an interface

The class `Built` could have been declared as an interface as follows:

```
interface Built
{
  public String identity();
}
```

and the classes `Car` and `Room` defined as implementing this interface `Built` as follows:

The class **Car**	The class **House**
```class Car implements Built { // Code as before }```	```class House implements Built { // Code as before }```

When combined with the fragment of code illustrated in Section 18.2.1 above the effect of running the code is the same.

18.3   An application to maintain details about a building

An application to maintain details about the different type of accommodation in a building is implemented by holding a collection of objects that represent the different types of accommodation in the building. Initially the application will only maintain details about two types of accommodation, a room and an office.

The application is required to give details about the individual areas in the building in response to a user's selection of an area number. For example, the user might ask about details of area 422 in the building.

Details stored about a room include a description of its location. Whilst for an office, the details stored are all those details for a room, plus the number of people who will occupy the room.

The responsibilities of a Room are as follows:

Method	Responsibility
Room	Creates an instance of a room.
describe	Delivers a string containing a description of the room.
room_number	Delivers the room's number.

The implementation of the class Room is as follows:

```
class Room
{
  private int     the_room_number;    //Number of room
  private String the_use;             //Use made of the room

  public Room( int number, String use )
  {
    the_room_number = number;
    the_use         = use;
  }
  public int room_number()
  {
    return the_room_number;
  }
  public String describe()
  {
    return the_use;
  }
}
```

The responsibilities of a Office are all those of a Room plus the following additional responsibilities.

Method	Responsibility
Office	Creates an instance of an Office.
describe	Returns a String describing an office.

The implementation of the class Office is as follows:

```java
class Office extends Room
{
  private int the_occupiers = 0;        //People in room

  public Office( final int number, final String use,
                 final int occupiers )
  {
    super( number, use );                //call constructor in Room
    the_occupiers = occupiers;
  }

  public String describe()
  {
    return use() + " occupied by " +
      String.valueOf( the_occupiers )  + " people ";
  }

}
```

18.4   Heterogeneous collections of objects

The real benefits of polymorphism accrue when a heterogeneous collection of related items is created. For example, when dealing with a building the individual areas in the building are represented by a heterogeneous collection of rooms and offices. An example of such a collection is illustrated in Figure 18.2.

Figure 18.2 Heterogeneous collection of Rooms and Offices.

18.5   The class **Building**

A class Building, which is used as a container to store and retrieve details about the different types of accommodation in a building, has the following responsibilities:

Method	Responsibility
add	Adds a description of a 'room'.
describe	Returns a description of a specific 'room'.

As adding a new type of accommodation to the building may fail due to lack of space an exception class BuildingException is defined so that an appropriate exception can be throw if this eventuality occurs. The class BuildingException is defined as follows:

```
class BuildingException extends Throwable
{
  BuildingException( String s )
  {
    super( s );
  }
}
```

The implementation of the class `Building` is as follows:

```
class Building
{
  int the_max_size;                    //Number of rooms
```

The heterogeneous collection is defined as an array of instances of the class `Room`. However, to this array may be assigned an instance of any class that is a subclass of Room.

```
Room the_rooms[];                      //Heterogeneous collection
int the_next_free = 0;                 //Next free slot
```

The constructor allocates `size` units of storage for the different types of accommodation.

```
public Building( int size )
{
  the_max_size = size;                 //Set maximum rooms
  the_rooms = new Room[the_max_size];
}
```

The method `describe` in the class `Building` uses a linear search to find the selected area in the collection, and when found sends the message `describe` to the selected object in the array `the_rooms`.

The resultant method `describe` that is called will return a string that describes the type of accommodation. However, the actual method `describe` that is called will of course depend on the type of the accommodation object selected. The code for the method `describe` is as follows:

```
public String describe( final int room )
{
  for ( int i=0; i<the_next_free; i++ )
  {
    if ( the_rooms[i].room_number() == room )
      return the_rooms[i].describe();
  }
  return "Room not known";
}
```

The method `add` adds a new type of accommodation to the building. Remember, that to this collection can be assigned any instance of the class `Room` or instance of a class that is inherited from the class `Room`.

A formal parameter can also be passed an object that is a subclass of its type. Hence to the method `add` can be passed any objects that have as their superclass `Room`. The object passed to the formal parameter `a_room` is then assigned to the next free element of the collection.

```
public void add( Room a_room ) throws BuildingException
{
  if ( the_next_free < the_max_size )
  {
    the_rooms[ the_next_free++ ] = a_room; return;
  }
  throw new BuildingException("Full");
}
}
```

18.5.1   Putting it all together

The classes `Room`, `Office` and `Building` are used to build an application to allow visitors to a building to find out details about individual rooms. To simplify the input and output interaction between the end user and the application an instance of the class `TUI` (see Section 5.5.1) is used to perform these transactions. The demonstration application is as follows:

```
class Main
{
  public static void main( String args[] )
  {
    TUI screen = new TUI();                          //I/O
    Building watts = new Building(10);
    try
    {
      watts.add( new Room(420,"Reception") );
      watts.add( new Office(414,"QA",4) );
    }
    catch ( BuildingException e )
    {
      System.err.println("Error building " + e.getMessage() );
    }
    loop: while ( true )
    {
      int room = screen.dialogue_int( "Enter room number: ");
      if ( room < 0 ) break loop;
      else
      {
        screen.message("Room " + room + " : " + watts.describe(room) );
      }
    }
  }
}
```

18.5.2   Putting all together

When the above application is compiled and run the results produced are as follows:

```
Enter room number: 420
Room 420 : Reception
Enter room number: 414
Room 414 : QA occupied by 4 people
Enter room number:
```

18.6   Advantages and disadvantages of polymorphism

Advantages

Additions and modifications to an application or applet are simplified. For example, in the above application, the introduction of a new type of accommodation would simply require the creation of a new subclass. The code which deals with the processing requests for details about a room would not change.

This mean that changes to the application are encapsulated in any new class which is implemented.

Disadvantages

Just by looking at the source code of the application or applet it is not possible to determine what code is executed. Not all applications or applets are amenable to the use of a polymorphic approach to their construction.

18.7   Downcasting

Downcasting is the conversion of an instance of a superclass to an instance of a subclass class. This conversion is normally impossible as extra information needs to be added to the instance of the superclass object to allow it to be turned into an instance of a subclass object. However, it is possible to assign a subclass object to an instance of a superclass. This will usually occur when for example using a heterogeneous collection. When this assignment takes place no information is lost, so although the compiler knows the object as an instance of the superclass in reality it is still an instance of the subclass.

18.7.1   The operator `instanceof`

The operator `instanceof` will return true for the expression:

```
object instanceof A_Class
```

if `object` is an instance of the class A_Class or if `object` is an instance of any of A_Class's superclasses. Hence the expression below will always return true.

```
an_arbitrary_object instanceof Object
```

18.7.2   Example of downcasting

The conversion from a superclass to a subclass type must, of course be possible. For example, the following code fragment copies the instances of the class `Office` in the heterogeneous array `accommodation` into the array `offices`. In implementing this code the operator `instanceof` is used to determine the real type of an object.

```
int MAX = 4;
Room accommodation[] = new Room[ MAX ];
accommodation[0] = new Room(420,"Reception");
accommodation[1] = new Office(414,"QA",4);
accommodation[2] = new Office(416,"Marketing",7);
accommodation[3] = new Room(430,"Meeting room");

Office offices[] = new Office[ MAX ];
int no_offices = 0;
for ( int i=0; i<accommodation.length; i++ )
{
  if ( accommodation[i] instanceof Office )
  {
     offices[no_offices++] = (Office) accommodation[i];
  }
}
for ( int i=0; i<no_offices; i++ )
{
  System.out.println( "Office " + offices[i].room_number() +
                      " contains " + offices[i].occupiers() +
                      " people" );
}
```

*Note: The operator **instanceof** returns true if the object is an instance of the specified class.*
That the operation to cast the object extracted from the array `accommodation` *to an instance of* `Office` *would fail with the exception* `ClassCastException` *if the object extracted is not of type* `Office` *or a subclass of* `Office`.

The above code when augmented with suitable wrapper code and declarations and compiled and run will produce the following output:

```
Office 414 contains 4 people
Office 416 contains 7 people
```

18.8   Maintenance and polymorphism

To modify the application in Section 18.3 so that details about executive offices in the building are also displayed would involve the following changes:

- The creation of a new subclass `Executive_office`.

- Adding extra code to populate the building with instances of an `Executive_office`.

No other components of the application would need to be changed. In carrying out these modifications, the following points are evident:

- Changes are localized to specific parts of the application.

- The modifier of the application does not have to understand all the details of the application to carry out maintenance.

- Maintenance will be easier.

Thus, when an application or applet is constructed carefully using polymorphism there can be considerable cost saving when the program is maintained/updated.

18.9   Self-assessment

- What is the difference between static and dynamic binding?

- Can you use the operator `instanceof` to tell which specific class an object is an instance of?

- What is a heterogeneous collection of objects? Describe one way a heterogeneous collections of objects is created and used in Java?

- How does the use of polymorphism help in simplifying application or applet maintenance?

- Can you convert a subclass to a superclass? Can you convert a superclass to a base class? Are these conversions safe? Explain your answer?

18.10   Exercises

Construct the following:

- The class `Executive_office` which will extend a normal office by including biographical details about the occupants. For example, "Ms C Lord, Programming manager".

- A new information application for a building which will include details about rooms, offices and executive offices. You should try and re-use as much code as possible.

- An application to record transactions made on different types of bank account. For example, the application should be able to deal with at least the following types of account:

  - A deposit account on which interest is paid.

  - An account on which no interest is paid and the user is not allowed to be overdrawn.

19. File I/O

This chapter illustrates the file handling classes. By using these classes data can be read from and written to local files, read from strings and even read from files on remote machines.

19.1　Reading and writing to a character file

An instance of the class `java.io.FileOutputStream` is a stream object that is responsible for writing data to a file.

This stream is then wrapped by an instance of the class `java.io.PrintWriter` to deliver an object that is used to facilitate the writing of character representations of binary data values to a file. As the data is written using a character representation it may be read by a human reader and manipulated with a word processor or text editor. For example, the following application writes 5 integer numbers to the file `file.dat`.

```java
import java.io.*;

class Main
{
  public static void main( String args[] )
  {
    try
    {
      final int NUMBER = 5;
      FileOutputStream ostream = new FileOutputStream("file.dat");
      PrintWriter pw          = new PrintWriter( ostream );

      pw.println( NUMBER );
      for ( int i=1; i<=NUMBER; i++ )
      {
        pw.print( " " ); pw.print( i );
      }
      pw.flush();
      ostream.close();
    }
    catch ( IOException e )
    {
      System.out.println("IOException : " + e.getMessage() );
    }
  }
}
```

The major methods in the class `java.io.PrintWriter` are:

Method	Responsibility
`checkError()`	Flushes the stream and return true if an error has occurred.
`close()`	Closes the stream.
`flush()`	Flushes all output to the output source. Output is buffered internally for efficiency reasons, hence, the most recent output may not have been written.
`print( t )`	Prints an instance of an: `boolean, char, char[], int, long, float, double, String`.
`println( t )`	Prints an instance of an: `boolean, char, char[], int, long, float, double, String` then print a new line.
`write( t )`	Writes an instance of an: `char[], char, string` or part of a `char[], string`.

Note: There are no exceptions generated by the methods of the class. To determine if an error has occurred the methods `checkError` should be used.

The major methods in the class `java.io.FileOutputStream` are:

Method	Responsibility
`FileOutputStream(s)`	Constructs a stream to write to the file in string s. A second parameter of `true` will append data to a file.
`close()`	Closes the stream.
`write( bytes )`	Writes the array of `bytes` to the stream.
`write( bytes, n )`	Writes the first n bytes of the array of `bytes`.

Note: The exception `IOException` or its subclasses will be thrown by members of this class.

19.1.1   Exception classes

The class `java.io.IOException` is a superclass of the following major exceptions:

```
FileNotFoundException    EOFException           IOInterruptedException
MalformedURLException    ObjectStreamException  SocketException
```

by catching the exception `IOException` any of the above IO exceptions will also be caught.

19.1.2   Appending to a character file

To append output to an existing file, the following constructor of the class `FileOutputStream` is used to create an output stream object:

```
FileOutputStream( string file_name, boolean append );
```

For example, to append text to the file `file.dat` created in the previous example, the following code would be used to create an instance of the class `PrintWriter`.

```
FileOutputStream ostream = new FileOutputStream("file.dat", true);
PrintWriter pw          = new PrintWriter( ostream );
```

19.1.3   Reading from a character file

The following application reads character data from the file `file.dat`. An instance of the class `FileInputStream` is wrapped by an instance of `BufferedInputStream` to provide an input stream of characters. The method `read` reads the next character from the stream. The end of file on the stream is indicated by the method `read` returning the value –1. Hence, the character read returned as an integer value so that -1 can be distinguished from a validly read character. The following application reads and prints the contents of the file `file.dat`.

```java
import java.io.*;

class Main
{
  public static void main( String args[] )
  {
    try
    {
      FileInputStream istream = new FileInputStream("file.dat");
      BufferedInputStream bis = new BufferedInputStream( istream );

      int c = bis.read();
      while ( c != -1 )
      {
        System.out.print( (char) c );
        c = bis.read();
      }

      bis.close();
      System.out.println();
    }
    catch ( IOException e )
    {
      System.out.println("IOException : " + e.getMessage() );
    }
  }
}
```

Note: The exception `EOFException` *is generated if an attempt is made to read past the end of file.*

The major methods in the class `java.io.BufferedInputStream` are:

Method	Responsibility
`close()`	Closes the stream.
`read()`	Reads the next byte of data from the input stream. The byte will be in the range 0—255, if no more data then – 1 is available. If no data is available the method will block till data becomes available.
`skip( n )`	Skips over n bytes of data.
`available()`	Returns the number of bytes that can be read without blocking.

The major methods in the class `java.io.FileInputStream` are:

Method	Responsibility
`FileInputStream(s)`	Constructs a stream to read from the file in string s.
`close()`	Closes the stream.

19.1.4   Putting it all together

When both applications are compiled and run the output from the second application is as follows:

```
1 2 3 4 5
```

19.2   Reading and writing to the standard streams

The class `java.io.FileDescriptor` has the following visible fields:

Field	Represents
`out`	An object representing the standard output stream. Writing to this will cause information to be written to the Java console.
`in`	An object representing the standard input stream.
`err`	An object representing the standard error stream. Writing to this will cause information to be usually written to the Java console.

To write data to the standard output stream for console output, the stream `FileDescriptor.out` is wrapped by an instance of the class `FileOutputStream`. This process is illustrated in the following demonstration application.

```
import java.io.*;

class Main
{
  public static void main( String args[] )
  {
    FileOutputStream fos = new FileOutputStream( FileDescriptor.out );
    PrintWriter      pw  = new PrintWriter( fos );

    pw.print("Writing string : "); pw.println( "text" );
    pw.print("Writing int    : "); pw.println( 42 );
    pw.print("Writing float  : "); pw.println( 3.14f );
    pw.flush();                                        //Must have
  }
}
```

Note: The use of the method `flush` *to force any outstanding output to the console.*

19.2.1   Putting it all together

When the above application is compiled and run the output produced is as follows:

```
Writing string : text
Writing int    : 42
Writing float  : 3.14
```

19.2.2   Auto flush of output

After every `println` or the writing of the character `'\n'` the output is automatically flushed to the output source if the output stream is created as follows:

```
FileOutputStream fos = new FileOutputStream( FileDescriptor.out );
PrintWriter      pw  = new PrintWriter( fos, true );
```

Note: The second parameter `true` *to the* `PrintWriter` *constructor.*

19.3   Reading and writing to a binary file

An instance of the class `FileOutputStream` is a stream object that is responsible for writing data to a file.

This stream is then wrapped by an instance of the class `DataOutputStream` to deliver an object that is used to facilitate the writing of binary data values to a file. It is important to remember that as the stream is binary the resultant file cannot be read by a human reader or edited with a normal word processor or text editor. For example, the following application writes 5 integer numbers in binary to the file `file.dat`.

```java
import java.io.*;

class Main
{
  public static void main( String args[] )
  {
    try
    {
      final int NUMBER = 5;
      FileOutputStream ostream = new FileOutputStream("file.dat");
      DataOutputStream dos      = new DataOutputStream( ostream );

      dos.writeInt( NUMBER );
      for ( int i=1; i<=NUMBER; i++ )
      {
        dos.writeInt( i );
      }
      dos.flush();
      ostream.close();
    }
    catch ( IOException e )
    {
      System.out.println("IOException : " + e.getMessage() );
    }
  }
}
```

To append data to a file the stream is created as follows:

```java
FileOutputStream ostream = new FileOutputStream("file.dat", true);
DataOutputStream dos      = new DataOutputStream( ostream );
```

*Note: The second parameter with value `true` to the `FileOutputStream`
constructor.*

The major methods in the class `java.io.DataOutputStream` are:

Method	Responsibility
`DataOutputStream(s)`	Constructs a stream.
`writeInt( i )`	Writes the `int` i as a binary pattern. Also in the same style: `writeByte`, `writeBytes`, `writeChar`, `writeDouble`, `writeFloat`, `writeLong` and `writeUTF`.
`flush()`	Flushes the stream.

19.3.1   Reading from a binary file

The following application reads the binary data that was written to the file `file.dat` illustrated in the previous example.

```java
import java.io.*;

class Main
{
  public static void main( String args[] )
  {
    try
    {
      FileInputStream istream = new FileInputStream("file.dat");
      DataInputStream dis      = new DataInputStream(istream);

      int items = dis.readInt();

      for( int i=1; i<=items; i++ )
      {
        int n = dis.readInt();
        System.out.print( n + " " );
      }
      System.out.println();
      istream.close();
    }
    catch ( IOException e )
    {
      System.out.println("IOException : " + e.getMessage() );
    }
  }
}
```

The major methods in the class `java.io.DataInputStream` are:

Method	Responsibility
`DataInputStream(s)`	Constructs a stream.
`readInt( i )`	Reads the `int` i as a binary pattern. Also in the same style: `readByte`, `readBytes`, `readChar`, `readDouble`, `readFloat`, `readLong` and `readUTF`.
`flush()`	Flushes the stream.

19.3.2   Putting it all together

When both applications are compiled and run the output from the second application is as follows:

```
1 2 3 4 5
```

19.4   The stream tokenizer

The stream tokenizer reads character data as tokens. At its simplest a token is a grouping of letters and digits or a punctuation character. For example, the following are all individual tokens:

Token	Type of token
class	Word
1234.56	Number
"Java is an OO programming language"	Quoted string
{	Char

A tokenized stream is created with the following declarations:

```
FileInputStream    istream  = new FileInputStream( "file.dat" );
InputStreamReader  br       = new InputStreamReader( istream );
BufferedReader     re       = new BufferedReader( br );
StreamTokenizer    sto      = new StreamTokenizer( re );
```

In essence a tokenized stream is a wrapper around a normal input stream. The major methods in the class `java.io.StreamTokenizer` are:

Method	Responsibility
StreamTokenizer(s)	Constructs a stream.

nextToken()	Reads the next token and returns the type of the token.
	TT_EOF -> End of file reached
	TT_EOL -> End of line reached
	TT_NUMBER -> Number read
	        field nval contains the number.
	TT_WORD -> Word read
	        field sval contains the word.

lineno()	Returns the current line number. ·
toString()	Contains a string representation of the current token.

19.4.1   An application to read tokens

The following application opens a file as a tokenized stream writing the token and its type to the standard output stream.

```java
import java.io.*;

class Main
{
  public static void main( String args[] )
  {
    for ( int i=0; i<args.length; i++ )
    {
      System.out.println("File is : " + args[i] );
      try
      {
        FileInputStream    istream = new FileInputStream( args[i] );
        InputStreamReader  br      = new InputStreamReader( istream );
        BufferedReader     re      = new BufferedReader( br );
        StreamTokenizer    sto     = new StreamTokenizer( re );
```

After opening the file as a tokenized stream, individual tokens are read and categorised. The method `nextToken` returns the next token and the field `ttype` contains the type of this token. If the token read is a number or word then `sval` will contain the word token as an instance of `String` and `nval` will contain the number token as an instance of a `double`.

```java
        sto.nextToken();
        while ( sto.ttype != StreamTokenizer.TT_EOF )
        {
          switch ( sto.ttype )
          {
            case StreamTokenizer.TT_NUMBER :
              System.out.println( "Number    : " + sto.nval );
              break;
            case StreamTokenizer.TT_WORD :
              System.out.println( "Word      : " + sto.sval );
              break;
            case StreamTokenizer.TT_EOL :
              System.out.println( "EOL       : " );
              break;
            case '"' : case '\'' :
              //Quoted string
              System.out.println( "Q String  : " + sto.sval );
              break;
            default :
              System.out.println( "Character : " + (char) sto.ttype );
          }
          sto.nextToken();
        }
        istream.close();
      }
```

```
      catch ( IOException e )
      {
        System.out.println("Fail : " + e.getMessage() );
      }
    }
  }
}
```

19.4.2   Putting it all together

Using the data file `hello.java` that contains the following text:

```
class Hello //Hello world in Java
{
  public static void main( String args[] )
  {
    System.out.println("Hello world");
  }
}
```

the above application when compiled and run with an argument of `hello.java` produces the following results:

```
File is : Hello.java
Word      : class
Word      : Hello
Character : {
Word      : public
Word      : static
Word      : void
Word      : main
Character : (
Word      : String
Word      : args
Character : [
Character : ]
Character : )
Character : {
Word      : System.out.println
Character : (
Q String  : Hello world
Character : )
Character : ;
Character : }
Character : }
```

Note: The Java style comment is ignored.

19.5   Reading from an instance of the class **String**

An instance of the class `java.lang.String` may also be used as an input source for the file handling classes. An instance of the class `StringReader` is a stream from which the characters of a nominated string may be read. For example, the following fragment of code reads using the normal input mechanisms characters from the string data.

```java
import java.io.*;

class Main
{
  public static void main( String argsx[] )
  {
    try
    {
      String data       = "First line\nSecond line\nThird line";
      StringReader sr    = new StringReader( data );

      int c = sr.read();
      while ( c != -1 )
      {
         System.out.print( (char) c );
         c = sr.read();
      }

      System.out.println();
    }
    catch ( IOException e )
    {
      System.out.println("IOException : " + e.getMessage() );
    }
  }
}
```

Which when compiled and run will produce the following results:

```
First line
Second line
Third line
```

The major methods in the class `java.io.StringReader` are:

Method	Responsibility
`StringReader(s)`	Constructs a string reader stream.
`read()`	Read a single character.

19.6   Reading from an URL

An instance of the class `java.net.URL` is used to represent a URL. The URL may then be read from as if it were a normal file. The code for this process is illustrated below:

```java
import java.io.*;
import java.net.URL;

class Main
{
  public static void main( String args[] )
  {
    try
    {
      URL url = new URL( args[0] );
      InputStreamReader isr =new InputStreamReader( url.openStream() );
      BufferedReader    bis =new BufferedReader( isr );

      int c = bis.read();
      while ( c != -1 )
      {
        System.out.print( (char) c );
        c = bis.read();
      }

      bis.close();
      System.out.println();
    }
    catch ( IOException e )
    {
      System.out.println("Fail : " + e.getMessage() );
    }
  }
}
```

Which when compiled and run from the command line with the following command line argument:

```
java Main http://www.brighton.ac.uk/java/home.html
```

will list the HTML text of the home page for this book.

The major methods in the class `java.net.URL` are:

Method	Responsibility
URL(s)	Creates an instance of a URL object from a `String s` representing a URL (Uniform Resource Locator)
openStream()	Returns an input stream to the URL.
getFile()	Returns the file name used in the URL.
getHost()	Returns the host name in the URL.

19.6.1   Reading tokens from a string

Other file handling classes may be used to take input from a string. For example, the following declarations will allow the stream tokenizer to read data from an URL.

```
URL url = new URL( a_url );
InputStreamReader isr = new InputStreamReader( url.openStream() );
BufferedReader     br  = new BufferedReader( isr );
StreamTokenizer    sto = new StreamTokenizer( br );
```

19.7   Case study: a text file de-archiver

To save space and to allow global editing on many files, a single text archive of the individual text files is created. The archive consists of a header record followed by lines of the file. Each line of the file is prefixed with the symbol + so that it cannot be confused with the header record. For example, two text files each containing two lines would be held in a single file as follows:

```
@@ file_one.dat @@
+Line 1 of file_one.dat
+Line 2 of file_one.dat
@@ file_two.dat @@
+Line 1 of file_two.dat
+Line 2 of file_two.dat
```

However, only text files can be stored in this archive.

19.7.1   A de-archiver application

The specification for a de-archiver application is as follows:

> To repeatedly take a line of text from the source until the end of file is reached. For each line containing a header record close the old Sink and open a new output Sink using the file name extracted from a line header record. For all other lines, output the line to the current output Sink.
>
> In the specification the terms Source and Sink are used to denote input and output sources.

One scheme for solving this problem in Java is to identify the major verbs and nouns in the problem. The nouns indicated in bold become the objects. The verbs indicated in bold and italics become the methods or functions in the object.

To repeatedly *take* a **line** of text from the **source** until the end of file is reached. For each **line** *containing* a header record *close* the old **Sink** and *open* a new output **Sink** using the file name *extracted* from a **line** header record. For all other **lines**, *output* the **line** to the current output **Sink**.

The major objects and verbs identified are:

Objects (nouns)	Messages (verbs)
Line Sink Source	close containing extracted open output take

On these objects are performed the following actions:

Line

> Take line from the current source.
> Output the line to the current sink.
> Ask if the current line contains a header record.
> Ask if the end of file was reached when this line was extracted.

Source

> Close the input file.

Sink

> Open a new output file.

It is more appropriate to deal with classes than to deal with objects. For example, Line is the class to which the object line belongs. Using this approach the messages sent to these classes can be refined into the following list:

19.7.2 Major classes

The messages sent to instances of the major classes in the application are show below:

Class	Message	Responsibility of method
Line	fill_from	Fills the line from the current source.
	empty_to	Empties the current line to the current sink.
	is_a_command	Returns true if the line is a command.
	at_eof	Returns true if this line represents the end of file.
	deliver_file_name	Delivers the file name extracted from the current line.

Source	get_line	Reads the next line.
	open_file	Closes any previous source that was open. Opens the file as the current source input.
	close_file	Closes the current source file.

Sink	put_line	Writes the line.
	open_file	Opens the file as the current sink output.
	close_file	Closes the current sink file.

19.7.3   Object diagram

An object diagram for the application Exp using the above classes is illustrated in Figure 19.1.

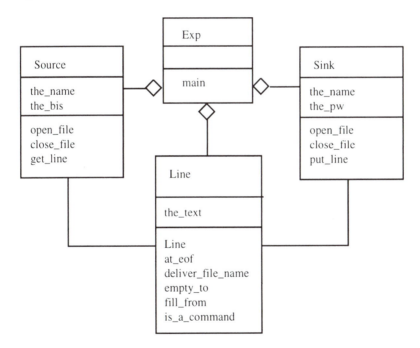

Figure 19.1 Object diagram for the application.

19.7.4   Sequence diagram

The sequence diagram for the text de-archiver is shown below in Figure 19.2. This controls the overall process of extracting files into individual files from the text archive.

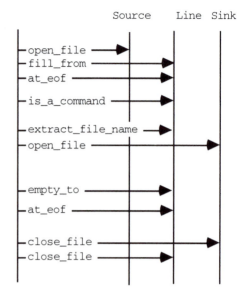

Figure 19.2 Sequence diagram for the de-archiver.

19.8   The application

The implementation of the class Exp follows the sequence diagram directly. In implementing the class the following library classes are used:

```
import java.io.FileOutputStream;
import java.io.FileInputStream;
import java.io.IOException;
import java.io.EOFException;
import java.io.PrintWriter;
import java.io.BufferedReader;
import java.io.BufferedInputStream;
import java.io.FileNotFoundException;
```

The class Exp contains the single method main that implements the sequence diagram shown earlier in Section 19.5.4.

```
class Exp
{
    private Source the_input        = new Source();      //input
    private Sink   the_output       = new Sink();        //output
    private Line   the_current_line = new Line();        //line
```

```
  public static void main( String args[] )
  {
    ( new Exp() ).expand( args );                          //Create object
  }

  public void expand( String args[] )
  {
    if ( args.length != 1 )
    {
      System.out.println("Usage: extract file");           //Usage
      System.exit(-1);                                      // error
    }

    if ( !the_input.open_file(args[0]) )                    //Archive
    {
      System.out.println("Cannot open " + args[0]);         //Open
      System.exit(-2);                                      // error
    }

    the_current_line.fill_from( the_input );                //Get line
    while ( !the_current_line.at_eof() )                     //While !eof
    {
      if ( the_current_line.is_a_command() )                // If command
      {
        String fn=the_current_line.extract_file_name(); //  Filename
        if ( !the_output.open_file( fn ) )                  //  Open
        {
          System.out.println("Cannot create " + fn);
        } else {
          System.out.println("Extracting file " + fn);
        }
      } else {                                              // Else
        the_current_line.empty_to( the_output );            //  Write line
      }                                                     // End if
      the_current_line.fill_from( the_input );              // next line
    }                                                       //End while
    the_output.close_file();                                //close all
    the_input.close_file();
  }
}
```

The class Source is responsible for reading lines from the archive when the end of file is detected a line containing "@END@" is returned.

```
class Source
{
  private String            the_name = "";                 //File name
  private BufferedInputStream the_bis  = null;
  public  static int EOF = -1;
```

The method `open_file` opens the file containing the archive.

```java
public boolean open_file( final String text )
{
  try
  {
    close_file();
    the_name = text;
    FileInputStream istream = new FileInputStream(text);
    the_bis = new BufferedInputStream( istream );
  }
  catch ( Throwable e )
  {
    System.out.println("Input " + text + " : " + e.getMessage());
    return false;
  }
  return true;
}
```

The method `close_file` simply closes the file where possible.

```java
public void close_file()
{
  if ( the_bis != null )                //Can close
  {
    try
    {
      the_bis.close();                  //close
      the_bis = null;                   //mark as closed
    }
    catch ( Throwable e )               //
    {
      System.out.println("Close " +the_name +" : " +e.getMessage());
    }
  }
}
```

The method `get_line` returns a string containing the line read.

```java
public String get_line()
{
  if ( the_bis == null ) return "@END@";   //No input stream
  String line = "";                        //Initial contents
  try
  {
    int ch = the_bis.read();               //Read character
    while ( ch != '\n' && ch != EOF )      //while current line
    {
      line += (char) ch;                   // Append char
      ch = the_bis.read();                 // get next char
      if ( ch == '\r' ) ch = the_bis.read();  // ignore ''
    }
```

A special check is made for the end of archive and a read error, in both cases a special line is returned to signify the end of input.

```
    if ( line.equals("") && ch == EOF )         //Real end of file
      return "@END@";
    return line;                                //Read line
  }
  catch( IOException exp )
  {
    return "@END@";                             //Say end of file
  }
}
}
```

The class `Sink` is responsible for creating and writing to the individual files that are represented by the text archive.

```
class Sink
{
  private String      the_name;                 //Of file
  private PrintWriter the_pw;                    //
```

The method `open_file` creates a new file where possible.

```
  public boolean open_file( final String text )
  {
    close_file();
    the_name = text;
    try
    {
      FileOutputStream ostream = new FileOutputStream(text);
      the_pw = new PrintWriter( ostream );
    }
    catch ( Throwable e )
    {
      System.out.println("Output "+text+" : "+e.getMessage());
      return false;
    }
    return true;
  }
```

The method `close_file` closes the output file where possible.

```java
public void close_file()
{
  if ( the_pw != null )                        //Can close
  {
    try
    {
      the_pw.close();                          //close
      the_pw = null;                           //Mark as closed
    }
    catch ( Throwable e )                      //
    {
      System.out.println("Close "+the_name+" : "+e.getMessage());
    }
  }
}
```

The method `put_line` writes a string representing a line to the created file.

```java
public void put_line( final String str )
{
  if ( the_pw != null )
    the_pw.write( str  + "\n" );
}
}
```

An instance of the class `Line` holds a line of text read from the archive. In addition this class is responsible for classifying the held line as a text line or a command line.

```java
class Line {
  private String the_text = "";                //Line to process

  public void fill_from( Source s )
  {
    the_text = s.get_line();
  }
```

The method `empty_to` is responsible for writing the line to the output sink.

```java
public void empty_to( Sink s )
{
  if ( the_text.length() >= 1 )                //OK line
  {
    s.put_line( the_text.substring(1) );
  }
}
```

The method `is_a_command` determines if the line contains a command action.

```
public boolean is_a_command()
{
  return the_text.length() >=2 &&                    //@@ filename @@
         the_text.substring(0,2).equals("@@");
}
```

The method `at_eof` returns true when the line read represents the command end of file.

```
public boolean at_eof()
{
  return the_text.equals("@END@");                   //
}
```

The method `extract_file_name` returns as a string the file name contained in the command line. Obviously the exact rules about what characters are valid in a file name will depend on the individual system.

```
public String extract_file_name()
{
  String fn = "";
  the_text = the_text.toLowerCase();
  for(int i=2; i<the_text.length(); i++)            //
  {
    char c = the_text.charAt(i);
    if ( (c >= 'a' && c <= 'z') ||
         (c >= '0' && c <= '9') ||
         c == '.' || c == '_' ||
         c == '+' || c == '-' || c == '\\' || c == '/' )

      fn += c;
  }
  return fn;
}
}
```

19.9   Self-assessment

● In the application for a text de-archiver are there sufficient checks in the code to prevent an attempt to read or write to a non-existent file?

19.10   Exercises

Construct the following applications

- *Text archive creator*
  Write an application that creates the archive file used by the text de-archiver.

- *Web site downloader*
  An application that will download the contents of a web site.
  Your application should have the following features:

  - Allows the user to specify a depth of download.

  - Allows the user to choice whether or not to download images

- *A simple web browser*
  A simple web browser that recognizes at least the following tags:

Feature	Tags used
Paragraph	`<P>`
Line break	` `

The Unordered list
• Item 1
• Item 2
	`<UL>`
	`  <LI> Item 1`
	`  <LI> Item 2`
	`</UL>`

Header	`<H1> Header </H1>`

20. Object serialization

This chapter looks at how objects can be serialized and deserialized. This process allows the state of an object to be saved to a file for later retrieval. By using this process, the lifetime of an object can be extended beyond the lifetime of the application or applet that created it.

20.1   Introduction

Instances of the two classes `ObjectOutputStream` and `ObjectInputStream` are used to serialize and de-serialize objects. In effect this process makes an object persistent by allowing its state to be saved and restored from a file.

Any object that is to be serialized must implement the `Serializable` interface. Objects that are to be serialized fall into two distinct categories:

- Objects that do not use linked storage and / or contain objects that implement the serializable interface.

- Objects that use linked storage or contain other objects that do not implement the serializable interface.

In the first case for the class to be made serializable all that is required is for the class to implement the interface `Serializable`. This interface is defined as:

```
interface Serializable
{
}
```

As can be seen this interface is a place-holder only, there are no methods to implement.

20.1.1   The class `java.io.ObjectOutputStream`

The major methods of the class `java.io.ObjectOutputStream` which are used as part of the serialization process are:

Method	Responsibility
`close()`	Closes the stream.
`flush()`	Flushes the stream.
`writeInt( integer )`	Writes an `int` value. Also in the same style: `writeByte`, `writeChar`, `writeDouble`, `writeFloat` and `writeLong`.
`writeObject( o )`	Writes the object `o` to the stream.
`writeString( str )`	Writes the string `str` in UTF format.

20.1.2 The class `java.io.ObjectInputStream`

The major methods of the class `java.io.ObjectInputStream` which are used as part of the deserialization process are:

Method	Responsibility
`close()`	Closes the input stream.
`readInt()`	Reads and returns an `int` value. Also in the same style: `readByte`, `readChar`, `readDouble`, `readFloat` and `readLong`.
`readObject()`	Reads and returns the object as type `Object`. This is usually cast to its real type.
`readUTF()`	Reads and returns a UTF formatted string.

20.2 Serialization of objects with no linked storage

The class `Account_S` that implements a serializable bank account is defined as follows:

```java
import java.io.*;

class Account_S implements Serializable
{
  private double the_balance     = 0.0d;  //Balance of account
  private double the_min_balance = 0.0d;  //Minimum balance

  public Account_S() {
     the_balance = the_min_balance = 0.00;
  }
 // Code for the methods
 //   account_balance, withdraw, deposit, set_min_balance

}
```

Note: This class is identical to the class `Account` as seen in Section 5.2.5 except that it now implements the interface `Serializable`.

20.2.1 Putting it all together

The following writer-application illustrates the use of the serializable class `Account_S`. The application saves instances of the class `Account_S` to the file `accounts.dat`.

```
class Main
{
  public static void main( String args[] )
  {
    try
    {
      Account_S mike    = new Account_S();
      Account_S corinna = new Account_S();
      mike.deposit(100.00);
      corinna.deposit(200.00);

      FileOutputStream ostream = new FileOutputStream("accounts.dat");
      ObjectOutputStream oos   = new ObjectOutputStream(ostream);

      oos.writeObject( mike );
      oos.writeInt( 123 );
      oos.writeObject( corinna );

      oos.flush();
      ostream.close();
    }
    catch ( Throwable e )
    {
      System.out.println("Fail : " + e.getMessage() );
    }
  }
}
```

The following reader-application restores instances of the class `Account_S` from the file `accounts.dat`.

```
class Main
{
  public static void main( String args[] )
  {
    try
    {
      Account_S mike;
      Account_S corinna;

      FileInputStream istream = new FileInputStream("accounts.dat");
      ObjectInputStream ois   = new ObjectInputStream(istream);

      mike          = (Account_S)ois.readObject();
      int an_int = ois.readInt();
      corinna       = (Account_S)ois.readObject();

      System.out.println( "Mike's Balance     = " +
                      mike.account_balance() );
```

```
    System.out.println( "The integer value    = " + an_int );

    System.out.println( "Corinna's Balance    = " +
                        corinna.account_balance() );
    istream.close();
  }
  catch ( Throwable e )
  {
    System.out.println("Fail : " + e.getMessage() );
  }
}
```

When both applications are compiled, and run the results from the second application
are:

```
Mike's Balance      = 100.0
The integer value   = 123
Corinna's Balance   = 200.0
```

20.3   Serialization of objects with linked storage

When an object contains linked storage or contains objects that do not implement the
serializable interface the builder of the class must define how the object is to be
serialized / deserialized by implementing the two methods:

```
private void writeObject( ObjectOutputStream out )
  throws IOException

private void readObject( ObjectInputStream in )
  throws IOException, ClassNotFoundException
```

The method `writeObject` implements the writing of the objects state to an
instance of the stream `ObjectOutputStreama` and the method `readObject`
implements the reading of the stored object's state from the stream
`ObjectInputStream`.

20.3.1   A serializable collection

The demonstration class `Numbers` shown below implements a simple container for
`double` numbers. This class has the following methods:

Method	Responsibility
add(d)	Adds a `double` to the collection.
holds()	Returns a `double` array that holds all the numbers in the collection.

The implementation of the class creates a chain of numbers using a linked approach. The growing chain is illustrated in Figure 20.1 below:

Stage of creation	Illustration of the resultant chain
An empty chain	
After adding the number 1.76	
After adding the number 1.5	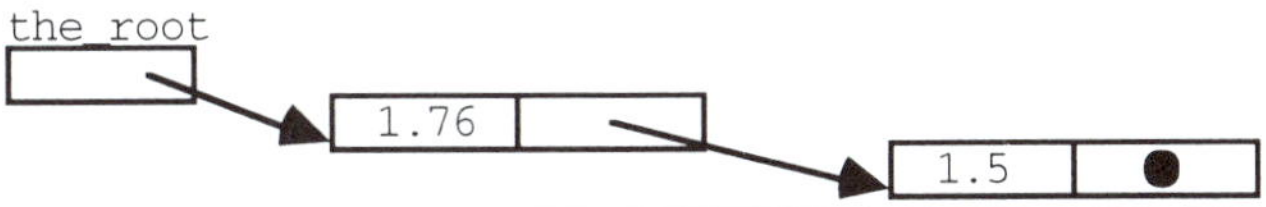

Figure 20.1 Stages of creation of the chain.

The implementation of the class `Numbers` is as follows:

```java
import java.io.*;

class Numbers implements Serializable
{
```

The contained class `Node` holds a number and a possible successor node. As objects are represented by a handle that points to the storage of the object, the successor node forms the next element of the chain. If no successor node then `the_next` contains the value `null`.

```java
  class Node
  {
    public Node     the_next;                   //Next Number
    public double   the_number;                 //Number
    public Node( final double n, final Node next )
    {
      the_next = next; the_number = n;
    }
  }
}
```

The root of the chain of nodes is rooted at `the_root` and the `the_number_held` holds the number of numbers in the chain.

```java
  private Node  the_root       = null;
  private int   the_number_held = 0;
```

The implementation of the method `add` is in two parts:

- If the chain is empty.
  Then a newly created node is assigned to the root.

- If the chain is not empty.
  Then iterate down to the last node in the chain and replace its next node that will have the value `null` with the newly created node.

By chaining the new `double` values to the end of the chain, the process of restoring the object is simplified as the method add can be used to re-create the state of the object.

```
public void add( final double n )
{
  Node tmp = new Node( n, null );                //New Node
  if ( the_root == null )                        //Empty chain
  {
     the_root = tmp;                              //Add at root
  } else {
    Node current = the_root;                      //Non empty chain
    while ( current.the_next != null )
    {
      current = current.the_next;                //Next element
    }
    current.the_next = tmp;                       //Chain at end
  }
  the_number_held++;                              //1 more
}
```

The method `holds` returns an array containing the elements of the collection.

```
public double[] holds()
{
  double results[] = new double[the_number_held]; //Array for results
  Node current = the_root;                         //
  int pos = 0;
  while ( current != null )
  {
    results[pos++] = current.the_number;           //Populate
    current = current.the_next;
  }
  return results;                                  //Return as result
}
```

As the class contains linked storage the method `writeObject` is provided to write a representation of the object to an instance of the class `ObjectOutputStream`.

```
private void writeObject( ObjectOutputStream out )
{
  try
  {
    Node current = the_root;
    out.writeInt( the_number_held );              // Number of numbers
    while ( current != null )                     //Scan down chain
    {
      out.writeDouble( current.the_number );      //Writing numbers
      current = current.the_next;
    }
  } catch ( Throwable e )
  {
    System.out.println("Fail : " + e.getMessage() ); //Disaster
  }
}
```

The methods `readObject` initializes a new instance of the class to the state that is saved. The state is read in from an instance of the class `ObjectInputStream`.

```
private void readObject( ObjectInputStream in )
{
  try
  {
    int number = in.readInt();                      //Size
    for ( int i=0; i<number; i++ )
      add( in.readDouble() );                       //Add to chain
  } catch ( Throwable e )
  {
    System.out.println("Fail : " + e.getMessage() );
  }
}
}
```

20.3.2   Putting it all together

The following demonstration application creates an instance of the class `Numbers`, populates this object with the height of three people and then serializes the contents of the object to the file `store.dat`.

The serialized object in the file `store.dat` is then deserialized into a new object `restored`.

```
class Main
{
  public static void main( String args[] )
  {
    Numbers heights  = new Numbers();
    Numbers restored = null;;
    heights.add( 1.76 );
    heights.add( 1.50 );
    heights.add( 1.45 );                   // Add to heights
    print( "Before  ", heights.holds() );
    try
    {
      FileOutputStream ostream = new FileOutputStream("store.dat");
      ObjectOutputStream oos   = new ObjectOutputStream(ostream);
      oos.writeObject( heights );
      oos.flush();  ostream.close();

      FileInputStream istream = new FileInputStream("store.dat");
      ObjectInputStream  ois = new ObjectInputStream(istream);
      restored = (Numbers) ois.readObject();
      istream.close();
    }
    catch ( Throwable e )
    {
      System.out.println("Fail : " + e.getMessage() );
      System.exit(-1);
    }
    print( "Restored", restored.holds() );
  }
```

The static method `print` prints the `double` array passed as a parameter.

```
public static void print( String str, final double values[] )
{
  System.out.print( str + " : " );
  for ( int i=0; i<values.length; i++ )
  {
    System.out.print( values[i] );
    if ( i != (values.length-1) ) System.out.print(", ");
  }
  System.out.println();
}
}
```

Which when compiled and run produces the following results, that show that the contents of the restored object are the same as the original object.

```
Before    : 1.76, 1.5, 1.45
Restored : 1.76, 1.5, 1.45
```

20.4   Standard classes that implement serialization

Many of the standard classes implement the interface `serializable`. For example, the following classes all implement the serializable interface:

An array	The inbuilt array.
Container classes	`ArrayList`, `HashMap`, `HashSet`, `Hashtable`, `LinkedList`, `Stack`, `TreeMap`, `TreeMap`, `Vector`. These are fully described in Chapter 22 on Collection classes.

20.5   Self-assessment

- When might an object be serialized?

- Why would it be difficult to provide object serialization as an automatic property of an object?

20.6   Exercises

- *Resumable draughts*
  Re-implement the game of draughts as seen in Chapter 15 so that a partially played game may be saved and subsequently restored at a later time.

21. Simple containers

This chapter examines some of the simple container objects provided as part of the standard class library. By using the standard container objects rather than an array the construction of an application can in many cases be simplified.

21.1   Introduction

So far to store a collection of objects an array has been used. However, an array has several disadvantages, these include:

- The maximum number of objects that can be stored is fixed when the arrays storage is allocated.

- Objects may not be inserted into an arbitrary position or removed from the array without explicitly moving already stored objects.

21.2   The `java.util.Vector` container

Unlike an array a vector is not declared to hold items of a specific type. The vector container is predefined to hold objects of type `Object`. As every class is derived from the class `Object` the vector container can hold instances of any class. A consequence of this is that it may hold a heterogeneous collection. A heterogeneous collection is composed of objects belonging to potentially many different classes.

However, a vector cannot hold instances of the inbuilt types such as `int` or `float`. If it is required to hold an instance of one of the standard types, then a wrapper class can be used to convert the standard type into an instance of the wrapper class.

The major responsibilities of a vector container are :

Method	Responsibility
`Vector()`	Constructs an instance of a vector.
`add(o)`	Adds the object o to the end of the vector. (JDK 1.2)
`addElement(o)`	Adds the object o to the end of the vector.
`size()`	Returns the number of items in the vector.
`elementAt(i)`	Returns the object at element i .
`insertElementAt(o, i)`	Inserts object o at position i .
`removeElementAt(i)`	Removes the object at position i .
`removeAllElements()`	Removes all the elements from the vector.

Key   o is an instance of the class `Object` or has the class `Object` as its superclass. All objects must have `Object` as their superclass. i is an instance of an `int`

A `Vector` container has the following advantages over an array:

- No maximum size for the container is specified when it is created.
- Items can be inserted into an arbitrary position in the container.
- Items are deleted from the container without leaving holes.

However, the cost of using a vector to store data (time and space) may be greater than that of using an array. Additionally as objects are placed in the vector container, when an item is extracted it must be converted back to its original type before it can be used.

21.2.1 Using the `Vector` container

As a `Vector` container holds a heterogeneous collection of items, once inserted into the collection an individual object loses its static type. Hence if an object is extracted from the vector container the programmer must explicitly convert the object back to its original type if it is to be used as an instance of that type.

For example, the following code inserts an instance of the class `Room` into a vector collection `the_rooms`.

```
Vector the_rooms = new Vector();

the_rooms.addElement( new Room() );    //Save
```

To extract this object and save it in an instance of `Room`, the extracted object must be cast back to a `Room`. This process is known as downcasting and is illustrated in the code fragment below:

```
Room a_room = (Room) the_rooms.elementAt(i)
```

Note: The term downcasting is used to describe the process of casting a superclass object to a subclass object. Obviously this can only take place if the object is really a subclass object masquerading as a superclass object.

This process will lead to an error, if the object placed in the vector container was not an instance of the class `Room` or an instance of class that was subclassed from the class `Room`. See Section 18.7.1 for a description of how this operation can be done safely.

21.2.2 Putting it all together

The class `Building` implemented in Section 18.5 used an array to hold the list of rooms. The responsibilities of this class are:

Method	Responsibility
add	Adds a description of a 'room'.
describe	Returns a description of a specific 'room'.

A room implements the following methods:

Method	Responsibility
describe	Delivers a string containing a description of the room.
room_number	Delivers the room's number.

A re-implementation of this class using the Vector container is shown below:

```
class Building
{
  Vector the_rooms;              //Heterogeneous collection

  public Building()
  {
    the_rooms = new Vector();  //Allocate storage for 0 rooms
  }

  public String describe( int room )
  {
    for ( int i=0; i<the_rooms.size(); i++ )           //All rooms
    {
      Room current = (Room) the_rooms.elementAt(i);   //Downcast
      if ( current.room_number() == room )
        return current.describe();
    }
    return "Room not known";
  }

  public void add( Room a_room )
  {
    the_rooms.addElement( a_room );                    //Save
  }
}
```

21.3 The `java.util.HashMap` container

Like a vector a HashMap container can only hold instances of the class Object or its subclasses. If it is required to hold an instance of one of the standard types, then a wrapper class must be used to convert the standard type into an instance of the wrapper class.

A HashMap is composed of (key, data) pairs. A data object is inserted with its object key into the HashMap. The data object is retrieved by quoting the object key.

The major responsibilities of a HashMap container are:

Method	Responsibility
HashMap()	Constructs an instance of a HashMap.
clear()	Clears the HashMap of all its key data pairs.
containsKey(key)	Returns true if key is in the HashMap.
get(key)	Returns the data associated with key.
put(key,data)	Adds the (key, data) pair to the HashMap.

| remove(key) | Removes the key and its associated object. |
| size() | Returns the number of keys in the HashMap. |

Key   key and data are instances of the class Object or have the
                         class Object as their superclass. All objects must have Object
                         as their superclass.

*Note: The container Hashtable also implements the above methods. The container
        Hashtable must be used for versions prior to JDK 1.2.
        Access to a HashMap and Hashtable are not synchronized and hence
        problems may occur if two threads attempt access.*

A HashMap container has the following advantages over an array:

● No maximum size for the HashMap container is specified when it is created.

● The index can be any object with any value.

● Random access to a data object is efficient.

However, the cost of using a HashMap to store data (time and space) may be greater
than that of using an array.

21.3.1   Using the **HashMap** container

The class Building implemented in Section 18.5 used an array to hold the list of
rooms. A re-implementation of this class using the container HashMap is shown below:

```
class Building
{
  HashMap the_rooms;                          //Heterogeneous collection

  public Building()
  {
    the_rooms = new HashMap();                //Allocate empty map
  }

  public String describe( int room )
  {
    Integer room_number = new Integer( room );    //Wrapper class
    if ( the_rooms.containsKey( room_number ) )    //Present in map
    {
      Room current = (Room) the_rooms.get( room_number );
      return current.describe();
    } else {
      return "Room not known";
    }
  }
}
```

```
  public void add( Room a_room )
  {
    Integer room_number = new Integer( a_room.room_number() );
    the_rooms.put( room_number, a_room );                    //Save
  }
}
```

21.3.2   The `Hashtable` container

Originally in the Java class library there were only two containers:

-    A `Vector`
-    A `Hashtable`

Java 2 introduced a family of containers, to which the original two containers where retro fitted, allowing legacy Java code to still run. The `Hashtable` container has for all practical purposes been replaced by the `HashMap` container.

21.4   Keys and the `Hashtable`/`HashMap` containers

If using an instance of a user defined class as the key to the containers `Hashtable` or `HashMap` then the method `hashCode` must be overridden in the class. The method `hashCode` returns an integer hashcode value for an object. A requirement of the `hashCode` method is that it returns the same integer number for objects that are equal according to the `equals` method. Hence when the method `equals` is overridden in a subclass the method `hashCode` will usually also be overridden. For example, a new version of the class `Account` that overrides both the methods `equals` and `hashCode` is shown below:

```
class Account
{
  private double the_balance     = 0.0d;  //Balance of account
  private double the_min_balance = 0.0d;  //Minimum bal

  //   The constructor(s)
  //   Account() and Account( final double opening_balance )

  public boolean equals( Account other )
  {
    return ( ( the_balance == other.the_balance ) &&
             ( the_min_balance == other.the_min_balance ) );
  }

  public int hashCode()
  {
    int hashcode = 0;
    long as_bits_bal = Double.doubleToLongBits(the_balance);
    long as_bits_m_b = Double.doubleToLongBits(the_min_balance);
    return (int)( as_bits_bal ^ (as_bits_bal>>32) ^
                  as_bits_m_b ^ (as_bits_m_b>>32) );
  }
```

```
    // Code for the methods
    //   account_balance, withdraw, deposit, set_min_balance
}
```

Note: The method `doubleToLongBits` *is a static method of* `Double` *and delivers a* `long` *bit representation of the* `double` *number. Also the method* `floatToIntBits` *returns an integer number representation of the* `float`.

The above class `Account` is then used in the following demonstration application.

```
class Main
{
  public static void main(String args[])
  {
    Account mike        = new Account(50.00);
    Account corinna     = new Account(50.00);
    Account miranda     = new Account(100.00);

    test( "mike.equals(mike)    " , mike.equals( mike ) );
    test( "mike.equals(corinna)" , mike.equals( corinna ) );
    test( "mike.equals(miranda)" , mike.equals( miranda ) );

    test( "mike == mike        " , mike == mike );
    test( "mike == corinna     " , mike == corinna );
    test( "mike == miranda     " , mike == miranda  );

    System.out.println("mike    = " + mike.hashCode() );
    System.out.println("corinna = " + corinna.hashCode() );
    System.out.println("Miranda = " + miranda.hashCode() );
  }

  public static void test( final String mes, final boolean res )
  {
    System.out.println("Assertion: " + mes + " is " +
                       ( res ? "true" : "false " ) );
  }
}
```

21.4.1   Putting it all together

Which when compiled and run will produce the following output:

```
Assertion: mike.equals(mike)     is true
Assertion: mike.equals(corinna)  is true
Assertion: mike.equals(miranda)  is false
Assertion: mike == mike          is true
Assertion: mike == corinna       is false
Assertion: mike == miranda       is false
mike    = 1078525952
corinna = 1078525952
miranda = 1079574528
```

Note: This code ensures that the objects `mike` and `corinna` are equal and will be regarded as equal when used with a `Hashtable` or `HashMap` container.

21.5 Self-assessment

- What are the advantages of using an instance of the class Vector, Hashtable or HashMap to hold a collection of objects rather than a normal array.

- What are the disadvantages of using an instance of the class Vector, Hashtable or HashMap to hold a collection of objects rather than a normal array.

21.7 Exercises

Use the container class Vector or HashMap to implement:

- *Address list*
  An application to maintain a list of names and addresses. The application should be able to:

  - Allow new names and addresses to be stored.

  - Allow the retrieval of a person's name using as a key their name.

- *Diary*
  An application to maintain a series of appointments for different days.

  - Allow a new appointment to be added for a particular day.

  - Allow the retrieval of all appointments for a specific day.

22. Collection classes

This chapter looks at the collection classes. Instances of these classes provide a generalized way of storing and manipulating collections of objects. In addition common algorithms to manipulate these collections of objects are provided. Hence with careful design, a programmer may change the data structure used to hold their data, but not need to change the application code that manipulates this data. These classes have been present in the class library since JDK 1.2.

22.1 Overview of the collection classes

The following table lists selected containers together with their major properties that are provided in the Java package `java.util`.

Container (class name)	Properties
ArrayList	Resisable array. The array grows in `capacityIncrement` units
HashMap	A collection of [key, data] pairs. The order that the [key, data] pairs are held is not guaranteed.
HashSet	A set implemented using a hash table. The order that the objects are held in is not guaranteed.
Hashtable	A collection of [key, data] pairs. The order that the [key, data] pairs are held is not guaranteed.
LinkedList	A linked list.
Stack	Last In First Out (LIFO) data structure.
TreeMap	A collection of (key, data) pairs. The [key,data] pairs are held in ascending key order.
TreeSet	A set implemented as a tree. Objects are held in ascending key order.
Vector	Resisable array. The array grows in `capacityIncrement` units. Access to the array is synchronized.

Note: HashMap, Hashtable, LinkedList, Stack, TreeSet and Vector implement the interfaces Cloneable and Serializable.

The class hierarchy of the collection classes is shown in Figure 22.1.

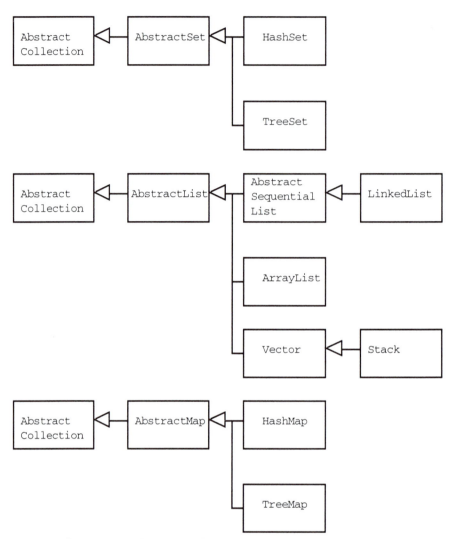

Figure 22.1 Class diagram of the major collection classes.

Note: The class `AbstractCollection` *is inherited from the class* `Object`*.*
The classes starting with `Abstract` *are as the name implies abstract and*
cannot be instantiated.

To allow interoperability between instances of the different collection classes, the individual classes implement the following interfaces.

Collection	Implements the interfaces
`ArrayList`	`List, Cloneable, Serializable`
`HashMap`	`Map, Cloneable, Serializable`
`HashSet`	`Set, Cloneable, Serializable`

Hashtable	Map, Cloneable, Serializable
LinkedList	List, Cloneable, Serializable
Stack	List, Cloneable, Serializable
TreeMap	SortedMap, Cloneable, Serializable
TreeSet	SortedSet, Cloneable, Serializable
Vector	List, Cloneable, Serializable

The hierarchy of interfaces is shown in Figure 22.2 below:

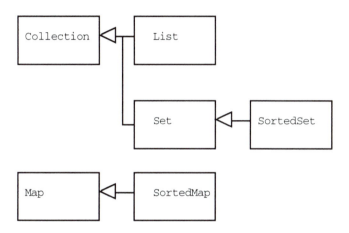

Figure 22.2 Class diagram of the interfaces used by the collection classes.

Hence, code that uses the following interfaces could operate on an instance of any of the following collection classes:

Interface	Supported by
List	ArrayList, LinkedList, Stack, Vector
Set	HashSet, TreeSet
SortedSet	TreeSet
Map	HashMap, TreeMap, Hashtable
SortedMap	TreeMap

22.2   The class **java.util.Collections**

The class Collections contains various static methods to manipulate data items held in collections that implement the interfaces Collection, List, Map, Set or SortedMap. A selected list of algorithms from the class Collections is shown below:

Signature	Implements
static int	binarySearch(List l, Object key) Searches for key in l using a binary search. Returns its position if found otherwise a negative number. The modulas of the negative number is where the key would be inserted.
static void	copy(List d, List s) Deep copy from s to d.
static Object	max(List l) Return the largest item in the collection;
static Object	min(List l) Return the smallest item in the collection;
static void	sort(List l) Sort the collection into ascending order.
static List Δ	synchronizedCollection(List l) Returns a synchronized List. This may then be accessed by multiple threads.
static List Δ	unmodifiedCollection(List l) Returns an unmodified (copy) of the List.

Note: Δ Other versions for Collection *(the root interface),* Map, Set,
SortedMap *and* SortedCollection.

22.3   The collection classes based on the interface `List`

The following collection classes support the `java.util.List` interface:

- LinkedList
- ArrayList
- Vector
- Stack

Hence any methods that are supported by the list interface can be used to manipulate
data in any of collection classes that implement the list interface.

Signature	Implements
void	add(Object o) Append the object o to the end of the collection .
boolean Δ	add(index, o) Add the object o to the list at position index. Returns true if can do this operation.
listIterator	listIterator() Returns a ListIterator to the collection.
boolean	contains(Object o) Returns true if the list contains Object o.
Object Δ	remove(int index) Removes the object at position index. Returns the removed object.

boolean Δ	remove(Object o) Remove object o from the list, returns true if this is performed.
int	size() Returns the size of the list.
void	clear() Removes all the items from the list.

Note: Methods marked Δ are not mandatory for all containers. If the method is called and it is not supported then the exception:

```
UnsupportedOperationException
```

is thrown.

22.4   Using the collection classes

The following application manipulates the colours (represented as strings) of a rainbow.

22.4.1   Algorithms

The following demonstration class contains two static methods that:

- Populates a rainbow with colours.
- Prints information about the colours in the rainbow.

The method `populate` that populates the rainbow with colours is implemented as follows:

```
class Rainbow
{
  public static void populate( List a_rainbow )
  {
    a_rainbow.add("Violet");
    a_rainbow.add("Blue");
    a_rainbow.add("Green");
    a_rainbow.add("Yellow");
    a_rainbow.add("Orange");
    a_rainbow.add("Red");
  }
```

Note: The parameter to the method `populate` *may be any collection class that supports the* `List` *interface.*

The method `about_the` displays the following information about the colours in a rainbow:

- The lowest and highest collating colours.
- The names of the colours in the rainbow.
- Whether red, green or brown are colours in the rainbow.

The code to determine the lowest and highest collating colours in the rainbow is implemented as follows:

```java
public static void about_the( List a_rainbow )
{
  System.out.print("The lowest  collating colour in a rainbow is ");
  System.out.print( (String) Collections.min( a_rainbow ) );
  System.out.println();
  System.out.print("The highest collating colour in a rainbow is ");
  System.out.print( (String) Collections.max( a_rainbow ) );
  System.out.println();
```

To print the colours of the rainbow an iterator to the collection is created and stepped through the individual elements of the collection.

```java
System.out.println("The colours of the a_rainbow are :");
Iterator cur = a_rainbow.iterator();
while ( cur.hasNext() )
{
  System.out.print( (String) cur.next() + " " );
}
System.out.println();
```

The following code tests if the colours in the string array some_colours are contained in the rainbow:

```java
String some_colours[] = new String[3];
some_colours[0] = "Red";
some_colours[1] = "Pink";
some_colours[2] = "Brown";

for ( int i=0; i<3; i++ )
{
  String colour = some_colours[i];
  int where = Collections.binarySearch( a_rainbow, colour );
  System.out.print("The colour " + colour );
  if ( where >= 0 )
  {
    System.out.println(" is at position " + where +
                        " in the a_rainbow" );
  } else {
    System.out.println(" is not a colour in the a_rainbow" );
  }
}
}
}
```

The following test application uses an instance of a vector as the collection.

```
class Main
{

  public static void main()
  {
    System.out.println( "Collection: Vector" );
    Vector a_rainbow = new Vector();

    Rainbow.populate( a_rainbow );          //Colour the a_rainbow
    Collections.sort( a_rainbow );          //Sort data
    Rainbow.about_the( a_rainbow );         //All about the a_rainbow
  }
}
```

22.4.2   Putting it all together

When compiled and run the output produced is as follows:

```
The lowest  collating colour in a rainbow is Blue
The highest collating colour in a rainbow is Yellow
The colours of the a_rainbow are :
Blue Green Orange Red Violet Yellow
The colour Red is at position 3 in the a_rainbow
The colour Pink is not a colour in the a_rainbow
The colour Brown is not a colour in the a_rainbow
```

22.4.3   Using other containers

The representation of the container declared in the method `main` may be changed and the same results will be printed. For example, the code for main could be rewritten as follows to use an instance of a linked list container to store the colours of the rainbow.

```
class Main
{

  public static void main()
  {
    System.out.println( "Collection: LinkedList" );
    LinkedList a_rainbow = new LinkedList();

    Rainbow.populate( a_rainbow );          //Colour the a_rainbow
    Collections.sort( a_rainbow );          //Sort data
    Rainbow.about_the( a_rainbow );         //All about the a_rainbow
  }
}
```

22.5　Self-assessment

● What collection class should you choose when you want to store the following information:

　● The names of all members of a football team.

　● The names and telephone numbers of your friends. You wish to use the collection in an application that will allow you to enter your friends' name and the application will return their telephone number.

● What are the disadvantages of using an instance of the class List to hold a collection of objects rather than a normal array.

22.6　Exercises

Construct the following class:

● *Bank*
Re-implement the class Bank shown in Section 10.8 to use a collection class for the storing of individual account.

23. Threads

This chapter looks at how several concurrently executing threads may be created and managed in a Java application or apple. By using threads an application or applet can respond effectively to events that occur from many different sources. However, when using concurrently executing threads in an application or applet, access to modify or read shared data must be serialized. In addition there is the danger of deadlock when a thread cannot proceed because it requires a resource that another thread cannot or will not give up.

23.1   The thread mechanism

A Java application or applet may contain sections of code that are executed simultaneously. An independently executing section of code is known as a thread or lightweight process. A thread shares the same address space as the main application or applet and hence can access data that is also visible to the main application or applet and any other concurrently executing threads. Hence, great care must be exercised in accessing shared data as one thread may be modifying the shared data whilst another thread is reading it.

The exact details of how a thread is implemented will depend on the machine on which the application or applet is run. On a multiprocessor machine, there can be true simultaneous execution of threads, whilst on a uni-processor machine this simultaneous execution is simulated by switching rapidly between the individual threads to give the illusion of simultaneous execution.

For example, a Java application that tests if a number is prime can perform this calculation as a thread whilst executing other activities The static method is_prime in the class Useful tests if a long number is prime or not. However, this process will take some time if the number is large. The code for the class Useful is shown below:

```java
class Useful
{
  public static boolean is_prime( long n )
  {
    if ( n  <= 0 || n%2 == 0) return false;        //no
    long root_n = (long) ( Math.sqrt( (double) n ) ) + 1; //upto
    for ( long i = 3; i<=root_n; i+=2 )            //Odd numbers
      if ( n % i == 0 ) return false;              //Divisible
    return true;                                   //Prime
  }
}
```

To create an active object, a function object is created that implements the interface Runnable. The interface Runnable defines a single method run that is overloaded with a method that will eventually be run as a separate thread. The interface Runnable is defined as follows:

```
interface Runnable
{
  public abstract void run();
}
```

The class Prime that implements the interface Runnable is defined as follows:

```
class Prime implements Runnable
{
  private long    the_number;              //Input data
  private boolean the_result;              //Output data
```

The constructor records any input data required by the thread. In this particular case, the number that is to be tested to see if it is a prime.

```
  public Prime( final long n )             //Input data
  {
    the_number = n;
  }
```

The method run implements the calculation to determine if the number is prime. The body of this method calls the static method is_prime to actually carry out the calculation.

```
  public void run()                        //Thread run
  {
    the_result = Useful.is_prime( the_number );
  }
```

The method result is used to return the result of the calculation that has been stored in the boolean variable the_result.

```
  public boolean result()                  //Return result
  {
    return the_result;
  }
}
```

Note: The method result will only deliver the correct answer if the method run has finished.

23.1.1 Putting it all together

An instance of the class `Prime` is first created that has responsibility for implementing the actions performed by the thread:

```
Prime  prime  = new Prime( 99 );            //Function object
```

Note: This class implements the interface `Runnable`*.*

The object `prime` is then wrapped by an instance of the class `Thread` to create the active object `thread`.

```
Thread thread = new Thread( prime );        //Construct thread
```

The active object `thread` is started by sending it the message `start`.

```
thread.start();                             //Start
```

This will set-up a new separately executing thread that executes the method `run` in the class `Prime`. This process is illustrated in Figure 23.1, which shows the start of the execution of the newly created thread.

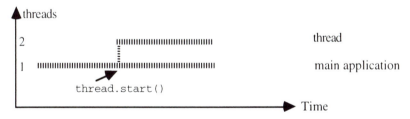

Figure 23.1 Illustration of two separately executing threads.

To be able to successfully retrieve the calculated results from the object `prime` the calculation must have finished. A call on the method `join` in the class `Thread` will cause a temporary wait till the thread has finished executing. For example, the following code will cause a wait till the independently executing thread `thread` has finished.

```
thread.join();                              //Wait till finishes
```

Figure 23.2 shows the main application waiting for the active object `thread` to finish executing after calling its method `join`. The main application is suspended until the join can take place. Naturally if the active object had already finished executing then the main application would be resumed immediately.

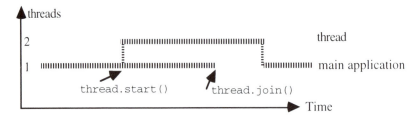

Figure 23.3 The main application waits for the thread to finish before resuming.

23.1.2   The complete application

The complete application to create a separately executing thread to check if the number
99 is a prime number is shown below. Whilst this calculation is taking place the main
application can simultaneously perform other calculations.

```
class Main
{
  public static void main( String args[] )
  {
    try
    {
      long number = 99;                        //Is prime

      Prime  prime  = new Prime( number );     //Function object
      Thread thread = new Thread( prime );     //Construct thread
      thread.start();                          //Start

      //Other work

      thread.join();                           //Wait till finishes


      System.out.println( "The number " + number + " is " +
                          (prime.result() ? "" : "not ") + "prime" );

    }
    catch ( InterruptedException exc )
    {
    }
  }
}
```

Note: The need to provide an exception handler for the exception
InterruptedException. Which in this case is effectively ignored.

23.2   The class `java.lang.Thread`

The major methods of the class Thread are:

Method	Responsibility
Thread() Thread(name) Thread(fo) Thread(fo, name)	Creates a new thread with name name. Creates a new thread that will run the function object fo that implements the interface Runnable.
activeCount()	Returns the number of active threads in this thread group.
destroy()	Destroys the thread. There is no cleanup.
getName()	Returns the name of the thread.
isAlive()	Returns true if the thread is alive.
join()	Waits for the thread to die.
join(delay)	Waits at most delay milliseconds for the thread to die.
run()	Runs the thread's function object that implements the interface Runnable.
sleep(delay)	Causes the thread to sleep for delay milliseconds.
start()	Causes the thread to start, the run method in the thread is called.
yield()	After pausing the thread allow other threads to continue.

Methods in the class java.lang.Object that interact with threads

Method	Responsibility
notifyAll()	Wakes up all threads that are waiting on this object. A thread enters the wait state when it calls one of the wait methods.
notify()	Wakes up a single thread that is waiting on this object.
wait(delay)	Waits until either of the following two conditions occur: ● One of the methods notify or notifyall is called from another thread on this object. ● The time delay in milliseconds has passed.
wait()	Waits until one of the methods notify or notify all is called from another thread on this object.

23.3   Inheriting from class `Thread`

An alternative way of implementing a thread in Java is to inherit directly from the class Thread. For example, the previous application could have been written as follows:

```
class Prime extends Thread
{
  private long   the_number;            //Input data
  private boolean the_answer;           //Output results
```

```
public Prime( final long number )                //Input data
{
  the_number = number;
}

public void run()                                //Thread run
{
  the_answer = Useful.is_prime( the_number );
}

public boolean result()                          //Return result
{
  return the_answer;
}
}
```

Then after an instance of the class `Prime` is created its `run` method is invoked by calling the method `start`. A new complete application is shown below that uses the new class `Prime` to implement a separately executing thread.

```
class Main
{
  public static void main( String args[] )
  {
    try
    {
      long number = 99;                        //Is prime

      Prime thread = new Prime(number);        //Construct thread
      thread.start();                          //Start

      //Other work

      thread.join();                           //Wait till finishes

      System.out.println( "The number " + number + " is " +
                          (thread.result() ? "" : "not ") + "prime" );
    }
    catch ( InterruptedException exc )
    {
    }
  }
}
```

23.4   Mutual exclusion and critical sections

In many cases of realtime working, sections of code must not be executed concurrently. The classic example is the adding or removing of data in a shared buffer. For example, to perform a copy operation between two separate devices a shared buffer can be used to even out the differences in response-time. This is illustrated diagrammatically in Figure 23.3.

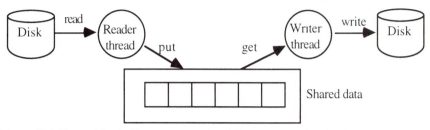

Figure 23.3 Copy with a buffer to even out the differences in read and write rates.

The problem is how to prevent both the read and write threads accessing the buffer simultaneously, causing the consequential corruption of indices and data.

Java allows the creation of a monitor. In essence a monitor is an object with special synchronized methods. Only one of the synchronized methods can be executed at any one instance in time. If another thread attempts to access a synchronized method whilst another synchronized method is being executed the request is queued until the currently executing synchronized method finishes.

In Java a monitor is implemented as a class whose methods are declared as synchronized. When a message is sent to a method that has been declared as synchronized the method is only invoked when there is no lock held on the object. If the object is locked the process that sent the message is temporary halted till the object is unlocked. An object is locked by the invocation of a synchronized method and unlocked when the method is exited.

A method can explicitly cause an object to be unlocked by executing the method wait. However, this will cause the method to be suspended until another thread sends the message notify or notifyAll to the object. A reactivated thread that was held on the wait method will once again lock the object. Obviously if there are two threads waiting on wait only one of the threads can be reactivated.

23.5   Implementation

The implementation of an application to perform an efficient disk to disk copy using an in store buffer to even out any differences in access time is implemented as two threads and a monitor. The monitor is used to provide serialized access to the shared data buffer. Data can be added to the buffer and removed from the buffer but the operations cannot occur simultaneously. This arrangement is illustrated in Figure 23.4 below.

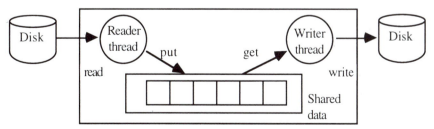

Figure 23.4 Copy implemented using two tasks and a protected object buffer.

The responsibilities of the individual components shown above are as follows:

Class	Instance is a	Responsibilities
Reader	thread [reader]	Read data from the input file and then pass the data to the buffer. Note: The task will block if the buffer is full.
Writer	thread [writer]	Take data from the buffer and write the data to the output file. Note: The task will block if the buffer is empty.
Buffer	monitor [buffer]	Serialize the storing and retrieving of data to and from a buffer.

23.5.1   The class **Buffer**

The buffer class contains two synchronized methods put and get to allow entry and retrieval of data respectively from the buffer. The buffer is implemented as a queue. Thus the first item entered into the buffer will be the first item to be removed from the buffer. The implementation of the queue uses an array to simulate the properties of a queue. To make this process general the queue is implemented as a collection of items of type Object. Hence any object can be entered into the queue. Figure 23.5 illustrates a queue of four objects a, b, c and d that have been entered into the queue. Objects are entered at the tail of the queue and removed from the head.

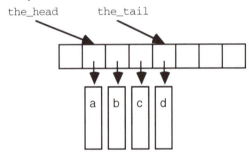

Figure 23.5 Illustration of a queue of objects implemented as an array.

```
import java.io.*;

class Buffer
{
```

The queue in Figure 23.5 is implemented as an array with integer pointers to represent the head and tail of the queue. The field the_no_of_objects contains a count of the current number of items in the queue. This field is used to avoid the ambiguity between a full and an empty queue.

```
private static final int QUEUE_SIZE = 5;        //Size
private static final int LAST = QUEUE_SIZE-1;   //Last index
```

```
private Object the_queue[] = new Object[ QUEUE_SIZE ];
private int the_no_in_queue = 0;                    //# items
private int the_head = 0;                           //Head of
private int the_tail = 0;                           //Tail of
```

The synchronized method get tests if there are any items in the queue. If there are then the head item is removed from the queue and returned as the result. However, if there are no objects in the queue the method is suspended with wait and hence the lock on the object is removed. The method will remain suspended until woken by the method notifyAll called by another thread. Just before exiting the method notifyAll is called to wake up any other threads that may be waiting.

```
public synchronized Object get()
{
  while ( the_no_in_queue <= 0 )
  {
    try {wait();} catch (InterruptedException e) {} //Suspend
  }
  Object res = the_queue[the_head];                 //Remove
  the_head = the_head == LAST ? 0 : the_head+1;     //Cycle
  the_no_in_queue--;                                //1 less
  notifyAll();                                      //Wake up
  return res;
}
```

The synchronized method put works in a similar way to the method get but this time an item is added when possible to the queue.

```
public synchronized void put( final Object value )
{
  while ( the_no_in_queue >= QUEUE_SIZE )
  {
    try {wait();} catch (InterruptedException e) {} //Suspend
  }
  the_queue[the_tail] = value;                      //Add
  the_tail = the_tail == LAST ? 0 : the_tail+1;     //Cycle
  the_no_in_queue++;                                //1 more
  notifyAll();                                      //Wake up
  }
}
```

23.5.2 The class Reader

The class Reader is implemented as a subclass of Thread as follows:

```
class Reader extends Thread
{
  private Buffer the_buffer;              //Shared buffer
  private String the_file_name;           //File to read from
  private static final int EOF = -1;
```

The constructor records the file from which data is to be read, and the buffer object used to hold data items. The class `Buffer` has synchronized methods for `put` and `get` to ensure that it is impossible to both enter a data item and retrieve a data item simultaneously.

```
public Reader( final String file_name, Buffer buffer )
{
  super( "Reader" );                       // Name the thread
  the_buffer    = buffer;
  the_file_name = file_name;
}
```

The method `run` contains the active part of the object and will be invoked when the instance of the class `Reader` is sent the message `run`.

```
public void run()
{
  try
  {
    FileInputStream istream = new FileInputStream( the_file_name );
    BufferedInputStream bis = new BufferedInputStream( istream );
```

Once the input file has been successfully opened, each line of data from the input file is converted into a string and added to the buffer. Remember, an instance of the class `Buffer` may be sent any object.

```
    int ch = bis.read();                    //
    while ( ch != EOF )                     //While not eof
    {
      String line = "";                     // Empty line
      while ( ch != '\n' && ch != EOF )     // While not eol
      {
        line += (char) ch;                  //  build line
        ch = bis.read();
      }                                     // End line
      the_buffer.put( line );               //
      ch = bis.read();                      // Next char
    }
    bis.close();                            //Close file
  }
```

Any exceptions that may occur are handled by the catch blocks shown below.

```
  catch ( EOFException e )
  {
    System.out.println("R] IOException :" + e.getMessage() );
  }
```

```
    catch ( FileNotFoundException e )
    {
      System.out.println("R] File problem: " + e.getMessage() );
    }
    catch ( IOException e )
    {
      System.out.println("R] I/O error   : " + e.getMessage() );
    }
```

When the end of file is reached or an error occurs a `null` object is added to the buffer to signify that there will be no more objects added to this shared buffer.

```
    the_buffer.put( null );                          //End
  }
}
```

23.5.3   The class `Writer`

An instance of the class `Writer` is used to retrieve instances of the class `String` from the shared buffer and write the retrieved strings to the output file.

```
class Writer extends Thread
{
  private Buffer the_buffer;               //Shared buffer
  private String the_file_name;            //File to write to
  private static final int EOF = -1;
```

The constructor records the file to which data is to be written, and the buffer object used to hold the shared objects.

```
public Writer( final String file_name, Buffer buffer )
{
  super( "Writer" );            // Name the thread
  the_buffer    = buffer;
  the_file_name = file_name;
}
```

The implementation of the method `run` first opens the output file into which the retrieved strings from the buffer are to be written

```
public void run()
{
  try
  {
    FileOutputStream ostream = new FileOutputStream( the_file_name );
    PrintWriter pw           = new PrintWriter( ostream );
```

The main processing loop retrieves instances of the class String from the buffer and writes these extracted strings to the output file. An empty buffer is signified by the return of a null value for an extracted object.

```
    Object line = the_buffer.get();          //Get line
    while ( line != null )                    //While not eof
    {
      pw.print( (String) line + "\n");        // Write line
      line = the_buffer.get();
    }                                         //End file
    pw.flush();                               //Close down
    ostream.close();
  }
```

Any I/O errors are caught and the nature of the error reported back to the user of the application.

```
    catch ( IOException e )
    {
      System.out.println("W] IOException: " + e.getMessage() );
    }

  }
}
```

23.5.4   The class Copy

The class Copy creates two active objects, reader and writer. These active objects are created with parameters representing the file to be read from or writen too and the monitor used to hold the shared data.

Once started the two threads execute independently adding and extracting data from the shared buffer until the reader thread has exhausted the input stream. Once both threads have terminated the application will be exited.

```
class Copy
{
  public static void main (String args[])
  {
    if ( args.length == 2 )
    {
      Buffer buffer = new Buffer();                    //Shared data
      Reader reader = new Reader( args[0], buffer ); //Read thread
      Writer writer = new Writer( args[1], buffer ); //Write thread
      writer.start();                                  //Start
      reader.start();                                  // threads
    } else {
      System.out.println("Usage: copy source destination");
    }
  }
}
```

23.5.5 Putting it all together

When the above application is compiled and run it performs a copy operation using an internal buffer to even out any differences between the speed of the input and output streams. For example, to copy the contents of the file from.dat to the file to.dat a user would enter on the command line:

```
java Copy from.dat to.dat
```

the above command line invocation of the application.

23.6 Temporary thread suspension

Execution of a thread can be temporarily delayed for a specific number of milliseconds. For example, to implement a delay of 1.5 seconds in an application the following static method of the class Thread is used.

```
   Thread.sleep( 1500 );                // 1500 milliseconds delay
```

When the time limit expires execution continues.

23.7 Self-assessment

• What is a thread or lightweight process?

• How is an active object implemented in Java?

• What problems can occur when separately executing threads share access to data?

• What is a synchronized method and why is it needed?

23.8 Exercises

Construct the following:

• *Fibonacci*
A class Fibonacci that is used to create an active object which delivers an array of terms containing n terms from the fibonacci series.

24. Networking

Inter-program communication is based around the *de facto* standard of TCP/IP. By using the TCP/IP protocol a Java application can communicate with other applications or applets running on the same machine or running on other machines anywhere in the world. This assumes of course that the separate computers are connected to the internet.

24.1   Introduction

TCP/IP is a set of protocols that allows two programs to communicate over a communications channel. This is achieved by creating a data connection between the two programs. Once established, the connection is viewed by the two programs as a file to which the sender writes and the receiver reads. A two-way communications channel is established by allowing both programs to read and write.

This process is illustrated in Figure 24.1 in which a client program establishes contact with a server program running on a different machine. By using this approach, transactions can be sent to other machines to be processed.

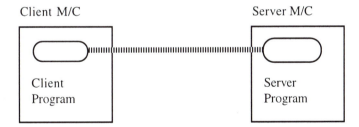

Figure 24.1 Client and Server.

The following table discusses the role of a client and server:

Client	A client application or applet sends transactions to a server application or applet for processing.
Server	A server application or applet processes transaction on behalf of one or more clients.

24.1.1   The name of a machine

Every machine that is connected to the internet is know by a unique IP address. An IP address is currently a 32 bit integer number that is usually written as four octets in the form: 193.62.183.86. However, as this is a very unfriendly way of naming a computer a symbolic domain name is usually used.

A domain name is of the form `hyperion.brighton.ac.uk` and is read as the machine `hyperion` is in the domain `brighton` that itself is in the domain `ac` that itself is in the domain `uk`. The top-level domains are allocated by international agreement, lower levels by the organization or person responsible for that domain. Using this strategy every computer in the world will have a unique domain name yet still retain an easily remembered form.

24.1.1.1   `localhost`

On many systems the name of your local machine has an alias of `localhost`. Thus if you only want to communicate with another application or applet running on your machine then you can use the name `localhost` for the name of the machine.

This allows testing of programs that use networking without the machine itself having to be connected to the internet. Of course networking software must be installed on your machine for this to work.

24.1.2   Ports

As there may be many programs running on an individual machine a logical port number is used to uniquely identify the program that a user wishes to communicate with. A port number is represented by an integer number currently in the range 1—65536. Port numbers in the range 1 .. 1024 are reserved for specific programs so should be avoided. For example, the FTP suite of program uses port numbers 20 and 21 to communicate between an FTP client and server. Using one of these numbers would probably prevent you from using an FTP client on your machine as well as getting strange results when connecting to other machines.

Unfortunately higher numbered ports are also used by some programs.

24.1.3   Client

A program that asks a server to perform some task on its behalf. The client initiates the conversation with the server. A thin client does very little local work delegating most of the task to the server, whilst a thick client does most of the work itself.

24.1.4   Server

A program that performs tasks on behalf of a client or clients. The server may communicate with the client to return the results of its request.

24.1.5   Socket

A socket is an endpoint in a communications connection between two programs. In essence the socket is the programmer's view of the connection between the two programs. When creating a socket there are two cases:

- A client program binding to a socket that will form a connection to a named port on a named machine.

- A server program binding to a socket that is connected to a named port on the host machine. This connection is not complete, and will only be completed when a client program binds to the host's port.

24.1.6   Summary

Figure 24.2 illustrates two computers `janus` and `strong` running client programs (Programs B and C) that communicate with a server program (Program A) running on the machine `hyperion`. The machines are all in the domain `brighton.ac.uk`.

The two client programs create a local socket that they bind to port `99` on the machine with domain name `hyperion.brighton.ac.uk`. The machine `hyperion.brighton.ac.uk` is running a server program (Program A) that is constantly listening for connections on the hosts port `99`.

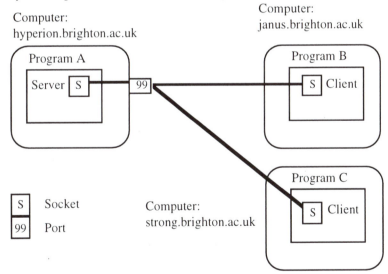

Figure 24.2 Illustration of two clients talking to a server.

The important concepts discussed in networking are summarized below:

IP Address	Currently an IPv4 (IP Version 4) uses a 32 bit integer value, for the address usually written as 4 bytes in the form: 193.62.183.86. Note: The format for an IP address will soon be expanded to IPv6 (IP Version 6 this will allow for 128 bit addresses) to allow for an even greater number of machines to be connected to the internet.
domain name	A symbolic name for a machine or group of machines. Each domain owner can register other names in that domain. For example, the University of Brighton [`brighton.ac.uk`] can choose the names of machines or other sub domains in its domain. Each domain will usually have a DNS (Domain Name Server) that will map the name of a machine within its domain to the true IP address. A DNS is a computer that is able to provide an IP address for a domain name or be able to ask another DNS to provide this information.
TCP	Transport Control Protocol. A protocol that guarantees that when a connection is established and kept open, the receiving machine will get the sent messages. The message will be split into packets, that may be sent by any route to the destination, however the TCP protocol guarantees to re-assemble these individual packets into the correct order for delivery to the receiver.
UDP	User Datagram Protocol. Messages are split into packets and sent to the destination but there is no guarantee that the packets will arrive in the correct order or even arrive at all.
IP	Internet Protocol. A collection of protocols of which TCP and UDP are members. Hence TCP/IP.
port number	A number in the range 1—65536, examples of used port numbers include: **Port Used by** 20-21 File transfer programs using FTP 23 Terminal emulators (Telnet) 79 Finger programs
Host	The machine on which the program is running.

24.2   A demonstration application

The following two applications implement a trivial client server relationship. The first program the client sends a transaction (a string) to another application the server that writes out the number of characters in the transaction message. This is illustrated in Figure 24.3.

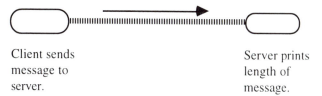

Client sends
message to
server.

Server prints
length of
message.

Figure 24.3 Client sending message to a server.

24.2.1   The client

An object diagram for the client is illustrated in Figure 24.4. In essence the client uses an instance of the class Net_Writer to write to the connection.

Figure 24.4 Object diagram for the client.

24.2.2   The client application

The following application illustrates a simple client that will send a request to a server application. The client application is run from the command line with the following command line parameters:

- The name of the machine on which the server application is running.
- The port number that the server listens on for connections.
- The message that is to be sent to the server.

An example run of the client application is shown below:

```
java Client localhost 2000 "Message sent to server"
```

The application is implemented as follows:

```
import java.lang.*;
import java.net.*;
import java.util.*;
import java.io.*;
```

The method main is responsible for decoding the command line parameters that represent:

- The name of the machine on which the server application runs.
- The port number that the server application will listen on.
- A string representing a message that is to be sent to the server

```
class Client
{
  public static void main( String args[] )
  {
    try
    {
      if ( args.length == 3 )
      {
        process( args[0], Integer.parseInt( args[1] ), args[2] );
        return;
      }
    }
    catch ( Exception err ) { }
    System.out.println( "Usage Client M/C port message" );
  }
```

The method process does the work of connecting to the server and sending to the server the message. Firstly a socket object is created, the parameters to this are the server's host machine name and the port on which the server listens. Then an instance of the class Net_Writer is created that allows information to be written a line at a time to the server application. The responsibilities of this class are:

Method	Responsibility
putLine	Write the string to the communications channel.
close	Close the channel down.

The implementation of the method process is:

```
public static void process( String host, int port, String message )
{
  try
  {
    Socket      socket = new Socket( host, port );
    Net_Writer out     = new Net_Writer( socket );
    out.putLine( message );                        //Send to server
    out.close();                                   //Close
  }
  catch ( Exception err )
  {
    System.out.println("Error : " + err.getMessage() );
  }
}
}
```

24.2.3 The class Net_Writer

The class Net_Writer is used to simplify the writing of data to a channel obtained from a socket. The constructor for the classes uses the supplied socket to create a buffered output stream, which in turn is used to create an instance of a PrintWriter object which is saved for later use.

```
class Net_Writer
{
  private PrintWriter     the_out;              //Output
  private String          the_message = null; //

  public Net_Writer( Socket s )
  {
    try
    {
      BufferedOutputStream bos =
          new BufferedOutputStream( s.getOutputStream() );

      PrintWriter out = new PrintWriter( bos );

      the_out = out;
    }
    catch( Exception err )
    {
      System.out.println("Error Net_Writer: " + err.getMessage() );
    }
  }
```

The method `putLine` is responsible for writing a string to the communications channel.

```
public void putLine( String message )
{
  the_out.println( message );            //Send Message
  the_out.flush();                       //Make sure gone
}
```

The method `close` closes the channel to the remote machine.

```
public void close()
{
  try
  {
    the_out.close();
  }
  catch ( Exception err ) {}
}
```

24.2.4   The server

An object diagram for the server is illustrated in Figure 24.5. In essence the server uses an instance of the class Net_Reader to read from the established connection.

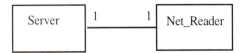

Figure 24.5 Object diagram for the client.

24.2.5   The server application

For a server to be useful it will need to be left running on a machine that is connected to the internet or an intranet. The client will send the server a single line of text and the server will display this line of text on its default output device. The server application is run from the command line with the following command line parameter:

- The port number that the server will listen on for connections.

An example run of the server application is shown below:

```
java Server 2000
```

The server application is implemented as follows:

```
import java.lang.*;
import java.net.*;
import java.util.*;
import java.io.*;
```

The method `main` is responsible for decoding the single command line parameter that represents:

- The port on which the server should listen on.

```
class Server
{
  public static void main( String args[] )
  {
    try
    {
      if ( args.length == 1 )
      {
        process( Integer.parseInt( args[0] ) );
        return;
      }
    }
    catch ( Exception err ) { }
    System.out.println( "Usage Server port" );
  }
```

The method process does the work of listening for a connection from a server. Firstly an endpoint to the channel is created using the class `ServerSocket`. The method `accept` blocks till a client establishes a contact with the server. Then an instance of the class `Net_Reader` is created that allows information to be read a line at a time from the server application. The responsibilities of the class `Net_Reader` are:

Method	Responsibility
getLine	Reads a line from the communications channel.
close	Closes the channel down.

```
public static void process( final int port )
{
  try
  {
    ServerSocket server_socket = new ServerSocket( port );
    Socket        socket       = server_socket.accept();    //Accept

    Net_Reader in = new Net_Reader( socket );

    String action = in.getLine();
    System.out.println( action );
  }
  catch ( Exception err ) {}
}
```

Note: Once a connection has been made the server application will exit. This is not a good idea if the server is responsible for processing multiple requests.

24.2.6   The class **Net_Reader**

The class `Net_Reader` is used to simplify the reading of data from a channel obtained from a socket. The string EOF ("\rEOF") is returned when an end of file is detected on the channel or an error occurs. This string however, cannot occur naturally as it contains the character '`\r`' which is never returned as part of the received text message.

The usual reason for an error occurring is that the channel has been closed from the other end. In which case returning an EOF is an appropriate action.

```
class Net_Reader
{
  public  final static String EOF = "\rEOF";      //Cannot occur
  private BufferedInputStream the_in;              //Input
  private String                the_message = null; //
```

The constructor uses the socket to create a buffered output stream.

```java
public Net_Reader( Socket s )
{
  try
  {
    BufferedInputStream in =
        new BufferedInputStream( s.getInputStream() );
    the_in = in;
  }
  catch( Exception err )
  {
    System.out.println("Error Net_Reader: " + err.getMessage() );
  }
}
```

The method `getLine` reads a line of data from the communications channel, any errors are treated as if an end of file. The special marker string returned when an end of file or error on the channel is found cannot normally be read as it contains a return character.

```java
public String getLine()
{
  try
  {
    String res = "";                    //Accumulating line

    while ( true )
    {
      int c = the_in.read();            //Next character
      if ( c == '\n' ) return res;      //End of line
      if ( c == -1   ) return EOF;      //End of file (EOF)
      if ( c != '\r' )                  //Ignore ''
      {
        res += (char) c;                // Append
      }
    }
  }
  catch ( Throwable e ) { }             //I/O error

  return EOF;                           //Treat as EOF
}
```

The method `close` closes down the channel in an orderly way.

```java
public void close()
{
  try { the_in.close(); } catch ( Exception err ) {}
}
```

24.2.7   Putting it all together

When compiled and run the following results are produced:

	Client (Application)	Server (Application)
Command line	`java Client` `localhost 2000 a_message`	`java Server  2000`
Output from application		`a_message`

Note: The two applications are run in separate windows.
The server application must be started first.
The command line to start the client is shown as two lines so that it will fit in the
space provided. In reality of course this should be typed as a single line.

24.3   A better server application

A better implementation of the server application is to have it constantly looping waiting
for a connection and then when a connection is established processing the request. So
that several client data can be processed simultaneously a separate thread is created to
handle the processing of the request from each client. This is illustrated in Figure 24.6.

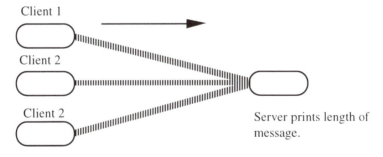

Client(s) send message to server.

Figure 24.6 Multiple clients sending a message to a server.

24.3.1   The better server

An object diagram for the better server is illustrated in Figure 24.7. In essence the server
uses instances of the class `T_Process_transactions` to read from connections
established by multiple clients.

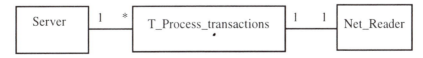

Figure 24.7 Object diagram for the server.

24.3.2   The better server application

The new version of the server, starts off in the same way as the previous version by decoding the command line parameter representing the port on which it will listen on for connections from client applications.

```java
import java.lang.*;
import java.net.*;
import java.util.*;
import java.io.*;

class Server
{
  public static void main( String args[] )
  {
    try
    {
      if ( args.length == 1 )
      {
        process( Integer.parseInt( args[0] ) );
        return;
      }
    }
    catch ( Exception err ) { }
    System.out.println( "Usage Server port" );
  }
```

The main method of the server application is now an endless loop, that waits for a connection from a client and then creates a new separately executing thread to deal with each request. In this way multiple clients may use the server without having to wait for another client's transaction(s) to finish.

```java
  public static void process( final int port )
  {
    try
    {
      ServerSocket socket = new ServerSocket( port );
      while( true )
      {
        Socket connection = socket.accept();       //Wait for connection
        T_Process_transactions thread =
          new T_Process_transactions(connection);//Create thread
        thread.start();                            //Start thread
      }
    }
    catch ( Exception err )
    {
      System.out.println("Error : " + err );
    }
  }
}
```

An instance of the class `T_Process_transactions` is an active object that processes a request from a single client. The constructor for the active object stores the socket used to create the communications channel. The method `run` overrides the method `run` in the class `Thread` and is called when the task is activated.

```
class T_Process_transactions extends Thread
{

  private Socket the_socket;                    //Socket used

  public T_Process_transactions( Socket s  )    //Construct
  {
    the_socket = s;
  }

  public void run()                             //Execution
  {
    Net_Reader in = new Net_Reader( the_socket );
    String action = in.getLine();               //From client
    System.out.println( action );
    in.close();                                 //Close
  }
}
```

24.3.3 Putting it all together

When compiled and run the following results are produced:

	Client (Application)	Server (Application)
Command line used	`java Client` `localhost 2000 a_message`	`java Server 2000`
Results returned		`a_message`

Note: Now there may be many client sending a message to the server.
The server will run forever unless terminated.
The command line to start the client is shown as two lines so that it will fit in the
space provided. In reality of course this should be typed as a single line.

24.4 Two-way communication between server and client

When a channel is created it may be written to as well as read from. By creating both a reader and a writer on a channel a two-way dialogue may be established between a client and a server. The next demonstration client—server relationship is where the client sends multiple transaction messages to a server, the server sends back to the client the length of each message. The client displays this information on its local terminal. This process is illustrated in Figure 24.8.

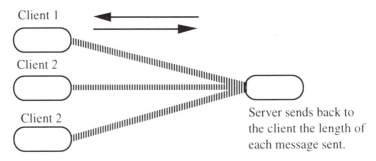

Client 1

Client 2

Client 2

Server sends back to the client the length of each message sent.

Client sends messages to the server and displays the returned result.

Figure 24.8 Multiple clients sending a message to a server.

24.4.1 The client

The following demonstration client passes a series of messages to a server, which returns for each message sent the length in bytes of the message.

```
import java.lang.*;
import java.net.*;
import java.util.*;
import java.io.*;
```

The main difference between this version of the client and the previous example is that:

- Many messages are sent by the client

- For each message sent the server sends back the length of the message in bytes, this information is displayed by the client onto the local terminal.

```
class Client
{
  public static void main( String args[] )
  {
    try
    {
      if ( args.length >= 3 )
      {
        process( args[0], Integer.parseInt( args[1] ), args );
        return;
      }
    }
    catch ( Exception err ) { }
    System.out.println( "Usage Client M/C port message(s)" );
  }
```

The method process is responsible for the actual sending and receiving of results from the server.

```java
public static void process( String host, int port, String message[] )
{
  try
  {
    Socket socket = new Socket( host, port );

    Net_Writer out = new Net_Writer( socket );
    Net_Reader in  = new Net_Reader( socket );

    for ( int i = 2; i<message.length; i++ )
    {
      out.putLine( message[i] );                //Transaction
      String response = in.getLine();           // Answer
      System.out.println("Length of [" +
                        message[i] + "]  is " +
                        response );
    }
    out.close();
  }
  catch ( Exception err )
  {
    System.out.println("Error : " + err );
  }
}
}
```

24.4.2   The server

An object diagram for the better server is illustrated in Figure 24.9. In essence the server uses instances of the class `Net_Reader` to read from connections established by multiple clients who wish to communicate with the server.

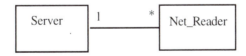

Figure 24.9 Better server.

24.4.3   The server application

The server is very similar to the previous versions, except that multiple transactions are received from an individual client and a response to the transaction is now returned on the communications channel back to the client.

```
import java.lang.*;
import java.net.*;
import java.util.*;
import java.io.*;

import Net_Reader;
import Net_Writer;

class Server
{
  public static void main( String args[] )
  {
    try
    {
      if ( args.length == 1 )
      {
        process( Integer.parseInt( args[0] ) );
        return;
      }
    }
    catch ( Exception err ) { }
    System.out.println( "Usage Server port" );
  }
```

The method process creates an active instance of the class T_Process_transactions for each client that connects to the server. This active object is responsible for processing the individual transactions from the client.

```
  public static void process( final int port )
  {
    try
    {
      ServerSocket socket = new ServerSocket( port );
      while( true )
      {
        Socket connection = socket.accept();      //Wait for connection
        T_Process_transactions thread =
          new T_Process_transactions(connection);//Create thread
        thread.start();                           //Start thread
      }
    }
    catch ( Exception err )
    {
      System.out.println("Error : " + err );
    }
  }
}
```

The class T_Process_transactions is used to create an active object that reads the transaction message(s) from the client and returns the number of characters in each message back to the client.

```
class T_Process_transactions extends Thread
{
  private Socket the_socket;                          //Socket used

  public T_Process_transactions( Socket s )           //Construct
  {
    the_socket = s;
  }

  public void run()                                   //Execution
  {
    Net_Reader in  = new Net_Reader( the_socket );
    Net_Writer out = new Net_Writer( the_socket );

    while ( true )
    {
        String action = in.getLine();                //From Client
        if ( action.equals( Net_Reader.EOF ) ) break;//No more data

        System.out.println( action );
        out.putLine( "" + action.length() );         //Response
    }

    in.close();                                       //Close Read
    out.close();                                      //Close Write

    try
    {
      the_socket.close();                             //Close Socket
    }
    catch ( Exception err ) {}
  }
}
```

24.4.4   Putting it all together

When compiled and run the following results are produced:

	Client (Application)	Server (Application)
Command line	`java Client` `localhost 2000 a bc def g`	`java Server  2000`
Output from application	1 2 3 1	

Note: Now there may be many clients sending a message to the server.
The server will run forever unless terminated.
The command line to start the client is shown as two lines so that it will fit in the
space provided. In reality of course this should be typed as a single line.
The server now produces no output to the terminal.

24.5   Case study a chatline

The following GUI based client and server implement a chatline, that allows multiple people to communicate with each other over the internet. Each chatter runs a client that sends messages to a central server, the central server then sends these messages back to each client. This process is illustrated in Figure 24.10.

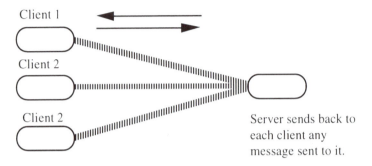

Client 1

Client 2

Client 2

Server sends back to each client any message sent to it.

Client sends messages to the server.
Displays any messages sent back.

Figure 24.10 Overview of chat line.

An illustration of two chatters communicating is shown below:

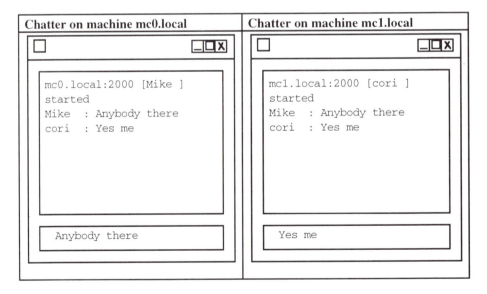

Chatter on machine mc0.local	Chatter on machine mc1.local
☐ ▢▢🗙	☐ ▢▢🗙

`mc0.local:2000 [Mike ]`
`started`
`Mike  : Anybody there`
`cori  : Yes me`
	`mc1.local:2000 [cori ]`
	`started`
	`Mike  : Anybody there`
	`cori  : Yes me`

`Anybody there`	`Yes me`

The clients and the server communicate using port 2000.

24.5.1 The `Client`

The chat line client is composed of the following classes:

Class	Brief overview
Application	Creates and manages the communication components.
Client	Starts the client.
TextArea	The awt visual text area.
Net_Reader	Read information from a remote server.
Net_Writer	Write information to a remote server.
TextField	The awt visual component.
Transaction	The call-back object for an instance of a TextField.

The object diagram for the client is shown in Figure 24.11.

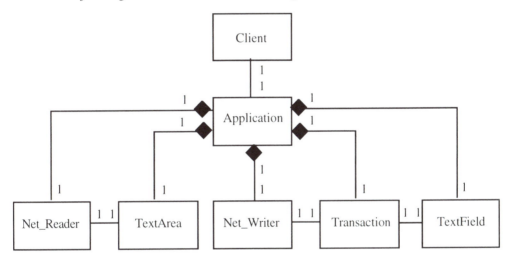

Figure 24.11 Class diagram for the client.

24.5.2 The `Client` implementation

The GUI based application is implemented as follows:

```
import java.awt.*;
import java.awt.event.*;
import java.net.*;
import java.io.IOException;

import Net_Reader;
import Net_Writer;
```

The client is started by creating an instance of the class Application that is a subclass of Frame.

```
class Client
{
  public static void main( String args[] )
  {
    Application client = new Application();    //Set up GUI
    client.show();                            //Show GUI
    client.start( args );                     //Start app
  }
}
```

The class `Application` a subclass of frame contains the major objects used in the GUI application.

```
class Application extends Frame
{
  private static final int H = 400;          //Height of Window
  private static final int W = 300;          //Width of Window

  private TextField    the_input;            //Visual Text Field
  private TextArea     the_output;           //Visual Text Area

  private String the_mc   = "localhost";     //Server
  private int    the_port = 2000;            //Port
  private String the_user = "Guest";         //User of chatline

  private Net_Reader the_reader;             //Coms line reader
  private Net_Writer the_writer;             //Coms line writer
```

The constructor for the class `Application` sets up two windows:

- An output window, `the_output` an instance of the class `TextArea`.

- An input window, `the_input` an instance of the class `TextField`.

The output window is used to display the currently taking place conversations on the chatline and the input window is used so that the local chatter can contribute to the conversations.

```
  public Application()
  {
    setLayout(null);                         //Set layout manager
    setSize( W, H );                         //Size of Window

    Font font =
      new Font("Monospaced",Font.PLAIN,12);  //Font Used

    the_input  = new TextField();            //Input area
    the_input.setBounds(10,H-50,W-20,40);    //          Size
    the_input.setFont( font );               //          Font
    add( the_input );                        //Add to canvas
```

```
  the_output = new TextArea( 10, 40 );       //Output area
  the_output.setBounds(10,30,W-20,H-100);    //            Size
  the_output.setFont( font );                //            Font
  add( the_output );                         //Add to canvas
  Transaction cb = new Transaction();        //Add listener
  the_input.addActionListener( cb );         //(Call-back)
}
```

The method `start` is responsible for the main processing loop of reading messages received from the server and displaying the messages in the output window. This can only take place if a connection has been established. The destination machine, port used and the chatter's name are supplied as command line parameters that the method `params` decodes.

```
public void start( String args[] )
{
  the_output.append( params( args ) + "\n");//Initial values
  String res = set_up_connection();          //Set up connection
  if ( res != null )
  {
    the_output.append( res + "\n" ); return;//Failure
  }
  the_output.append( "Started\n" );          //Display
  while ( true )
  {
    String message = the_reader.getLine();  //Message received
    if ( message.equals( Net_Reader.EOF ) ) //Server dead / Closed
    {
      the_output.append( "Server died\n" );
      return;
    }
    the_output.append( message +"\n" );      //Display
  }
}
```

The `method` params, decodes the command line parameters, where an inconsistency is found in the supplied parameters an appropriate default value is substituted.

```
public String params( String args[] )
{
  String prefix = "";
  try
  {
    if ( args.length == 3 )
    {
      the_mc   = args[0];                            //Machine
      the_port = Integer.parseInt( args[1] );        //Port
      the_user = (args[2] + "     ").substring(0,5); //Chatter
    } else {
      prefix = "Defaulted to ";
    }
  }
```

```
  catch ( Exception err )
  {
    prefix = "Defaulted to ";
  }
  return prefix + the_mc + ":" + the_port + " [" + the_user + "]";
}
```

The method `set_up_connection` is responsible for setting up the connection to the server machine.

```
public String set_up_connection()
{
  Socket socket;
  try
  {
    socket = new Socket( the_mc, the_port ); //Socket host.port
    the_reader = new Net_Reader( socket );
    the_writer = new Net_Writer( socket );
    return null;
  }
  catch ( Exception err )
  {
    return err.getMessage();
  }
}
```

The method `Transaction` implements the call-back action for the input text area. The method `actionPerformed` is called after a user has entered a message and pressed the return key.

```
class Transaction implements ActionListener
{
  public void actionPerformed( ActionEvent e )
  {
    String user_input = the_input.getText();
    if ( the_writer != null )
      the_writer.putLine( the_user +  " : " + user_input );
  }
}
}
```

24.5.3   The server

The server reads text messages from clients and sends back these text messages to all clients that are currently connected to the server. The chatline server is composed of the following classes:

Class	Brief overview
Net_Reader	Read information from a remote server.
Net_Writer	Write information to a remote server.
Person	Creates an active object that communicates with the client.
Server	Starts the server.
T_Chat_Manager	Manages the communication between the client and server.
T_Client_Reader	Creates an active object to read information from the client and provides an interface for non-blocking access to the read information.

In essence the server creates multiple instances of the class `Person` to handle individual chatters. An instance of `T_Chat_manager` is an active object that manages the flow of messages between the individual chatters. An object diagram for the chatline server is illustrated in Figure 24.12.

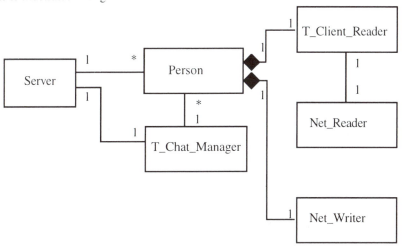

Figure 24.12 The chatline server.

```
import java.lang.*;
import java.net.*;
import java.util.*;
import java.io.*;
import Net_Reader;
import Net_Writer;

import java.lang.Thread;
```

The class `Server` implements the main processing loop of the chatline server. In essence chatters make contact with the server. For each contact a separate active object is created to manage communication with the chatter. In addition a separate process is created that polls each chatter in turn to see if they have made contact with the server to send a message, if they have, then the message is rebroadcast to all chatters.

```
class Server
{

  public static void main( String args[] )
  {
    try
    {
      if ( args.length == 1 )
      {
        process( Integer.parseInt( args[0] ) );
        return;
      }
    }
    catch ( Exception err ) { }
    System.out.println( "Usage Server port" );
  }

  public static void process( final int port )
  {
    try
    {
      T_Chat_Manager chat_manager = new T_Chat_Manager();
      chat_manager.start();

      ServerSocket socket = new ServerSocket( port );
      while( true )
      {
        Socket connection = socket.accept();     //Wait for connection

        chat_manager.add( new Person( connection ) );
      }
    }
    catch ( Exception err )
    {
      System.out.println("Unexpected communications failure");
    }
  }
}
```

24.5.4   The class T_Chat_Manager

The class T_Chat_Manager manages instances of class Person. Each instance of the class Person is an active object that is held in the array the_chatters. The role of an instance of the class Person is to communicates with an individual chatter.

```
class T_Chat_Manager extends Thread
{
  private static int MAX_PERSONS = 10;        //Max chatters
  private Person the_chatters[];              //
```

```
public T_Chat_Manager()
{
  the_chatters = new Person[ MAX_PERSONS ]; //Set up storage
  for ( int i=0; i<MAX_PERSONS; i++ )
  {
    the_chatters[i] = null;                    //Initially null
  }
}
```

The method `add` adds a news person to its collection of managed chatters. This is a synchronized method to prevent corruption and misuse of the shared resource `the_chatters`. The collection `the_chatters` is added to and accessed by different concurrently executing threads.

```
public synchronized void add( Person p )
{
  for ( int i=0; i< MAX_PERSONS; i++ )        //Add a new chatter
  {
    if ( the_chatters[i] == null )
    {
      the_chatters[ i ] = p;
      return;
    }
  }
}
```

Note: The bug that if there are MAX_PERSONS chatters already the new chatter is lost.

The method `remove` removes an inactive chatter from the managed collection.

```
public synchronized void remove( int i )
{
  the_chatters[i] = null;                      //Not active
}
```

The method `getMessage` returns a message from a chatter, if the chatter has not transmitted a message then `null` is returned. This method will not block as each chatter in the collection `the_chatters` is an active object that continuously monitors the communication line between it and the client.

```
public synchronized String getMessage( int i )
{
  String message = null;                       //Set none
  if ( the_chatters[i] != null )
  {
    message = the_chatters[i].getLine();       //Potential message
    if ( message != null  &&
         !message.equals(Net_Reader.EOF) )     //Real message
    {
      if ( the_chatters[i].getName() == null )  //Not Known
      {
        String name = message.substring( 0, 5 );
        the_chatters[i].setName( name );       //So save
      }
    }
  }
  return message;                              //
}
```

The method `getName` returns the name of a chatter.

```
public synchronized String getName( int i )
{
  if ( the_chatters[i] != null )
    return the_chatters[i].getName();         //Name of chatter
  return "?????";
}
```

The method `putMessage` writes a message to the chatter.

```
public synchronized void putMessage( int i, String message )
{
  if ( the_chatters[i] != null )
  {
    the_chatters[i].putLine( message );     //Write message
  }
}
```

The method `send_to_all` sends a message to all chatters, including the originator.

```
public void send_to_all( String message )
{
  for ( int i=0; i<MAX_PERSONS; i++ )          //Send message to all
  {
    putMessage( i, message );
  }
}
```

The method `run` implements the active part of the object which is a continuous loop, polling each chatter in turn to see if they have sent a text message. If they have then the text message is resent to all chatters. If the name of the chatter is currently unknown then the name sent as part of the text message is used as the chatter's name.

If a chatter has finished, an EOF message will be received, in which case the other chatters are informed that the chatter has left.

```java
public void run()
{
  while( true)
  {
    for ( int i=0; i<MAX_PERSONS; i++ )         //All chatters
    {
      String message = getMessage(i);
      if ( message != null )                    //Chatter spoke
      {
        if ( message.equals( Net_Reader.EOF ) )//Chatter died
        {
          message = getName(i) +                //Who left
                    " : left chat area";
          remove( i );                          //Remove
        }
        send_to_all( message );                 //Send message to all
      }
    }
    try {
      Thread.sleep( 500  );                     //Delay
    }
    catch( InterruptedException e ) {}
  }
}
```

24.5.5   The class `Person`

The class `Person` is used to create an active object that continuously monitors the communication connection to the client looking for a new text message. This functionality is implemented in an instance of the class `T_Client_Reader`.

In essence, the class `Person` provides a clean interface to the objects that are responsible for reading and writing to and from the communications channel.

```java
class Person
{
  private T_Client_Reader the_in;         //Input from client
  private Net_Writer      the_out;        //Output to client
  private String          the_name = null; //Name of chatter

  public Person( Socket s )
  {
    the_in  = new T_Client_Reader( new Net_Reader( s ) );
    the_out = new Net_Writer( s );
    the_in.start();                       //Start reading
  }
```

```
public String getLine()
{
  return the_in.getLine();           //Return message from client
}

public void putLine( String message )
{
  the_out.putLine( message );        //Write to client
}

public void setName( String name )
{
  the_name = name;                   //Set name of chatter
}

public String getName()
{
  return the_name;                   //Return name of chatter
}
}
```

24.5.6   The class `T_Client_Reader`

The class `T_Client_Reader` is used to create an active object that will continuously monitor the communications line to a chatter waiting for a text message to be sent. So that this process will not block a 1 unit buffer is used to hold the received text message. The buffer is checked for a message rather than the communications line. Thus, a non-blocking request can be made to see if the buffer contains a message. As waiting for a text message on the communications channel will block, this functionality is performed by the active part of the object.

The class is implemented as follows:

```
class T_Client_Reader extends Thread
{
  private Net_Reader the_in;              //Input from client
  private String     the_message = null;  //Data received

  public T_Client_Reader( Net_Reader in )
  {
    the_in = in;
  }
```

The method run, implements the active part of the object. When a text message is received from the chatter it is placed into the 1 unit buffer. Operations on this buffer are synchronized to prevent corruption etc.

```
public void run()
{
  while ( true )
  {
    String message = the_in.getLine();   //Will block if no data
    while ( !store_if_space( message ) )
    {
      try {
        Thread.sleep( 500 );                // 500 milliseconds delay
      }
      catch( InterruptedException e ) {}
    }
    if ( message.equals(Net_Reader.EOF) )
      return;
  }
}
```

The method `store_if_space` will only store the text message if space is available in the buffer.

```
public synchronized boolean store_if_space( String message )
{
  if ( the_message == null )
  {
    the_message = message;              //Space so store
    return true;                        //
  } else {
    return false;                       //No space
  }
}
```

The method `getLine` returns the text message stored in the buffer. If no message is stored in the buffer then `null` is returned.

```
public synchronized String getLine()
{
  if ( the_message != null )
  {
    String tmp = the_message;            //Message available
    the_message = null;                  //Clear
    return tmp;
  } else {
    return null;                         //No message
  }
}
```

24.6   Self-assessment

● Why is the client server relationship important?

● What is an IP Address?

● What is a domain name?

● How can you communicate with an application or applet running on another machine?

24.7   Exercises

Construct the following:

● *Time server*
A pair of applications that implements a time server and a client to access this data. The server delivers the current time of day and the client prints this retrieved time.

● *Remote file store*
A pair of applications that implements a remote file store. The client sends request to the server to store and retrieve files. The server processes these requests saving and retrieving the data from its local file store.

● *Better chatline server*
Remove the problem of a client unable to join the chatline because there are already MAX_PERSONS connected.

Allow a visual interface to the server so that there is a constant display of the number of connections.

● *Improved chatline (server & client)*
Re-write the chat line pair of applications so that the following additional features are provided:

   ● To be able to ask how many users are connected to the chat line.
   ● To be able to send a message to just one member of the chat line.
   ● An improved interface
   ● A moderator that has the ability to control the messages sent.

Remove the problem that will occur if more than MAX_CHATTERS attempt to connect to the server.

25. Remote Method Invocation

Normally when a message is sent to an object the object resides in the same address space as the code that sent the message. In essence the interacting objects are contained in a single program. However, by using RMI (Remote Method Invocation) a message can be sent to an object residing in an another program, which may be executing in a distant machine.

25.1 Introduction to Remote Method Invocation

RMI (Remote Method Invocation) allows an application or applet to communicate with objects residing in programs running in remote machines. In essence, instead of creating an object the programmer binds the remote object to a local stub. The local stub is then sent messages as if it were the real object. The stub accepts any messages sent to it and sends these messages onto the distant object, which invokes the appropriate methods. The result of the method invocation on the distant object is then sent back to the stub that then returns the result to the caller.

Apart from the binding of the distant object to the stub the code written by a programmer required to communicate with a distant object is the same as if the object were contained in the local application or applet.

25.2 Overview of the process

Figure 25.1 illustrates an application (the client application) running on machine A sending a message to a remote object contained in an application (the server application) running on machine B.

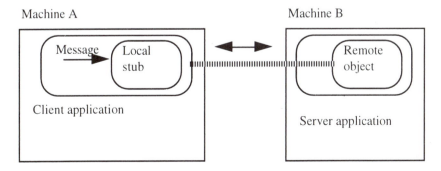

Figure 25.1 Sending a message to a remote object.

When the client application sends a message to the local stub of the remote object, the request is transmitted to the machine containing the actual object where the method is invoked and any result returned back to the local stub so that the client application can receive the appropriate response.

25.2.1   The class `java.rmi.Naming`

The class `Naming` contains the following static methods that allow access to remote objects using a URL to specify the name and location of the remote object.

Method	Responsibility
`bind(url,object)`	Binds a name to the remote object. The name is specified as a URL.
`list(url)`	Returns an array of strings representing the URL's in the registry.
`lookup(url)`	Returns the remote object (A stub) associated with the URL.
`rebind(url,object)`	As for bind but replaces any previous association.
`unbind(url)`	Removes the association between the remote object and the URL.

The URL is in the form: `rmi://host:port/object_name` where

Component of URL	Defaults to	Specifies
`rmi`	`rmi`	The access method (must be rmi).
`host`	`localhost`	The host machine.
`port`	`1099`	The port number to use.
`object_name`		The name of the remote object.

25.2.2   The application `rmiregistry`

The server application `rmiregistry` is used to:

● Register a name and a location of a remote object.
This would be performed by a server that holds the remote object. The code in the server would be of the form:

```
Naming.rebind( "rmi://host/name", object );
```

Where `"rmi://host/name"` is the location of the remote object and `object` is the object that is to be called remotely. In addition the `rmiregistry` application must be running on the same machine as the server application that contains the remote object.

● Allow a client to bind a local stub that will allow access to the remote object held in the server application.
The client application binds to the remote object by using the method `lookup` to return an object that allows access via the stub to the remote object. The code in the client to perform this action is of the form:

```
Naming.lookup( "rmi://host/name" );
```

In essence, the application `rmiregistry` acts as a registry for objects that are to be accessed remotely. Objects are entered into the registry and bound to a local stub by using methods in the class `Naming`. The class `Naming` is in the package `java.rmi`.

25.2.3 The whole process

Figure 25.2 illustrates the whole process of a client application running on machine A accessing a remote object held in a server application running on machine B.

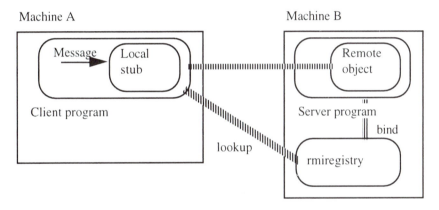

Figure 25.2 Overview of accessing a remote object using `rmiregistry`.

The sequence of steps involved is as follows:

Set-up

● The `rmiregistry` application is started on machine B.
● The server application containing the remote object is started on machine B.
● The server application binds (`bind` or `rebind`) the remote object to the `rmiregistry` application.
● The client application is started on machine A.
● The client application looks up (`lookup`) the remote object and binds this to a local stub.

Access

● Messages are sent to the local stub on machine A that are then forwarded to the server holding the actual object. The method corresponding to the message is invoked and the result returned.

Note: The rmiregistry *application must be run on the same machine as the server application that holds the remote object.*

An important class used in the RMI process is the class Naming. The major responsibilities of class Naming are:

Method	Responsibility
bind(str, o)	Binds the name str to the remote object o.
lookup(str)	Returns a stub associated with the name str. By sending messages to the stub access is made to the remote object
rebind(str, o)	Rebinds the name str to a new remote object.
unbind(str)	Removes the association between the remote object and the name str.

25.3   Accessing a bank account remotely

The following applications illustrate a client—server relationship where the server application contains a bank account object that is accessed remotely from a client application. The bank account class is based on the class Account seen earlier in Section 5.2.5. The bank account class has the following responsibilities:

Method	Responsibility
account_balance()	Returns the amount of money held in the account.
deposit	Deposits money into the account.
withdraw(money)	Withdraws money from the account. But only if the account balance would not be taken below £0.00.

As an instance of this class is to be accessed remotely it must extend the class UnicastRemoteObject that is in the package java.rmi.server and implement the interface Remote_Account. The interface Remote_Account is discussed in more detail in the following Section 25.3.2.

In addition each method in the class must be able to throw the exception RemoteException.

25.3.1   The class R_Account

The implementation of the class R_Account is as follows:

```
import java.rmi.*;

class R_Account extends      java.rmi.server.UnicastRemoteObject
               implements Remote_Account
{
  private double the_balance      = 0.0d;  //Balance of account
```

```
    public R_Account() throws RemoteException
    {
      super();
      the_balance = 0.00;
    }

    public double account_balance() throws RemoteException
    {
      return the_balance;
    }

    public double withdraw( final double money ) throws RemoteException
    {
      if ( the_balance - money >= 0.00 )
      {
        the_balance = the_balance - money;
        return money;
      } else {
        return 0.00;
      }
    }

    public void deposit( final double money ) throws RemoteException
    {
      the_balance = the_balance + money;
    }

}
```

Note: The class extends `java.rmi.server.UnicastRemoteObject` *and implements the protocol* `Remote_Account`.
Each method can throw the exception `RemoteException`.

25.3.2   The interface `Remote_Account`

The interface `Remote_Account` defines the protocol that the remote object will implement. It is defined as follows:

```
import java.rmi.*;
import java.io.*;
import java.rmi.server.UnicastRemoteObject;

interface Remote_Account extends Remote
{
  public double account_balance() throws RemoteException;
  public void    deposit( final double money) throws RemoteException;
  public double withdraw( final double money ) throws RemoteException;
}
```

The interface extends the interface `Remote` and each method in the interface may throw the exception `RemoteException`.

Note: This interface must be defined, it is not correct to have the class `R_Account` *implement the interface* `Remote` *directly.*

25.3.3 The client application

The client application will be run from the command line with a command line parameter of the URL that represents the location of the remote object. For example, if both the server and client are run on the same machine then the URL only need specify the name of the remote object as follows:

```
java Client Mike
```

The code for the client is illustrated below. The static method `main` extracts the URL as a string and passes this to the static method `process` that has responsibility for contacting and accessing the remote object.

```java
import java.rmi.*;

class Client
{
  public static void main( String args[] )
  {
    if ( args.length == 1 )
    {
      process( args[0] );
    } else {
      System.out.println("Usage: client url" );
    }
  }
}
```

Using early version of Java a security manager is required to allow access to the remote object, however, with Java 2 this is not required. The method `process` uses the method `lookup` to return a stub to the remote object. The stub is then accessed as it were a normal local object.

A message sent to the stub is converted to a form that can be sent to the remote object by way of a network connection. If a result is returned from the remote object this is delivered as the result of sending the message to the local stub.

```java
static void process( String url )
{
  // Uncomment for legacy JDK 1.1 systems
  //System.setSecurityManager( new RMISecurityManager() );
  Remote_Account mike;
  try
  {
    mike = (Remote_Account) Naming.lookup( url );

    double obtained;
```

```
        System.out.println( "Mike's Balance    = " +
                            mike.account_balance() );
        mike.deposit(100.00);
        System.out.println( "Mike's Balance    = " +
                            mike.account_balance() );

        obtained = mike.withdraw(20.00);
        System.out.println( "Mike has withdrawn  : " + obtained );
        System.out.println( "Mike's Balance    = " +
                            mike.account_balance() );

    }
    catch ( Exception err )
    {
        System.out.println("Error: " + err.getMessage() );
    }
  }
}
```

Note: The installation of a security manager required for legacy systems that use JDK
        1.1.
        The look up of the remote object. In true Java tradition an object of type
        `Object` is returned which must be cast to the interface `Remote_Object`.

```
mike = (Remote_Account) Naming.lookup( url );
```

25.3.4   The server application

The server application simply creates an instance of the R_Account object and binds
this to the URL that is supplied as a command line parameter. For example, if both the
server and client are run on the same machine then the URL only need specify the name
of the remote object as follows:

```
java Server Mike
```

The implementation of the server application is as follows:

```
import java.rmi.*;
import java.io.*;

class Server
{
  public static void main( String args[] )
  {
    if ( args.length == 1 )
    {
      process( args[0] );
    } else {
      System.out.println("Usage: Server url" );
    }
  }
```

The static method process creates an instance of the class R_Account and binds the object to the supplied URL.

```
static void process( String url )
{
  try
  {
    // Uncomment for legacy JDK 1.1 systems
    //System.setSecurityManager( new RMISecurityManager() );
    R_Account mike = new R_Account();

    Naming.rebind( url, mike );
    System.out.println( "Bound mike to: " + url );
  }
  catch ( Exception err )
  {
      System.out.println("Error: " + err.getMessage() );
  }
}
}
```

Note: The server application will not exit.

25.4   Compiling and running the applications

In the following description of how to compile and run the above applications, the standard JDK development kit is used. This development kit consists of a command line compiler and interpreter to run the generated byte code. See Appendix G for a fuller description of these components. In describing the process the following files contain the following classes and interfaces:

File	Contains
Remote_Account.java	The interface Remote_Account
R_Account.java	Contains the class R_Account
Client.java	Contains the class Client
Server.java	Contains the class Server

25.4.1   Compiling the applications

Using a command line compiler the applications are compiled in the following way:

```
javac Remote_Account.java
javac R_Account.java
javac Client.java
javac Server.java
```

However, a stub must also be generated for the remote object. This is performed by the command line rmi compiler as follows:

```
rmic R_Account
```

25.4.2 Running the applications

Firstly on the server machine the `rmiregistry` application is started using the following command line:

```
rmiregistry
```

then the server application is started using the command line interpreter:

```
java Server rmi://Hyperion/Mikes_Account
```

then on another machine the client is started

```
java Client rmi://Hyperion/Mikes_Account
```

which will print

```
Mike's Balance      = 0.0
Mike's Balance      = 100.0
Mike has withdrawn  : 20.0
Mike's Balance      = 80.0
```

If this is run again the output produced will be

```
Mike's Balance      = 80.0
Mike's Balance      = 180.0
Mike has withdrawn  : 20.0
Mike's Balance      = 160.0
```

25.5 A web-based client using RMI

The client naturally may also be an applet. However, in this case there are some minor changes to the strategy required to access the remote object. In essence these is:

● It is assumed that the web-based applet is loaded from the machine that contains the remote object. The methods:
```
getCodeBase().getHost()
```
are used to obtain the name or IP address of the machine on which the server runs.

25.5.1 Overview of applet

This demonstration applet is based on the applet illustrated in Section 8.8.1. The applet has an input area and an output area into which are written the results of any interactions with the applet.

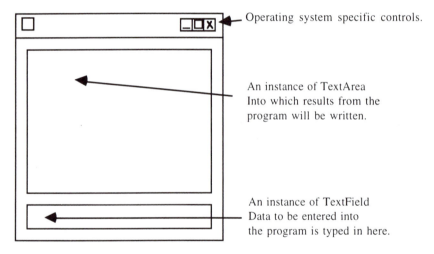

Operating system specific controls.

An instance of TextArea
Into which results from the
program will be written.

An instance of TextField
Data to be entered into
the program is typed in here.

Transactions to the applet are of the form:

```
D 100.00            // Deposit 100 into the bank account
W 20.00             // Withdraw £20 from the account
B                   // Display the balance
```

25.5.2 Implementation

The complete applet is implemented as follows:

```
import java.awt.*;
import java.awt.event.*;
import java.applet.*;
import java.rmi.*;
```

```
public class Account_Applet extends Applet
{
  private static final int H = 400;        // Height of window
  private static final int W = 300;        // Width  of window

  private TextField  the_input;            //Visual Text Field (Input)
  private TextArea   the_output;           //Visual Text Area  (Output)
  private Transaction    the_cb = new Transaction();
  private Remote_Account the_account;
```

The method `int` creates the visual components of the interface and looks up and binds the remote object to a local copy of the interface. To ascertain the host name from where the web page was downloaded the following two methods are used:

Method	In class / Responsibility
getCodeBase()	In the class `Applet`: Returns an instance of the class URL that represents the URL used to load the file.
getHost()	In the class URL: Returns the host part of the URL as a string.

```
public void init()
{
  setLayout(null);                       //Set layout manager (none)
  setSize( W, H );                       //Size of Window

  Font font = new Font("Monospaced",Font.PLAIN,12);

  the_input = new TextField();           //Input area
  the_input.setBounds(10,H-50,W-20,40);  //              Size
  the_input.setFont( font );             //              Font
  add( the_input );                      //Add to canvas
  the_input.addActionListener( the_cb );

  the_output = new TextArea( 10,40 );    //Output area
  the_output.setBounds(10,30,W-20,H-100); //             Size
  the_output.setFont( font );            //              Font
  add( the_output );                     //Add to canvas

  try
  {
    String url = "rmi://" + getCodeBase().getHost() + "/Account";
    System.out.println(url);
    the_account = (Remote_Account) Naming.lookup( url );
  }
  catch ( Exception err )
  {
    System.out.println("Error: " + err.getMessage() );
  }
}
```

The call-back method `Transaction` is called each time a user enters a transaction into the input text field and presses return.

```
class Transaction implements ActionListener
{
  public void actionPerformed( ActionEvent e )
  {
    String user_input = the_input.getText() + "  ";//Make safe
    char action       = user_input.charAt(0);        //Transaction
    String rest       = user_input.substring( 1 ); //Data
    double value      = 0.0;
    try
    {
      value = Double.parseDouble( rest );             //Data val
    }
    catch ( NumberFormatException ex )
    {
      the_output.append( "Error in # [" + rest + "]\n" );
    }
    try
    {
      double res = 0.0;
      switch ( action )
      {
        case 'D' : case 'd' :                         //Deposit
          if ( value >= 0.00 )
          {
            the_account.deposit( value );
            the_output.append( "Deposited  : " + value + "\n");
          } else {
            the_output.append( "Amount must be positive\n" );
          }
          break;
        case 'W' : case 'w' :                         //Withdraw
          if ( value >= 0.00 )
          {
            res = the_account.withdraw( value );
            if ( res == value )
              the_output.append( "Withdrawn  : " + value + "\n");
            else
              the_output.append( "Sorry not possible\n" );
          } else {
            the_output.append( "Amount must be positive\n" );
          }
          break;
        case 'B' : case 'b' :                         //Balance
          res = the_account.account_balance();
          the_output.append( "Balance    : " + res + "\n" );
          break;
        default  :
          the_output.append( action + " - Error\n" );
      }
    }
    catch ( Exception ex ) { }
  }
}
```

25.5.3 Putting it all together

When compiled and run with the following transactions entered into the input text field:

```
D 200
B
W 20
```

the applet will display the following information.

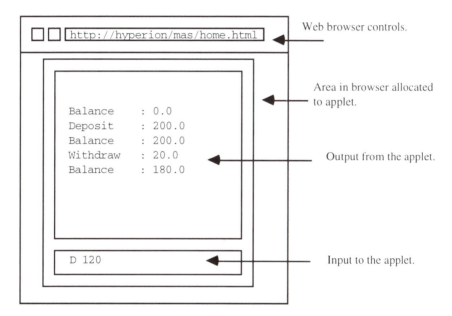

Web browser controls.

Area in browser allocated to applet.

Output from the applet.

Input to the applet.

25.6 Self-assessment

- What is RMI?

- What does the `rmiregistry` application do?

- Why is a new security manager required when using an application for the client and server?

- What are the advantages / disadvantages of using a remote object approach to the implementation of a client server application or applet rather than a stream based approach ?

25.7   Exercises

Construct the following:

- *Remote file store*
  Implement a class File_Manager that provides the ability to create, read, and write to and from files. Create a server application that makes this class visible and then use this to read and write files on the remote machine.

- *Better remote file store*
  Add password protection to the files created by the remote file system.

- *Chat ine application*
  Re-implement the chatline application from the previous chapter using remote objects.

26. Reflection

The reflection mechanism allows an application or applet at runtime to acquire information about a class.

26.1   Introduction

In an object-oriented methodology every object belongs to a specific class. So the question arises what class do classes belong to? The answer is a meta-class. In Java this class is the class `Class`. For example, using the previously seen class `Account`, the following fragment of code creates an object that the class `Account` is an instance of. This object is then used to acquire information about the class `Account`:

```
Account an_account    = new Account();
Class   account_class = an_account.getClass();

System.out.println("toString : " + account_class.toString() );
System.out.println("getName  : " + account_class.getName () );
```

Note: The method `getClass` returns an instance of the class that represents the class
that an object is an instance of.
The initial definition of the method `getName` is in the class `Object`.

When this code is incorporated into a complete application and compiled and run the results produced are as follows:

```
toString   : class Account
getName    : Account
```

Note: The method `getName` of the class `Class` is inherited from the class `Object`.

26.2   Reflection classes

The classes `Class`, `Method` and `Constructor` are all used to find information about a class.

26.2.1 Selected methods in the class `java.lang.Class`

The major methods of the class `java.lang.Class` are:

Method	Responsibility
getName()	Returns the name of the class as a string.
getConstructors()	Returns an array of instances of Constructor representing the constructors in the class.
getMethods()	Returns an array of instances of Method representing the methods in the class.

26.2.2 Selected methods in the class `java.lang.reflect.Method`

The major methods of the class `Method` are:

Methods	Responsibility
getDeclaringClass()	Returns an instance of Class representing the class that declared this method.
getParameterTypes()	Returns an array of instances of Class representing the parameters to the method.
getReturnType()	Returns an instance of Class representing the return type of the method.
getName()	Returns the name of the method as a string.
invoke(object o, object p[])	Invokes this method on o with parameters contained in the array p returning the result.

26.2.3 Selected methods in the class `Constructor`

The major methods of the class `java.lang.reflect.Constructor` are:

Methods	Responsibility
getDeclaringClass()	Returns an instance of Class representing the class that declared this constructor.
getName()	Returns the name of the constructor as a string.
getParameterTypes()	Returns an array of instances of Class representing the parameters to the constructor.

26.3 Using the classes `Class`, `Method` and `Constructor`

The following demonstration class Useful contains the static method about that lists to the standard output details about the object passed as a parameter. The details are the constructors and methods contained in the class to which this object is an instance of.

For each method or constructor in the class the following information is printed: its type (method or constructor), the returned result, the name of the method or constructor, and the parameters to the method or constructor.

```
class Useful
{
  public static void about( Object object )
  {
    Class object_class = object.getClass();              //Meta class

    System.out.println( object_class.toString() );
```

Firstly the constructors in the objects class are printed.

```
    Constructor c[] = object_class.getConstructors();   //Methods in
    for ( int i=0; i<c.length; i++ )                    // For each
    {
      String line = "C ";
      Class in  = c[i].getDeclaringClass();             //Declared in
      line += in.equals(object_class) ? "L " : "I ";
      line += c[i].getName() + "(";
      Class p[] = c[i].getParameterTypes();             // Parameters
      for ( int j=0; j<p.length; j++ )                  //  For each
      {
        line += p[j].getName();                         //  Type
        if ( j != p.length-1 ) line += ",";
      }
      line += ")";
      System.out.println( line );
    }
```

Secondly the methods in the objects class are printed.

```
    Method m[] = object_class.getMethods();             //Methods in
    for ( int i=0; i<m.length; i++ )                    // For each
    {
      String line = "M ";
      Class in  = m[i].getDeclaringClass();             //Declared in
      line += in.equals(object_class) ? "L " : "I ";
      Class rt  = m[i].getReturnType();                 //Return Type
      line += rt.getName() + " " + m[i].getName() + "(";
      Class p[] = m[i].getParameterTypes();             // Parameters
      for ( int j=0; j<p.length; j++ )                  //  For each
      {
        line += p[j].getName();                         //  Type
        if ( j != p.length-1 ) line += ",";
      }
      line += ")";
      System.out.println( line );
    }
  }
}
```

26.3.1   Putting it all together

The following example application lists all the methods and constructors of an instance of the class `Account_with_statement`. This class is shown in Chapter 12 on Inheritance.

```
class Main
{
  public static void main( String args[] )
  {
    System.out.println("Key");
    System.out.print  ("C - Constructor      ");
    System.out.println("M - Method");
    System.out.print  ("I - Inherited Method ");
    System.out.println("L - Local Method");
    System.out.println();
    Useful.about ( new Account_with_statement() );
  }
}
```

Which when compiled and run produces the following output:

```
Key
C - Constructor      M - Method
I - Inherited Method L - Local Method

class Account_with_statement
C L Account_with_statement()
C L Account_with_statement(java.lang.String)
M I boolean equals(java.lang.Object)
M I java.lang.Class getClass()
M I int hashCode()
M I void notify()
M I void notifyAll()
M I java.lang.String toString()
M I void wait()
M I void wait(long)
M I void wait(long,int)
M I double account_balance()
M I void deposit(double)
M I void set_min_balance(double)
M I double withdraw(double)
M L java.lang.String statement()
```

*Note: The inclusion of methods from `Account_with_statement` superclasses
          `Account` and `Object`.*

26.4 Self-assessment

- Would it be possible to have reflection with a compiled language?

- What is a meta class?

- Why is reflection important in Java?

26.5 Exercises

Construct the following class method in the class `Useful` that has the following signature:

- *Object call(Object o, String method, Object prams[])*
  That will send the message contained in the string `method` to the object o with parameters held in the array `prams`. If the method does not exist then the exception `Exception_method_not_there` is to be thrown. If the process succeeds then the result of result of calling the method is returned.

  Hint: Use the method invoke in the class Method.

27. Layout of visual components

This chapter examines the different layout managers that are used in an application or applet to automatically position visual components in a window according to the designers' guidelines. By using a layout manager a change in the size of the displayed application or applet window can be accommodated automatically whilst still retaining the implementor's desired format guidelines.

27.1   Introduction

If visual components are placed at fixed positions on the visual window that represents the running application or applet, then a re-sizing of the window may result in some of the components in that window not being displayed as they were intended. This may occur for example, when a user running the application or applet has only a small monitor screen on which to view the application or applet window.

Rather than force designs of GUI-based applications to recalculate where each visual component should be placed when a re-size of an application or applet window occurs, a layout manager will perform this re-organization of the visual components automatically. By choosing a layout manager or a combination of layout managers the implementor's desired format guidelines are adhered too.

27.2   Layout managers

The package `java.awt` provides several layout managers that will re-organize automatically the position of visual components on a window when it is re-sized. By using layout managers, the developer of an application or applet does not have to be concerned with the re-calculation of the position of visual components when a window is re-sized.

27.3   The class `java.awt.FlowLayout`

This is the default layout manager and has the simplest strategy of all layout managers for arranging components in a window. In essence visual components flow one after another in a displayed window. If a component will not fit in the current row a new row is started. The items are by default centred in the row in which they are placed. Figure 27.1 illustrates the effect of the flow-layout manager after re-sizing a window that contains five visual components.

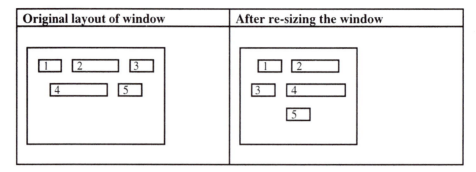

Original layout of window	After re-sizing the window

Figure 27.1 Effect of the flow-layout manager after re-sizing a window.

The class `java.awt.FlowLayout` implements the following major responsibilities:

Method	Responsibility
`FlowLayout()`	Creates an instance of a flow layout.
`FlowLayout(hgap,vgap)`	Creates an instance of a flow layout with a horizontal gap of `hgap` and vertical gap of `vgap`.
`getAlignment()`	Returns the current alignment.
`getHgap()`	Returns the horizontal gap between components.
`getVgap()`	Returns the vertical gap between components.
`setAlignment(align)`	Sets the alignment for components. May be: CENTER, LEFT, RIGHT, LEADING and TRAILING.
`setHgap(pixels)`	Sets the horizontal gap between components.
`setVgap(pixels)`	Sets the vertical gap between components.

For example, the following code uses the class `FlowLayout` to distribute 5 buttons in a window.

In this demonstration class an instance of the class `Panel` is created as a container for the five instances of the visual class `Button`. On this panel is set an instance of the class `FlowLayout` as the layout manager.

The class `java.awt.Panel` is inherited from `Container` that has the following inherited major responsibilities:

Method	Responsibility
`add( component )`	Adds a `component` to the panel.
`add( component, constraint )`	Adds a `component` with `constraint`.

A demonstration application to illustrate the flow layout is shown below:

```
class Application extends Frame
{
  private static final int H = 200;
  private static final int W = 300;
```

```
Application()
{
  setSize( W, H );                          //Size of Window

  Panel panel = new Panel();                //Create panel
  panel.setLayout( new FlowLayout() );      //Type of layout

  Button first  = new Button( "1 First");
  Button second = new Button( "2 Second long name");
  Button third  = new Button( "3 Third");
  Button Fourth = new Button( "4 Fourth long name");
  Button fifth  = new Button( "5 Fifth" );

  panel.add( first );                       //Add to panel
  panel.add( second );
  panel.add( third );
  panel.add( Fourth );
  panel.add( fifth );

  add( panel );                             //Add to window
  setTitle("FlowLayout");
}
}
```

27.3.1 Putting it all together

When compiled with suitable declarations and run the application distributes the buttons in the window according to the flow-layout manager. The right-hand example below illustrates the default layout generated and the left hand example shows the effect of a re-sizing of the window by reducing its width:

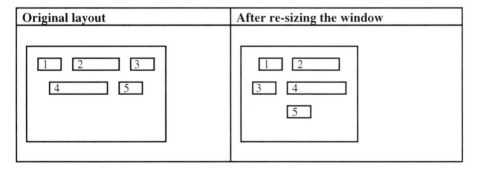

27.4   The class `java.awt.BorderLayout`

In this layout the window is divided into 5 named regions into which visual components may be placed. These five regions are named `North`, `East`, `South`, `West` and `Center`. The approximate positions of these regions in a window is illustrated in Figure 27.2 below:

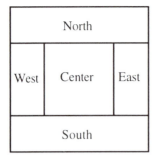

The North and South regions are like a header and a footer, whilst the West, Center (US spelling) and East regions form a band across the middle.

Figure 27.2 The approximate position of the five regions in a border layout .

The class java.awt.BorderLayout implements the following major responsibilities:

Method	Responsibility
BorderLayout()	Creates an instance of a borde layout.
BorderLayout(hgap, vgap)	Creates an instance of a borderlayout with a horizontal gap of hgap and vertical gap of vgap.
getHgap()	Returns the horizontal gap between components.
getVgap()	Returns the vertical gap between components.
setHgap(pixels)	Sets the horizontal gap between components.
setVgap(pixels)	Sets the vertical gap between components.

The following demonstration class places buttons in each of the five regions. Again a panel is used as a container on which this time an instance of the class BorderLayout is used as the layout manager.

```java
class Application extends Frame
{
  private static final int H = 300;
  private static final int W = 300;

  Application()
  {
    setSize( W, H );                           //Size of Window
    Panel panel = new Panel();                 //Create panel
    panel.setLayout( new BorderLayout() );     //Type of layout

    Button north  = new Button( "North" );     //North
    Button east   = new Button( "East" );      //East
    Button south  = new Button( "South" );     //South
    Button west   = new Button( "West" );      //West
    Button center = new Button( "Center" );    // Note US Spelling

    panel.add( north,  BorderLayout.NORTH );   // Add to panel
    panel.add( south,  BorderLayout.SOUTH );
    panel.add( east,   BorderLayout.EAST );
    panel.add( west,   BorderLayout.WEST );
    panel.add( center, BorderLayout.CENTER );
```

```
      add( panel );                              //Add
      setTitle("BorderLayout");
   }
}
```

27.4.1   Putting it all together

When compiled with suitable declarations and run the application distributes the buttons as illustrated below. Also shown is the effect of a re-sizing of the window, the re-sizing reduces the width of the window:

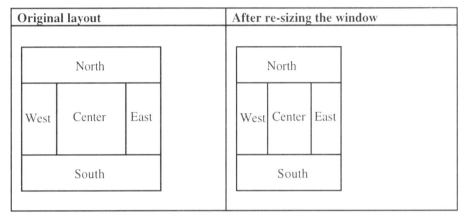

Original layout	After re-sizing the window

27.5   Nesting layouts

When constructing an interface a layout manager may be nested inside another layout manager. In the following demonstration application a boarder layout is used to hold six buttons. Two of the buttons are held in the East position. This is achieved by creating a panel to contain the two buttons. This panel is then added to the original panel that obeys the boarder layout. The following application illustrates this nesting of layouts:

```
class Application extends Frame
{
  private static final int H = 300;
  private static final int W = 300;

  Application()
  {
    setSize( W, H );                          //Size of Window

    Panel panel = new Panel();                //Create panel
    panel.setLayout( new BorderLayout() );    //Type of layout

    Button north  = new Button( "North" );    //North
    Button south  = new Button( "South" );    //South
    Button west   = new Button( "West" );     //West
    Button center = new Button( "Center" );   //Center
```

```
    Panel east_panel = new Panel();              //Create panel2
    east_panel.setLayout( new FlowLayout() );    //Type of layout
    Button east1 = new Button( "1" );            //East 1st button
    Button east2 = new Button( "2" );            //East 2nd button
    east_panel.add( east1 );                     //Panel2 contains
    east_panel.add( east2 );                     // second & third

    panel.add( north,      BorderLayout.NORTH ); // Add to panel
    panel.add( south,      BorderLayout.SOUTH );
    panel.add( east_panel, BorderLayout.EAST );
    panel.add( west,       BorderLayout.WEST );
    panel.add( center,     BorderLayout.CENTER );

    add( panel );                                //Add
    setTitle("BorderLayout");
  }
}
```

27.5.1 Putting it all together

When compiled with suitable declarations and run the resultant layout of the buttons in their window are shown below:

Layout	Commentary
 North / West / Center / 1 2 / South	The buttons named North, South, West and Center fill their regions whilst the buttons for 1 and 2 are placed in a row in the east position. The size of these buttons is sufficient to allow the display of their title.

27.6   The class `GridLayout`

In a grid layout visual components are arranged evenly to fill a grid. The size of each cell of the grid is the same. For example, if a window were split into a grid of two rows by three columns then the six elements of the grid would be as illustrated in Figure 27.3 below.

Note that each of the regions are the same size.

Figure 27.3 A grid layout of three columns by two rows.

The class `java.awt.GridLayout` implements the following major responsibilities:

Method	Responsibility
GridLayout(rows,cols)	Creates an instance of a grid layout of rows by cols.
GridLayout(rows,cols, hgap,vgap)	Creates an instance of a grid layout of rows by cols with a horizontal gap of hgap and vertical gap of vgap.
getRows()	Returns the number of rows in the grid layout.
getHgap()	Returns the horizontal gap between components.
getVgap()	Returns the vertical gap between components.
setHgap(pixels)	Sets the horizontal gap between components.
setRows(rows)	Sets the number of rows to be rows.
setVgap(pixels)	Sets the vertical gap between components.

The following demonstration class creates a grid layout of two rows by three columns and places in this grid five buttons.

```
class Application extends Frame
{
  private static final int H = 300;
  private static final int W = 300;

  Application()
  {
    setSize( W, H );                         //Size of Window

    Panel panel     = new Panel();           //Create panel
    GridLayout gb   = new GridLayout(2,3);   // 2 rows 3 cols

    panel.setLayout( gb );                   //Type of layout

    Button first  = new Button( "First" );
    Button second = new Button( "Second ");
    Button third  = new Button( "Third" );
    Button fourth = new Button( "Fourth" );
    Button fifth  = new Button( "Fifth"  );

    panel.add( first );                      //Add to panel
    panel.add( second );
    panel.add( third );
    panel.add( fourth );
    panel.add( fifth );

    add( panel );                            //Add to window
    setTitle("GridLayout");
  }
}
```

27.6.1   Putting it all together

When compiled with suitable declarations and run the resultant layout of the buttons in the window of the application is shown below:

Layout	Commentary
First Second Third Fourth Fifth	Note though allocated the sixth region has no visual component.

27.7   The class `java.awt.CardLayout`

A card layout allows different layout to be chosen, from a pre-defined set of layouts. This operates like a deck of playing cards in that the exposed layout hides the other layouts. By using the layout manager `CardLayout` different graphical components can be displayed in a visual form. For example, an application that allows a user to set a value either as an absolute value or as an approximation using buttons has the following two visualizations:

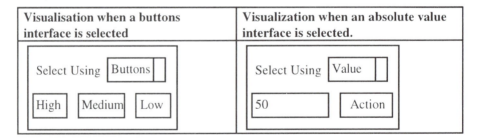

Visualisation when a buttons interface is selected	Visualization when an absolute value interface is selected.
Select Using Buttons High Medium Low	Select Using Value 50 Action

The pop-up menu is used to select which visualisation is to be shown. When the pop-up menu has `Buttons` selected the bottom of the form shows three buttons which are used to select either a high, medium or low value. When the pop-up menu has `Value` selected the bottom of the form has a text box into which the user can type an absolute value and press the action button to select this specific value.

The class `java.awt.CardLayout` implements the following major responsibilities:

Method	Responsibility
`CardLayout()`	Creates an instance of a card layout.
`CardLayout(hgap,vgap)`	Creates an instance of a card layout with a horizontal gap of `hgap` and vertical gap of `vgap`.
`getHgap()`	Returns the horizontal gap between components.
`getVgap()`	Returns the vertical gap between components.
`setHgap(pixels)`	Sets the horizontal gap between components.
`setVgap(pixels)`	Sets the vertical gap between components.

The following demonstration class implements the above visual frame:

```
class Application extends Frame
{
  private static final int H = 100;
  private static final int W = 300;

  Panel cards_stack;                        // Selection

  Application()
  {
    setSize( W, H );                        //Size of Window
    String OPT1 = "Buttons";                //Choice - Buttons
    String OPT2 = "Value";                  //Choice - by value

    Panel panel = new Panel();              //For border layout
    panel.setLayout( new BorderLayout() );  //
```

The next section of code creates the north panel that contains the pop-up menu used to select either the buttons interface or the text box interface for the lower part of the form. This effect is implemented by the call-back function `itemStateChanged` that is a member of the class `Action`. An instance of this class is registered as a listener for the instance of the pop-up menu `choice`.

```
    Panel  north  = new Panel();            //North panel
    Choice choice = new Choice();           //Pull down list
    choice.add( OPT1 );                     // item 1
    choice.add( OPT2 );                     // item 2

    Action ct = new Action();               //Called on change
    choice.addItemListener( ct );           //
    north.add( new Label( "Select using" ) );
    north.add( choice );                    //North panel
```

The south part of the form contains the two possible layouts, either buttons or value:

```
Panel choice1 = new Panel();              //Choice 1
choice1.add( new Button( "High" ) );      // Button - High
choice1.add( new Button( "Medium" ) );    // Button - Medium
choice1.add( new Button( "Low" ) );       // Button - Low

Panel choice2 = new Panel();              //Choice 2
choice2.add( new TextField( "50", 10) );  // Text Field
choice2.add( new Button( "Action" ) );    // Button - Action
```

The object `cards_stack` an instance of `Panel` is allocated the card layout manager. The two possible layouts are then added to this instance of a `Panel`.

```
cards_stack = new Panel();                //For cards layout
cards_stack.setLayout( new CardLayout() );
cards_stack.add( OPT1, choice1 );         // Choice 1
cards_stack.add( OPT2, choice2 );         // Choice 2
```

The main `panel` which uses a border layout has the pop-up menu as its north component and the card layout as its south component.

```
panel.add( north,       BorderLayout.NORTH );//North panel
panel.add( cards_stack, BorderLayout.SOUTH );//South panel

add( panel );                             //Add
setTitle("CardLayout");
}
```

The call-back function `itemStateChanged` interrogates the pop-up menu for the currently selected item (`getItem()`) and requests `cards_stack` to display this selected layout.

```
class Action implements ItemListener
{
  public void itemStateChanged( ItemEvent evt )
  {
    CardLayout cl = (CardLayout) cards_stack.getLayout(); //Layout
    String     selected = (String) evt.getItem();        //Selected
    cl.show( cards_stack, selected );                    //Show
  }
}
}
```

27.7.1 Putting it all together

Which when compiled and run will produce the following output as illustrated in Figure 27.4.

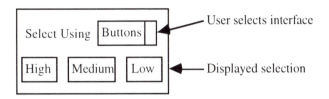

Figure 27.4 Annotated illustration of output when using the card layout manager.

27.8 Self-assessment

- What are the advantages of using layout managers rather than using absolute positioning of components on the screen?

- Can the layout managers shown cope with all situations?

27.9 Exercises

- Re-implement an application that you have already written using a layout manager?

28. Graphics

This chapter looks at the graphic features of the Java language. Using graphics, diagrams can be drawn in a canvas and if required animated to produce moving images.

28.1   Introduction

Line graphics are drawn onto a canvas with coordinates that represent individual pixels on the user's screen. A pixel is an individual picture element and on a high-end colour monitor looks like an individual coloured dot displayed on the screen.

For example, Figure 28.1 illustrates a canvas of 150 pixels wide by 200 pixels deep onto which has been drawn a rectangle (50 pixels wide by 100 pixels deep). The top left-hand corner of the rectangle is at position (50,50) and the bottom right-hand corner is at position (99,149).

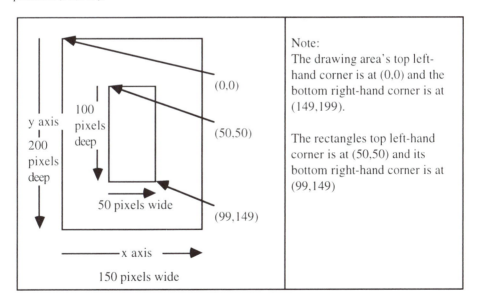

Figure 28.1 A rectangle drawn on a canvas of 100 by 200 pixels.

To draw the above rectangle the method `drawRect` in the class `java.awt.Graphics` is used as follows:

```
canvas_context.drawRect( 50, 50, 50, 100 )
   // Parameters 1st the top left x coordinate
   //            2nd the top left y coordinate
   //            3rd the width  of the rectangle in pixels
   //            4th the height of the rectangle in pixels
```

Note: The object canvas_context *is an object that implements the methods in the abstract class* graphics.

28.2   Graphic primitives

The following is a selected list of graphical methods in the abstract class java.awt.Graphics. The class is abstract so that a concrete implementation can be subclassed from it to deal with a specific device. A programmer however, does not need to worry about specific devices and simply requests a graphic context (an instance of a subclass of Graphics) that implements these graphic primitives on the specific output device the application is displaying to.

28.2.1   Shapes that can be drawn

The class Graphics contains the following major methods for drawing shapes:

Method	Explanation	Example
drawRect(x, y, width, height)	Draws a rectangle in the current colour.	
fillRect(x, y, width, height)	Draws a rectangle and fills with current colour.	
drawOval(x, y, width, height)	Draws an oval in the current colour.	
fillOval(x, y, width, height)	Draws a filled oval in the current colour.	
drawLine(x1, y1, x2, y2)	Draws a line in the current colour from (x1, y1) to (x2, y2)	
drawRoundRect(x, y, width, height, archeight, arcwidth)	Draws a round rectangle with corners that are made up of an arc with height and width which are arc height and arc width.	
fillRoundRect(x, y, width, height, archeight, arcwidth)	Draws a filled round rectangle in the current colour.	
drawArc(x, y, width, height, startangel, endangle)	Draws an arc from start to end. 0 degrees is at 3'oclock, end angle is the angular extent, which is in an anti-clockwise direction.	

fillArc(x, y,
         width, height,
         startangel, endangle)
	As for drawArc but the arc is filled in the current colour.	

drawPolygon(poly)	Draws a polygon. (The argument poly is an instance of the class Polygon.) See Section 29.2.2.3.	
fillPolygon(poly)	As for drawPolygon but the polygon is filled in the current colour.	

28.2.2   Example of drawing shapes

The following table illustrates some example calls of the graphic primitives. In these calls, the object g is an instance of a subclass of the class Graphics.

28.2.2.1   Drawing a line

A line is drawn from a point (x1, y1) to another point (x2, y2) on the drawing surface. The following example illustrates the drawing of a diagonal line from 0, 0 to 99, 99 in a drawing area of 100 pixels wide by 100 pixels high.

Example drawing a line	line drawn
g.drawLine(0, 0, 99, 99)	(0,0) (99,99)

28.2.2.2   Drawing an arc

The parameters to the methods fillarc are as follows:

```
fillArc( x, y, width, height, start_angel, end_angle )
```

In drawing an arc, the start_angel is relative to the position 3'oclock, a positive angular value (in degrees) will take you in an anticlockwise direction whilst a negative angular value takes you in a clockwise direction from this point.

The arc is drawn to position end_angel which again is relative to the position 3'oclock, a positive angular value (in degrees) will take you in an anticlockwise direction whilst a negative angular value takes you in a clockwise direction from this point.

Example drawing an arc	Shape drawn

`g.fillArc( 0, 0, 100,100, 0, 90 )`
or
`g.fillArc( 0, 0, 100,100, -270, -90 )`
	(0,0)
	
	(99,99)

`g.fillArc( 0, 0, 100,100, 0, -90 )`
or
`g.fillArc( 0, 0, 100,100, 270, 90 )`
	(0,0)
	
	(99,99)

`g.fillArc( 0, 0, 100,100, 270, -90 )`
or
`g.fillArc( 0, 0, 100,100, -180, +90 )`
	(0,0)
	
	(99,99)

28.2.2.3   Drawing a polygon

A polygon is drawn with the aid of the class `Polygon` that is used to create an instance of an object that holds the points of a polygon. The class `Polygon` has the following major methods:

Method	Responsibility
`Polygon(int x[],int y[],int n )`	Creates an instance of a polygon with n points initialized to the points in the x and y arrays.
`Polygon()`	Creates an empty polygon.
`addPoint( int x, int y )`	Adds the point (x, y) to the polygon.
`contains( Point p )`	Returns true if the polygon contains point p. An instance of the class `Point` holds an x, y pair. For example, `new Point(1,2)`.

The following example, illustrates the drawing of a diamond in a drawing area of 100 pixels wide by 100 pixels high.

Example drawing a polygon	Shape drawn

`int x[] = { 50, 100,  50,  0 };`
`int y[] = { 0,   50, 100, 50 };`
`Polygon poly = new Polygon( x, y, 4 );`
`g.drawPolygon( poly );`
	(0,0)
	
	(99,99)

Note: If the start and end point of the points that represent the polygon are not the same then the polygon is closed by drawing a line from the start point to the end point.

28.2.3 The colour of the draw shape

The colour of the draw shape is manipulated by the following methods in the class Graphics:

Method	Explanation
setColor(colour)	Set the colour of any object drawn.
getColor()	Return the current drawing colour.

The class java.awt.Color defines the following public variables:

black	blue	cyan	darkGray
gray	green	lightGray	magenta
orange	pink	red	white
yellow			

Thus, to set the drawing colour to magenta the following code can be used:

```
setColor( Color.magenta )
```

If the available colours are insufficient, then a custom colour can be created from the individual RGB values as follows:

```
setColor( Color( 255, 0, 10 ) )    // Color( red, green, blue )
```

that sets the drawing colour to a red which has had a touch of blue added to it.

28.2.4 Writing text to the image

The following method allows a string to be written to the image:

Method	Explanation
drawString(string, x, y)	Write the string in the current colour, font and point size with the first character starting at position x, y. The coordinate y is the position of the baseline of the character.

A character has three important attributes when drawn, that are illustrated in Figure 28.2.

Ascender line

Baseline

Descender line

Figure 28.2 Illustration of character attributes.

These attributes are:

- Ascender line: This is the top of any character
- Baseline: This is the bottom of most characters.
- Descender line: This is the bottom of characters that descend below the base line.

28.2.5   Changing the font and point size

The class `Font` is used to create a specific instance of a font to be used by a visual component. The class `Font` has the following major constructor:

Method	Explanation
`Font( font_face, style, size )`	Creates an instance of the font class for a `font_face` in `style` and `point size`. For example, `Font("Monospaced",Font.PLAIN,12)`

The font name may be a specific name of a font face or a logical name chosen from the following predefined list: `Dialog`, `DialogInput`, `Monospaced`, `Serif`, `SansSerif` or `Symbol`.

The style is chosen from the following predefined styles: `Font.BOLD`, `Font.ITALIC` and `Font.PLAIN`.

For example, to set the style of the label used on a button to a monospaced font in a plain typeface and 12 point in size, the following code is used:

```
Font font = new Font("Monospaced",Font.PLAIN,12);
Button north = new Button( "North" );
north.setFont( font );
```

Alternatively, this font could be set on the container for the visual objects and all text displayed would then be in a monospaced font in plain typeface and 12 point.

28.3   Ball mover application

The following application demonstrates the use of graphics by allowing a user to move a coloured ball up, down, left and right on the screen. The application has the following visualization:

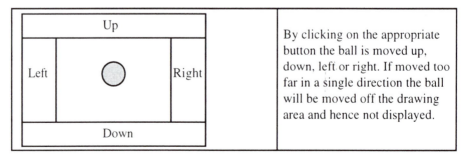

28.4   Implementation

The ball mover application uses the following packages:

```
import java.awt.*;
import java.awt.event.*;
import java.io.IOException;
import java.util.*;
```

The application starts by declaring an instance of the ball that is moved together with objects representing the visual representation of the ball and buttons used to move the ball.

```
class Application extends Frame
{
  private static final int H = 400;      // Height of window
  private static final int W = 300;      // Width  of window

  private Ball          the_ball;        //Ball
  private Ball_Observer  the_ball_canvas; //View of ball (Visual)
  private Button        the_left;        //Buttons (Visual)
  private Button        the_right;       // "    "
  private Button        the_up;          // "    "
  private Button        the_down;        // "    "
```

The declared objects belong to the following classes and have the following responsibilities:

Class	Responsibility
Ball	Holds the position and size of the ball.
Ball_Observer	Implements a visual view of the ball.
Button	Implements a visual button. Standard awt button (java.awt.Button).

The constructor for the class `Application` sets up the visual interface using the boarder layout manager.

```
public Application()
{
  super();
  setSize( W, H );                              //Size of Window

  Font font = new Font("Monospaced",Font.PLAIN,12);

  the_left  = new Button( "Left" );             //Left
  the_right = new Button( "Right" );            //Right
  the_up    = new Button( "Up" );               //Up
  the_down  = new Button( "Down" );             //Down
```

```
    Button_Action cb = new Button_Action();        //Action
    the_left .addActionListener( cb );             //Set call-back
    the_right.addActionListener( cb );             // "
    the_up   .addActionListener( cb );             // "
    the_down .addActionListener( cb );             // "

    Panel panel = new Panel();                      //Panel
    panel.setLayout( new BorderLayout() );

    the_ball        = new Ball( W/2, H/2, 20 );     //Ball
    the_ball_canvas = new Ball_Observer( the_ball );//View of Ball
    the_ball.addObserver( the_ball_canvas );        //Add observer

    panel.add( the_up,         BorderLayout.NORTH ); // Layout pos
    panel.add( the_down,       BorderLayout.SOUTH ); //
    panel.add( the_right,      BorderLayout.EAST );  //
    panel.add( the_left,       BorderLayout.WEST );  //
    panel.add( the_ball_canvas, BorderLayout.CENTER );//

    add( panel );                                   //To window
    setTitle("Ball");                               //Title
    the_ball.notifyObservers();                     //Changed
  }
```

Note: The observer object the_ball_canvas *that observes the object* the_ball.
*By using an observer the ball implementation has no responsibility for displaying
a representation of the ball.*

The inner class Button_Action implements the ball movement. This is
achieved by sending the message move_by to an instance of the ball. The parameters to
this method represent the number of pixels to move in the x and y direction. Once
moved; the ball's observer is notified about the change to the position of the ball using
the notifyObservers method.

```
  class Button_Action implements ActionListener
  {
    public void actionPerformed( ActionEvent event )
    {
      Object object = event.getSource();
      if      ( object == the_left ) the_ball.move_by( -5, 0 );
      else if ( object == the_right) the_ball.move_by( +5, 0 );
      else if ( object == the_down ) the_ball.move_by(  0, +5 );
      else if ( object == the_up   ) the_ball.move_by(  0, -5 );
      the_ball.notifyObservers();
    }
  }
}
```

28.4.1 The class `Ball`

The attributes of the class `Ball` are its size and position in an x, y coordinate system.

```
class Ball extends Observable
{
  private int the_x;          //Ball's x coordinate
  private int the_y;          //Ball's y coordinate
  private int the_size;       //Ball's size

  public Ball( final int x, final int y, final int size )
  {
    the_x = x; the_y = y; the_size = size;
  }

  public synchronized int x() { return the_x; };
  public synchronized int y() { return the_y; };
  public synchronized int get_size() { return the_size; };
```

The method `move_by` moves the ball by a relative amount to a new position in the coordinate system:

```
  public synchronized void move_by( int x_inc, int y_inc )
  {
    the_x += x_inc; the_y += y_inc;
    setChanged();
  }
```

whilst the method `set_size` changes the size of the ball.

```
  public synchronized void set_size( int size )
  {
    the_size += size;
    setChanged();
  }
}
```

Note: Though the classes are synchronized the extraction of the (x,y) coordinates should be done as an atomic action.

28.4.2 The class `Canvas`

The class `Canvas` (`java.awt.Canvas`) represents a visual image of a blank rectangle. This class may be subclassed to create custom visual components. The class `Canvas` is itself a subclass of `Component`.

To create a new visual component the following steps are required:

- Create a subclass of `Canvas` to represent the new visual component

- In this subclass override the methods:
  ```
  void paint(Graphics g)  // from Canvas
  void update(Graphics g) // From Component
  ```

The two methods `paint` and `update` are called when:

Method	Called when
paint(Graphics g)	The visual image is first displayed or if the image has been damaged.
update(Graphics g)	An update of the image has been requested. An update of the image is requested by sending an instance of the class the message `repaint()`.

Note: When an application is loaded one of the actions it performs is to ask each of its visual components to display a representation of itself on the screen. This is accomplished by calling each visual component's `paint` method.

28.4.3   The class `Ball_Observer`

The class `Ball_Observer` is responsible for displaying an image of the ball onto the screen. This class extends the class `Canvas` and implements the interface `Observable`.

The implementation of the class is shown below:

```
class Ball_Observer extends Canvas implements Observer
{
  private Ball the_ball;                //Observing
  private int the_last_x;               //Last position
  private int the_last_y;

  Ball_Observer( Ball a_ball )
  {
    the_ball = a_ball;                  //Observing object
    the_last_x = the_ball.x();          //Initial position
    the_last_y = the_ball.y();
  }
```

The overridden method `update( Observable o, Object arg )` is called by an instance of the class `Ball` when its position has changed. The implementation of this method calls `repaint` that will call the classes `update( Graphics g )` method.

```
public void update( Observable o, Object arg  )
{
  repaint();                          //Re paint canvas as ball moved
                                      //Will call update(Graphics g)

}
```

The method `paint` will be called automatically by the application on start-up or if the representation of the displayed image is damaged. This method is overridden in the class and its implementation calls the method `re_display` that does the work of displaying the image.

```
public void paint ( Graphics g )      //First show or damaged
{
  re_display( g );
}
```

Update is called when an update of the image is required. This will be called when for example, code that manipulates the internal representation of the image requires that the image be updated to reflect changes in data values. In this case, the implementation of the method calls the method `re_display` that will do the work of updating the whole image.

```
public void update ( Graphics g )     //Update of view requested
{
  re_display( g );
}
```

The method `re_display` is responsible for drawing the image of the ball on the screen. However, before the image can be re-drawn the old image must first be erased. The strategy used is as follows:

- Erase the old image of the ball by drawing a new image of the ball over it in the background colour.

- Draw a new image of the ball in its new position.

```
public void re_display( Graphics g ) //Re-display the object
{
  int hs = the_last_size/2;                    //Half size
  g.setColor( Color.white );
  g.fillOval( the_last_x-hs, the_last_y-hs,    //Center
              the_last_size, the_last_size ); //Last x , y

  the_last_x    = the_ball.x();                //Remember
  the_last_y    = the_ball.y();                // last position
  the_last_size = the_ball.get_size();         // last size
  hs = the_last_size/2;
```

```
        g.setColor( Color.red );
        g.fillOval( the_last_x-hs, the_last_y-hs,    //Center
                    the_last_size, the_last_size ); //Last x, y
    }
}
```

Note: The ball is drawn centred on the x, y position. As the drawing method
*   fillOval draws from the top left-hand corner, the starting position of the*
*   drawing is moved left and up by half the ball's size. This results in the ball being*
*   drawn centred on the x, y position obtained from* `the_ball`.

28.4.4   The class `Main`

The class `Main` creates an instance of the class `Application` and starts the
application by sending it the message `show`.

```
class Main
{
  public static void main( String args[] )
  {
    (new Application()).show();
  }
}
```

28.4.5   Putting it all together

Once compiled and run, the application will display the following image onto the user's
screen.

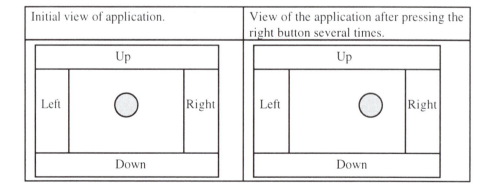

Initial view of application.	View of the application after pressing the right button several times.

28.5 Animated ball

The ball in the ball mover application can be animated so that it constantly inflates and deflates. This new application allows this moving graphic itself to be moved. This addition requires a new class `Ball_Inflater` that has the responsibility of animating the inflating and deflating ball.

28.5.1 The class `Ball_Inflater`

The class `Ball_Inflater` is used to create an active object that will continuously inflate and deflate the ball. Its implementation is as follows:

```
class Ball_Inflater extends Thread
{
  public Ball          the_ball;             //Ball moved
  public int           the_initial_size;     //Initial size

  public Ball_Inflater( Ball a_ball, int size )
  {
    the_ball        = a_ball;
    the_initial_size = size;
  }

  public void run()
  {
    int size = the_initial_size;             //Initial size
    boolean inflate = true;                  //Inflate

    while ( true )
    {
      if ( size > 90  ) inflate = false;     //Deflate as too big
      if ( size <  1  ) inflate = true;      //Inflate as too small
      size = size + ( inflate ? 1 : -1 );    //New size
      the_ball.set_size( size );             //Set
      the_ball.notifyObservers();            //Tell observer changed
      try {
        Thread.sleep( 50  );                 //50 milliseconds delay
      }
      catch( InterruptedException e ) {}
    }
  }
}
```

28.5.2 The class `Application`

The class `Application` is amended to accommodate the active object `the_ball_mover` as follows:

```
class Application extends Frame
{
  // Declaration as before

  // + declaration of active object

  private Ball_Inflater the_ball_inflater;  //Ball inflater

  public Application()
  {
    // code as before

    // + Initialization and activation of the active object
    //    the_ball_inflater

    the_ball_inflater = new Ball_Inflater( the_ball, 25 );
    the_ball_inflater.start();                        //Start inflating
  }

  class Button_Action implements ActionListener
  {
    public void actionPerformed( ActionEvent event )
    {
      Object object = event.getSource();
      if       ( object == the_left ) the_ball.move_by( -5, 0 );
      else if ( object == the_right) the_ball.move_by( +5, 0 );
      else if ( object == the_down ) the_ball.move_by(  0, +5 );
      else if ( object == the_up   ) the_ball.move_by(  0, -5 );
    }
  }
}
```

Note: The object the_ball_inflater *animates the ball by continuously inflating*
        and deflating the ball. Hence, there is no need for the method
        ActionPerformed *to request an update of the image when the ball is moved.*

28.5.3   Putting it all together

Once compiled and run, the application will display the following image onto the user's
screen.

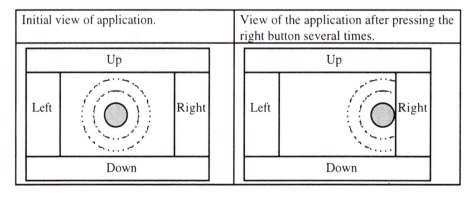

28.5.4 Image flicker

If you run this application occasionally, the moving ball will flicker. This is because the strategy for animation is to erase the image and then redraw the image whilst it is being displayed. Whilst not too annoying, this flickering does destroy the effect of a smooth animation.

This flickering can be easily removed by using double buffering. In double buffering a new image is created off-screen and when the image drawing is completed this off-screen image is written to the display. By using this technique of double buffering smooth image animation is achieved.

28.6 Animated ball (using double buffering)

By changing the implementation of the `re_display` method in the class `Ball_Observer` to use double buffering the flicker from the inflating ball can be removed.

28.6.1 The new implementation of the method `re_display`

In this new implementation an off-screen graphic context `the_os_image` is created. Information written to `the_os_image` is not displayed immediately. When the drawing on the off-screen graphic context is completed the whole context is written to the display in a single operation using the method:

```
g.drawImage( the_os_image, 0, 0, this );
```

thus preventing flickering. The modified code for the ball inflater that does not flicker is shown below:

```
public void re_display( Graphics g ) //Re-display the object
{
  Dimension d = getSize();              //Size of image

  //See if image resized or first time

  if (  ( the_os_graphics == null )  ||
        ( d.width  != the_os_dimension.width ) ||
        ( d.height != the_os_dimension.height ) )
  {
    the_os_dimension = d;
    the_os_image     = createImage( d.width, d.height );
    the_os_graphics  = the_os_image.getGraphics();
  }
```

Note: *The method* getsize() *returns an instance of the class* Dimension *that describes the size of the drawing area. The public fields* width *and* height *are used to access the size of the component.*
The method createImage(width, height) *in the class* Component *the superclass of class* Canvas *returns an instance of the class* Image *that is used for double buffering.*
The method getGraphic() *in the class* Image *returns a graphics context for drawing the off-screen image.*

The new position of the ball is drawn in the off-screen graphics context as follows:

```
int hs = the_last_size/2;

the_os_graphics.setColor( Color.white );
the_os_graphics.fillOval( the_last_x-hs, the_last_y-hs,
                               the_last_size, the_last_size );

the_last_x    = the_ball.x();
the_last_y    = the_ball.y();
the_last_size = the_ball.get_size();

hs = the_last_size/2;
the_os_graphics.setColor( Color.red );
the_os_graphics.fillOval( the_last_x-hs, the_last_y-hs,
                               the_last_size, the_last_size );
```

Finally the off screen graphics context is written to the screen in a single operation so removing flicker.

```
   g.drawImage( the_os_image, 0, 0, this );
}
```

28.7   Drawing text graphically

As described in Section 28.2.4 characters draw on the screen have three important characteristics. These are illustrated again in Figure 28.3

Ascender line

Baseline
Descender line

Figure 28.3 Illustration of character attributes.

28.7.1 The class `java.awt.Font`

The class Font is used to create and manipulate a font that is used for displaying text onto the screen. The class Font has the following major methods:

Method	Responsibility
Font(name,style,size)	Creates a new font with name name style style and point size size.
getName	Returns a string representing the name of the font.
getSize	Returns the size of the font in points.
getStyle	Returns the style used for the font. (Possible values are: Font.PLAIN, Font.BOLD and Font.ITALIC.)
getFamily	Returns a string representing the family name of the font.

28.7.2 The class `java.awt.FontMetrics`

To work on a graphical surface which is measured in pixels, a process is required to determine the size in pixels of displayed characters. An instance of the class FontMetrics is used to provide this information. The class FontMetrics has the following major methods:

Method	Responsibility
FontMetrics(font)	Creates a new font metric object for the font font.
charWidth(c)	Returns the width in pixels of the character c.
getAscent()	Returns the distance between the baseline and the ascending line in pixels.
getDescent()	Returns the distance between the baseline and the descending line in pixels.
getHeight()	Returns the height in pixels between the baselines of two lines of text. This is equivalent to getAscent() + getDescent() + getLeading().
getLeading()	Returns the size in pixels of the leading between lines.
getMaxAscent()	Returns the maximum ascent for a character in this font. This may be more than the value returned by getAscent.
getMaxDescent()	Returns the maximum descent for a character in this font. This may be more than the value returned by getDescent.
stringWidth(str)	Returns the width in pixels of the string str.

28.8   A demonstration application using text

Figure 28.4 illustrates the visual appearance of an application that displays the text "Hello world" followed by 2 lines about the font used.

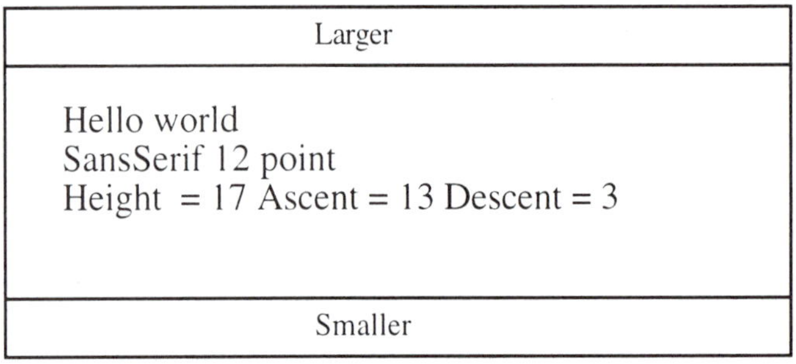

<table>
<tr><td colspan="2">Larger</td></tr>
<tr><td>Hello world
SansSerif 12 point
Height = 17 Ascent = 13 Descent = 3</td></tr>
<tr><td colspan="2">Smaller</td></tr>
</table>

Figure 28.4 An application to display text using the method drawText.

The size of the font may be changed either upwards or downwards by pressing the buttons marked Larger or Smaller respectively.

28.8.1   The implementation of the application

The main application class Application creates the visual interface and uses the following classes:

Class	An instance of which
Text	Records the text to be displayed and the point size to be used.
Text_Observer	Displays a visual representation of the text plus details about the font used.

to facilitate the display of the message "hello world" and information about the font used.

The implementation of the class Application is shown below:

```
class Application extends Frame
{
  private static final int H = 200;
  private static final int W = 600;

  private Text            the_text;         //Text and point size
  private Text_Observer   the_text_canvas;  //View of text (Visual)

  private Button          the_up;           // "    "
  private Button          the_down;         // "    "
```

The constructor for the class creates instances of the visual objects that are used. Each button uses the same listener to process the button pressed action.

```
public Application()
{
  setSize( W, H );                                //Size of Window
  Font font = new Font("SansSerif",Font.PLAIN,12);
  setFont( font );                                //Font Used

  the_up    = new Button( "Larger" );             //Increase
  the_down  = new Button( "Smaller" );            //Decrease

  Button_Action cb = new Button_Action();         //Action
  the_up   .addActionListener( cb );              // "
  the_down .addActionListener( cb );              // "

  Panel panel = new Panel();                      //Panel
  panel.setLayout( new BorderLayout() );

  the_text        = new Text("hello world", 12);  //Text
  the_text_canvas = new Text_Observer( the_text );
  the_text.addObserver( the_text_canvas );        //Add observer

  panel.add( the_up,        BorderLayout.NORTH );  // Layout pos
  panel.add( the_down,      BorderLayout.SOUTH );
  panel.add( the_text_canvas, BorderLayout.CENTER );

  add( panel );                                   //To window
  setTitle("Text");                               //Title
  the_text.notifyObservers();                     //Changed
}
```

When a button is pressed the method `actionPerformed` in the class `Button_Action` is responsible for determining which button was pressed. When the button pressed has been determined either an increase or decrease in font size is implemented by sending the object `the_text` an instance of the class `Text` the message `font_changed`.

```
class Button_Action implements ActionListener
{
  public void actionPerformed( ActionEvent event )
  {
    Object object = event.getSource();
    if      ( object == the_down ) the_text.font_change( -1 );
    else if ( object == the_up   ) the_text.font_change( +1);
    the_text.notifyObservers();
  }
}
}
```

The class `Text` has the following responsibilities:

Method	Responsibility
`Text(str, size)`	Creates an instance of a text object that represents the string `str` with point size `size`.
`get_size()`	Returns the point size of the text.
`get_text()`	Returns the string that is displayed.
`font_change( n )`	Changes the relative size of the font by n points.

The class is implemented as follows:

```java
class Text extends Observable
{
  private String the_text;                 //Text message
  private int    the_size;                 //Text point size

  public Text( String text, final int size )
  {
    the_size = size;                        //Text to display
    the_text = text;                        //Initial point size
    setChanged();                           //Cause re-display
  }

  public int    get_size() { return the_size; };
  public String get_text() { return the_text; };

  public void font_change( int size )
  {
    the_size += size;
    setChanged();
  }
}
```

The observer for the class `Text` performs the actual display of the text using double buffering techniques.

```java
class Text_Observer extends Canvas implements Observer
{
  private Text      the_text;              //Observing
  private Graphics  the_os_graphics;       //Off-screen graphics
  private Dimension the_os_dimension;
  private Image     the_os_image;

  Text_Observer( Text a_text )
  {
    the_text = a_text;                      //Observing object
    repaint();
  }

  public void update( Observable o, Object arg  )
  {
    repaint();                              //Re paint canvas as text moved
                                            //Will call update
  }
```

```
public void paint ( Graphics g )      //First show or damaged
{
  re_display( g );
}
public void update ( Graphics g )     //Update of view requested
{
  re_display( g );
}
```

The method `re_display` implements the actual display of the text. Instances of the classes `Font` and `Fontmetrics` are used to determine the characteristics of the displayed text.

```
public void re_display( Graphics g )
{
  Dimension d = getSize();                        //Size of image
  //See if image resized or first time
  if (   ( the_os_graphics == null )          ||
         ( d.width  != the_os_dimension.width ) ||
         ( d.height != the_os_dimension.height ) )
  {
    the_os_dimension = d;
    the_os_image     = createImage( d.width, d.height );
    the_os_graphics  = the_os_image.getGraphics();
  }

  the_os_graphics.setColor( Color.white );        //Background
  the_os_graphics.fillRect(0,0, d.width,d.height);//Clear
  the_os_graphics.setColor( Color.black );        //Writing in

  Font original_font = the_os_graphics.getFont(); //Old font
  Font font = new Font(original_font.getName(),   //New font
                    original_font.getStyle(),  //
                    the_text.get_size() );

  the_os_graphics.setFont( font );
                                    //Attributes
  int    font_size  = font.getSize();             // Font size
  String font_name  = font.getName();             // Font name

  FontMetrics fontmetrics = the_os_graphics.getFontMetrics();
  int    font_ascent  = fontmetrics.getAscent();  //About font
  int    font_descent = fontmetrics.getDescent(); // in pixels
  int    font_height  = fontmetrics.getHeight();  //

  String line1 = the_text.get_text();
  String line2 = font_name + " " + font_size + " point";
  String line3 = "Height  = " + font_height +  " Ascent = " +
                  font_ascent +  " Descent = " + font_descent;

  the_os_graphics.drawString( line1, 0, font_height   );
  the_os_graphics.drawString( line2, 0, font_height*2 );
  the_os_graphics.drawString( line3, 0, font_height*3 );
  g.drawImage( the_os_image, 0, 0, this );
}
}
```

The class `Main` creates an instance of the class `Application` and starts the application by sending it the message `show`.

```
class Main
{
  public static void main( String args[] )
  {
    (new Application()).show();
  }
}
```

28.9   Graphical version of noughts and crosses

In Chapter 10 on arrays, an application to play the game of noughts and crosses was developed. In this application a text user interface was used to present the results of play to a player. Whilst this shows the state of the noughts and crosses game the information presented and mode of data entry could be made clearer. In particular:

●   The square that the user plays their counter on is selected by typing its square number using the keyboard. A mouse click over the appropriate square would be more user friendly.

●   The representation of the board is textual; graphical symbols for O and X would be more visually stimulating for the players.

Figure 28.5 below illustrates the original interface for the noughts and crosses game together with a new interface using graphics.

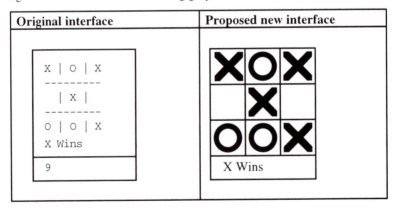

Figure 28.5 Old and proposed new graphical interface for the game of noughts and crosses.

28.9.1   The revised application

This graphical version of the game of noughts and crosses will re-use the class `Board` described in Chapter 10. This class `Board` has the following responsibilities:

Method	Responsibility
add	Adds the player's counter to the board. The player's move is specified by a number in the range 1 to 9 and their counter by a character X for ✗ and O for ◯.
check_move	Returns true if the move is valid. The method checks that the move is in the range 1 to 9 and that the specified cell is not occupied.
position	Returns the character occupying a cell on the noughts and crosses board.
situation	Returns the current state of the noughts and crosses board.

In the code for the application shown below, (based on the code in Section 16.5) the constructor builds the user interface. In particular the following initialization is performed:

- Create a visual object the_output that is used to display messages about the state of the game.

- Create an observer the_brd_canvas of the noughts and crosses board.

- Create a listener for mouse events and add this listener to the_brd_canvas. The listener will action any mouse events.

- Add the observer the_brd_observer to the noughts and crosses board the_oxo.

- Create a boarder layout for managing the the_brd_canvas and the_output.

```
public Application()
{
  setSize( W, H );                              //Size of Window
  Font font = new Font("Monospaced",Font.PLAIN,12);

  the_output = new TextArea( 4, 40 );           //Output area
  the_output.setFont( font );                   //            Font

  Transaction cb  = new Transaction();

  the_board_canvas = new Board_Observer( the_oxo );
  the_oxo.addObserver( the_board_canvas );

  Panel io_area = new Panel();                   //Area used for I/O
  io_area.setLayout( new BorderLayout() );
  io_area.add( "North", the_output );            //Messages

  Panel game_brd = new Panel();                  //Game board
  game_brd.setLayout( new BorderLayout() );

  game_brd.add( "Center", the_board_canvas );//Board display area
  game_brd.add( "South",  io_area );             //I/O Area

  add( game_brd );                               //
  setTitle("Noughts & crosses");

  the_board_canvas.addMouseListener( cb );       //Add listener

  the_game.display_who_plays( the_output );      //Display player to move
  the_oxo.notifyObservers();
}
```

28.9.2   Mouse events

The interface `MouseListener` contains the following methods:

Method	Called when
mouseClicked	The mouse button is clicked.
mouseEntered	The mouse enters.
mousePress	The mouse is pressed.
mouseReleased	The mouse button is released.
mousesExited	The mouse exits.

Note: A mouse click will usually generate three events: mousePress, MouseRelease and MouseClicked.

The class `MouseAdapter` implements this interface with methods that perform no action. By inheriting from `MouseAdapter` rather than implementing `MouseListener` only methods for events that are to be processed need be provided.

28.9.3   The inner class `Transaction`

The inner class `Transaction` extends `MouseAdapter` and is responsible for handling transactions from the mouse. To make life simple, only the `mousePressed` event will be overloaded with an action. When a mouse event is received information about the event is obtained from an instance of the class `MouseEvent`. The class `MouseEvent` has the following major methods:

Method	Called when
getX()	Return the x coordinate of the mouse.
getY()	Return the y coordinate of the mouse.

When the mouse is pressed, the coordinates of the mouse are obtained and is converted to a row and column position in the noughts and crosses board.

```java
class Transaction extends MouseAdapter
{
  Point the_point = null;                  //Point on canvas
  public void mousePressed( MouseEvent e )
  {
    int x = e.getX();
    int y = e.getY();
    if ( the_point == null )
    {
      the_point = new Point( x, y );
    } else {
      the_point.x = x;
      the_point.y = y;
    }
```

```
      Dimension d = the_board_canvas.getSize();      //Size of image
      int a_third_x = d.width/3;
      int a_third_y = d.height/3;
      int row = 0, column = 0;
      for ( int i=0; i<3; i++)
      {
        if ( x > i*a_third_x ) column = i;
        if ( y > i*a_third_y ) row    = i;
      }
      the_game.action( the_output, "" + ( row*3+(column+1) ) ) );
    }
  }
}
```

28.9.4   The class `Board_Observer`

The constructor for this class stores the observed object to simplify later access, when
the state of the object is required.

```
class Board_Observer extends Canvas implements Observer
{
  private Board the_oxo;                //Observing

  private Image     the_os_image;       //Off-screen image
  private Dimension the_os_dimension;   //Off-screen size
  private Graphics  the_os_graphics;    //Off-screen context

  Board_Observer( Board a_oxo )
  {
    the_oxo = a_oxo;                    //Observing object
  }
```

The `update` method is called when the observed object has changed its state and a
request is made to re-display the object. This method calls `repaint` to effect the
normal re-display mechanism.

Both `paint(Graphics  g)` and `update(graphics  g)` call the method
`re_display` to re-draw the whole noughts and crosses board.

```
  public void update( Observable o, Object arg  )
  {
    repaint();                          //Re paint canvas calls update
  }

  public void paint( Graphics g )    //First show or damaged
  {
    re_display( g );
  }

  public void update( Graphics g )   //Update of view requested
  {
    re_display( g );
  }
```

Double buffering is used to prevent flicker when a new X or O is added to the board. Whilst initially looking complex the method `re_display` is divided into the following code fragments. The first fragment creates, if necessary, a new version of the off-screen graphics context.

```
public void re_display( Graphics g )  //Re-display the object
{
  Dimension d = getSize();              //Size of image

  //See if image resized or first time

  if (   ( the_os_graphics == null )  ||
         ( d.width  != the_os_dimension.width )  ||
         ( d.height != the_os_dimension.height ) )
  {
    the_os_dimension = d;
    the_os_image     = createImage( d.width, d.height );
    the_os_graphics  = the_os_image.getGraphics();
  }
```

Note: This will only need to be recreated, if this is the first call or the canvas has been re-sized.

The next fragment draws the lines of the noughts and crosses board. The lines split the canvas into thirds both horizontally and vertically.

```
  the_os_graphics.setColor( Color.black );
  int a_third_x = d.width/3;
  int a_third_y = d.height/3;
  for ( int i=1; i<3; i++ )
  {
    the_os_graphics.drawLine(i*a_third_x, 0, i*a_third_x, d.height);
    the_os_graphics.drawLine(0, i*a_third_y, d.width, i*a_third_y);
  }
```

The final fragment, calculates the position of each cell on the noughts and crosses board and passes the top left corner of each cell to the method `draw_cell` that is responsible for drawing the contents of an individual cell.

```
  for ( int i=0; i<9; i++ )
  {
    char who = the_oxo.position(i+1);
    int x_top = (i % 3) * a_third_x;
    int y_top = (i / 3) * a_third_y;
    draw_cell( the_os_graphics, who,
               x_top, y_top, a_third_x, a_third_y );
  }

  g.drawImage( the_os_image, 0, 0, this );
}
```

The method `draw_cell` uses appropriate graphic primitives to draw a circle and a cross. The main complication with the code is that the circle or cross are drawn not to fill the cell but to have a 10% wide (of cell) margin around each cross or circle.

```
private void draw_cell( Graphics where, char who,
                        int x, int y, int x_size, int y_size )
{
  int x10pc = x_size/10;      //10% of size of cell in x direction
  int y10pc = y_size/10;      //10% of size of cell in y direction
  int x_top = x + x10pc;      //X start of drawing area used
  int y_top = y + y10pc;      //Y start of drawing area used
  switch ( who )
  {
    case 'O' :
      where.setColor( Color.red );
      where.fillOval( x_top , y_top, x_size-x10pc*2, y_size-y10pc*2);
      where.setColor( Color.white );
      where.fillOval( x_top+x10pc , y_top+y10pc,
                      x_size-x10pc*4, y_size-y10pc*4 );
      break;
    case 'X' :
      where.setColor( Color.blue );
      {
        int x_bottom = x_top + x_size - x10pc*2;
        int y_bottom = y_top + y_size - y10pc*2;
        Polygon line1 = new Polygon();
        line1.addPoint( x_top-x10pc/2, y_top );
        line1.addPoint( x_top+x10pc/2, y_top );
        line1.addPoint( x_bottom+x10pc/2, y_bottom );
        line1.addPoint( x_bottom-x10pc/2, y_bottom );

        Polygon line2 = new Polygon();
        int bias = x_size-x10pc*2;
        line2.addPoint( x_top+bias-x10pc/2, y_top );
        line2.addPoint( x_top+bias+x10pc/2, y_top );
        line2.addPoint( x_bottom-bias+x10pc/2, y_bottom );
        line2.addPoint( x_bottom-bias-x10pc/2, y_bottom );

        where.fillPolygon( line1 );
        where.fillPolygon( line2 );
      }
      break;
  }
}
```

The logic of the game implemented by the class Game is the same as that shown in Section 16.5 except that as the board is displayed graphically the message area is cleared before messages for the current move are displayed. The message area only contains the request for the current user to enter their move, and when they make an invalid move a request to re-enter their move.

28.9.5   Putting it all together

When compiled with the class `Board` a typical interaction would be as illustrated below in Figure 28.6:

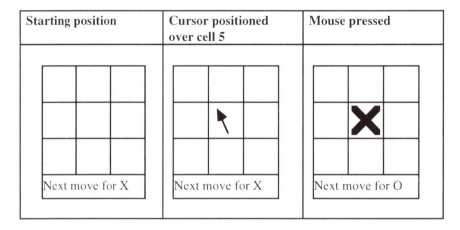

Figure 28.6 A typical interaction for a first move.

Note: The displayed message is actually "Next move for Player X""but as this would not fit in the re-drawn example in Figure 28.6, I shortened it.

28.10   Self-assessment

●   How would you draw the following shapes?

●   How do you prevent flicker when creating an animation?

28.11   Exercises

●   Re-implement the game of draughts described in Chapter 15 using a graphical representation of the board. In this game of draughts the mouse is used to indicate how a player moves.

●   Implement the game of reversi as described in the exercises in Chapter 15 this time using a graphical interface with players' moves indicated using the mouse.

29. Compiling systems

This chapter looks at ways of compiling a computer program into a form in which it can be executed on a computer system. In particular attention is given to the process by which a Java application or applet is turned into a form that can be executed.

29.1 Anatomy of a compiler

A compiler for a high-level language is a computer program that reads the source code for a program and produces as output, an executable representation. The executable representation, when run, will implement the actions specified by the programmer or programmers who constructed the program.

Internally, a compiler is usually split into two distinct components:

Component	Description
The front-end	The front-end itself is usually split into four parts: ● The lexical analysis phase: This splits the source program up into lexical tokens. For example, the expression: <pre>money = money + gift;</pre>is split into the 6 lexical tokens: money, =, money, +, and gift. ● The syntax analysis phase: Checks that the tokens conform to the grammar of the language. The grammar of the language defines the order in which tokens can occur. For example, that if is followed by a (. ● The semantic analysis phase: Checks that the meaning of the constructs used in the program are consistent. For example, in the construct: <pre>if (holiday)</pre>that the variable holiday is of type boolean. ● The code generation phase: Produces a representation of the program in a form that is suitable for easy conversion into real machine code. The internal representation of the program is then passed to the back-end.

Component	Description
The back-end	This generates the instructions for a particular machine architecture. The output from the back-end itself may need to be linked with other previously compiled code to form an executable image.

The following table illustrates different types of errors detected by the compiler.

Type of error	Example code fragment containing error
| Syntax error | ```
int number = 10;
if number > 20.0 )
     ^ '(' expected
``` |
| Semantic error | ```
int number = 10.0;
         ^ Incompatibility between number and 10.0
           cast required for conversion
``` |

In some compilers the interface between the front-end and the back-end of the compiler is through an abstract machine code. The abstract machine code represents an instruction set for a hypothetical machine. The back-end of the compiler then converts the abstract machine code into the specific machine code for the target computer. This process is illustrated in Figure 30.1.

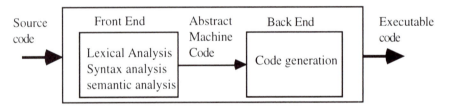

Figure 30.1 The major components in a compiler.

Note: Some compilers may not produce executable code, but rather object code that is then linked with other compiled code to form a complete program.

29.1.1   Anatomy of an interpreter

An interpreter is similar to a compiler except that instead of generating executable machine code, abstract machine code is generated. To run the program the abstract machine code is executed by an interpreter.

An interpreter is a program that simulates the action of a hypothetical computer that runs the abstract machine code. In some cases the compiler and interpreter are combined into a single development environment.

29.1.2   Comparison between a compiler and an interpreter

The following table summarizes the major differences between a compiler and an interpreter.

Criteria	Compiler	Interpreter
Speed of compilation	Usually slower	Usually faster
Speed of execution of the resultant program	Usually faster	Usually slower
Diagnostics produced when the running program fails	Usually worse	Usually better
Size of the resultant program	Usually larger	Usually smaller
The produced 'code' can be run on many different machine architecture's.	No	Yes

Note: The difficulty in being more definite about performance issues in the comparison is simply that the implementation quality for a specific compiler or interpreter may be significantly better.

29.1.3   Speeding up an interpreter

As an interpreted program is usually considerably slower in execution than a compiled program, ways have been sought of speeding up the execution of the interpreted code. An early technique was that implemented by Brown (Brown, P.J. 1976) in his throw away compiling scheme. In this approach each line of a Basic program was compiled into real machine code as it was run. When space in memory for the compiled program code was exhausted, the code was simply thrown away, and subsequently executed lines were re-compiled into machine code into the now free memory area. This system was designed to allow a program to run in a very small space, yet still retain the speed of a compiled program.

Note: Remember, most programs consist of loops that repeatedly execute the same lines of code.

29.2   Compiler portability a brief history

In 1958 Mock (Mock, O. et al. 1958) proposed a universal low-level machine code that would help make high -evel languages easily available on all machines. The idea was that the compiler for each high-level language would produce not real machine code, but an abstract machine code UNCOL. Each machine would have a translator that turned the UNCOL code into the real machine code for that machine. Using this idea instead of the need to write a total of L (Languages) * M (Machines) compilers only L compilers + M translators would need to be written. This process is illustrated in Figure 30.2 showing current languages and machines.

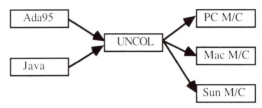

Figure 30.2 UNCOL as an intermediate language.

For political as well as practical reasons, the idea however never took off. In those far off days, every machine cycle counted and the overhead due to the two levels of conversion would have been excessive.

Martin Richard (Richards, M. 1971) described how he used OCODE as an intermediate language in bootstrapping the BCPL compiler to a new machine. In essence, the BCPL compiler was provided in two forms: as BCPL source code, and as OCODE instructions. An implementor of BCPL for a new machine would simply implement a program to translate the OCODE instructions into the machine code for the target machine. Once this program has been completed it is used to translate the compiler (in OCODE) into machine code. The resultant program can now be run in native mode on the target machine. As the BCPL compiler produces OCODE as its output any new programs written in BCPL can be compiled using this compiler and have their OCODE representation translated into the machine code of the new machine.

Around 1977 the UCSD Pascal system was implemented in a similar way. This time the intermediate code was called P-Code. However, a translator from P-Code to machine code was rarely provided. A software interpreter was usually responsible for executing the P-Code instructions. To make this a truly portable system an operating system was also encoded in P-Code. Hence the whole UCSD environment could be run on any machine that had a P-Code interpreter.

Hence the UCSD development system was easily provided on many popular contemporary micro computers. One novel feature at the time was that a UCSD Pascal program could be developed on one micro computer and run on another micro computer that had a different hardware architecture.

Soon after this the Pascal micro engine was produced. This was a recording of the micro code of a PDP-11 to allow it to execute P-Code directly. This greatly increased the execution speed of a UCSD Pascal program.

29.3   Java

Java was initially designed for the implementation of software contained in embedded systems. To enable a Java application or applet to run on many different machines a byte code (Abstract machine code) is generated by the compiler rather than the more traditional machine code representation. This byte code is then interpreted on the target machine.

The Java programming environment consists of:

- A Java compiler to turn source Java into a bytecode representation.
- An interpreter for the bytecode.
- An extensive class library that includes the ability to access and use: Containers, Windowing components, Networking, Graphics.

More recently JIT (Just In Time) translators have been introduced. A JIT translator converts the bytecode (abstract machine code) into real machine code instruction before execution. Although this process takes longer than interpreting the abstract machine code directly, it will usually produce a faster executing program as the resultant compiled code will be executed many times. Usually program code consists of loops that repeatedly execute the same lines of code.

29.3.1   A Java application

A Java application is very like a traditional program. However, as an abstract machine code is produce by the compiler, the resultant program can be run on any machine that has an interpreter or just in time compiler for the bytecode. This process is illustrated in Figure 30.3.

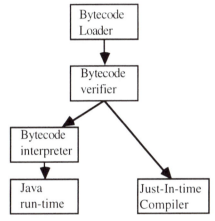

Figure 30.3 Executing a Java application on a computer.

In Figure 30.3 two ways of executing a loaded Java application are shown:

●   A Bytecode interpreter
●   A Just-In-Time translator or compiler.

29.3.2   A Java applet

With the rise of the internet and the need for more than static web pages, a Java applet provides a mechanism that enables code to be downloaded and executed in a web browser. By using this mechanism, a web page can have dynamic or interactive components. This process is illustrated in Figure 30.4.

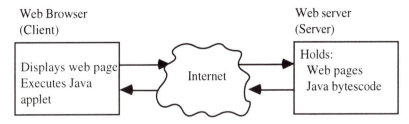

Figure 30.4 A web browser accessing information on.

The HTML tag <APPLET .. > in a web page, instructs the browser to download the Java applets bytecode from the web server and to start executing the downloaded applets bytecode. Obviously this process has grave security implications. To make this process secure the following security processes are undertaken:

● A static check is made on the downloaded bytecode to make sure that it does not try and perform any actions that would compromise security. This is performed by the bytecode verifier.

● The running Java applet is not allowed to access resources outside the virtual machine in which it is run. A consequence of this is that the applet cannot access the client computer's file system.

Note: There is still the problem of a denial of service attach, in which a rogue applet consumes resources on the user's machine.

Figure 30.5 illustrates the process of a Java applet being downloaded into a Web browser before its subsequently execution.

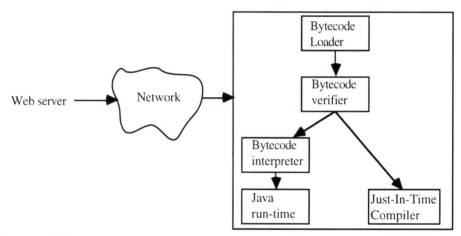

Figure 30.5 Executing a Java applet in a web browser.

29.4   Self-assessment

- What is the difference between syntax and semantic errors?

- What are the advantages and disadvantages of using a compiling system based on interpretation rather than compilation?

- Why is portability an important issue today in computing?

- Why was the UNCOL idea not taken up in the early days of computing?

- Explain why it is safe or unsafe to run an applet downloaded from the web?

- Can a rogue applet downloaded from the web cause problems when run on a user's machine?

- Would Java have been successful if implemented in the 80's, 70's or 60's?

29.5   References

Brown, P.J. (1976), 'Throw away compiling', Software Practice and Experience, vol 6, no 3, pp 423—454.

Mock, O. et al.. (1958). 'The problem of programming communications with changing machines: a proposed solution' Comm. ACM, 1, 8 12—18.

Richards, M. (1971). 'The portability of the BCPL compiler' Software Practice and Experience, 1, 135—146.

Appendix A: The main language features of Java

Variable and object declarations in Java

```
char    c;      //A 16-bit Unicode character
byte    b;      //An 8 bit integer
short   s;      //A 16 bit integer
int     i;      //A 32 bit integer
long    l;      //A 64 bit integer
float   f;      //A 32 bit floating point number IEEE 754
double  d;      //A 64 bit floating point number IEEE 754

Account mike;   // Object declaration
```

Class implementation

```java
class Account
{
  //private    visible only within class
  //protected visible only within class, subclass and package
  //public     visible to all who can see object

  private double the_balance      = 0.0d;  //Balance of account

  public Account()                          //Constructor
  {
    the_balance = 0.00;
  }

  public Account( final double money )     //Constructor
  {
    the_balance = money;
  }

  final public double account_balance()    //May not be overridden
  {
    return the_balance;
  }

  public double withdraw( final double money )
  {
     // code for withdraw
  }

  public void deposit( final double money )
  {
    the_balance = the_balance + money;
  }
}
```

Inheritance

```
class Interest_Account extends Account
{
  private static double the_interest_rate = 0.00026116;;
  private double        the_accumulated_interest;

  public Interest_Account()
  {
    super(0.00);                    //Constructor in superclass
    the_accumulated_interest = 0.0d;
  }

  public Interest_Account(final double initial)
  {
    this();                         //Constructor in this class
    deposit( initial );             //Set initial amount
  }

  public void end_of_day()
  {
    interest_accumulate(
      account_balance() * the_interest_rate );
  }

  public void interest_credit()
  {
    deposit( the_accumulated_interest );
    the_accumulated_interest = 0.0d;
  }

  protected void interest_accumulate( final double ai )
  {
    the_accumulated_interest += ai;
  }
}
```

Objects

```
Account mike = new Account();      // Create object

mike.deposit( 100.00 );            // Send the message deposit £100.00
                                   //  to the object mike

Account copy_mike = mike;          // Shallow copy assignment
Account deep_mike = mike.clone(); // Deep copy or clone
```

Arrays

```
int numbers[]  = new int[5];                //Array of 5 integers;
numbers[0] = 123;

int numbers[]   = { 10, 11, 12, 13, 14 };  // Initialized

Account bank[] = new Account[3];            //Array of objects
bank[0] = new Account();
bank[1] = new Account();
bank[2] = new Account();


Account bank[] = { new Account(), new Account(), new Account() };

for ( int i=0; i<bank.length; i++ )         // Visit each element
{
  bank[i].deposit( 10.00 );        // Gift
}
```

Life-time of variables

```
class Life_Time
{
  private static int        the_red;      //Of the program
  private int               the_blue;     //Of the object
  private final static int  the_green=2;  //Of the object (immutable)

  public void method()
  {
    int       red_cars = 4;  //Of the method (mutable)
    final int blue_cars= 6;  //Of the method (immutable)
  }

}
```

Casts

```
float number = (float) 2;                              //Simple cast

Vector bank = new Vector(0);                            //Collection
bank.add( new Account() );                              //Add to
bank.add( new Interest_Account() );                    //Add to

for ( int i=0; i<bank.size(); i++ )
{
   Account cur = (Account) bank.elementAt(i);          //Extract
   System.out.println( "The amount in account #" +
                       i + " : " +
                       cur.account_balance() );
}
```

The type of an object (`instanceof`)

```
Account bank[] = { new Account(), new Interest_Account() };
for ( int i=0; i<bank.length; i++ )
{
  if ( bank[i] instanceof Interest_Account )
  {
    System.out.println( "Account # " + i +
                        " is an Interest bearing Account" );
  }
}
```

Compound statement

```
{
  int number;
  number = 2; System.out.println( "The number is " +  number );
}
```

Selection statements

```
if ( temperature > 16 ) System.out.println("Warm");

if ( temperature > 16 )
  System.out.println("Warm");
else
  System.out.println("Cool");

switch ( number )
{
  case 2 + 3 : System.out.println("Number = 5");
              break;
  case 7     : System.out.println("Number = 7");
              break;
  default    : System.out.println("Number not 5 or 7");
}

System.out.println( temperature > 16 ? "Warm" : "Cool" );
```

Looping statements

```
while ( raining ) work();              // While it is raining work

do                                     // Play while it is sunny
  play();
while ( sunny );

for( int i = 1; i < MAX ; i++ ) System.out.println( "#" + i );
```

Changing the flow of control in a loop

```
do_work: while ( raining )
{
  work();
  if ( tied() ) break do_work;                 // Exit from loop now!
  work();
}

do_work: while ( raining )
{
  work()
  if ( stopped_raining() ) continue do_work:; // Goto start of loop
  work();
}
```

Exceptions

```
try {

  //Code which may raise an exception
  throw new InternalError("It went wrong");

}
catch ( Exception err )
{
  System.out.println(" err.GetMessage() );
}
```

Arithmetic operators

```
res = a + b;  //Plus
res = a - b;  //Minus
res = a * b;  //Multiplication
res = a / b;  //Division
res = a % b;  //Modulus (Remainder)
```

Logical operators

```
res = a << 2;   //Shift a left  2 binary places
res = a >> 2;   //Shift a right 2 binary places (sign propagated)
res = a >>> 2;  //Shift a right 2 binary places (sign not propagated)

res = a & b;    //Logical and of a b
res = a | b;    //Logical or  of a b
res = a ^ b;    //logical xor of a b
res = !a;       //logical not of a
res = ~a;       //1's complement of a
```

Conditional expressions

```
if( a == b )   //Equal to
if( a > b )    //Greater than
if( a < b )    //less than
if( a != b )   //Not equal
if( a >= b )   //Greater or
               //equal
if( a <= b )   //Less or
               //equal
```

```
if( wet && monday )   //and
if( dry || tuesday )  //or
```

```
if ( cost > 15 && number <= 100   )
{
    System.out.println( "Cost greater than 15 and the number of" +
                        " items is less than 100" );
}
```

Note: *The conditional expression will only be evaluated as far as necessary to produce the result of the condition. Thus in the* `if` *statement:*

```
if ( method _one() || method _two() ) perform();
```

`method _two()` *will not be called if* `method _one()` *delivered true.*

Short cuts

```
a++;              //equivalent to a = a + 1;
a--;              //equivalent to a = a - 1;
res += a * b;     //equivalent to res = res + (a * b)
                  //also for -=, *=, /=, %= etc.
```

Class modifiers

The following modifiers may be applied to a class

Modifier	Description
«none»	A non-public class that is only accessible in its package.
abstract	The class contains un-implemented methods and hence cannot be instantiated.
final	The class may not be subclassed.
public	The class is accessible anywhere that its package is accessible.
static	A top-level class, not an inner class.

Note: «none» represents no modifier

Interface modifiers

The following modifiers may be applied to an interface:

Modifier	Description of effect
«none»	A non-public interface that is only accessible in the package.
abstract	As an interface is abstract this is an optional addition to an interface declaration.
public	The interface is accessible anywhere that its package is accessible.

Method modifiers

The following modifiers may be applied to a method:

Modifier	Description of effect
«none»	Is only visible within the package that the class is a member of.
abstract	The method has no body. Its signature is followed by a semicolon. The class that it is in must also be abstract.
final	The method may not be overridden.
private	The method is not visible outside the class.
protected	The method is only visible in a class that subclasses the class that the method is directly or indirectly in. A method is indirectly in a class if it is inherited. Also visible inside the package that contains the class.
public	The method is visible wherever the class is visible.
static	The method may not access instance variables. A class method.

Variable / Object declaration modifiers

The following modifiers may be applied to variables or object declarations.

Modifier	Description of effect
«none»	Is only visible within the package that the class is a member of.
final	The variable is read only. For an object it's the handle to the object that is read only and not the actual contents of the object.
private	The variable is not visible outside the class.
protected	The variable/object is only visible in a class that subclasses the class that the variable/object is directly or indirectly in. A variable/object is indirectly in a class if it is inherited. Also visible inside the package that contains the class.
public	The variable/object is visible wherever the class is visible.
static	The variable/object is a class member. There is but a single copy of this variable/object which is shared between all instances of the class.

Appendix B: Reserved words and operators in Java

Reserved words in the Java language

abstract	boolean	break	byte	case
cast	catch	char	class	const
continue	default	do	double	else
extends	final	finally	float	for
goto	if	implements	import	instanceof
int	interface	long	native	new
null	package	private	protected	public
return	static	super	switch	synchronized
this	throw	throws	transient	try
void	volatile	while		

However, the following reserved words are not currently used but are reserved for possible future use.

```
const        goto
```

Operators

~	^	!	!=	%
%=	&	&&	&=	*
*=	+	++	+=	-
--	-=	/	/=	:
<	<<	<<=	<=	=
^=	==	>	>=	>>
>>=	>>>	>>>=	?	|
|=	||	instanceof		

Priority of operators

Associates	Operators in Java:	Notes
Left to Right	( ) [ ]	Highest priority
Right to Left	++ -- + - ! ~ (type)	Monadic operators
Left to Right	* / %	
Left to Right	+ -	
Left to Right	<< >> >>>	
Left to Right	< <= > >= **instanceof**	
Left to Right	== !=	
Left to Right	&	
Left to Right	^	
Left to Right	|	
Left to Right	&&	
Left to Right	||	
Right to Left	? :	conditional expression
Right to Left	= *= /= etc.	Lowest priority

Appendix C: String and character escape sequences

The following are the escape sequences for introducing control characters into a string or character constant.

\ "	A double quote " character
\ '	A single quote ' character
\b	Backspace
\DDD	The character with octal value DDD
\f	Form Feed
\n	A new line
\r	Return
\t	Tab
\uDDDD	A 4 digit hexadecimal Unicode character DDDD
\ \	The \ character

Using the above escape sequences the following statement:

```
System.out.println("\"A String\"\n\tWith embedded escape sequences")
```

would print:

```
"A String"
  With embedded escape sequences
```

Appendix D: Fundamental data types

The following fundamental data types are provided in the language.

Type	Comment	Representation	Initial value
boolean	A boolean value	1 bit	false
byte	A whole number	8 bit 2's complement no.	0
short	A whole number	16 bit 2's complement no.	0
char	A character	16 bit Unicode character	'\u0000'
int	A whole number	32 bit 2's complement no.	0
float	A number with decimal paces	32 bit IEEE 754	0.0F
long	A whole number	64 bit 2's complement no.	0L
double	A number with decimal places	64 bit IEEE 754	0.0D

Range of values held for each of the integer data types:

Type	Range of values that can be held	Size (bits)
byte	-128 ... +127	8
short	-32768 ... +32767	16
int	-2147483648 ... +2147483647	32
long	-9223372036854775808 ... +9223372036854775807	64

Range of values held for each of the floating point data types:

Type	Range of values that can be held (approximately)	
float	+/- $1.4 * 10^{-45}$ ...	$3.4 * 10^{38}$
double	+/- $4.9 * 10^{-324}$ ...	$1.8 * 10^{308}$

Appendix E: Literals in Java

A literal in Java has a type, which will effect the way it is processed.

Literal	Example	Type	Commentary
Character	`'A'`	`char`	16 bit Unicode character
Decimal number	`123456`	`int`	32 bit number
Octal number	`01234`	`int`	A leading 0 denotes an octal number
Hexadecimal number	`0xCAFE` `0Xfacade`	`int`	Leading 0x or 0X denotes a hexadecimal number.
Large number	`1L`	`long`	Suffix of L or l Also for octal and hexadecimal number.
Real number	`1.23F`	`float`	Suffix of F or f
Large real number	`1.23` `1.23D`	`double`	May also have suffix of D or d
String	`"mas"`	`String`	A string of Unicode characters

Note: *By default a real number (e.g. 1.23) has type* `double`.
A leading 0 to an integer means that the number is octal.
The `long` *hexadecimal constant* `FFFF0000FFFF0000` *is written as:*
`0xFFFF0000FFFF0000l`.

Appendix F: Selected interfaces and classes

`java.Cloneable`

```
public interface Cloneable extends Object
{
}
```

`java.Serializable`

```
public interface Serializable extends Object
{
}
```

`java.lang.System`

The major fields of this class are:

Field	Object is:
`final InputStream in`	The current input stream.
`final PrintStream out`	The current output stream.
`final PrintStream err`	The current error stream.

The major methods of this class which are all `public static` are:

Signature	Responsibility
`long`	`currentTimeMillis()` Returns the current time in milliseconds since January 1st 1970 UTC.
`void`	`exit( int n )` Exits the Java application or applet with code n.
`void`	`gc()` Explicitly calls the garbage collector.
`Properties`	`getProperties()` Returns the current properties.
`String`	`getProperty( String s )` Returns the property identified by s.
`SecurityManager`	`getSecurityManager()` Returns the current security manager.

Signature	Responsibility
int	identityHashCode(Object o) Returns the hashcode for object o and not its potentially overridden hashcode.
void	load(String lib) Loads the specified library .
void	loadLibrary(String lib) Loads the specified system library.
void	runFinalization() Runs now, the finalization methods of objects that have been identified as candidates for garbage collection.
void	setErr(OutputStream err) Sets the current error stream to be err.
void	setIn(InputStream in) Sets the current input stream to be in.
void	setOut(OutputStream out) Sets the current output stream to be out.
void	SetProperties(Properties p) Sets properties.
void	setSecurityManager(SecurityManager s) Sets the security manager.

java.lang.Object

The methods of this class are:

Signature	Responsibility
	Object() constructs an object.
final Class	getClass() Returns the classes class.
int	hashCode() Returns a unique number for each instance of this class.
boolean	equals(o) Returns true if the object equals o.
Object	clone() Δ Returns a clone copy of this object.
String	toString() Returns a string representation of this object.
final void	notify() Wakes up a single thread that is waiting on this object monitor.
final void	notifyAll() Wakes up all threads waiting on this object.

Signature	Responsibility
final void	wait() The currently executing thread releases control of this object's monitor.
final void	wait(delay) As per wait() but will also awaken if nothing happens after delay microseconds. Also wait(delay, nanoseconds) provides finer control.
void	finalize() Δ Called by the garbage collector just before releasing the storage of the object. If an exception occurs in the method the finalization of the object is abandoned, but the exception is not propagated.

Note: Methods marked Δ are protected, the rest are public.

java.lang.Character

The major public methods of this class are:

Signature	Responsibility
	Character(char c) Constructs an instance of a character object.
char	charValue() Returns the integer value of this character object.
static int	digit(char c, int radix) Returns the numeric value of this digit in radix.
boolean	equals(Object o) Returns true if o contains the same character as the object.
static boolean	isDigit(char c) Returns true if c is Unicode digit.
static boolean	isLetter(char c) Returns true if c is Unicode letter.
static boolean	isLetterOrDigit(char c) Returns true if c is Unicode letter or digit.
static boolean	isLowerCase(char c) Returns true if c is a lower-case character.
static boolean	isSpace(char c) Return true if this is a ISO Latin-1 space character.
static boolean	isUpperCase(char c) Returns true if c is an upper-case character.
static char	toLowerCase(char c) Returns the lower-case equivalent of the Unicode character. If no lower-case character returns the character c.
static char	toUpperCase(char c) Returns the upper-case equivalent of the Unicode character. If no upper-case character returns the character c.

`java.lang.Throwable`

The public methods of this class are:

Signature	Responsibility
	`Throwable()` `Throwable( String s )` Constructs a new instance of a throwable object. The string `s` may be obtained retrieved using the method `getMessage()`.
`Throwable`	`fillInStackTrace()` When an exception is caught, this method may be used to return the thrown exception so that it can be rethrown after partial error recovery has been performed.
`String`	`getLocalMessage()` Returns a message that may be changed by overriding this method in a subclass. If the method is not overridden will return the same as `getMessage()`.
`String`	`getMessage()` Returns a detailed message about this throwable object.
`void`	`printStackTrace( PrintStream ps )` Writes the exception and stack trace to the stream `ps`.
`void`	`printStackTrace( PrintWriter pw )` Writes the exception and stack trace to the stream `pw`.
`void`	`printStackTrace()` Writes the exception and stack trace to the standard error output.
`String`	`toString()` Returns a short description of this object.

Appendix G: Java JDK command line tools

Javac

This is the Java compiler and converts Java source code into the interpretable byte code.

Synopsis

```
javac [options] program.java @file_list
```

Options summary

```
-classpath classpath
```
      Sets the class path.
```
-d directory
```
    Set the destination directory.
```
-g
```
    Create local information for debugging.
```
-O
```
    Optimize the code produced. May make debugging difficult.
```
-verbose
```
    Lots of information about how the compiling process is proceeding.

Example

```
javac Game.java
```

Java

The Java byte code interpreter.

Synopsis

```
java [options] class [arguments]
java [options] -jar file.jar [arguments]
```

Options summary

```
-classpath classpath
```
      Sets the class path
```
-d directory
```
    Set the destination directory.
```
-g
```
    Create local information for debugging.
```
-O
```
    Optimize the code produced. May make debugging difficult.
```
-verbose
```
    Display information about classes loaded.

    Additional qualifiers.

`:class`	When this class is loaded.
`:ge`	Report when garbage collector used.

Example

```
java Game
```

`javadoc`

The Java byte code interpreter.

The application `javadoc` automatically creates HTML pages to document an Application or Applet. So that the generated documents to be of greatest use, the programmer can embed comments in their program which are extracted by `javadoc` and included in the generated documentation. These doc comments take the form:

```
/**
 * @tag  description
 */
```

Note: *The extra * at the start of the /* comment.*
As the documentation is produced to be viewed in a web browser HTML tags may also be used in the description.

where `tag` describes the type of doc comment and `description` is an elaboration of the tag. The different types of doc comments are described below:

Synopsis
```
javadoc files @filename
```

Options summary
```
-overview filename
```
The contents of the file Δ are placed after the alphabetic links in the index file `packages.html`.
Δ Only information between the HTML tags `<BODY> </BODY>`
```
-public
```
Only `public` items shown (e.g. public fields and public classes)
```
-protected
```
Only `public` and `protected` items shown.
```
-private
```
Shows all classes and members.
This is the option you are most likely to want to use if you want to document the non public classes in your application or applet.
```
-classpath classpath
```
Use this class path as well in finding files.

Example
```
javadoc -private  Game.java
```

List of documentation tags

Tag	Brief description
@author *text*	The text names the author of the application or applet.
@depreciated *text*	The text indicates that the method should not be used as it has been replaced by a better version.

@exception *class*	Adds a description of the fully qualified class that will be thrown if an error occurs.
	For example
	    @exception NumberFormatException
	        throw for an invalid number

@return *value*	Adds a description of the returned item to the method documentation.

@see *classname*	Add a hypertext link to *classname* in the form:
	    See Also
	        <u>Character</u>
	For example
	  @see Character
	  @see Character#charValue
	  @see lang.Character#charValue
	  Note format classname#member

@since *text*	The text names a time since the feature was implemented.
@version *text*	The text describes the version of the document
@link	As for see but the hypertext link is placed immediately in the text without a see also reference.
@since *text*	The text names a time since the feature was implemented.
@throws *classname desc*	The text names a time since the feature was implemented.

Where tags may be used:

Package documentation tags

see	link	since	deprecated

Class and interface documentation tags

see	link	since	deprecated
author	version		

Field documentation tags

see	link	since	deprecated
serial	serialfield		

Constructor and method tags

see	link	since	deprecated
param	return	throws	serialdata

Example of use

The class `Account` is shown below with suitable doc comments.

```
/**
 * @author  Michael Alexander Smith
 * @version 1.4
 */
class Account implements Account_protocol
{
  /**
   * Holds the balance of the account
   */
  private double the_balance     = 0.0d;  //Balance of account
```

```
  /**
   * Sets balance and min_balance to 0.00
   */
  public Account() {
    the_balance = 0.00;
  }
```

```
  /**
   * Returns the balance of the account
   * @return The amount of money in the account
   */
  public double account_balance()
  {
    return the_balance;
  }
```

```
  /**
   * Withdraw money from the account
   * @param  money The amount of money to withdraw
   *               must be +ve
   * @return The amount of money actually withdraw
   */
  public double withdraw( final double money )
  {
    if ( the_balance - money >= 0 )
    {
      the_balance = the_balance - money;
      return money;
    } else {
      return 0.00;
    }
  }
```

```
  /**
   * Deposit money into the account
   * @param  money The amount of money to deposit
   */
  public void deposit( final double money )
  {
    the_balance = the_balance + money;
  }
}
```

Example output from `javadoc`

The exact format of the documentation generated will depend on the version of javadoc used. The documentation produced is hypertext linked together, which unfortunately cannot be shown in a conventional book. However, the general form of the documentation generated is illustrated below:

Summary information about the class

```
Class Account

java.lang.Object
   |
   +----Account


class Account extends Object


Field Summary

double     the_balance
                Holds the balance of the account

Constructor Summary

Account()
                Sets balance to 0.00

Method Summary

double     account_balance()
                Returns the balance of the account
void       deposit(double)
                Deposit money into the account
double     withdraw(double)
                Withdraw money from the account
```

More detailed information about the class. This may be accessed by using the hypertext links from the summary information.

```
Constructor Detail

Account

 public Account()

     Sets balance to 0.00

Method Detail

account_balance

 public double account_balance()

     Returns the balance of the account

     Returns:
            The amount of money in the account
```

```
withdraw

 public double withdraw(double money)

    Withdraw money from the account

    Parameters:
         money - The amount of money to withdraw must be +ve
    Returns:
         The amount of money actually withdraw
deposit

 public void deposit(double money)

    Deposit money into the account

    Parameters:
         money - The amount of money to deposit
```

In addition an index of the items found in the class and any other classes that were processed by javadoc is created. Illustrated below is the style of index created for all items starting with A.

```
Index

Index of all Fields and Methods

A

Account(). Constructor for class Account
     Sets balance and min_balance to 0.00
account_balance(). Method in class Account
     Returns the balance of the account
```

rmic

The Remote Method stub compiler

Synopsis

```
rmic [options] package.classname
```

Options summary

```
-verbose
```
    Verbose output about what is being done.

Example

```
rmic R_Account
```

will generate the following files:

`R_Account_Skel.class` and `R_Account_Stub.class`

    _Skel A class used on the server side to receive requests from a client to call a method in the remote object. Will send the result of executing the remote method back to the client.

    _Stub A class used on the client side to send requests to a remote object and receive back the result of executing the remote methods.

`rmiregistry`

Starts a remote object registry. A server will register a remote object with this running application. Clients contact the `rmiregistry` program to facilitate communication with remote objects. The server application is run on the same machine as the `rmiregistry` program.

Synopsis

```
rmic [port]
```

Options summary

`port`
> The port to use, if no port is given then port 1099 is used.

`jar`

Combines files into a single compressed jar file

Synopsis

```
jar [options] filename class_files
```

Options summary

`c`
> Creates a new archive.

`t`
> List all files in the jar archive.

`x [files]`
> Extract all files or just the named `files`.

`v`
> Verbose output.

`m file`
> Include manifest information from `file`.

`u`
> Update an existing jar file with new files.

`f file`
> Names the jar file to be processed.

Examples

```
jar cvf mas.jar *.class
```
> Add the class files in the current directory to a newly created jar file `mas.jar`.

```
jar vtf mas.jar
```
> List all the files in the jar archive `mas.jar`.

Appendix H: HTML formatting tags

The basic layout of an HTML document and the resultant information displayed by a browser is shown below:

HTML markup	Displayed by browser

```<HTML>```
 	
 ```<HEAD>```
 `  <TITLE>Title web page </TITLE>`
 ```</HEAD>```
 	
 ```<BODY>```
 `An example of a simple`
 `<B>web</B>`
 `page.`
 ```</BODY>```
 	
 ```</HTML>```
	An example of a simple **web** page.

The tags used are in above HTML document are:

Tag	Purpose
`<HTML>  </HTML>`	Defines the extent of the HTML markup text.
`<HEAD>  </HEAD>`	Contains descriptions of the HTML page. This meta information is not displayed as part of the web page.
`<TITLE> </TITLE>`	Describes the title of the page. This description is usually displayed by the browser as the title of the window in which the web page is displayed. This information is also used by some search engines to compile an index of web pages.
`<BODY> </BODY>`	Delimits the body of the web page. In the body is the text to be displayed as well as HTML markup tags to hint at the format of the text.
`<B>  </B>`	Displays the enclosed text in a bold typeface.

Other simple tags that may be used include:

` `	Start a new line.
`<I>  </I>`	Italicise the enclosed text.
`<P>`	Start a new paragraph.
`<TT> </TT>`	Write the enclosed text in a teletype font.

Appendix I: Selected solutions

Introduction to programming

If the answers to the paper exercises at the end of the chapter, on an introduction to programming, are compiled and run then the displayed results are not always what is expected. The reason for this is that floating point numbers are held only to a fixed number of places and the result of a calculation may produce a number that is almost but not quite the exact answer. For example, the result of executing the Java statement:

```
System.out.println( 3 * 2.4 )
```

is

```
7.199999999999999
```

and not as might be expected 7.2. This is not wrong, but just a consequence of the use of floating point numbers in an arithmetic calculation and the effect of displaying the resultant calculation without specifying how it is to be formatted.

Chapter 11 describes how numbers may be formatted to be displayed with a specific precision to overcome the above difficulties.

Write out your name and address

```
System.out.println("Mike Smith");
System.out.println("School of Computing");
System.out.println("University of Brighton");
```

Calculate the total weight of 27 boxes of paper.
Each box of paper weighs 2.4 kilograms.

```
int boxes_of_paper;
double weight_of_box;

boxes_of_paper = 27;
weight_of_box  = 2.4;

System.out.print( "Total weight = " );
System.out.println( boxes_of_paper * weight_of_box );
```

or

```
System.out.print( "Total weight = " );
System.out.println( 27 * 2.4 );
```

However, to a reader of the program code the purpose of the code is not as obvious. In addition the output produced gives no indication about what was produced.

Write out the text message "Happy Birthday" 3 times.

```
int i;
i = 1;
while ( i <= 3 )
{
  System.out.println("Happy Birthday");
  i = i + 1;
}
```

Print a 5 times table.

```
int times_table;
int row;
times_table = 5;
row        = 1;

while ( row <= 12 )
{
  System.out.print( times_table );
  System.out.print( " * " );
  System.out.print( row );
  System.out.print( " = " );
  System.out.print( times_table * row );
  System.out.println();
  row = row + 1;
}
```

Print a table listing the weights of 1 to 20 boxes of paper, each box of paper weighs 2.4 kilograms.

```
int    boxes_of_paper;
double weight_of_box;
boxes_of_paper = 1;
weight_of_box  = 2.4;

while ( boxes_of_paper <= 20 )
{
  System.out.print( "The weight of " );
  System.out.print( boxes_of_paper );
  System.out.print( " box(es) of paper : " );
  System.out.print( boxes_of_paper * weight_of_box );
  System.out.println();
  boxes_of_paper = boxes_of_paper + 1;
}
```

Print a multiplication table for all values between 1 and 5.

```
System.out.println("   |  1  2  3  4  5");
System.out.println("-------------------");

int row;
int col;
row = 1;
while ( row<=5 )
{
  System.out.print( row );
  System.out.print( "  |" );
  col = 1;
  while ( col<=5 )
  {
    System.out.print(" ");
    System.out.print( row * col );
    col = col + 1;
  }
  row = row + 1;
  System.out.println();
}
```

Java introduction 1

An application to print the numbers 1 to 25.

```
class Main
{
  public static void main()
  {
    for ( int number=1; number<=25; number++ )
    {
      System.out.println( number );
    }
  }
}
```

An application to print the 7 times table.

```
class Main
{
  public static void main()
  {
    int times_table = 7;

    for ( int row=1; row<=12; row++ )
    {
      System.out.println( row + " * " + times_table + " = " +
                          ( times_table * row ) );
    }
  }
}
```

An application to print a conversion chart from miles to kilometres.

```
class Main
{
  public static void main()
  {
    final double KILOMETRES_IN_MILE = 0.609244;
    System.out.println("Miles" + "\t" + "Kilometres" );
    for ( int miles=1; miles<=25; miles++ )
    {
      System.out.println( "" + miles + "\t" +
                          ( (double) miles / KILOMETRES_IN_MILE ) );
    }
  }
}
```

An application to print all numbers in the fibonacci sequence up to the first number over 50000.

```
class Main
{
  public static void main()
  {
    int first  = 1;                     //First number in window
    int second = 1;                     //Second number in window

    System.out.println( first );
    System.out.println( second );

    int next;
    do
    {
      next = first + second;            //Next term
      System.out.println( next );
      first = second; second = next;    //Slide window

    } while ( next < 50000 );
  }
}
```

Java introduction 2

An application to print the Unicode characters between 65 and 69.

```
class Main
{
  public static void main()
  {
    for ( char uc=65; uc<=69; uc++ )
    {
      System.out.println( "The Unicode character " + uc +
                          " has internal value " + (int) uc );
    }
  }
}
```

An application to print all prime numbers between 3 and 1000.

```
class Main
{
  public static void main()
  {
    for ( int pos_prime=3; pos_prime<=1000; pos_prime++ )
    {
      boolean is_prime = true;
      check: for ( int factor=2; factor<pos_prime; factor++ )
      {
        if ( pos_prime % factor == 0 )
        {
          is_prime = false;            //Divisible so not prime
          break check;                 //Give up check
        }
      }
      if ( is_prime )
        System.out.println("" + pos_prime + " is a prime number" );
    }
  }
}
```

An application to print all perfect numbers between 3 and 1000.

```
class Main
{
  public static void main()
  {
    for ( int pos_perfect=3; pos_perfect<=1000; pos_perfect++ )
    {
      int sum = 0;
      for ( int factor=1; factor<pos_perfect; factor++ )
      {
        if ( pos_perfect % factor == 0 )      //Divisible
        {
          sum = sum + factor;                 //Add factor
        }
      }
      if ( sum == pos_perfect )
      {
        System.out.println("" + pos_perfect + " is a perfect number" );
        System.out.print("Factors are: " );
        for ( int f=1; f<pos_perfect; f++ )   //Re-work out factors
        {
          if ( pos_perfect % f == 0 )
          {
            System.out.print(" " + f );       //Print factor
          }
        }
        System.out.println();
      }
    }
  }
}
```

Anatomy of a method

An application to process transactions for a small cinema.

```
import TUI;                                 // See Section 5.5.1

class Performance
{
  private int the_seats_left = 0;           //Seats left

  public Performance( final int no_seats )  //Constructor
  {
    the_seats_left = no_seats;              //Set seats performance
  }

  public int book_seats( final int no_seats )  //Book seats
  {
    if ( the_seats_left - no_seats >= 0 )
    {
      the_seats_left = the_seats_left - no_seats;
      return no_seats;
    } else {
      return 0;
    }
  }

  public int seats_left()                   //Seats left
  {
    return the_seats_left;
  }
}
```

```
class Transaction
{
  public static void process( Performance a_performance, TUI screen )
  {
    int      amount;                 //Seats processed

    screen.menu("Book", "Available", "Main menu", "", "" );

    loop: while ( true )
    {
      switch ( screen.chose_option() )
      {
        case Menu_item.M_1 :
          amount = screen.dialogue_int("Seats to book");
          if ( amount >= 0 )
          {
            a_performance.book_seats( amount );
          } else {
            screen.message("Number of seats must be positive");
          }
          break;
        case Menu_item.M_2 :
          {
            String mes = "Number of setas left = "  +
                         a_performance.seats_left();
            screen.message( mes );           //"Seats left ... "
          }
          break;
        case Menu_item.M_3 :
          break loop;                        //Exit this menu
      }
    }
  }
}
```

```
class Main
{
  public static void main( String args[] )
  {
    Performance first  = new Performance(200);    //2pm
    Performance second = new Performance(200);    //5.30pm
    Performance third  = new Performance(200);    //8pm
    Performance Fourth = new Performance(100);    //11pm

    TUI screen = new TUI();

    while ( true )
    {
      screen.menu( "2pm", "5.30", "8pm", "11pm", "" );
      switch ( screen.chose_option() )
      {
        case Menu_item.M_1 :  Transaction.process( first, screen );
                              break;
        case Menu_item.M_2 :  Transaction.process( second, screen );
                              break;
        case Menu_item.M_3 :  Transaction.process( third, screen );
                              break;
        case Menu_item.M_4 :  Transaction.process( Fourth, screen );
                              break;
      }
    }
  }
}
```

Appendix J: On-line resources

World wide web references

http://java.sun.com/

The Sun web site that contains the latest version of the JDK (Java Development Kit) and in particular the hypertext linked documentation for the class libraries.

Index